UNIVERSAL

A Comparative Approach to
Representation in Eurasian History

EDITED BY

PETER FIBIGER BANG

AND

DARIUSZ KOŁODZIEJCZYK

CAMBRIDGE
UNIVERSITY PRESS

CAMBRIDGE
UNIVERSITY PRESS

University Printing House, Cambridge CB2 8BS, United Kingdom

Cambridge University Press is part of the University of Cambridge.

It furthers the University's mission by disseminating knowledge in the pursuit of education, learning and research at the highest international levels of excellence.

www.cambridge.org
Information on this title: www.cambridge.org/9781107527478

© Cambridge University Press 2012

First published 2012
First paperback edition 2015

A catalogue record for this publication is available from the British Library

Library of Congress Cataloguing in Publication data
Universal empire : a comparative approach to imperial culture and representation in Eurasian history / edited by Peter Fibiger Bang and Dariusz Kołodziejczyk.
pages cm
Includes bibliographical references and index.
ISBN 978-1-107-02267-6
1. Imperialism – History.   2. Kings and rulers – History.   3. Imperialism – Social aspects – History.   4. Imperialism – Philosophy.   5. Political culture – History.   6. Civilization – History.   7. World history.   8. World politics – To 1900.   9. Eurasia – History.   10. Eurasia – Politics and government.   I. Bang, Peter F. (Peter Fibiger)   II. Kołodziejczyk, Dariusz.
JV61.U64   2012
306.2 – dc23   2012015658

ISBN 978-1-107-02267-6 Hardback
ISBN 978-1-107-52747-8 Paperback

UNIVERSAL EMPIRE

The claim by certain rulers to universal empire has a long history stretching as far back as the Assyrian and Achaemenid empires. This book traces its various manifestations in Near Eastern and classical antiquity, the Islamic world, Asia and Central America as well as considering seventeenth- and eighteenth-century European discussions of international order. As such it is an exercise in comparative world history combining a multiplicity of approaches, from ancient history, to literary and philosophical studies, to the history of art and international relations, and historical sociology. The notion of universal imperial rule is presented as an elusive and much-coveted prize among monarchs in history, around which developed forms of kingship and political culture. Different facets of the phenomenon are explored under three, broadly conceived, headings: symbolism, ceremony and diplomatic relations; universal or cosmopolitan literary high cultures; and, finally, the inclination to present universal imperial rule as an expression of cosmic order.

PETER FIBIGER BANG is Associate Professor of History at the Saxo Institute, University of Copenhagen, and holds a doctorate from the University of Cambridge. He is a Roman historian interested in comparative and world history. From 2005 to 2009 he was Chair of the European research network, Tributary Empires Compared, funded by COST (http://tec.saxo.ku.dk) and he has been a Visiting Professor at the universities of Tübingen and Heidelberg. He has authored, edited or co-edited seven other volumes, most importantly *The Roman Bazaar: A Comparative Study of Trade and Markets in a Tributary Empire* (Cambridge, 2008) and with C. Bayly *Tributary Empires in Global History* (2011). With Walter Scheidel he is about to publish *The Oxford Handbook of the State in the Ancient Near East and Mediterranean*.

DARIUSZ KOŁODZIEJCZYK is Professor of Early Modern History at the University of Warsaw and at the Polish Academy of Sciences. He has published extensively on the Ottoman empire, the Crimean Khanate, and international and intercultural relations in eastern Europe. He is currently Vice-President of the Comité International des Études Pré-ottomanes et Ottomanes (CIEPO) and he has been a Visiting Professor at the Collège de France, University of Notre Dame and Hokkaido University. His most important publications include *Ottoman–Polish Diplomatic Relations (15th–18th Century): An Annotated Edition of 'Ahdnames and Other Documents* (2000), *The Ottoman Survey Register of Podolia (ca. 1681): Defter-i Mufassal-i Eyalet-i Kamaniçe* (2004), and *The Crimean Khanate and Poland-Lithuania: International Diplomacy on the European Periphery (15th–18th Century): A Study of Peace Treaties Followed by Annotated Documents* (2011).

Cymbeline: Well,
          My Peace we will begin. And Caius Lucius,
          Although the victor, we submit to Caesar
          And to the Roman empire, promising
          To pay our wonted tribute, from the which
          We were dissuaded by our wicked Queen,
          Whom heavens in justice both on her and hers
          Have laid most heavy hand.
Soothsayer: The fingers from the powers above do tune
          The harmony of this peace. The vision
          Which I made known to Lucius ere the stroke
          Of this yet scarce-cold battle, at this instant
          Is full accomplished. For the Roman eagle,
          From south to west on wing soaring aloft,
          Lessened herself, and in the beams o'th'sun
          So vanished; which foreshowed our princely eagle,
          Th'Imperial Caesar, should again unite
          His favour with the radiant Cymbeline,
          Which shines here in the west.

William Shakespeare

Contents

vii

Figures

Maps

Notes on the contributors

DIMITER ANGELOV is Fellow in Byzantine History at the University of Birmingham. His main interests lie in the political and intellectual history of the Byzantine empire during the thirteenth, fourteenth and fifteenth centuries. He is the author of *Imperial Ideology and Political Thought in Byzantium, 1204–1330* (Cambridge, 2007) and recently published an analytical study of the uses and textual history of the Donation of Constantine during the late Byzantine period in the volume *Church and Society in Late Byzantium* (2009) edited by him.

PETER FIBIGER BANG is Associate Professor at the Saxo Institute, University of Copenhagen, and holds a doctorate from the University of Cambridge. He is a Roman comparative historian, interested in political economy, the sociology of power, state-formation and world history. He was chair of the COST research network Tributary Empires Compared 2005–9 (www.tec.saxo.ku.dk) pioneering comparison between the Roman, Mughal and Ottoman empires. He has published *The Roman Bazaar: A Comparative Study of Trade and Markets in a Tributary Empire* (Cambridge, 2008) and six other edited volumes, including, with C. A. Bayly (eds.), *Tributary Empires in Global History* (2011). With Walter Scheidel he is editing *The Oxford Handbook of the State in the Ancient Near East and Mediterranean* (in press).

GOJKO BARJAMOVIC is Associate Professor of Assyriology at the University of Copenhagen. His research is focused on early historical economy and the political, social and intellectual history of the ancient Near East with particular emphasis on the Old- and Neo-Assyrian periods. He is the author of *A Historical Geography of Anatolia in the Old Assyrian Colony Period* (2011); *Ups and Downs at Kanesh: Observations on Chronology, History and Society in the Old Assyrian Period* (with T. Klitgaard Hertel and M. Trolle Larsen, 2012) and is editing three volumes on various aspects of intellectual history, including *Libraries before Alexandria* (with K. Ryholt, forthcoming).

GARTH FOWDEN is attached to the Centre for Greek and Roman Antiquity, National Research Foundation, Athens. His books include *Empire to Commonwealth: Consequences of Monotheism in Late Antiquity* (1993) and *Qusayr 'Amra: Art and the Umayyad Elite in Late Antique Syria* (2004). His current research develops those works' concern with culture, religion and empire during the first millennium, with special reference to emergent Islam. In preparation: *Before and after Muḥammad: The First Millennium Refocused*.

PETER HALDÉN holds a PhD from the European University Institute, Florence and is currently a researcher at the Department of Peace and Conflict Research at the University of Uppsala, Sweden. He has specialised in the history of the Holy Roman Empire during the early modern era and is the author of *Stability without Statehood: Lessons from Europe's History before the Sovereign State* (2011). His current research interests include state-formation/state-building, constitutions, European and German history, African and Central Asian societies, and international security.

JOHN A. HALL is James McGill Professor of Comparative Historical Sociology at McGill University, Montreal and a visiting professor at the Saxo Institute, University of Copenhagen. His interests roam widely from nations, states and empires to sociological theory and intellectual history. Among his many publications are *Powers and Liberties* (1985), *International Orders* (1996), *Ernest Gellner: An Intellectual Biography* (2010) and *Power in the Twenty-First Century: Michael Mann in Conversation with John Hall* (2011).

JUDITH HERRIN is Professor of Late Antique and Byzantine Studies at King's College, London. Her research interests include: Ravenna in Late Antiquity, early church structures, and women in the Byzantine world. Recent publications: 'Book Burning as Purification', in Philip Rousseau and Manolis Papoutsakis (eds.), *Transformations of Late Antiquity: Essays for Peter Brown* (2009), 205–22; 'The Acts of Trullo (692) as a Continuation of Chalcedon', in Richard Price and Mary Whitby (eds.), *Chalcedon in Context: Church Councils 400–700* (2009), 148–68. A revised edition of *The Formation of Christendom* is forthcoming.

EBBA KOCH is a professor of Asian art at the Institute of Art History, University of Vienna and a senior researcher at the Institute of Iranian

Studies, Austrian Academy of Sciences. Professor Koch was visiting professor at Harvard (2008/9), Oxford (2008), Sabanci University (2003) and the American University in Cairo (1998), and held an Aga Khan Program for Islamic Architecture Fellowship at Harvard (2002). Since 2001 she has been global advisor to the Taj Mahal Conservation Collaborative, and she was Austrian delegate to the Management Committee of COST Action 36 'Network of Comparative Empires' of the European Commission (2005–9). Her research interests are Mughal art and architecture, the political and symbolic meaning of art, and the artistic connections between the Mughals and their neighbours and Europe. Her publications include *Mughal Architecture* (1991), *Mughal Art and Imperial Ideology* (2001), and *The Complete Taj Mahal and the Riverfront Gardens of Agra* (2006). She has co-authored, with Milo Beach and Wheeler Thackston, *King of the World: The Padshahnama: An Imperial Mughal Manuscript from the Royal Library, Windsor Castle* (1997).

DARIUSZ KOŁODZIEJCZYK is associate professor at the Institute of History, University of Warsaw and has published widely on Ottoman and eastern European history. His most important work has focused on the relationship between early modern Poland-Lithuania and its Muslim neighbours and includes *Ottoman–Polish Diplomatic Relations (15th–18th Century): An Annotated Edition of 'Ahdnames and Other Documents* (2000), *The Ottoman Survey Register of Podolia (ca. 1681): Defter-i Mufassal-i Eyalet-i Kamaniçe* (2004), and *The Crimean Khanate and Poland-Lithuania: International Diplomacy on the European Periphery (15th–18th Century): A Study of Peace Treaties Followed by Annotated Documents* (2011).

JUSTYNA OLKO is associate professor at the Institute for Interdisciplinary Studies 'Artes Liberales', University of Warsaw. She specializes in Aztec/Nahua ethnohistory, Nahuatl philology and cross-cultural transfers between Europe and New Spain. She has authored several books, including *Turquoise Diadems and Staffs of Office: Insignia of Power in Aztec and Early Colonial Mexico* (2005) and *Insignia of Rank in the Nahua World* (University Press of Colorado, in press) as well as of numerous journal papers and book chapters. She has conducted extensive archival research in Mexico, Spain and USA where she received fellowships at Dumbarton Oaks and John Carter Brown Library; she currently directs an international team project on contact-induced change in older Nahuatl within the Focus Programme of the Foundation for Polish Science.

VELCHERU NARAYANA RAO is currently Visiting Distinguished Professor of South Asian Studies at Emory University. For thirty-eight years, he taught Telugu and Indian literatures at University of Wisconsin-Madison. His publications include *Girls for Sale: A Play from Colonial India,* a translation of *Kanyasulkam* by Gurajada Apparao (2007), and several books in collaboration with David Shulman and Sanjay Subrahmanyam, including, with the former, *Srinatha: The Poet who Made Gods and Kings* (2012).

EVELYN S. RAWSKI holds a Ph.D. in History and Far Eastern Languages from Harvard University and is currently Distinguished University Professor of History at the University of Pittsburgh. She has published books on sixteenth- and eighteenth-century Chinese agricultural development, elementary literacy, and the emperors and imperial institutions of the Qing dynasty, which ruled China from 1644 to 1911. Among her books is *The Last Emperors* (1996).

ROLF MICHAEL SCHNEIDER studied classical archaeology, ancient history and Byzantine art history in Hamburg, Heidelberg and Rome. He has lectured in Heidelberg, Marburg, Munich and Cambridge where he also was Curator of the Museum of Classical Archaeology and Fellow of Downing College. He is currently Professor of Classical Archaeology at the Ludwig-Maximilians-Universität, Munich. His research interests revolve around image and (con)text, cultural readings of marble, the 'Other' in Greece and Rome, anthropology of emotions, Classics in South Africa and beyond. He has published extensively in these fields (www.klass-archaeologie.lmu.de/) and is co-editor of the series ICON (Berlin).

SANJAY SUBRAHMANYAM is Professor and Doshi Chair of Indian History at the University of California at Los Angeles (UCLA). Since 2005, he has also directed the Center for India and South Asia at UCLA. He earlier taught in Delhi and Paris, and held a chair in Indian History and Culture at Oxford. His recent publications include *Textures of Time* (with V. Narayana Rao and David Shulman) (2003); *Explorations in Connected History,* 2 vols. (2005); *Three Ways to Be Alien: Travails and Encounters in the Early Modern World* (2011); and, with Muzaffar Alam, *Indo-Persian Travels in the Age of Discoveries, 1400–1700* (2007) and *Writing the Mughal World* (2011).

Preface

This collection of essays explores the notion of universal empire in Eurasian and world history from antiquity till the dawn of modernity. It is the result of a long journey and one of the main outcomes of a European-based network to compare tributary empires which we are grateful to acknowledge was boldly and generously financed by COST (www.tec.saxo.ku.dk). This brought historians together from a number of fields who had not usually had a great deal of contact with each other and enabled them to meet several times annually for an extended period. In this connection, we want to extend our thanks to all the many participants in this series of meetings and our hosts, as well as to the contributors to the present volume for all the enthusiasm and curiosity they have brought to this endeavour to promote comparative history. In relation to this volume, however, we thank in particular Adam Ziółkowski, who helped organise one of the meetings on which this volume builds, and C. A. Bayly, who acted as co-chair of the network for its entire duration and also commented on a first draft of our introduction. It is also a great pleasure to thank both Michael Sharp and his staff at Cambridge University Press for working hard on bringing our manuscript into print, as well as the two anonymous readers who offered much valuable advice. René Lindekrone Christensen, finally, provided much appreciated technical assistance with the images for this book.

For the past decade or so, imperialism, globalisation and world history have been high on the agenda both of the historical disciplines and of the public in general. Unsurprisingly, both discourses have been dominated by the experience of modernity and colonial empire. (Bayly 2004 is exemplary.) But as these debates are rapidly changing our image of the world, past and present, and are themselves responses to an ongoing seismic shift in the current world order, older forms of history can ill afford to ignore this development; they must find ways of addressing the concerns of the evolving more global perspective on the past or risk consigning themselves to obscurity and irrelevance. Fortunately, there is a growing sense among students of more ancient forms of history of the need not to study their topics in isolation, but to reach out to neighbouring fields and allow their enquiries to be informed and shaped by more general problems of world history. This is what we have been aiming for in this volume; we radically cut across both conventional chronology and cultural geography to illuminate our theme on the broadest possible canvas. In doing so, we join ranks with a small but accumulating number of studies and projects dedicated to the comparative history of pre-modern empires (Alcock *et al.* 2001; Bang and Bayly 2003 and 2011; Bang 2008; Hurlet 2008; Mutschler and Mittag 2008; Scheidel 2009; Morris and Scheidel 2009). It is a particular joy to mention the project on Rome and Han China led by Walter Scheidel and the network of ancient and modern imperialisms co-ordinated by Phiroze Vasunia, both of whom were present at several of our meetings. Such initiatives are crucial to reinvigorate and renew fields that are both blessed and burdened with a long tradition of scholarship. Perhaps, the most significant and fruitful experience of the dialogue that emerged within our network was to be confronted with the unfamiliar or little known, but not in the broad anthropological sense of 'meeting the other' in general, important as that may be. Rather, it was the engagement with a number of historical societies specifically selected for the general characteristics they had in common, but not usually treated together, which helped us to broaden our own horizons, inspire new questions and shake our firm beliefs, and tempted us to step out of our accustomed mental and intellectual frameworks to explore other vistas. If this volume offers a modest impression of this experience and the excitement it brought, our efforts will not have been in vain.

Peter Fibiger Bang   Dariusz Kołodziejczyk
Copenhagen   Warsaw

CHAPTER I

'Elephant of India': universal empire through time and across cultures

Peter Fibiger Bang with Dariusz Kołodziejczyk

> The Imperial Assemblage is over, and Her Majesty has been duly proclaimed Empress of India... The roads to the plain presented a strange and animated spectacle... Gaudily-trapped elephants and camels, the many-coloured dresses of the crowd, quaint vehicles, and dust such as has never been seen in England, formed purely Oriental features... Soon after 11 most of the officials and Chiefs had taken their seats... each could be identified by the banner presented to him last week... These banners were of satin, and were shaped like those in the pictures of Roman triumphs.
>
> *The Times*, 2 January 1877 (p. 5)

On 1 January 1877, it was officially announced in Delhi by Lord Lytton, the British Viceroy, that Queen Victoria had assumed the title of 'Empress of India'. Readers of the *Times of London* would have found this dispatch, telegraphed from Delhi via Teheran, reporting the events in the paper of the following day. The wonder of modern technology brought metropolitan society in close and immediate contact with its imperial possessions, literally thousands of miles away. There was a mastery of distant colonial theatres never achieved before by any legendary conqueror or grand potentate in history. Operating at the level of daily routine, this is an emblematic example of the new-found powers to gather information, systematise knowledge and put in taxonomic order subject societies enjoyed by states and ruling elites during the age of colonialism. Yet this triumph of modern streamlined, even electrified, imperial power cultivated a self-consciously archaic image. The imperial proclamation of Victoria was organised as a grand historicist extravaganza – a timeless medley of Roman, feudal and Indian symbolism.[1] Royal pomp and circumstance were mobilised in a

---

[1] The fundamental analysis of the assumption of the imperial title by Victoria, the politics involved and the accompanying imperial ceremony, pageantry and symbolism is by Cohn (1983) and further Cannadine (1983 and 2001: 44–57) with a vivid sense of the Victorian era penchant for historicist extravaganza displays. References to ancient Greek and Latin texts below are given by author name, and where necessary by title and the standard conventional book and chapter numbering.

Fig. 1.1 Elephants photographed in procession through the streets of Delhi during the Coronation Durbar in 1903 for which the 1877 celebration of Victoria's imperial title had set the model.

display of might on a scale to match and better any standards set by previous generations. A great throng of Indian chiefs and rulers had been invited to Delhi with their vast retinues to pay homage to their imperial overlord and confirm their commitment to British rule. The staged ritual took great care to muster all the standard metaphors and trappings in the repertoire of universal lordship. Victoria was presented not as a mere monarch, among others, but as a ruler superior to everyone else; she was the supreme lord to whose throne the royalty of India flocked in loyal service. Typical of such occasions, the diversity of subjects put on parade was used to reflect the wide reach and unsurpassed sway of the monarch. Arranged to emphasise variety in dress, colour and equipment, the spectacles showed 'that mixture of splendour and squalor so characteristic of the East', as the correspondent put it.[2]

---

[2] *The Times*, 1 January, 5. Roberts (1897: 331–5), an eye witness account by one of the central participants in the organisation of the event, gives a good impression of how the British authorities wished the Durbar to appear.

This last observation is significant. In the public *imaginaire* of Britain, the well-established grammar of imperial grandeur was now intimately linked with prevailing notions of the exotic and the strange, exhilarating, but also dangerous (fig. 1.1). The parliamentary debates preceding the decision that Victoria should be invested with an imperial title were not a little acrimonious. Disraeli, the prime minister whose idea this had been, encountered tough opposition in both the Commons and the Lords.[3] This was, he insisted, 'a step which will give great satisfaction not merely to the Princes, but to the nations of India. They look forward to some Act of this kind with intense interest, and by various modes they have conveyed to us their desire that such a policy should be pursued.'[4] Since the deposition of the Great Mughal after the Sepoy mutiny in 1857, a symbolic void had been left in India which it was now time to fill. Moreover, proclaiming Victoria Empress was not only congenial to Indian sentiment, it was also a strong demonstration of the firm commitment of Britain to hold on to her South Asian possession. The imperial title would serve to solidify the foundations of British rule. Neither of these arguments cut much ice with the opposition. To the first, Gladstone and other Liberals objected that they seriously doubted that the Indians liked to have subjection rubbed in their faces. They saw little indication that the government proposal echoed the wishes of the Indian population. British rule ought to be progressive rather than oppressive. Creating a special imperial title for the Queen was likely to breed hostility and resentment in India.[5] If the first part met with serious criticism, the second part of Disraeli's argument earned him little but ridicule. The whole idea of an emperor as a supreme monarch was simply risible. Worse still, to think that an imperial title would help to shore up British rule against competition from other powers, Russia in particular, was a claim 'impossible to treat . . . seriously', the earl of Rosebery scornfully remarked; 'it reminded him of the warlike proceedings of the Chinese [i.e. under the Opium wars] – also, by-the-by, governed by an Emperor – who put their chief trust in wooden swords, and shields painted with ugly faces'.[6]

[3] The Royal Titles bill was presented to the House of Commons on 17 February 1876. Debates in both chambers of the British parliament took place from February till April (the three readings in the Commons: 17 February, 9 March, 23 March 1876).

[4] *Hansard Parliamentary Papers* (House of Commons, 17 February 1876), vol. 227 c. 410.

[5] *Hansard Parliamentary Papers* (House of Commons, 17 February 1876), vol. 227 cc. 410–14; (House of Commons, 9 March 1876), vol. 227 cc. 1735–39; (House of Commons, 23 March 1876), vol. 228 cc. 480–2, 486–92 and 512–13.

[6] *Hansard Parliamentary Papers* (House of Lords, 3 April), vol. 228 c. 1084.

Enfeebled relic or romanticist desire, the notion of an Emperor provoked very different responses in political life, but about one thing opinions converged. Both sides of parliament were united in the belief that the title was, predominantly, a foreign thing and unsuitable for Britain itself. To be sure, there were nuances. In some respects the critics played this card the hardest. Next to the concerns that the imperial title might prove offensive to Indians, because of the blatant inequality implied by its rejection for England, they did at the same time not shy away from appealing to anti-Semitic prejudice in satirical cartoons mocking Disraeli's fascination with the 'foreign' trappings of empire and rank. He, on the other hand, also pointed to some aspects of the English cultural heritage which seemed compatible with the imperial title.[7] Nevertheless, the government did not find it difficult to sooth concerns that English freedom was being corrupted by a foreign import. Victoria would rule as Empress in India, but in British affairs she would remain Queen, the government repeatedly reassured its critics.[8] As Sir George Bowyer observed during the debates, the title was derived from Roman models and the idea was Oriental.[9] The easy, almost unconscious, relegation of the Roman imperial monarchy to the cultural sphere of the East may strike us as curious. But this figure of thinking was common currency at the time. The history of the Roman emperors was widely received as a story of their gradual descent and decline into an Oriental despotism. Supreme monarch, ruler of the world, such claims were increasingly relocated on the European mental map to the exotic confines of Asia. The whole arrangement was, in short, a textbook example of *Orientalism*, albeit of a much more embattled, contested and frayed

---

[7] See Taylor 2004 and more generally on the Liberals and Disraeli's imperialism, Wohl 1995 and Durrans 1982. Racism or ethnic stereotyping, thus, was not only on the government side, the impression given by Cohn (1983: 184), nor did it dominate the formation of opinions completely. On both sides, it entered as only one strand in a complex set of views. While the Liberals objected to the application of a different set of values to India, their resistance to the imperial title was nevertheless firmly grounded in nationalist resistance to foreign influence and oriental corruption, cf. the speech made in a Lords committee by the Earl Shaftesbury dismissing 'Emperor' as connected with 'Mahomedan' misrule and decline. The English should not revive the loathed memories of the Mughals, but guide India to freedom by example and 'imbue them with British feeling...teach them that...the noblest expression of a genuine Briton is to fear God and honour the King' (*Hansard Parliamentary Papers* 3 April 1876, vol. 228 cc. 1039–47). The Conservative position, on the other hand, was more ready to contemplate the use of 'Emperor/Empress' in English culture, both historically, and for the present. As Disraeli reminded the Commons, according to Edward Gibbon it was under the Roman Antonine emperors that mankind had been most happy. *Hansard Parliamentary Papers* (House of Commons, 9 March 1876), vol. 227 c. 1721.

[8] Also after the bill had been passed, cf. the exchange in the House of Lords between Lord Selborne and the then Chancellor of the Exchequer: *Hansard Parliamentary Papers* (House of Lords, 2 May 1876), vol. 228 cc. 1953–81).

[9] *Hansard Parliamentary Papers* (House of Commons, 17 February 1876), vol. 227 c. 419.

kind than Said was generally willing to acknowledge.[10] It is characteristic of these debates that the title under discussion was at all times the English 'Empress'. When a proclamation was first issued from the court on 28 April 1876, making the assumption of the new title official, only two versions were included: 'Imperatrix Indiae' or alternatively 'Empress of India'.[11]

But what would be the Indian equivalent of these Latinate (Western) forms, a couple of critics asked without first receiving an answer. By the time of the Delhi Durbar, the British government had settled on the grandiose 'Kaiser-i-Hind'. This caused disagreement to flare up again briefly, in parliament and in the newspapers. 'Kaiser' was a German title – in fresh memory as it had just been assumed by the ruler of the recently united nation – Sir George Campbell noted with dismay. But here the government gleefully, and not without condescension, countered with the backing of confident Orientalist scholarship; 'Kaiser' was also current in Persian – a language which owing to the Mughals was widespread in India. The term could already be found in the classic epic of Firdausi and was generally the name under which people in the Orient, including India, would refer to the Ottoman sultan.[12] To this, one of the protagonists in the newspaper debate added, teasingly, the further observation that 'Kaiser', as was well known, derived from the Roman Caesar. According to one (spurious) legend, this name had entered the Julian family during the wars with Carthage and meant elephant in Punic: '"Elephant of India", then, is not so bad a style and title after all, for it smacks both of poetry, heraldry and predominance.' That might all well be, Campbell answered, but at the end of the day no amount of learning or classical lore could hide the fact that, in an Indian cultural context, the title was 'as new to the "ordinary native" as an English title', and, to add insult to injury, even put in a clumsy masculine format.[13] The titles current in Indian usage such as *padishah*, on the other hand, were felt by the European experts to have lost force, damned by their connection to the moribund regimes of the past. And yet, when hard pressed by the opposition to provide evidence that there was any wish in India to have Victoria invested with a new imperial title, the government representatives had referred to a few isolated episodes where groups of Indians had used

[10] Said 1978.   [11] *The Times*, 29 April 1876, p. 10.
[12] *Hansard Parliamentary Papers* (House of Commons, 1 March 1877), vol. 232 cc. 1211–12; *The Times*, 2 March 1877 (W. Nassau Lees), p. 4.
[13] *The Times*, 5 March 1877, p. 8. During the parliamentary debates of the previous year, Campbell had already made the point that the Indian/Mughal political traditions deserved more respect than generally accorded to them and that, in relation to India, there was little reason to change in the European-style titulature of Victoria as Queen, see *Hansard Parliamentary Papers* (9 March 1876), vol. 227, cc. 1730–1.

precisely titles of this sort in flattering addresses to the Queen.[14] Instead of following such precedents, however, the government had chosen to invent a new convention which could claim some foundation in Indo-Persian culture; but more importantly, it was within the purview of the English cultural horizon and could be used to match and mirror the contemporary claims to grandeur posed by other European great powers subscribing to the same Roman tradition, be it the German Kaiser or the Russian Tsar.[15] Under the pretext of an alleged Oriental craving for inflated titles and distinctions, the government set about 'reinventing' the British monarchy. For, as Disraeli remarked, 'It is only by the amplification of titles that you can often touch and satisfy the imagination of nations.'[16]

Controversial and in between, Roman as well as Oriental, European and Asian, endlessly emulated and historically loaded: the contributions to this volume roam widely to cut through these conventional oppositions and explore the notion of a universal emperor and empire, charting its career through time and across cultures in Eurasia, from antiquity till the dawn of colonialism. The following chapters combine perspectives ranging from the history of diplomacy to art history, to illuminate the many facets of this phenomenon. Together they represent a new foray into world history that joins recent attempts to pioneer comparison and stimulate much needed dialogue among students of vast pre-industrial empires, East and West.[17] Below we establish the basic comparative framework for this exercise and offer a synthesis that seeks to pull the many different threads together in a shared analytical model, sketch a common historical chronology and identify a set of thematic keys under which to study our topic.

UNIVERSAL EMPIRE: THE DYNAMICS OF HEGEMONIC PRE-EMINENCE

Victoria's imperial investiture had become an instrument in the tool box of invented traditions which the builders of modern 'imagined communities' employed to stir the emotions of mass publics; it was basically a piece of theatricality, still powerful and evocative, but perhaps not quite in keeping

---

[14] *Hansard Parliamentary Papers* (House of Commons, 9 March 1876), vol. 222 cc. 1750–1: 'Sháhán-sháh-i-Hind Zil-i-Subháni', according to the Chancellor of the Exchequer, and he added, the envoy of the Persian government should also have recognised that the Queen ought to be styled as *pádsháh*.

[15] Cohn 1983: 201 with further analysis of the scholarship proposing the Kaiser-i-Hind title.

[16] *Hansard Parliamentary Papers* (House of Commons, 9 March 1876), vol. 227 c. 1724; Oriental desire for elaborate titles, c. 1750 (on which Cohn 1983: 184). On the reinvention of the British monarchy in more imperial fashion, see Cannadine 2001, ch. 8.

[17] Bang 2008; Scheidel 2009; Mutschler and Mittag 2008; Morris and Scheidel 2009; Bang and Bayly 2003 and 2011; Alcock *et al.* 2001.

with the modern age. Increasingly, the notion of emperors and universal empire was felt to be a thing of the past, a relic of more romantic ages that progress had left behind or relegated to the more exotic margins of history. In his private journal of the embassy to the Chinese court led by Macartney in 1793, his audience with the Qianlong emperor provoked this telling observation: 'Thus I have seen "King Solomon in all his glory." I use the expression, as the scene recalled perfectly in my memory a puppet show of that name which I recollect to have seen in my childhood, and made so strong an impression of my mind that I thought it a true representation of the highest pitch of human greatness and felicity.'[18] The connection between universalist emperors and a child-like universe was one frequently made during those days and crops up left, right and centre. Kierkegaard, the Danish philosopher, explained the fascination with wonders and curiosities, often prized as signs of imperial might, as the expression of a child's psychology. Nero, the Roman emperor, he commented, possessed everything in abundance and was bored with it, yet might momentarily draw satisfaction and amusement from the most insignificant surprises, mere trifles, like the joy of a child over toys and trinkets.[19]

This was the result of developments long in train. From the sixteenth century, a powerful discourse had emerged in Europe fiercely critical of aspirations to universal monarchy. In *Lords of All the World* Antony Pagden has tracked how these opinions grew out of opposition mainly to the Habsburg bid for mastery in Europe. The British parliamentary debates on Victoria's imperial title echoed much of this literature; that she would remain only a queen in Britain was for instance basically a repetition of an argument already advanced by the school of Salamanca in the sixteenth century. Dealing with Charles V, the Holy Roman Emperor, Francisco Vitoria had maintained that in his Spanish possessions Charles held the right not of an emperor, but merely of a king. The claim to universal empire was impossible. Such ideas were patently absurd, 'a silly notion', Hugo Grotius added scornfully, writing as he did from the renegade Dutch republics in the early seventeenth century.[20] These views found vindication

---

[18] The passage is quoted from the analysis of Hevia 1995: 107–8.

[19] S. Kierkegaard, *Enten Eller* (9th edn, Copenhagen, 1994), vol. II, 176 (*Either Or*, from *Part 2, the papers of B, second part*).

[20] Vitoria [Victoria], *De Indis* 2.1 (ed. J. B. Scott, Washington, DC, 1917; also the English translation in his *Political Writings* ed. A. Pagden and J. Lawrance in 1991) and Hugo Grotius, *De iure belli ac pacis*, lib. II, cap. xii, §13 (ed. J. B. Scott, Washington, DC, 1913; a recent translation by Richard Tuck was published in 2005) with Pagden 1995: ch. 2. The reading of Vitoria in Anghie 2005: ch. 1 is too inquisitorial: as a defence of colonialism Vitoria's thought was at least ambiguous and also concerned to rein in claims to universal monarchy in Europe.

on the battlefield. The Reformation and the Thirty Years War broke the
back of the universal ambitions of the Habsburgs.[21] Europe remained
split up between a number of regional, jealously competitive monarchies.
Without effective power and intellectually discredited, universal empire
was put to rest. As Henry VIII had asserted when severing the English
church from the Catholic, his kingdom was fully an empire in its own
right, not subject to the authority of any other power, be it pope or (Holy
Roman) emperor.[22] History and in time progress seemed to favour the
development of a plurality of independent states (and empires), sovereign,
equal and geographically bounded; it was on these principles that the
mainstream constructed modern doctrines of statehood and international
relations – discussed by Haldén in Chapter 12 below.[23] Still, the idea
of a universal unifying empire retained more of its allure than is often
supposed. After all, in professing their sovereignty, in Latin often simply
imperium or *summum imperium*,[24] European monarchs had arrogated to
themselves many of the prerogatives and trappings of universal empire.
Depictions of early modern European kings in Roman imperator costume
are without number. While the new (proto) national polities took shape,
they drew heavily on the imagery and ideology of universal empire, as
may be seen from the quotation from Shakespeare's *Cymbeline* which
serves as epigraph to this book.[25] None other than Napoleon, surging
out of a revolutionary France experimenting with nationalism, attempted
to breathe fresh life into the idea by proclaiming a new empire to order
his Europe.[26] Universal empire died hard; its demise was hardly a foregone
conclusion.

If we raise our perspective from Europe and the Atlantic to the global
level, this impression is confirmed. Far from being the era which experienced the end of moribund universal empire, the early modern period
saw imperial universalism vigorous and flourishing. At the dawn of the
age, the new Ming dynasty in China had proclaimed its universal sway

[21] Kennedy 1987: ch. 2.   [22] Muldoon 1999: 128, and more generally ch. 6.
[23] Creveld (1999: 41) reflects well in mainstream thinking the element of incomprehension with regard
to universal empire: 'to the extent these and similar claims did not correspond to reality they could
sometimes lead to comic results'. See his ch. 3 for an excellent account of the evolution of the
modern state, complemented by Watson 1992: chs. 17–18.
[24] E.g. in the writings of the seventeenth-century lawyer and leading exponent of modern international
law, Samuel Pufendorf, cf. his *De jure naturae et gentium* (ed. Frank Böhling, Berlin, 1998), book
VII, cap. 3–4.
[25] Yates 1975: 29–87 on the use of imperial imagery in the public construction of the English and
French monarchies in the second half of the sixteenth century.
[26] Huet 1999 and Nouvel-Kammerer 2007 for Napoleon's use of Roman symbolism. Further Forrest
and Wilson 2008.

by launching a series of grand, unprecedented naval expeditions into the Indian Ocean between 1405 and 1433. Built to impress, these gigantic fleets were to bring home rare objects and awe foreign princes to accept the 'son of heaven' as their tributary overlord.[27] A few decades later, in 1453, the conquest of Constantinople by Sultan Mehmed II sparked Ottoman and Muscovite/Russian claims to the succession of Rome.[28] As Constantinople had for centuries been capital of the ancient Mediterranean empire, geography favoured the Ottoman adoption of the title of *Kayser i-Rum*. But since the city had been founded by the first Christian emperor, religion could justify the ambitions of the Tsar through a postulated transfer inside the Orthodox family. The sixteenth century witnessed the further expansion of Ottoman territories until the new Muslim realm rivalled the extent of the Eastern Roman empire at the height of its powers during the reign of Justinian. It was not merely fanciful posturing when in 1623 Sultan Mustafa, addressing the Polish king Sigismund, boastfully referred to his own court as 'the refuge of sultans and the seat of felicity which feeds the lips of the Caesars of the epoch and is thronged by the mouths of the Khusraws of the age'. Royalty and artists alike gravitated to the throne of the Ottoman Caesars (see Kołodziejczyk, Chapter 7 below).[29] Meanwhile, a new Muslim dynasty was establishing itself in India. Under Akbar (r. 1556–1605) the Mughals rose to real prominence. Donning regnal names such as 'World Seizer/Jahangir' or 'King of the World/Shahjahan', the Mughal emperors made little secret of their confidence and pretensions to universal monarchy. Their enormous wealth and vast subject populations placed them as the only credible rival to the Ottomans for pre-eminence within the world of Islam.[30] Finally, the conquests in the new world made it seem as if the Habsburg domains were now surpassing all previous empires in recorded history. 'Plus ultra' or 'further beyond', their power had broken through the confines of the old world. Under Philip (r. 1556–98), the son of Charles V, the writ of the Spanish branch of the Habsburg dynasty literally circled the globe.[31]

These developments were the upshot of a much longer history, with roots stretching far back in Eurasian time. The claim to universal empire was already one trumpeted by rulers during antiquity. There we also find the

---

[27] Dreyer 2007. [28] Grala 1996.

[29] Quotation from Kołodziejczyk 2000: 388–401; the quoted fragment is on 390 (Turkish Ottoman text) and 396 (English translation). On 'Roman' Constantinople as capital of the Ottoman empire and its court as centre of artistic patronage, briefly Goffman 2002: 51–64 and 105–9, even of an Italian renaissance painter, cf. Jardine and Brotton 2000: 8.

[30] Farooqi 1989.

[31] For a comparison, see Subrahmanyam 2009. Rosenthal 1971 on the Habsburg motto.

idea that history could be organised as a succession of dominant empires. Most famous is the prophecy in the Old Testament Book of Daniel describing the Neo-Babylonian empire of Nebuchadnezzar as a giant on feet of clay, soon to be overtaken by a succession of powers before the establishment of an eternal kingdom of God over all the earth.[32] Rulers inscribed and measured themselves in and against such genealogies of imperial power (see Angelov and Herrin, Chapter 6 below). Rome, who liked to see herself as governing the *orbis terrarum*, became a well-established standard to emulate for later empire-builders, and, as we have seen, not just within Christianity. Alexander the Great, the Macedonian conqueror of the Persian world empire, had even wider geographical purchase.[33] A late antique Greek fairytale history, the so-called *Alexander Romance*, travelled far and wide across much of Eurasia and received countless translations and retellings. Alexander and the people in his ambience provided substance for literary and philosophical discourse within the Christian and Muslim worlds, an example of which is excavated by Garth Fowden (Chapter 5 below). In this league of imperial models can also be found famed and notorious Central Asian and Mongol conquerors like Genghis Khan and Timur Lenk.[34] The rather misty figure of Aśoka, ruler of the Indian Maurya empire, earned a place within Buddhist traditions. Mythologised, he came to typify the ideal Buddhist universal ruler, the wheel-turning/cakravartin lord; and, through a complex genealogy, he still featured as a model for the Qing emperors, roughly two millennia later.[35]

The notion of world rule connected with these models has posed an awkward challenge to students of empire. Since our general points of reference have been shaped by modern theories of statehood, 'universal empire' has seemed foreign and mysterious, and sometimes stubbornly to fly in the face of reality. No empire, after all, has ever actually held universal sway. Apart from dismissal, a common response therefore has been to treat it as the product of an 'other' civilisation and see it as an expression of a particular foreign culture. Much can be achieved in this way. The late C. R. Whittaker's *The Frontiers of the Roman Empire* (1994) is a particularly successful attempt to explain the Roman claim to universal power with reference to the specific cultural horizon and geographical mindset of Greco-Roman civilisation. Yet, as we saw above, the risk of succumbing to exoticism or ethnic stereotyping and essentialist arguments is never far off.

[32] Book of Daniel 2.   [33] Ray and Potts 2007.
[34] The Timurid aspect of Mughal imperial ideology is well illustrated in Beach, Koch and Thackston 1997: 25–7. For a broad survey of Timur's legacy, see Manz 2002.
[35] Crossley 1992: 1482–3 and, in more detail, 1999: ch. 5.

Historians of such empires have often had to contend with various cultur-
alist prejudices, for instance that rulers were caught up in rigid rituals and
cultural illusions, were unable to adjust in order to discern existing challenges correctly, did not properly understand where their power came to an
end, or even were unable to develop ways of engaging in diplomatic negotiations. Ultimately, explanations that confine the phenomenon within a
context of cultural uniqueness, exclusivity and particularism are bound
to run up against an intellectual barrier, as argued by James Hevia in his
study of the much debated Chinese tributary system, *Cherishing Men from
Afar*.[36] The notion of the universal emperor or empire exists across different
cultures and time periods; it is not the unique property of a single society,
nor the preserve of one specific group of historians and area specialists.
Historical comparison and a wider context are required. The basis for this
volume, therefore, is the identification of a set of shared broad 'commonalities' or recurrent features. Cultures are rarely clearly bounded entities
developing in isolation, but are porous and affected by their surround-
ings. The process of civilisation involves constant borrowing, emulation
and reinterpretation of other societies. Like monarchy or its rituals such
as the hunt, we approach the phenomenon of imperial universalism as a
specific form of political organisation or practice, culturally and historically
inflected but not an expression of absolute difference.[37]

At the heart of the notion of universal empire is a hierarchical conception of rulers and statehood (cf. Barjamovic, Chapter 2).[38] Possession
of extensive territories generally comes with the package, but it does not
preclude the existence of alternative centres of power. War was frequent
in agrarian societies, the paramount activity of rulers and states. In this
environment, conquest was a 'natural' constant, competition fierce and
the inclination to rank powers ingrained. We even find this phenomenon
in the culturally 'isolated' Precolumbian America, as argued by Olko in
Chapter II of this volume. A universal emperor staked out a claim to be the
supreme monarch in the sea of contentious and rival lordships; all others
ranked below him and were thus, in a sense, part of his hegemony, even
if they eluded direct control (see Kołodziejczyk, Chapter 7). Behind the
idea of world rule were imperial conglomerates comprising a vast variety
of relationships and degrees of submission, from directly controlled territories, to client kings and tribal chieftains, as well as distant kingdoms that
might occasionally send an embassy bringing gifts symbolically to confirm

[36] Hevia 1995: 25.   [37] Cf. Allsen 2006.
[38] For this and what follows, Hevia 1995: ch. 5 is one of the best analyses. Further, Watson 1992:
ch. 12; Wink 1986: 9–66. See also Sahlins 1988.

their allegiance or recognition of the emperor, the highest tributary lord. Tenth-century Byzantine diplomacy, for instance, related to the surrounding world as a family of kings subject to the emperor in Constantinople (see Angelov and Herrin, Chapter 6). There was little to distinguish a universal empire from an international society or inter-state system, and boundaries therefore were less important to define these entities than in our accustomed way of thinking of the state.[39] The notion of universal empire covered both the experience of the loosely structured Holy Roman Empire of the German Nation where imperial supremacy was mostly symbolical and the Qing empire with its empire-wide cadres of Han literati having passed through the state examination system. These empires, in short, represented a hierarchical ordering of diversity and were frequently presented as the embodiment of divine and civilisational order. Nevertheless, supremacy had constantly to be defended and maintained, also at the symbolical level as Bang argues in Chapter 3, an analysis of the Hellenistic monarchies informed by the work of Clifford Geertz.

For Roman emperors, Persia became something of a touchstone.[40] One of the acts which would later help Caligula (r. AD 37–41) earn notoriety was in fact a ritual staged to show that the Roman emperor surpassed even the greatest of Persian kings. Suetonius includes in his biography the story of how Caligula had a bridge of ships constructed across the Gulf of Baiae and then led a series of triumphal processions over it. This was an act of symbolic rivalry with the Achaemenid emperor Xerxes (r. 485–465 BC), of whom Herodotus relates that he bridged the Hellespont to take his army across to Europe in the invasion of Greece. But the Gulf of Baiae was wider and hence the 'achievement' of Caligula was greater.[41] In turn, the Greco-Roman world would be cast in a similar role in attempts to renew or reinvent the Persian imperial tradition.

When, after the Muslim conquests, Persians gradually emerged to reassert their position and status within the world of Islam, their old history of confrontation with Hellenism and the Roman empire was also mobilised. Under the Parthian and especially Sasanid dynasties, the Achaemenid past seems largely to have receded from historical memory, its place eventually taken by a meandering mythological and legendary universe.[42] But, as we have seen, Alexander was still vividly remembered. The epic resurrection of Persian royal ideology, the *Shahname* of the court poet Firdausi (c. 940–1020), claims the Macedonian king for Persia. He is portrayed as the son of

---

[39] Watson 1992: 128; Brummett 2007: 47–9. More generally Whittaker 1994; Gommans 2002.
[40] Cf. Parker 2008: 211.   [41] Suetonius *Caligula*, ch. 19; Herodotus VII, 33–7, 44–56.
[42] Wiesehöfer 2001: 224–7 for a discussion of Persian historical memory and the sources for Firdausi.

a Greek princess and the Persian emperor. Alexander's conquest of Persia is thus turned into a tale of how he defeats his tyrannical half-brother, then on the throne, before going on to position himself as a world ruler of unsurpassed might: intrepid, spirited and mindful of Persian sentiments.[43] With the death of Alexander, the Persian throne is left vacant in Firdausi's poem until the rise of the Sasanid dynasty. These Persian monarchs step into the void and establish themselves as new world rulers. In the fertile imagination of Firdausi, the humiliating defeats inflicted on the Romans during the third century AD are elaborated into a charming tale. The Persian king Shapur, as a seeker of wisdom, daringly travels to Rome to find out about his rival.[44] His cover broken by his natural royal charisma, the Persian ruler is taken captive and sewn into an ass's skin. Then the Roman emperor leads an invasion to ravage a Sasanian empire suffering under the lack of a king. But at the last minute, Shapur escapes his Roman captivity, returns to his kingdom and manages to snatch victory from the jaws of defeat. In a surprise attack, the hapless Roman emperor, busy enjoying the fruits of his conquests, is overwhelmed together with army and nobles. Now the roles are reversed. Taken prisoner, the vicious Roman emperor is brought low, mutilated and treated like a beast of burden. On humiliation then follows retribution; Roman territories are invaded, their armies are annihilated and finally a peace is concluded which high-mindedly leaves the enemy empire standing, but with the obligation to pay tribute and the Roman emperor still wasting away in shackles. His eventual death affords the grand Persian king of kings a final opportunity to demonstrate nobility of character and moral superiority: the corpse of the former emperor is magnanimously returned to Rome. This was an act worthy of a true world ruler.[45]

The archetype for these poetically embroidered tales of Persian imperial history is not difficult to identify. They employ many of the narrative

---

[43] The translation by Warner and Warner (London, 1920–5) of Firdausi is conveniently available from the homepage of Persian literature in translation hosted by the Packard Humanities Institute: http://persian.packhum.org/persian. The poem proceeds chronologically from reign to reign and the relevant parts are therefore easy to locate in this otherwise exuberant and sprawling epic. For Alexander and Dara, their contrasting personalities and contest, see Warner and Warner: VI, 25–85. Pages 85–187 relate the rest of Alexander's reign as a series of conquests and extraordinary adventures to the ends of the earth.

[44] Firdausi availed himself here of his poetical licence, not only to embroider and fictionalise the narrative, but also to change the chronology. The capture of the Roman emperor Valerian, which incident, however transformed, surely constitutes the discernible historical background to Firdausi's fairy tale, took place under the first Shapur, not the second as in the *Shahname*, cf. Wiesehöfer 2001, note 42 above.

[45] *Shahname*, reign of Shapur, son of Urmuzd, in the trans. of Warner and Warner: VI, 335–57.

elements of the *Alexander Romance*.[46] But whereas the third-century Greek version presents Alexander as the offspring of the last king of Egypt, Nektanebo, paternity now goes to Persia, thereby appropriating the conquering hero of Hellenism for the cause of Persian imperialism. Likewise Shapur's audacious trip to Rome mirrors episodes in the novel picturing Alexander tempting fate with similar feats of derring-do.[47] Persian imperial universalism is reconstructed and shaped along a pattern intimately linked with Hellenistic cultural models. But to this element of cultural emulation is added confrontation, assertion of autonomy and the proclamation of Persian superiority. The Sasanids rise above the Greco-Roman world, 'Rum' as it is invariably called by Firdausi whether he refers to the age of Alexander or to the remaining Byzantine realm of his own times. The notion of a universal empire, in other words, has not left a simple genealogy. The Achaemenids were far more present on the mental horizon of the Romans than to later Persian dynasties. Rather the notion was reproduced and constantly reinvented in a complex process of cultural transfer and competitive appropriation, emulation as well as differentiation.[48]

A WORLD HISTORICAL SKETCH

Nevertheless we may attempt to describe this experience through a set of broad, admittedly simplifying, world-historical phases. In his essay *Empire to Commonwealth* Garth Fowden analysed the Arab caliphate of the Umayyad and Abbasid dynasties as the culmination of classical antiquity. In the seventh century by simultaneously conquering the Sasanid empire and vast swathes of the Roman, the victorious Muslim armies had effectively united the old world from Sind in the East to the Pillars of Hercules in the West (map 1). This was the realisation of an old, more or less utopian, ambition. The Greek historian Herodian (fl. *c.* 170–240) makes

---

[46] For the complex processes of transmission of Alexander material into the Middle Eastern languages Syriac, Arabic and Persian, see recent discussions by Bladel 2007 and Venetis 2008.

[47] [Pseudo-Callisthenes], *Alexander Romance* (ed. W. Kroll, *Historia Alexandri Magni*, Berlin, 1926), I, 34 (Nektanebo, father of Alexander); II, 13–15 and III, 20–3 (Alexander recklessly risking his life by travelling under cover to an enemy ruler's court in order to get real experience of his opponent).

[48] Cf. Hekster and Fowler 2005: 34–8 and Canepa 2009 in particular, for the importance of competitive emulation and appropriation to the dissemination of models of kingship across cultures during antiquity. Our project, therefore, should not be seen as a new attempt to follow in the footsteps of Frazer's *Golden Bough* (1890) and produce an exercise in evolutionary anthropology. We approach the notion of a universal emperor as a constantly reinvented tradition or dynamic form of rule, not as an archaic custom like his 'divine' kingship, a fascinating or bizarre left-over in complex, literate cultures from man's more primitive ages. Brisch 2008 for a collection of empirical studies revisiting Frazer's notion of 'Divine Kingship'.

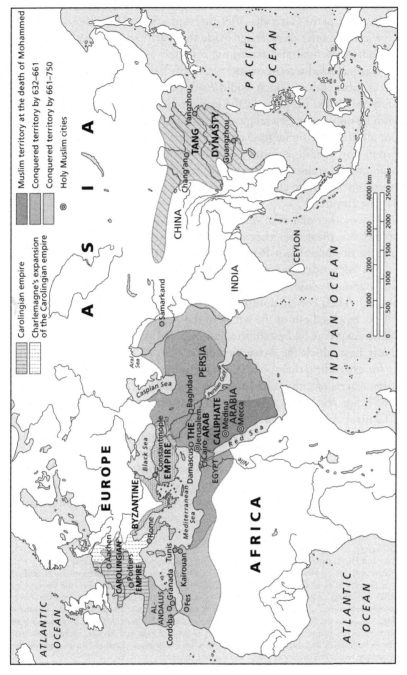

Map 1 The Arab caliphate in the so-called classical age and the Tang empire

Muslim territory at the death of Mohammed
Conquered territory by 632–661
Conquered territory by 661–750
◎ Holy Muslim cities

Carolingian empire
Charlemagne's expansion
of the Carolingian empire

PACIFIC OCEAN

TANG DYNASTY

CHINA

Changʼan · Yangzhou
Guangzhou

Samarkand

Aral Sea

Caspian Sea

PERSIA

Baghdad

Persian Gulf

THE ARAB CALIPHATE

INDIA

CEYLON

INDIAN OCEAN

A S I A

EUROPE

Black Sea

BYZANTINE EMPIRE

Constantinople

Jerusalem
Damascus ◎ Cairo
EGYPT

Nile

Red Sea

Medina ◎
Mecca ◎

ARABIA

Rome

Mediterranean Sea

CAROLINGIAN EMPIRE

Aachen
Poitiers

Tunis
Kairouan

AL-ANDALUS
Córdoba · Granada · Fes

AFRICA

ATLANTIC OCEAN

ATLANTIC OCEAN

0   1000   2000   3000   4000 km
0   500 1000 1500 2000 2500 miles

the Roman emperor Caracalla offer this aspiration as his official justifica-
tion for a mock-offer of marriage made to a Parthian princess; combining
the military potential and economic resources of the two major powers
of the classical Mediterranean and Near East held the promise of creating
'one irresistible empire' which would 'easily govern the whole world'.[49] This
task now fell to the caliph.[50] As the leader of Islam, the commander of the
faithful, he presided over a religion which was presented as the consumma-
tion of all previous divine revelation. There was truth to be found in both
Christian and Jewish scripture, but the divine teachings communicated
by Muḥammad transcended and perfected those of all previous prophets.
Islam embraced all the children of Abraham, its truths were universal and
so was the empire.[51]

Only two other phases of similar such unity across the old world can be
identified, one prior, the other after. Behind Caracalla's wedding plans was
the dream of obtaining a Parthian or Persian triumph in Alexander-like
style. But Alexander was not only the champion of Hellenism, he was
also in a certain sense 'the last of the Achaemenids', as Pierre Briant has
taught us.[52] Their Persian dominion had eventually, after a Neo-Babylonian
interlude, emerged out of the wreck of the Neo-Assyrian empire (934–605
BC). The Assyrians had established an imperial pattern of government in
the Near East which the Achaemenids (*c.* 550–330 BC) used as a stepping
stone for expanding their possessions incomparably. Their power brought
the dimensions of empire to an unprecedented pitch.[53] The Achaemenid
king of kings reached out to India, the eastern Mediterranean and deep
into Central Asia; the bounds of his territories prefigured those of the
caliphate in the classical age of Islam. It was this universal empire Alexander
miraculously conquered and briefly expanded before his early death in
Babylon (323 BC; map 2). The other phase is constituted by the Mongol
conquests of the thirteenth century. In an enormous explosion of power,
their armies darted out of Central Asia to create the largest land empire

[49] Herodian IV, 10, 2–4.
[50] Crone and Hinds (1986) are fundamental on the imperial nature of the early caliphs.
[51] Fowden 1993, ch. 6. Herodian, Roman and Sasanian universal imperial ambitions are treated in
ch. 1. Dreams of re-establishing the Achaemenid empire are mostly ascribed to the Persians by
sources of Roman origin. Fowden may give too much credit to those. As we have seen above,
concrete memories of the Achaemenids were weak and foggy in later Persian traditions. But there
is little reason to doubt Sasanian universal claims in general. Shapur celebrated his victories over
Roman emperors by proclaiming himself 'the king of kings of Eran and Aneran', in other words of
all lands both inside and outside Iran. On the titles, see Huyse 2006. Further Canepa 2009 on the
late antique symbolical rivalry of Rome and Sasanid Persia.
[52] Briant 1996; see also 2003.   [53] Taagepera 1978.

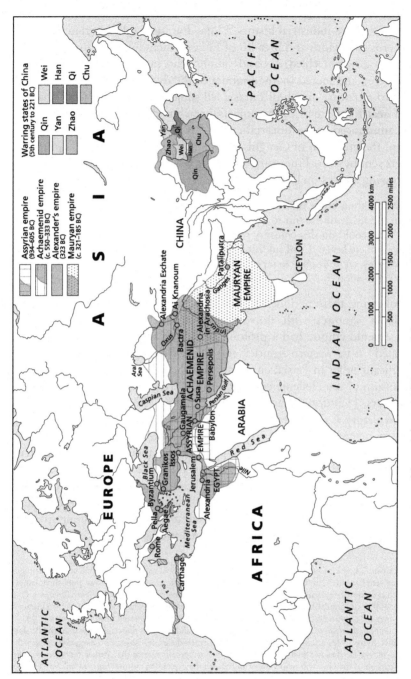

Map 2 Achaemenid Persia and the conquests of Alexander

in recorded pre-industrial history.[54] Like dominoes, old agrarian dynasties fell across the width and breadth of Eurasia, including the Southern Sung and the now enfeebled Abbasid caliphs who saw their capital Baghdad conquered and looted by the founder of the dynasty of the Il Khans. For close to a century, much of Eurasia fell subject to the Genghisid Khagan, the Great Khan (map 3); the universal reach and supremacy of his empire was announced in no uncertain terms to a trembling world. As Güyük Khan, the grandson of Genghis, wrote in a famous rebuke of 1246 to the letters sent by Pope Innocent IV bidding the Mongol ruler to abandon his harrowing attacks on Christian territories:

How dost thou know that such words as thou speakest are with God's sanction? From the rising of the sun to its setting, all the lands have been made subject to me. Who could do this contrary to the command of God? Now you should say with a sincere heart: 'I will submit and serve you.' Thou thyself, at the head of all the Princes, come at once to serve and wait upon us! At that time I shall recognize your submission.[55]

Following these periods of unification was the crystallisation of more 'regional' empires with universal aspirations. The formation of the Achaemenid empire had a profound effect on the neighbouring regions. Located on its western frontier, the Greek city-states did not just find a significant other in Persia; engaging with the great power also effected an expansion of the Hellenic cultural horizon. To explain victory in the Persian wars, Herodotus (420s BC) found that he effectively had to write a world history. A rival Greek universalism had already begun to evolve in the century preceding the conquests of Alexander. Xenophon (c. 430–350s BC) could present Persia as a land of opportunity for courageous Greek mercenaries while Isokrates (436–338 BC) might counsel concord among Hellenic communities and advocate a joint expedition to conquer the great empire to the East.[56] This Hellenistic culture followed in the train of Alexander's armies and nothing was yet settled at his death. But in the ensuing struggle among his generals, a number of regional monarchies of Greek cultural

[54] Di Cosmo, Frank and Golden 2009 for an extensive survey of the Mongol empire and its heritage.
[55] This letter, written in Persian, is preserved in the Vatican archives. It was published, along with a facsimile, by Paul Pelliot, 'Les Mongols et la Papauté', *Revue de l'Orient Chrétien* 3 (23) (1922–3), 3–30 (available online: www.catholicapedia.net/Documents/Revue-de-l.Orient-chretien/23-1922.1923_revue-de-l.orient-ch_paris.pdf). English translation quoted from Dawson 1955: 86.
[56] Xenophon, *Anabasis* relates the failed expedition of a band of Greek mercenaries to assist the Persian prince Kyros in his attempt to conquer the Achaemenid throne. Isokrates, *Panegyricus*, especially chs. 187–9. Further, see Hall 2002: ch. 6. It is not by coincidence that Parker (2008) opens his discussion of the Greco-Roman view of India with the expanding cultural horizon following in the wake of Achaemenid power and Alexander's conquests.

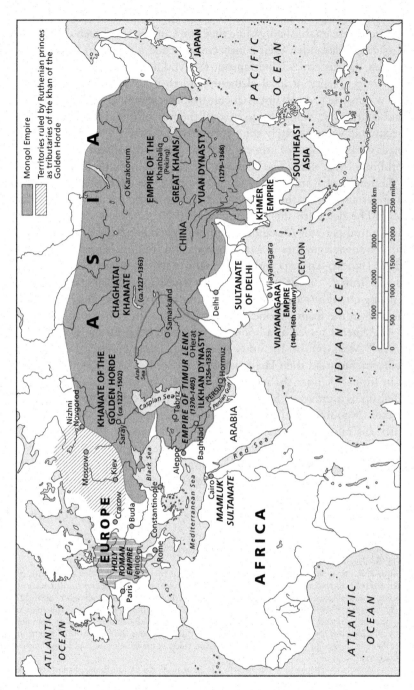

Map 3 The Mongol moment

Legend:
Mongol Empire
Territories ruled by Ruthenian princes as tributaries of the khan of the Golden Horde

ATLANTIC OCEAN

EUROPE

Paris
Buda
Cracow
HOLY ROMAN EMPIRE
Venice
Rome
Constantinople
Mediterranean Sea
Black Sea
Kiev
Moscow
Nizhni Novgorod

KHANATE OF THE GOLDEN HORDE
(ca.1227–1502)
Saraj
Caspian Sea
Aral Sea

CHAGHATAI KHANATE
(ca.1227–1363)

Samarkand

ASIA

Karakorum

EMPIRE OF THE GREAT KHANS/
YUAN DYNASTY
(1279–1368)

Khanbaliq
(Peking)

CHINA

JAPAN

PACIFIC OCEAN

EMPIRE OF TIMUR LENK
(1370–1405)
Tabriz
Herat
ILKHAN DYNASTY
(1256–1353)
PERSIA
Baghdad
Hormuz
Persian Gulf

Aleppo
Cairo
MAMLUK SULTANATE
Red Sea
ARABIA

AFRICA

ATLANTIC OCEAN

Delhi
SULTANATE OF DELHI

Vijayanagara
VIJAYANAGARA EMPIRE
(14th–16th century)
CEYLON

INDIAN OCEAN

KHMER EMPIRE
SOUTHEAST ASIA

0 500 1000 1500 2000 2500 miles
0 1000 2000 3000 4000 km

orientation were established. While they continued to rival each other over the legacy of Alexander, their courts consolidated a common Hellenising culture in the eastern Mediterranean, the Middle East, Central Asia and North India. Plenty of local elements had to be accommodated within this new construct. As all imperial cultures, this was an amalgam.[57] In the second century BC, when Rome entered the fray of the Hellenistic world, this ecumene was ultimately split in two. Around the Mediterranean, the Romans created a Greco-Latin empire more than big enough to constitute a world in its own right. The emperor liked to present himself as universal and the might of Rome as boundless: 'To other peoples have been given land of certain extent: the territory of the city of Rome and the orb is the same.'[58] The defeat to the Romans suffered by the Seleucids, successors to the central parts of Alexander's empire, opened the way for the return of more Iranian dynasties in Mesopotamia and Iran. As king of kings, the Parthian (140 BC–AD 224) and then Sasanid (AD 224–651) ruler co-existed with the Roman Caesar in uneasy competition (map 4). Neither power was strong enough to destroy the other, but rivalry remained and came to expression in the frontier zone. For long periods, the right to appoint the king of Armenia served as a bone of contention between the two mighty empires.[59] Meantime, at the other side of the Persian empire, the example of Achaemenid (and then Hellenic) universal power had spawned emulation in India.[60] Under the Maurya dynasty (c. 320–185 BC), Aśoka threw himself up as a universal lord, the Buddhist wheel-turning sage king and protector of godly, moral order, *dhamma* or *dharma*. After the fall of the dynasty, his model retained its allure. Powerful empires, like those of the Kushanas (fl. first to third centuries AD), cast themselves in this mould of Buddhist kingship, while the Guptas (fourth to sixth centuries AD) took it in a Hindu direction and continued to elaborate the tradition which in the language of Sanskrit was projected across much of South and South East Asia in the following centuries.[61] Less affected by these developments,

---

[57] Sherwin-White and Kuhrt 1993. Walbank 1992 for a general history.

[58] Ovid, *Fasti* II, 683–4. Best on this, Whittaker 1994.

[59] A ritual climax was reached under Nero when the Armenian king Tiridates, brother of the Parthian ruler, accepted to travel to Rome and have his dignity confirmed by the emperor through a set of carefully choreographed public ceremonies. Symbolically, the supremacy of Rome was re-affirmed, while a member of the Parthian royal lineage was tolerated on the throne of Armenia. This episode was described at length by Suetonius, *Life of Nero*, ch. 13 and Tacitus, *Annales* XV, 28–31. Sommer 2005 and Campbell 1993 for modern discussions. Later the Ottomans and Safavids would contend over the right to appoint Kurdish and Georgian client-rulers in the same region, see Tezcan 2000.

[60] Pollock 2006.

[61] Stein 1996: 73–104; Thapar 1997 (on Aśoka); Christian 1998: 210–18 (on the Kushanas); Pollock 2006 (on the dissemination of the Gupta courtly model and its Sanskrit culture).

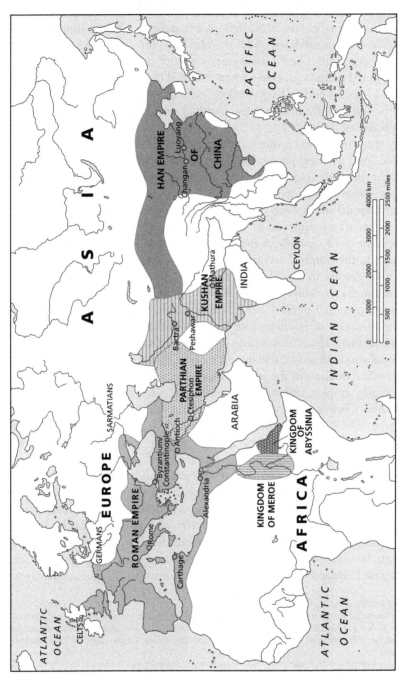

Map 4 Rome–Parthia–Han China

it was in the final centuries BC that a more separate Chinese imperial universalism was consolidated under the Qin (221–206 BC) and Han dynasties (206 BC–AD 220). The Chinese emperor ruled as *Huangdi*, a title which was adopted by the Qin rulers when they had conquered their neighbours and thus put an end to the so-called Warring States period. The *Huangdi* was the lord of 'all under heaven' and had surpassed the kings (*Wang*) of the preceding period.[62]

By the tenth century, our second period of unification was drawing to a close. As a political power, the Abbasid caliphate was a spent force and its territories were fragmenting into a number of volatile monarchies. The caliph, however, retained some of his symbolical and religious authority. Many regional rulers, even if they did not obey his commands, still sought the rubber stamp approval of the distant figure-head of Islam as a mark of legitimacy. For a while in the eleventh century, it even seemed as if the Seljuks, as the nominal servants of the caliph, might revitalise a powerful universal empire in the Muslim heartlands. But fragmentation prevailed and in the place of empire a Muslim commonwealth developed.[63] A similar situation obtained in the Christian lands to the west and north of Islam. Its combination of world empire and universal creed had been pioneered by the Romans after Constantine (r. 306–337) attached Christianity to the imperial monarchy. The collapse of Roman government in the West and its drastic reduction in the eastern Mediterranean left the idea of a Christian world empire somewhat embattled. Nevertheless both Byzantium and Latin Christianity continued to harbour and project such aspirations (map 1). On Christmas Eve 800 the Frankish king Charlemagne was crowned emperor by the pope and the empire revived in the West to rival the claims of the old Roman empire in the East.[64] This new Roman dominion would under various forms have a long career in European history. But with pope and emperor frequently at each other's throats, the Universal and Holy Roman Empire was always less than it promised, often only an ephemeral existence, yet still a prize worth fighting for.[65]

Our final phase of unification was the least durable. The Mongol empire had reached such dimensions that it was effectively impossible to maintain centralised rule and it quickly dissolved into a number of regional khanates.

---

[62] Bodde 1986: 53–4.   [63] Kennedy 2004 for a survey.

[64] McKitterick 2008 for a revisionist discussion of Charlemagne, trying to peel off the layers of myth and look at his reign with fresh eyes. Classen (1985) provides a clear analysis of the different claims read into Charlemagne's imperial title by the pope, Byzantium, Charlemagne and his Frankish court.

[65] The meandering course taken by Charlemagne's imperial dignity and heritage is usefully surveyed in Muldoon 1999.

Then in 1368 the Ming dynasty led a successful rebellion in China which ousted the Mongol Yuan less than a century after Kublai Khan had conquered the southern parts of China. But even if the Mongol 'moment' proved short-lived, its impact was profound on several levels. It brought the Chinese tradition of universal empire closer to the rest of Eurasia. Already during the Tang dynasty (618–907), much of the Buddhist tradition had been absorbed within the heavenly empire. The Mongols multiplied these links. It is fascinating to observe one of the first Ming emperors style himself with the Persian *pādshāh* (master-king) in his diplomatic correspondence with the successor of Timur.[66] Furthermore, the Mongols left a model of rulership which continued to spark emulation during the next centuries. The social organisation of nomadic warriors had now found a formula which enabled them more permanently to tax the more populous agricultural regions of Eurasia. This served to reinvigorate the (re)formation of classical agrarian empires.[67] Chinese unity, for instance, was the product of the Mongol conquests. The culmination of this development was the establishment during the early modern period of a string of post-nomadic agrarian empires, all with universal aspirations, across Eurasia (map 5): the Manchu, Qing dynasty (1644–1912) exercised hegemony over China, Tibet and substantial regions in Central Asia as well as the client-kingdom of Korea (Rawski); the Mughal empire governed much of India and even Afghanistan (Koch); the Ottomans from Constantinople, the old Roman capital conquered in 1453, controlled south-eastern Europe, the eastern Mediterranean and the Black Sea regions, Mesopotamia and the Hijaz; and finally Russia, as the conquest of the post-Genghisid Volgine khanates and Siberia was instrumental in shaping the imperial ambitions of Muscovian rulers.[68] Meanwhile, Hindu imperialism, modelled on the Guptas, had been resurgent in southern India. Flourishing from the mid fourteenth till the mid sixteenth century, great kings projected their power from their splendid capital Vijayanagara, the city of Victory (see Rao and Subrahmanyam, Chapter 9). In their construction or articulation of universal empire, all these ruling dynasties combined models from previous phases: Turkish Central Asian, Persian, Roman and caliphal in the Ottoman case; in the Mughal case, Genghisid in the style of Timur, Persian, caliphal and

---

[66] Crossley 1999: 39–40; Fletcher 1995: ch. II (China and Central Asia, 1368–1884), 212 (with quotation of the letter).
[67] Di Cosmo 1999.
[68] Fletcher 1995, ch. VII; Gommans 2007; Wink 2011. For the argument that Muscovy adopted and conformed to the steppe (i.e., Genghisid) tradition rather than challenged its rules, see Keenan 1967 and Pritsak 1967; cf. also Kołodziejczyk 2011: 444–5.

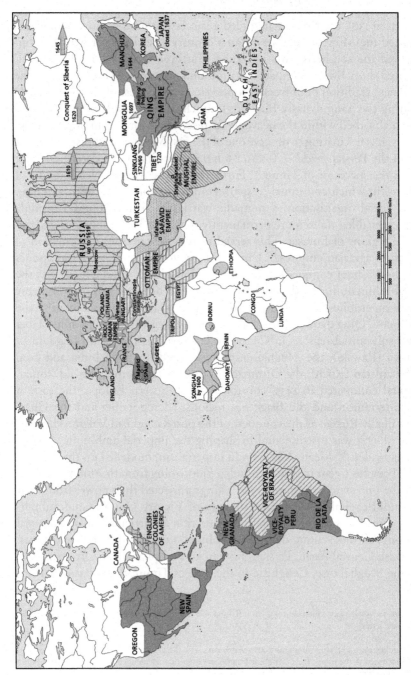

Map 5 The early modern Eurasian empires

Hindu; while the Manchus drew on the Mongol Khans, Tibetan Buddhism and the Han Chinese tradition, claiming to have won the mandate of heaven, and so on. Within these interconnected repertoires some examples of European iconography and forms of representation even began to crop up in the art sponsored by Asian courts as global contacts thickened in the wake of the so-called age of discoveries.[69]

This uneven sediment of historical models constituted a common or partly overlapping language of power which was fashioned, modulated and strategically employed to emphasise the pre-eminence of each ruling dynasty and articulate its relations to other powers, often with great flexibility as shown by the contributions of Rawski and Koch.[70] Akbar, the Great Mughal, entertained dreams of following in the footsteps of Timur Lenk (1336–1405). In a letter he pictured how his armies would cut through Central Asia all the way to 'Rum' and bring even the Ottomans to heel and accept their throne from the hands of the Indian Timurids as they had already done once before.[71] The sultans residing in Constantinople, however, also had competition closer to home. Under the Habsburgs during the sixteenth century, Latin Christian imperial universalism was reawakening.[72] Through deft matrimonial diplomacy, they managed to combine the surging force of Iberian expansionism, which at the Treaty of Tordesillas (1494) had pretended exclusively to divide the right to the new global worlds opening to their seafarers, with the old central European and Italian title to the Holy Roman Empire. But Ottoman power was at the height of its glory and would bow to no one. Not to be outdone, the Ottoman court seems quickly to have staged a response to the splendid imperial coronation by the pope of Habsburg Charles V in Bologna in 1530. On his progress towards Vienna in 1532, Süleyman the Magnificent paraded through the cities en route in Roman triumphal fashion. For this occasion, a fabulous four-tiered crown-helmet, set with marvellous precious stones, had been fabricated in Venice (fig. 1.2). Put on display during the processions, this awe-inspiring wonder quoted both holy-Roman imperial and papal regalia in its design. There was to be only one Caesar, one universal lord – this was the unmistakable claim – and that was the Ottoman sultan.[73]

---

[69] Koch 2001 (European influences on Mughal court art); Rawski 1998: 177 (the European Jesuit Castiglione serving as a painter at the eighteenth-century Manchu court); Subrahmanyam 1997a, cf. Jardine and Brotton 2000.

[70] Cf. Bayly 2004: 42–3.   [71] Farooqi 1989: 190.   [72] Pagden 1995, chs. 1–2; König 1969.

[73] Necipoğlu 1989. Further Ágoston 2007. On Charles' coronation, see Frieder 2008, ch. 4. Burke 1999 and Silver 2008 for the construction of the Habsburg imperial 'persona' in general.

SVLIMAN·OTOMAN·REX·TVRC· X·

Fig. 1.2 Augustino Veneziano: engraving of Sultan Süleyman, engraving 1535.

To the Dominican friar Tommaso Campanella this contest was destined
to play itself out differently. Writing some decades later at the turn of the
sixteenth century, he had his hopes firmly set on the Spanish monarchy:

and He [the Ottoman sultan] will also at this time already be called, *The Universal
Lord*; as the King of *Spain* is called, *The Catholic King*: So that these two Princes
seem now to strive, which of them shall attain to the Universal Monarchy of

the whole World . . . both these Princes are a part of the Roman Empire . . . But according to *Esdras*, the German, which is now the same that the Spaniard (as hath been said before) is the *Right Head*, but the Turk is the *Left Head* of the *Imperial Eagle*; after that Mahomet fell off from the Emperor *Heraclius*, during whose Reign the *Eagle* was divided: to whom notwithstanding there was no other promise, but that He should Devour the Middle Head, namely, the *Constantinopolitan*; whereas the Spaniard has this Promise made him, that he should devour the Left Head, that is to say the Turk.[74]

History, however, would soon give the lie to this apocalyptically inspired prophecy. As the English translator of the *De Monarchia Hispanica* remarked barely half a century later: 'the businesse hath miscarried, and the Spaniard hath not yet arrived, and perhaps now is never like to arrive to the end of [Universal Monarchy]'.[75] But this ought not, the publisher went on, to cool the English readership to the precepts and analysis of a perceptive political philosopher. Over the next century or so this judgment would be overturned. Increasingly as new theories of the state and international law, based on Hobbesian sovereignty, gained currency, thoughts such as Campanella's came to look like the outpourings of a fevered mind.[76] The new 'science' of politics was based on the principle of equality, rather than hierarchy, among sovereign states and would eventually come to see international society as constituted by so many individual nations. Disseminated during the age of colonial empires, this did in turn become a way of organising state power that was more universal in reach than the now old imperial universalisms, as Haldén observes in Chapter 12 below.

THREE THEMATIC KEYS

Around the elusive and much coveted prize of universal imperial rule developed forms of kingship and political culture. The chapters in the current volume examine different facets of the articulation of this phenomenon under three, broadly conceived, headings: (1) symbolism, ceremony and diplomatic relations, (2) universal or cosmopolitan literary high-cultures and, finally, (3) the inclination to present universal imperial rule as an expression of cosmic order. The key component in the grammar of

---

[74] T. Campanella, *A Discourse Touching the Spanish Monarchy* (London, 1654), 197 and 199 (ch. xxx); translation based on the 3rd Latin edition. Headley 1997 for a recent monograph on Campanella. Pagden 1990: ch. 2 for a discussion of his views of empire.

[75] From the translator's preface to Campanella, *A Discourse*. Running in a similar, but harsher vein was the assessment of Ludovicus Elzevirius in the dedicatory epistle to his 1640 Amsterdam edition of the Latin text: a clever, but flawed work.

[76] Watson 1992: chs. 14–18; Creveld 1999: 180–4; Pagden 1995: 38–9.

universal monarchy was the celebration of mastery over a multiplicity of lesser lords and subject populations and their need to pay homage and tribute to the supreme ruler. Enacted in ritual processions and fixed in works of art, imperial lords everywhere attempted to publicise their boundless might by putting on display the infinite diversity of people gravitating to their throne. This theme runs through history (and the contributions to this book), from the reliefs at Persepolis showing the great number of subjects bringing tribute to the Achaemenid great king (Barjamovic), and the use in Roman art of polychrome marble and personifications of provinces with various natural attributes to illustrate the enormous variety of resources at the command of the emperor (Schneider),[77] to the late eighteenth-century compilations of *Illustrations of Tributaries of the Qing Empire (Huang Qing zhigongtu)*.[78] For the Victorians in our opening example such gaudy spectacle was turning into a piece of Orientalism; it could still serve as a demonstration of vast imperial might, but the ritual had been subsumed under an evolving wider master-narrative about the power of progress, science and Western civilisation to reorder the world and had itself become an emblem of colonial subjection – 'that mixture of squalor and splendour' which the correspondent of *The Times* found so much more characteristic of Indian society, traditional and oriental, than the modern metropolitan nation.

Before that colonisation, however, this symbolical language had served to make manifest the power of imperial ruler(s) to absorb the foreign and the exotic, as Schneider argues in Chapter 4 (cf. figs. 1.3, 1.4a and 1.4b). Frequently this claim was grounded in theories of geographical determinism and humoral conceptions of the body. In the imperial centre came together the perfect mix of hot and cold, crude and refined, belligerency and subservience; it balanced all the properties and characteristics of individual regions and societies into a superior combination.[79] As such, imperial rulers generally claimed a position of supremacy for themselves and were reluctant to treat other monarchs and states on a basis of equality. Obviously even such over-mighty lords had to contend with limits to their power and accept that they could not command every other ruler around them. But the language of universal rule was flexible enough to handle this issue, a key point in Bang's analysis of the Hellenistic monarchies. In Chapter 8,

---

[77] On Roman pictorial strategies and imperial subjection, see further Schneider 1986 and Landskron 2006.

[78] Analysis of the latter in Crossley 1999: 332–6. And more broadly on this topic in Qing rulership, see Rawski 1998, especially 51–5 and 177.

[79] Bayly 2002: 50–5.

Fig. 1.3 Kneeling barbarian in polychrome marble.

Koch discusses how the Mughals, in appropriating Persian imperial culture for their monarchy in India, had to accommodate their contemporary
Iranian Safavid rivals. While the Mughals generally claimed that their rule
was the most universal, it is nevertheless possible to find some contexts
where the Safavids were referred to more courteously on equal terms.[80]
After the Manchu Qing dynasty had successfully conquered the Ming

[80] See further Farooqi 1989.

Fig. 1.4a The Chinese emperor depicted as a Tibetan, Buddhist monk.

rulers, they still tacitly tolerated that their Korean client-kings defiantly stuck to the calendar of the previous dynasty in their own internal documents, as Rawski shows in Chapter 10. Universal monarchy was capable of expressing itself in several registers from sublime arrogance to pragmatic conciliation (see also Kołodziejczyk, Chapter 7).[81]

At the heart of the symbolism of multiple subjects and ethnic variety was the aspiration of world conquest and global rule. Impossible and hyperbolic as critics have pointed out since Herodotus, but as a metaphor for extensive empire it worked well enough in a world where the speed of transport and communication was set by wind and animal power.[82] Among world

[81] Cf. Toby 1991: 202.
[82] Cf. the sophisticated comment made by the Greek geographer Strabo (64 BC – AD 25) that it was impossible to know all the world equally well. Even if the whole was united under just one ruler, regions far from the seat of government would still be much less familiar and also less important. The world-geography of a scholar serving an Indian ruler would thus be much different from his

Fig. 1.4b The Chinese emperor depicted as a hunter in European apparel.

historians, the term ecumene has gained currency.[83] In ancient Greek, 'oikoumene' spanned a range of meanings from 'the inhabited world' to Greek versus barbarian lands. Under Roman rule, the concept was frequently applied to the empire. Geographers were certainly aware that the

own, their horizons and worlds being in a certain sense not identical (*Geography* 1, 1, 16, pp. 32–5 in the parallel Greek text and English translation by H. L. Jones in the Loeb Classical Library). Further, see Fowden 1993: 13.

[83] Brummett 2007: 20–4 and 56–8 for an attempt to apply to the Ottoman empire this concept introduced by Marshall Hodgson (e.g. 1974: I, 109–10) and used e.g. by William McNeill 1986: 19 and 22.

oikoumene included more. But in general usage, empire and oikoumene could be thought of as coterminous, in which case the word came close to meaning something like 'the civilised world' or our world.[84] This conflation of empire and the civilised part of the earth is a recurrent phenomenon. By the same token, Ottoman sultans might be described as 'the prosperous padishah of the inhabited portion of the earth'.[85] In the ancient context, the notion of an imperial oikoumene is illustrated well by a second-century eulogy of Rome written by the Hellenic master orator Aristeides. The speech presents an idealised image of the empire as a military camp defending the internal oikoumene against outside intruders. The old distinction between Greek and Barbarian, the Hellenic author claimed, had been superseded by another one: Roman and non-Roman. Under the emperors a new and wider community of the 'best men' had been forged, transcending local loyalties.[86] In enumerating the blessings of this new community, urban and lettered, our rhetor is waxing not a little lyrical. Even so, it is an important characteristic that universal empires promoted cosmopolitan forms of discourse and identity (cf. Bang, Chapter 3). Emperors did not only celebrate the subjection of local diversity, they also encouraged the imitation of universal cultural standards and the formation of types of supra-local knowledge.[87] As Strabo, the Augustan geographer, observed, the expansion of imperial power widened geographical horizons and helped his branch of Greek learning to extend its grasp of the world. His was a 'colossal' work, Strabo insisted; it operated on a globular scale, dealing with elevated and important matters, the concerns of great generals, to convey the big picture instead of losing its way in trifling details. Geography, in short, was a grand affair, it was universal, it belonged to philosophy.[88] The notion of an ecumene captures well the emergence and dissemination of such kinds of hegemonic 'transcultural' knowledge and

---

[84] E.g. Philo, *Legatio ad Gaium*, chs. 8–10, 15–20; Nicolet 1991: ch. 2; Whittaker 1994: 12–18, 31–8; Mattern 1999: ch. 2. Cf. Appian, *Roman History*, preface, chs. 6–7 and further Isaac 2004: 371–80, the latter showing well the ambiguous position which the Parthians occupied on the Roman mental map combining traits of barbarian nomads with those of a civilised rival.

[85] *saʿadetlu padişah-i rubʿ-i meskun*: this expression was used by the Crimean khan, Islam III Giray in an instrument of peace from 1649 addressed to the Polish king, John II Casimir Vasa. The document is published in Kołodziejczyk 2011: 959–63.

[86] Aelius Aristeides, *To Rome*, chs. 9–10, 28–9, 31, 33 and 61 (the Roman empire is a world-empire; it rules the ecumene), 36, 59–64, 101 (a cosmopolitan Roman world of the 'best' men set against the barbarian), 81–2 (the empire ring-fenced by an army defending it against the outer barbarians).

[87] For Rome, see the analyses in Bang 2010 and Wallace-Hadrill 1997 with further bibliography.

[88] Strabo, *Geography* I, chs. 1–2, in particular ch. 2.1 (empire widens horizon); ch. 1, 16 (the handmaiden of great conquerors who unite peoples and states); ch. 1, 23 (grand affair, not trifling details, worthy of philosophy). Dueck, Lindsay and Pothecary 2005 for a recent collection of essays discussing Strabo's *kolossourgia*.

discourse. From the Roman empire the term entered Christian theology. Ecumenical is now most commonly connected with restoring and preserving the unity of church and belief in a Christian commonwealth. This is essentially a question about reaching a minimal degree of consensus around the interpretation of scripture and the performance of ritual to provide a basis for a shared community of faith reaching across local congregations. Constantine invested considerable time and prestige in securing a common creed for his church at the ecumenical council of Nicaea in 325.[89]

There is a strong link between universal religions and empire, sometimes fairly straightforward as in the formative phases of Islam, at other times more complex such as during the European Middle Ages (for the latter see Angelov and Herrin, Chapter 6).[90] But imperial cultural universalism also articulated itself in other modes than the theological: pictorial representation (Schneider, Koch), philosophy (Fowden) and literature/poetry (Rao and Subrahmanyam). Courts patronised complex and ornate forms of artistic and verbal expression.[91] Based on the command of a demanding canon of classical works, a careful selection of often arcane vocabulary and grammatically regimented, high forms of language served as means both of distinction and of communication. An exclusive and lettered idiom helped mark out as elite its practitioners from ordinary vernacular speakers. This level of proficiency could only be achieved through arduous study and careful cultivation. But if that characteristic barred access for the hoi polloi, the same quality facilitated the geographical dissemination of these languages far and wide. With a stable canonical kernel, which had to be mastered through a long and expensive education, the languages of power and high culture could be and were adopted by elites far from the centre of power.[92] Classical and imperial languages such as Greek, Latin, Sanskrit, Arabic, Persian and Han Chinese helped elites communicate with each other across vast geographical distances and cultural barriers – also long after the imperial base had ceased as a functioning political entity, as

---

[89] On Constantine and the so-called ecumenical council of Nicaea, see Barnes 1981: ch. 12 and Drake 2000: ch. 7 with differing emphases. Humfress 2007: ch. 8 and more broadly Millar 2006 for discussions of the relationship between imperial government and efforts to create a uniform set of Christian beliefs in late antiquity.

[90] Cf. Woolf 2009, a discussion of Jaspers' 'Achsenzeit'-thesis, pointing to the importance of the formation of vast world-empires for facilitating the spread of universal forms of personal belief and rational thought rather than the 'founding figures' at the centre of Jaspers' thinking such as Socrates and Confucius.

[91] Blake 1991: 130–40; Swain 1996; Schmitz 1997; Woolf 2003.

[92] Alam and Subrahmanyam 2007 and Whitmarsh 2001 explore these dynamics in terms of travel and exile, respectively, in the early modern wider Persian cultural sphere and in the ancient Greco-Roman world.

illustrated below by Fowden and by Angelov and Herrin.[93] They represent in pure form the horizontal integration of elites across local societies which Ernest Gellner saw as a distinguishing feature of agrarian civilisation.[94] But, so far, there has been surprisingly little effort to explore the sociology of such universal imperial languages through comparison. With this collection we hope, at least, to stimulate interest in this issue. A notable pioneer study is Sheldon Pollock's, though at times eccentric, *The Language of the Gods in the World of Men.* Comparing imperial Latin and the Sanskrit culture, roughly of the first millennium, he draws on the Stoic notion of the cosmopolis to describe a civilisational universe severed from local affiliations (discussed by Bang, Chapter 3).[95] The capacity to transcend place in the construction of these elite cultures is mirrored well by the contributions to this volume. Schneider, Koch and Rawski each analyse how conquerors, though outsiders, inscribed themselves in pre-existing universal discourses: the Romans in the Hellenistic world of the eastern Mediterranean, the Mughals by elaborating the Persian culture originating in Iran, and the Manchu dynasty claiming to take over the 'mandate of heaven' to rule from the Ming emperors. The latter had failed to govern as virtuous monarchs and thus forfeited the right to leadership.

Virtuous or righteous kingship was a central concern of many of the participants in the discourse of imperial ecumenes. Literati produced cascades of laudatory speeches and mirrors for princes in which the merits and moral disposition of the exemplary ruler were celebrated in painstaking and sermonising detail. The good king would rule in accordance with justice and the proper order of things.[96] In other words, his reign had to be in alignment with the forces of the cosmos, a moral and divine as much as a natural universe. 'And as the whole heavens is regulated in all its parts by one motion, that of the Prime Mover, and by a single motor, which is God . . . the human species is best served when it is regulated by one prince [i.e., emperor], like a single motor, and by one law, like a single movement', Dante reasoned in his treatise advocating the cause of Christian universal empire.[97] The link between empire and cosmology was not restricted to monotheism;[98] it is also a prominent theme of Olko's contribution on the Aztec empire or of Bang's discussion of Hellenistic

---

[93] Bennison 2002: 74–80 for a succinct analysis of Islam.
[94] Gellner 1983: ch. 2.   [95] Pollock 2006; see also 2003.
[96] Howard 2007; Bayly 1996: 14–36; Alam 2004 for a detailed analysis of Persian political culture in medieval India and the centrality of the so-called Akhlaq literature, drawing on Hellenistic philosophy and Muslim theology, in shaping the discourse of kingship. Roller 2001 and Noreña 2001 for the public construction of virtuous kingship in the Roman world.
[97] Dante, *De monarchia* 1, ix, 2 (our translation).   [98] A classic analysis was given in L'Orange 1953.

kingship as an 'axis mundi'. Fowden points out how late antique, pagan Neoplatonist philosophy fed into al-Suhrawardī's amalgam of Muslim and Iranian illuminationist thinking. This was appropriated by some Islamic dynasties, among those the Mughals, to bolster the claim they were august, perfect men, shadows of God on earth, and partakers in divine light (Koch, and Rao and Subrahmanyam). Akbar's flirtation with sun worship and religious experimentation raised the eyebrows more than a little among some of the more austere-minded members of the ulema. They thought him verging on blasphemy and elevating himself too high above the human lot.[99]

Whether the universal emperor was to be considered a servant of godly order and cosmic right or these were to be put in his service was a matter which was subject to constant debate and renegotiation between the monarch and the men of the book and other elites.[100] Medieval Christianity exemplifies the two ends of the spectrum, as Angelov and Herrin make clear in their discussion. Within Catholic Christianity two rivals, emperor and pope, the sword and the book, both claimed universal power – the latter with such success that a particularly hard-nosed pontiff famously forced the emperor 'to go to Canossa'. Among the Orthodox, the Byzantine emperor was able to assert a higher degree of control over the patriarch of Constantinople. Nevertheless, even in this case, the old notion of Caesaro-papism seems exaggerated. Collaboration was closer, the clerical establishment more submissive and dependent, but the Orthodox Church was not simply the handmaiden of the ruler. Theological controversies presented him with plenty of challenges; and on occasion the ecclesiastical hierarchy was able to resist attempts from the Byzantine emperors to arrogate more powers to themselves in the appointment of metropolitan bishops. Actual positions, in other words, fluctuated between the two poles of the spectrum, another example of which is provided by Rao and Subrahmanyam in their analysis of Vijayanagara emperorship and the smaller successor kingdom of the Nayakas. Paradoxically it was the successor dynasty which proclaimed itself divine whereas the Vijayanagara rulers had ostensibly respected the varna-based moral order of the Brahmins and their temples.

The languages of imperial cosmology regularly mobilised the widespread myth of a golden, paradisiacal age and the visions of ecstatic religious

[99] The Mughal court historian Abu'l Fazl (see Abu'l Fazl 1873: book I, ch. 77 and II, ch. 22) reveals the influence of illuminationist thought on the royal ideology of Akbar's court. For some discussions, see e.g. Richards 1978 and Khan 1997. Fundamental is Rizvi 1964.

[100] The observation by Woolf (2008: 256) that the Roman emperors 'were the lowest of the gods, and the greatest of men' captures well this ambiguity, albeit in its specific Greco-Roman religious context, but the problem reflects a wider phenomenon.

prophecy, eschatological and millenarian.[101] The ideal-typical case is provided by Vergil, who combined both figures in the sixth song of the *Aeneid*. This classic epic expression of Roman imperial universalism and cosmology saw Aeneas, the Trojan prince and founder of the Roman people, seek out the Cumaean Sibyl. She, fabled prophetess, was to act as his guide through the horrors of the underworld where he would have the destiny of Rome revealed to him by his dead father, Anchises. At the end of a long tableau of heroes, Augustus arrives as the culmination of Roman history (further discussed by Scheider in Chapter 4):

This man, he it is, whom you oftentimes have heard promised, Augustus Caesar, the god's progeny, who shall found the golden age anew through the fields of Latium as once governed by Saturn and extend empire's sway over the Garamantes and the Indians. Land situated beyond the stars, beyond the march of the year and the sun where heaven-carrying Atlas on his shoulders turns the star-studded glimmering vault.[102]

World empire would see a saviour-monarch return the age of Saturn and usher in a new blessed era of peace, justice and prosperity when nature freely yielded its produce without the toil of man. A popular mythological hero of this condition was the bard Orpheus. His heavenly play on the lyre was thought to have created harmony among the animals so that predators and prey would co-exist peacefully.[103] Vergil himself set this figure a lasting monument with the exquisite poem celebrating country life, the seasons and Italy, *The Georgics*. The final song concludes by narrating the captivating tale of how Orpheus with his art almost overcame death to bring back his wife Eurydice from the underworld. The success of the Orpheus legend was secured and would echo through centuries of Latin literary composition. The motif of Orpheus playing to the peacefully assembled animals also made it into a set of Florentine coloured stone mosaic plaques, so-called pietre dure work, which were presented as a gift to the Mughal

---

[101] Levin (1969) charts the basic components of the golden age and millenarian language and imagery.

[102] Vergil, *Aeneid* (ed. Mynors), VI, 791–7 (our translation). Zanker 1987 is fundamental on the golden age motifs in the art and culture of the Augustan court. Within the staggering corpus of Vergilian scholarship, Norden 1916 remains a classic commentary on the 6th song of the *Aeneid*. The messianic dimension of the golden age myth was further explored by Norden in his study (1924) of Vergil's 4th eclogue, a short poem celebrating the birth of a child with a prediction of the return of the golden age, and later taken to be a prophecy of the birth of Christ. The striking similarity in mythological contents was not a reflection of any proto-Christian beliefs on the part of Vergil – how could it possibly be, since the poem predated Jesus by about half a century – but an expression that both Christian theology and pagan poet drew on a common stock of mythological motifs with deep roots in the Fertile Crescent, including Egypt. Hardie 2006 is a recent study picking up on this theme. For a survey of the immense influence of Vergil's poetry on later ages, one may now start with Ziolkowski and Putnam 2008.

[103] Ovid, *Metamorphoses* X, 1–154 and XI, 1–66.

Fig. 1.5a The throne in the Hall of Public Audience in the Red Fort of Delhi.

emperor in the seventeenth century and then used to decorate the wall behind the elevated throne in the Hall of Public Audience in the new palace, the Red Fort of Delhi (fig. 1.5a and 1.5b). Only, as demonstrated in a classic study by Ebba Koch, to the Mughals the figure of Orpheus meant little. In their islamicate tradition, the motif was attached to the Jewish kings, David and in particular Solomon. But the message conveyed remained essentially the same. The Solomonic rule of the Mughal emperor represented the establishment of a paradisiacal age of justice where, as shown in numerous depictions, the lion and the lamb would lie next to each other.[104]

Fused with eschatological beliefs, the myth of the imperial golden age resonated powerfully in various versions and inflections through the centuries and across cultures. Empire was penned into religious accounts of the end of times and millenarian prophecy.[105] Campanella, as we encountered above, may have been an eccentric, but not because he expressed himself in a prophetic idiom. His times were rife with such beliefs, and not only among Christians. The Ottoman ecumene experienced a wave of similar millenarian teachings linked to the rule of Süleyman the Magnificent.[106] If expressed in a 'lower' linguistic key, as they often were, millenarian and apocalyptic prophecies of these kinds had the potential to appeal to a wider constituency and touch the 'little' traditions of the broad population, as Angelov and Herrin point out below. But that also brought with it a subversive potential and the capacity to stir discontent. For centuries after the suicide of Nero in AD 68, beliefs lingered in the eastern parts of the empire that he would return as an avenging saviour, or for some early Christians as the Antichrist who would wreak havoc upon the empire and the world before the final triumph of Christ. Several 'False Neroes' emerged in the decades following his fall at the head of regional rebellions in the Roman world.[107]

Cosmology and 'millenarian' prophecy, ecumenical literary high-cultures and the symbolism and hierarchical diplomacy of supreme monarchy, these

[104] Koch 2001: 61–129 (reprints the study originally published in 1988).
[105] Yates 1975 was path breaking and remains fundamental.   [106] Fleischer 1992.
[107] Augustine, *De Civitate Dei* xx, ch. 19; *Sibylline Oracles* IV, 115–39; V, 28–34, 117–54, 214–27 and 361–85. Dio Chrysostomus, *Orations* 21.10; Suetonius, *Life of Nero*, ch. 57; Tacitus, *Histories* II, 8–9. See Galivan 1973 and Charles 1920: 76–87 for discussions of various parts of this material. Henten 2000 seems misguided. That in the Sibylline oracles the Nero legend is mixed up with general stereotypes of the tyrannical ruler is, in fact, the whole point. This does not simply substitute a general generic avenger/Antichrist for Nero. Sober, coherent and unambiguous description is hardly to be expected from apocalyptic prophecy; it is polyvalent and operates on many levels. The allusions to Nero are hard to miss, and to dismiss them as insignificant ignores the contemptuous remarks of late antique Christian theologians such as Augustine (and Lactantius) about the lingering belief in Nero's return as Antichrist. Muldoon 1999: ch. 5 for parallel Joachite prophecies pitted on the return of Emperor Frederick II Hohenstaufen (1194–1250).

Fig. 1.5b Orpheus playing to the animals, pietre dure plaque, detail from the wall
decoration behind the throne.

are the three main themes that the chapters in this volume touch upon
in varying degrees. In this introduction, we have attempted to sketch a
basic model and chronology of the notion of universal empires. Such
an exercise in world history necessarily entails simplification, but with
the aim of generating a more nuanced interpretation. For we offer this
common framework to stimulate interest in historical comparison, on a
theme which so far has seen relatively little of this activity, and to inspire

further exploration of similarities and differences in greater depth. However, we have also hazarded this broad-brush historical outline to raise awareness of such commonalities and insist on their importance for understanding our phenomenon.[108] The chapters that follow have therefore been divided into only two parts. The first part, and by far the largest, seeks to follow the notion of universal empire across the span of Eurasia, or the so-called old world, from the first millennium BC till the dawn of modernity at the turn of the eighteenth century AD. Needless to say, with such a wide range, our sample of cases is far from exhaustive, but we hope to have included many of the most significant examples. The second part, *Contrasting universalisms – old and new world* attempts to place the Eurasian examples into perspective by two treatments, one a discussion of the Precolumbian Aztec claims to imperial supremacy, the other an analysis of how the gradual emergence of first the European and then later the global international system of sovereign states relates to previous, medieval notions of a universal monarchy. Finally, a conclusion, written by John Hall, attempts to tease out some implications of our 'quest' for world history and historical sociology.

---

[108] Cf. the efforts of Lieberman 2010 and 2008 (condensed) and Fletcher 1995: ch. x, though both very different in approach, execution and scope from this volume.

PART I

Eurasia – antiquity till early modernity

Propaganda and practice in Assyrian and Persian imperial culture

Gojko Barjamovic

At the beginning of my kingship, in the first year of my reign – when Shamash the judge of the four quarters had spread his beneficial shadow over me, when I had seated myself nobly upon the royal throne, and he had placed in my hand the sceptre for the shepherding of the people – I mobilized my chariotry and my army. I passed through difficult paths and rugged mountains that were unsuitable for chariots and troops and I marched them to the lands of Tummu. I conquered Libê, their fortified city, as well as the cities of Surra, Abuqu, Arura and Arubê, which lie between Mounts Urinu, Arunu and Etinu – mighty mountains. I massacred many of them and carried off their captives, possessions, and oxen . . . I dyed the mountain red like carmine wool with their blood, and the ravines and torrents of the mountain swallowed the rest of them. I razed, destroyed and burned their cities.

Assurnasirpal II, 883–859 BC

Based in grand palaces in newly founded imperial cities, the rulers of Assyria and Persia asserted their claim to universal hegemony through propagandistic writings, grand orchestrated spectacles, and monumental art and architecture on a hitherto unseen scale. In reality their power diminished with distance, and political control was dependent upon an imperfect network of communication and indirect representation through delegation and mandate. This complex relationship between universal ideology and real policy is the focus of this study: the proclamation of power by divine sanction and birthright on the one hand, and the pragmatic management of policy through arbitration on the other.

SOURCES

In spite of their close proximity in space and in time, the Neo-Assyrian and Persian empires in several ways represent counterpoints in regard to both the quantity and the nature of historical data available for study. The fact

that the Assyrian administration wrote its records on clay tablets, which
survive very well in the archaeological record, means a broad range of
sources has come down to us from the imperial bureaucracy. Thousands of
texts, including state treaties, administrative and judicial records, omens,
royal annals and a vast political correspondence add to an extensive graphic
record of narrative scenes carved on kilometre-long stone panels in the
royal palaces.[1] In contrast to most other states in antiquity, which used less
durable materials on which to note down records, the Assyrian imperial
administration left an extensive 'paper' trail that allows us to document
political conduct and contrast it to state propaganda.

Compared to Assyria, there is less contemporary evidence available for
the study of Persian imperial bureaucracy, and administrative records from
the imperial chancellery survive only in a few instances – above all in the
still mostly unedited clay tablets written in the poorly understood Elamite
language from the archives of Susa and Persepolis.[2] Also, the archaeological
record of the Persian empire is scantily documented, and apart from the
above-mentioned capital cities only a limited number of sites have been
excavated to help us understand the way in which the state was organised
on a larger scale. The few surviving royal inscriptions are mostly short
and laconic, with a tendency to favour topics of universalism and divine
legitimacy. Views of the Persian empire have instead been heavily dependent
upon a biased literary discourse and a set of cultural presuppositions and
ideological stereotypes reproduced from the Old Testament, and from
classical Greek and Roman authors.[3]

---

[1] The Royal Inscriptions of Mesopotamia Project based in Toronto has provided updated editions and
translations of all the Assyrian royal inscriptions from the third millennium down to 859 BC. The
annals of Tiglath-Pileser III have been edited in Tadmor 1994, the Khorsabad inscriptions of Sargon II
in Fuchs 1994, Sennacherib in Frahm 1997, Esarhaddon in Leichty 2011, and Assurbanipal in Borger
1996. The Neo-Assyrian Text Corpus Project has produced complete editions and translations of
the state archives from the rule of Sargon II onwards, see www.helsinki.fi/science/saa/cna.html. The
volumes cover state letters, treaties, and judicial, administrative, religious, literary and divinatory
texts. Additional letters and administrative texts have appeared in Friedrich 1940 and in the series
Cuneiform Texts from Nimrud. Lecoq (1997) has recently re-edited the Persian royal inscriptions, and
Kuhrt (2007) has assembled a general *Corpus of Sources from the Achaemenid Period*. A selection of
administrative texts from the Persepolis Treasury appear in Cameron 1948, some of the Persepolis
Fortification Tablets in Hallock 1969, and the texts from Malyan in Stolper 1984. Two central syntheses
on the Persian empire are Wiesehöfer 1994 and Briant 1996 (an updated English translation appeared
in 2002). For updated bibliographies, resources and news, consult www.achemenet.com. Persian
studies are currently moving at great pace, and during the editing of the present chapter alone a
number of important works on the textual evidence have appeared, e.g. Henkelman 2008: ch. 2, and
Briant, Henkelman and Stolper 2008.
[2] Additional evidence for the Persian imperial administration derives mainly from Egypt (Briant 2002:
472) and Babylonia (2002: 484–6). In general sources are scarce (2002: 8f.).
[3] Wiesehöfer 1994.

UNIVERSAL POWER

Taken at face value, the image of the Assyrian and Persian empires as monolithic autocracies incapable of dealing with political opposition except through violent retribution is corroborated by the subjective self-representations handed down in the state propaganda produced by the empires themselves. Assyria and Persia both combined advertisements of legitimacy and self-praise in texts and images to project their claim to supremacy. Focus is on ideals of masculinity, bravery and justice, as well as servile qualities of respectfulness and efficiency in reverence to the gods.

The royal titles present the kings as rulers of all lands and people, chosen by divine power to extend order and subjugate chaos. The standard Assyrian repertoire includes the phrases 'great king', 'king of all rulers', 'king of the universe', 'king of the four quarters', 'ruler of all lands' and 'king of all people' and lays claim to the right for the Assyrian king to rule all peoples and lands, including those beyond the imperial frontier. Some epithets, such as 'faithful shepherd' and 'sun of all people', underline the role of the king as leader and supreme adjudicator of his own people. Personal characteristics come into focus through phrases such as 'strong king', 'attentive prince' and 'valiant man'. Divine choice was always a crucial parameter in royal legitimacy, as reflected in the titles 'viceroy of divine Aššur', 'appointee of divine Enlil' and 'the king who is the desired object of the gods'.[4]

The Persian kings took over parts of the traditional Mesopotamian titulary but reorganised it to express novel concepts. Darius I was also 'king of kings', 'king of the countries containing all races' and 'king of this great earth even far off', but kingship was now tied specifically to the region of Persis and the dynastic line of Achaemenes as sanctioned 'by the favour of Ahura Mazda'.[5] There is often a strong focus on the personal virtues of the ruler, and the ideal sovereign was said to possess a particular set of physical and mental characteristics.

What is right, that is my desire. I am not a friend to a man who is a Lie-follower. I am not hot-tempered. What things develop in my anger, I hold firmly under control by my thinking power. I am firmly ruling over my own impulses . . . Trained am I both with hands and with feet. As a horseman I am a good horseman. As a bowman I am a good bowman both afoot and on horseback. As a spearman I am a good spearman both afoot and on horseback.[6]

---

[4] Cifola 1995; Holloway 2002.   [5] Wiesehöfer 1994: ch. 2.
[6] Translation from Briant 2002: 212.

Particular to Assyrian royal rhetoric was a deliberate broadcast of violent brutality in the form of complex textual and pictorial narratives as historical propaganda on a monumental scale. Natural and human-made obstacles were shown as a preamble to the Assyrian king and his army overcoming them. The atmosphere is one of invincible power and 'calculated frightfulness',[7] underlining the intimate relation between Assyria and the gods as opposed to the irreverent behaviour of its defeated foes:

They rose against me in battle like a swarm of locusts in spring. The dust from their march covered the face of the horizon, and they drew up for battle before me like a mighty sandstorm in freezing winter . . . I roared mightily, thundering like the Storm God, and by the command of Assur, the great lord, my lord, on flank and front, I pressed upon the enemy like a raging hurricane . . . I cut them down rapidly and I defeated them. I cut their throats like lambs. I severed their windpipes like a string. I spilled their blood onto the wide earth like the waters of a spring shower. The charging stallions of my chariot plunged into the mere of blood as into a lake. The wheels of my chariot – which crushes the wicked and the murdering – were immersed in their blood and filth. I filled the plain with the corpses of their warriors like grass. I cut off their lips, ruining their dignity. I chopped off their hands like ripe cucumbers. I collected the torques of gold and shining silver from their wrists . . . [The Elamite king and his allies] abandoned their tents, and to save their lives they trampled the bodies of their fallen army. Their hearts were hammering like that of a newly hatched pigeon held in the hand, and they wet themselves and they soiled their chariots.[8]

Persian state propaganda instead projected an image of static power and voluntary integration. Although the administrative template and state iconography were in large measure taken over from Mesopotamian predecessors, the Persian kings left no royal narratives in the true sense, in neither text nor image.[9] Instead they adopted the mechanics of a refined institutionalised court protocol tied to the setting of the royal palaces. Stylised etiquette and a rigid social hierarchy combined with strict rules of physical access and an appropriation of space were created in order to present an image of the universal empire with the king at its central axis. Both the Assyrian and the Persian capitals were built to celebrate the power of the imperial state and its ruler, and functioned as the physical arena in which

---

[7] Olmstead 1918.   [8] For the annals of Sennacherib, see Luckenbill 1924; Frahm 1997.

[9] The Iranian historical tradition appears to have been mainly oral in character (see Wiesehöfer 2009: 66–7). The only real exception to the general lack of written narrative is found in the display inscription of Dareios [Darius] I on the rock at Behistun – a text that is unique in both its character and purpose, being a state-sanctioned report on the political events that led to Dareios taking the Persian throne.

political and social power was negotiated and dispensed, where loyalties were affirmed, spectacles played out and foreign dignitaries received.[10]

A difference in the use of symbols and decoration is instructive of deeper differences in Assyrian and Persian state ideology. Whereas the earlier Assyrian palaces combined ritual scenes and displays of foreign tribute with dynamic displays of torture and violence (fig. 2.1), the visual syntax at Persepolis underlines the static aspects of kingship: the unchanging political and social hierarchy and the cosmic centrality of the supreme ruler. State art was created to emanate a notion of an eternal universal order in scenes of iconic quality. In contrast to the Assyrians, who emphasised assimilation and practised incorporative strategies that ultimately resulted in the formation of a new and broader, more inclusive, imperial Assyrian identity,[11] access to the Persian elite was restricted and reserved for ethnic Iranians. Subject peoples were integrated as opposed to assimilated, with ideological emphasis placed upon brotherhood and a shared political superstructure, but by no means uniformity or equality.

Structural differences are particularly evident at the level of discourse: in addition to the absence of violence, the tributaries portrayed in Assyrian royal palaces are reinterpreted in the Persian reliefs as voluntary gift-bearers holding the hand of their Iranian overlords. The gateway complex to the royal acropolis was known as 'the Gate of All Nations', and the multitudes incorporated in the realm became a point of ideology. Elites from near and far are pictured as taking part in a shared eclectic court culture, and together all imperial subjects are portrayed as holding up the king seated on the imperial throne (fig. 2.2). Artistic and religious symbols, as well as architectural elements characteristic of the subject territories, were joined and displayed in new combinations: Ionian columns stood beside Egyptian doorways with Assyrian sculpture and Babylonian tiles. The Persian royal propaganda is a statement of symbolic intertextuality, syncretism and commonality set in a new framework of brotherhood and collaboration:[12]

This palace, which I built at Susa, its materials were brought from afar . . . The cedar timber was brought from a mountain named Lebanon. The Assyrians brought it to Babylon; from Babylon the Carians and the Ionians brought it to Susa. The yakâ-timber was brought from Gandara and from Carmania. The gold was brought from Lydia and from Bactria, and was wrought here. The precious stones, lapis lazuli and carnelian, which were wrought here, were brought from Sogdia. The precious stone turquoise, which was brought from Chorasmia, was wrought here.

---

[10] Barjamovic 2011. [11] Lumsden 2001: 39. See also Machinist 1993.
[12] See Root 1979. For Persian imperial consumption as a display of imperial reach and diversity, see Sancisi-Weerdenburg 1993.

Fig. 2.1 Dynamic displays of torture and violence. Rebel leaders mutilated after the failed Babylonian revolt in 652–648 BC. Southwest Palace (Nineveh), Room 33.

Fig. 2.2 Manifestation of universal order. Imperial subjects carry the Persian king on his throne. Ethnic differences are emphasised through fashion; collaboration and brotherhood result from imperial rule. Persepolis: jamb of Throne Hall.

The silver and the ebony came from Egypt. The ornamentation with which the wall was adorned was brought from Ionia. The ivory that was wrought here was brought from Nubia, from India and from Arachosia. The stone columns, which were wrought here, were brought from a village named Abirâdu in Elam. The stone-cutters who wrought the stone were Ionians and Lydians. The goldsmiths who wrought the gold were Medes and Egyptians. The men who wrought the wood were Lydians and Egyptians. The men who wrought the baked brick were Babylonians. The men who adorned the wall were Medes and Egyptians.

DIPLOMACY

Both the Persian and the Assyrian king ruled over societies that ranged in complexity from undifferentiated groups to full-fledged states. Political activities conducted within such a heterogeneous international system could not be treated as uniform, and flexible options within a broad strategy of rule had to be applied to the various subjugated units.[13] As is often argued in the case of pre-modern imperial states, a unifying element in all such strategies was the demonstration of military force and a strong manifestation of an imperial ideology and symbolism of power towards the subjugated population. But a broader effort to secure the empire's frontiers and extract wealth and resources from its territories was made through the development of an administrative structure that defined norms of conduct, and was aimed as much at the imperial elite as at an external audience of client and foreign rulers. Such procedures are particularly evident in the Assyrian source material, which preserves both the official historical narratives and the everyday correspondence between imperial bureaucrats, delegates, informants and clients. A clear distinction can be drawn between the way in which official accounts present the political developments and the pragmatic policies reflected in the state archives.

Hundreds of letters survive in the Assyrian state archives, showing that the imperial foreign policy was directed from the capital. In order to prevent inconsistencies and avoid internal contradictions, a course of action was decided and plotted out in each new situation. Infrastructural difficulties were overcome by granting a broad mandate to a select group of provincial governors and imperial magnates, while a coherent foreign policy was upheld by following a strict set of guidelines and a clear structure of command. When an important change in local conditions took place

[13] Mann 1984; Hassig 1985; D'Altroy 1992; Alcock et al. 2001; Bang and Bayly 2003; Morris and Scheidel 2009. Two recent studies devoted specifically to the expansion and the imperial dynamics of the Neo-Assyrian empire are Lamprichs 1995 and Parker 2001.

officials were required to report it to the central court alongside any relevant facts and then wait for a decision prior to taking any further action. A stock phrase in the reports is 'Let the king, my lord, decide what his orders are and write me.' This does not imply that imperial foreign policy was directed unilaterally. Advice and carefully worded criticism is expressed in the letters to the king and suggests that policy was a matter of debate within the innermost circle of imperial advisors.[14]

Modern international law has accustomed us to think of international or inter-state relations in terms of a clear division between domestic/local and foreign affairs. But such a simplified dichotomy of 'inner' and 'outer' does not apply well to the Assyrian and Persian case and serves to obscure the vital social condition in which political power ultimately comes from one single person, who treated with all others as, in principle, hierarchically inferior and subjected to his throne.[15] In effect, everything apart from the ruler was 'external' in some sense, and therefore subject to constant arbitration, renewal and approval. Historians of diplomacy have often emphasised the diplomatic capabilities of the Byzantine empire, whose success is said to be rooted in a number of key internal and external factors that helped form the empire.[16] The obvious parallels these factors have to Assyrian and Persian conduct of foreign relations point to the conclusion that such strategies are in fact the rational consequence of the general challenges and constraints faced by pre-modern territorial empires. Byzantium made full use of all physical signs of unique superiority – the material wealth of art and architecture, grants of honorary titles and offices to subservient rulers, and the ideological supremacy as Christians being opposed to heretics;

[14] See e.g. the letter in Lanfranchi and Parpola 1990: text no. 203 (l. rev. 14ff.) in which an Assyrian provincial governor suggests a coercive tactic applied during diplomatic negotiations with the assembly in Babylon. The governor counsels the king in matters where he appears to feel competent even though Babylon lies far from his own provincial territory.

[15] The general state-centric perception dominating International Relations studies and the inability to accept individuals as actors instead of states often leads to an insufficient description of the type of interactions taking place inside the large hegemonic polities of antiquity. Note e.g. Wight (1977), who proposes the concept of 'suzerain states system' to describe cases such as the Roman empire, the ancient Chinese state or the British Raj in India where a dominant unit controls the relations between a permanent group of states inside and surrounding itself. Giddens (1985: 4) sees the emergence of international relations as coeval with the emergence of the nation-state, implying that Europe after 1500 AD represents the first and only historical example of an international system. However, note also the persistent drive towards a historical synthesis and the focus upon systems and continuity found in the so-called 'English School' of IR studies and its continued opposition to the perceived inadequacies of behaviourist and games theory interpretations (e.g. Watson 1992; Buzan and Little 2000). Especially the latter have suggested a less state-centric model that seems better suited for the general study of historical international systems.

[16] See e.g. Nicolson 1969: 8; Mookerjee 1973: 20; Watson 1992: 111; Hamilton and Langhorne 1995: 14–19.

it practised diplomatic marriages with foreign rulers; it kept a permanent store of disappointed claimants, defeated rebels and dispossessed rulers, ever ready to be used as negotiating material and comfortably accommodated at the imperial palace; it consciously divided its enemies to embroil them with each other; it oversaw a constant gathering of intelligence from all parts of the world and used this information to minimise the risks of war; and its protocol for official correspondence shows an elaborate notion of a 'family of kings' under the tutelage of the Byzantine emperor so that foreign rulers were referred to as being the emperor's friends and allies, sons or brothers.[17]

The use of art and architecture in propagandistic displays, diplomatic marriages, the maintenance of a large group of foreign nobles at the court, who were brought up in and stayed loyal to the empire, the policy of 'divide and rule' among the clients, an elaborate infrastructure and complex intelligence networks, and the use of an ideological language of kinship among clients and equals[18] are all standard elements in the Assyrian and (as far as it is attested) Persian imperial toolkit. In Assyria, where there is more preserved evidence for the activities of policy-making, one is able to follow the process of the king and his central administration continuously preparing, entering and administering a series of treaties with the imperial subjects.[19] Such treaties were a principal tool for guaranteeing external security, inner loyalty, and geographic, political and economic expansion, and in times of crisis they worked to legitimise actions within the international system.[20] There are only very minor differences between the way in which

---

[17] See Angelov and Herrin, Chapter 6 below.

[18] For a general analysis of this phenomenon (common throughout the history of the ancient Near East), see Liverani 2001: 135ff. For a specific Assyrian example, see e.g. Luukko and van Buylaere 2002: text no. 1 (lines 1–13): 'A tablet from Esarhaddon, king of Assyria, to Urtaku, king of Elam, my brother. I am well, your sons and daughters are well, my country and magnates are well. May Urtaku, king of Elam, my brother, be well, may my sons and daughters be well, may your magnates and your country be well! Aššur, Sîn, Šamaš, Bel, Nabû, Ištar of Nineveh, Ištar of Arbela and Manziniri have now fulfilled and confirmed what they promised, and have developed our friendship to its peak.' The letter was written at a time when the two royal houses had entered a peace treaty and had exchanged royal sons and daughters as palace hostages.

[19] Parpola and Watanabe 1988: xv–xxv; Parpola 2003: 1054–9 with further references.

[20] The 'international system' is used here as a shorthand way of referring to the nexus of actors and interactions that constitute the subject matter of international relations, conscious or not (Dunne 1998: 125; Buzan and Little 2000: 35–48). Lately the term has been defined as 'a group of states (or more generally, a group of communities) which not merely form a system, in the sense that the behaviour of each is a necessary factor in the calculations of the others, but also have established by dialogue and consent common rules and institutions for the conduct of their relations, and recognise their common interest in maintaining these arrangements' (Bull and Watson 1984: 1). As such the ancient world did not form an international society, since no supra-national institutions existed for the conduct of relations. A more recent definition is Buzan 1993: 327–52, who attempts

such sworn statements were set up with individuals 'inside' and 'outside' imperial territory. Treaties were not ratified by abstract entities, such as states, but were always tied to individuals. The Assyrian nobility, the governors, the priesthood and the army all swore personal oaths of loyalty to the king in front of divine witnesses in a manner similar to the subject rulers, tribal leaders and foreign dignitaries, and each agreement would be up for renewal upon the accession of a new ruler or crown prince. The 'inner' and 'outer' regions of the empire were defined in territorial terms, but all political and social power was delegated, held and administered by individuals who were personally bound to the king. In this respect there was little difference between the manner in which an 'internal' Assyrian governor and an 'external' foreign embassy were tied to the ruler.

Instrumental to the empire's success was the dissociation of individual subjects from loyalties to any institutions apart from the king and the breaking of the bonds which otherwise tied them to their own community. A straightforward expression of this strategy is found in the castration of a large part of the palace administration, literally severing the royal bureaucrats from the paramount social obligations to the family. Yet, in all aspects of daily conduct the imperial governors, delegates and envoys, who acted as the main executors of imperial foreign policy, were to perpetuate the same basic agenda with varying degrees of mandate. This strategy involved the continued maintenance of the harmony of interests between the king and his subjects, while at the same time nurturing a conflict of interests between his individual subjects.[21] When the structure was established and everyone had to compete for the attention of the sovereign the system could ideally function through structural force alone (as opposed to physical strength), and continue at least as long as the king was successful in providing his servants with a feeling of reward and potential social progression in return for their undivided loyalty. At the outset, this type of political power tends to be strong at the centre but not very far-reaching. In order to overcome

to distinguish between an 'international system' and an 'international society' and the system is seen as prerequisite for the society to evolve. The frequency with which the players can interact within the system (often a question of infrastructure) is perceived as a crucial factor in deciding when a system may become a society (1993: 331). By his definition the ancient world would form an international system, but not a society. Buzan goes against the thought that only units sharing a common culture may form an international system, especially referring to the ideas of Mann 1986. See also Bederman 2001. The degree to which such an international system may be pure fiction has been treated *in extenso* in Carr 1946 and Manning 1962: esp. ch. 3. The position is not unrelated to Anderson's discussion of 'imagined communities' – the process by which states bond their identities to a community that lies beyond their ability to experience directly (see Anderson 1983).

[21] Galtung 1971, Lamprichs 1995.

its fundamental logistical and infrastructural constraints, and to improve its capacity to penetrate local institutions and civil society and implement a logistical and political system throughout it, both Assyria and Persia made use of a developed network of state agents controlled by an extensive hierarchical administrative structure to keep an exclusive monopoly on power. Important tasks for the civil servants included the gathering and storing of information, enforcing the will of the state, and catering to subject elites.

Apart from monopolising the means of organised violence outside subjugated communities and the use of the imperial communication infrastructure, both Assyria and Persia allowed civil authority to remain fairly decentralised on a local level. Subjugated areas retained virtual autonomy in communal matters, and in most societies leaders were locally elected.[22] Ideally they were appointed by their peers to act as an instrument of the community, both internally and in relation to the imperial central power. In reality both Assyrian and Persian policy pursued the familiar paradigm of *divide et impera* by actively drawing the loyalty of local leadership away from its constituency so as to penetrate and co-ordinate aspects of society to which they had only limited direct access. Multiple overlapping and intersecting sociospatial networks of power constituted society on a local level.[23] Immersed in this multiplicity of power relations, the imperial agents sought to create a space in which to manoeuvre and play off various interest groups against each other for the benefit of imperial policy. As already argued, this may well have been the most important function of the imperial diplomacy: to act among the subjugated elites in order to create a sense of imperial unity at the expense of local social and political cohesion. Several of the letters in the state archives of Assyria illustrate such activities and, perhaps predictably, the concept of loyalty recurs as a central topic in most imperial self-representations, while letters written to the Assyrian king and his administration abound with declarations of personal fidelity as well as the denunciation of rivals in the social hierarchy:

Concerning the six men and one woman about whom I wrote to the king, my lord . . . the first crime of Kûti and Tûti: When my son commanded them, 'Bring me the horses, so that I can bring them to the king!,' they refused . . . The king, my lord, is the sun! I am a servant of the king . . . his words are within my ears. Let me see the face of the king, my lord.[24]

---

[22] Larsen 2000; Radner 2003; Barjamovic 2004. For a recent study of Assyrian diplomatic discourse, see Fales 2009.

[23] Mann 1986, 1.

[24] Luukko and van Buylaere 2002: 58–62 (text no. 63), see e.g. ch. 5 'Denunciations' for many additional examples.

THE GRAND IMPERIAL SPECTACLES

In addition to sworn agreements and continued negotiations, a key strategy in both Assyria and Persia was to reinforce notions of belonging and personal loyalty to the king at immense annual or bi-annual gatherings. On such occasions the public was literally drawn into the king's orbit at the royal palaces, and the imperial elite – the royal family, the governors, imperial delegates at client courts, army officials, intellectuals and the priesthood – greeted and filed past the king, carrying and receiving gifts and public recognition alongside foreign embassies and emissaries from the imperial client states (fig. 2.3).[25] Administrative texts inform us about the procurement of colourful garments, furniture and aromatic fumigants, the stocking of wine cellars, and the presence of musical performers, gardeners, cooks and confectioners at such occasions.[26] Extensive parks (what the Greeks called 'paradises') were built to incorporate plants and animals from across the empire, some as pleasure gardens and others as hunting grounds.[27] The enclosed gardens were regulated spaces that would demonstrate the king's control over territories and prosperity on a symbolical level, and in some cases regulate access to the king.[28]

The great gatherings were events at which to see and be seen, and they were often the only time when direct contact could be established between the imperial elite and its clients. On special occasions, such as the banquet held by Assurnasirpal II to celebrate the opening of his grand new capital at Kalhu, 69,574 guests are said to have attended a gigantic gathering that ran for ten days, including some 1,500 functionaries from the imperial palaces and 5,000 foreign dignitaries.[29]

There can hardly be any doubt that the sight of Assurnasirpal's palace made a lasting impact upon all of its many visitors. It was an architectural wonder in the true sense – a 28,000 m² multi-storeyed building made of the finest woods and magnificent stone, lavishly decorated with carved panels, carpets, wall-paintings, glazed bricks, sculptures and brightly painted reliefs.[30] It was a first of its kind in the world, and the model to be emulated by all later Assyrian and Persian kings. It was a complex built to impress. Its monumentality was simple and heavy, the architecture focused on large

---

[25] Parpola 2003: 1053.   [26] See e.g. Kinnier Wilson 1972; Fales and Postgate 1992.
[27] Weissert 1997; Briant 2002: 201f., 297ff.; Novák 2002.   [28] Brosius 2007: 40.
[29] Grayson 1991: 288–93. For a similar text relating to a feast at the royal Persian table, note Polayenus' collection of *Stratagems* (IV.3.32) discussed in Briant 2002: 286ff.
[30] For a general introduction to the palace at Nimrud (ancient Kalhu), see Oates and Oates 2001; Barjamovic 2011.

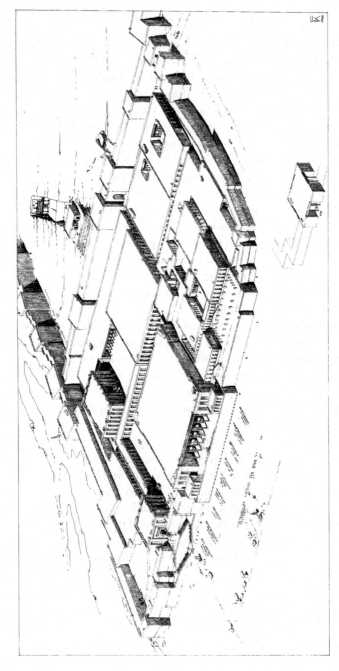

Fig. 2.3 Commonality and court culture. Dignitaries pass below the terrace of Darius' palace at Persepolis; others climb the monumental staircase and pass through the Gate of All Nations.

open spaces and long views, its niches and colossal statues were set to accentuate the main functional elements of the building, and paintings and reliefs were carefully placed to mirror the activities taking place in each sector of the building.[31]

Bersani and Dutoit, two scholars working in modern art and media, have compared certain scenes in the Assyrian reliefs to the powerful propagandistic images created by the Nazi filmmaker Leni Riefenstahl.[32] According to their analysis, the Assyrian sculptor and the German filmmaker realise the apotheosis of their leader by similar visual means, where an efficient off-set between undifferentiated 'bodies' and the individualised head-figure in both cases works to create a feeling of the unchanging, and unchallenged, presence of a *Führer* in a dangerously chaotic world. Indeed, the large courtyards of the Assyrian and Persian palaces would have provided a bombardment of such visual stimulants. Although stylistically far from the clean and repetitive principles of Speer's arena in Nuremberg, the function and use of space is similar. The artistic creation of an atmosphere of invincible power, elevation and sublimity would ideally rob its spectator of any feeling of individuality and reservation against the regime, and the repeated statement of absolute control would remove any sense of individualism in him. A unique characteristic of Assyrian artistic propaganda was the consistent tradition for authenticity in the narrative. Images of enemy cities were not simply made up, and deeds could not be usurped from a predecessor, as in the case of Egyptian or Mayan royal monuments. Yet, in all instances, the art and architecture served to create a feeling of belonging to an omnipotent political elite, and to remove the feeling of personal solidarity between the imperial client and his subjects back home. Once again, one may enlist Byzantine history to illuminate the ancient Near Eastern experience. A colourful representation of a comparable situation is found in Baynes' description of a royal audience in Constantinople:

Picture for a moment the arrival of a barbarian chieftain from steppe or desert in this Byzantine Court. He has been royally entertained, under the vigilant care of imperial officials; he has seen the wonders of the capital, and today he is to have an audience with the Emperor. Through a dazzling maze of marble corridors, through chambers with rich mosaic and cloth of gold, through long lines of palace guards in white uniforms, amidst patricians, bishops, generals and senators, to the music of organs and church choirs he passes, supported by eunuchs, until at last oppressed with interminable splendour he falls prostrate in the presence of the silent, motionless, hieratic figure of the Lord of New Rome, the heir of

---

[31] See e.g. Winter 1997; Lumsden 2004.   [32] Bersani and Dutoit 1985; note also Bahrani 2008.

Constantine, seated on the throne of the Caesars: before he can rise, Emperor and throne have been caught aloft, and with vestments changed since he last gazed the sovereign looks down upon him, surely as God regarding mortal men. Who is he, as he hears the roar of the golden lions that surround the throne or the song of the birds on the trees, who is he that he should decline the Emperor's behests? He stays not to think of the mechanism, which causes the lion to roar or the birds to sing: he can scarce answer the questions of the logothete speaking for his imperial master: his allegiance is won: he will fight for the Roman Christ and his Empire.[33]

In Assyria extensive royal annals were composed each year and presumably read out to the dignitaries and divinities present at the annual spectacles.[34] Supported by the wide-ranging pictorial record, they offer a vivid impression of the imperial discourse surrounding life at court and present an example of how subjects to the empire were urged to perceive themselves and their equals. The extensive programme of architecture and decoration at Persepolis, with its towering columned reception halls built on elevated platforms, makes a similarly awe-inspiring statement about unity in plurality under a universal ruler.[35] On the seemingly endlessly running reliefs of the palace were depicted guards, imperial magnates and the ceremonial gathering of representatives from the numerous communities of the Persian empire marching in procession bearing gifts and tribute to the omnipotent Great King. But neither set of imperial representation, Persian or Assyrian, lends itself easily to the study of imperial policy as it was put into practice. Empires maintain the fiction of invincibility at their peril, both in letter, in image and in action. The state-induced image of imperial invincibility can manipulate audiences even across the millennia,[36] and so when we have them, letters, judicial documents and administrative texts add crucial information on everyday policy-making as a contrast to the formalised narratives of the imperial annals and pictorial representations. The self-styled image of an empire held together for centuries by divine will, the pre-eminence of the royal lineage, and an omnipotent military force gives way to a more pragmatic understanding of the way in which policy was deliberated and administered. Power and ideology were not impersonal and had to be applied by individuals onto individuals. A supposed ambiguity about what was internal and what was external represents our inadequate grasp of

[33] Baynes 1925: 72–3.   [34] Oppenheim 1960.
[35] Cf. Briant 2002: 196–203 for the Persian royal festivals, processions and banquets as imperial rituals.
[36] An extensive literature on the issues of historiography, state propaganda and the Assyrian royal annals as a literary genre has appeared in the last three decades, especially in Italy (Liverani, Fales, Zaccagnini, Ponchia *et al.*) and Israel (Tadmor, Cogan, Ehp'al, Oded *et al.*). A useful overview with further references is available in Tadmor 1997.

how the ancient empires were structured rather than their shortcomings. Even if imperial conduct was submitted to an ideological agenda, it continued to be disseminated and implemented by and towards individuals whose relations were embedded in social and political reality. Physical force and ideological brands are rarely as efficient in keeping a state together as the proverbial social contract.

CHAPTER 3

Between Aśoka and Antiochos: an essay in world history on universal kingship and cosmopolitan culture in the Hellenistic ecumene

Peter Fibiger Bang

The Beloved of the Gods believes victory by *dhamma* to be the fore-most victory. And moreover the Beloved of the Gods has gained this victory on all his frontiers to a distance of six hundred *yojanas*, where reigns the Greek King named Antiochos, and beyond the realm of that Antiochos in the lands of the four kings named Ptolemy, Antigonos, Megas, and Alexander.[1]

ALEXANDER'S AXIAL MOMENT

Here is a fascinating reflection from an era of dramatically expanding horizons. This short passage offers surprising testimony that in the mid third century BC to the emperor Aśoka were known not only the Seleucid kings, claiming territories reaching to the very doorstep of India, but also the Hellenistic monarchies of the distant eastern Mediterranean. The arena into which the 'Beloved of the Gods' looked to extend his *dhamma* or righteous order was the creation of the shockwave which the conquests of Alexander (r. 336–323 BC) had sent through the old Near Eastern and Central Asian world circumscribed by the Achaemenid empire. In the early days of the British Raj, the restless and searching activities of travellers, administrators and scholars began to identify the edicts of Aśoka on rocks and columns around India. These new inscriptions combined with other finds to lend concrete shape to the distant memory of Alexander's exploits

---

[1] Aśoka 13th Major Rock Edict, translation quoted from Thapar 1997: 256. Appendix V provides basic translation of all his edicts. Hultzsch 1925 for a text-critical corpus, with translations. Greek and Roman authors are referred to in this chapter by name, title of work, and the standard chapter and paragraph divisions. Texts with parallel translation will often be conveniently available in the Loeb Classical Library Series. Patrick Olivelle very kindly discussed various problems in relation to Aśoka with me and also gave me access to a new article of his prior to publication. Patricia Crone and Kim Ryholt with equal generosity sent me some of their forthcoming material, while John Hall and Peter Garnsey offered incisive comments on drafts of this chapter. Finally, a seminar audience in Copenhagen offered valuable discussion. I am deeply grateful for this help and assistance. Need I say that responsibility for the final result rests, alas, solely with the author.

on both sides of the Hindu Kush.[2] Europeans would mirror themselves in the romance of the Macedonian conqueror as they went about their projects of exploration and domination. Kipling's famous short story 'The Man Who Would Be King' has captured well for posterity the atmosphere of adventure, thrill and anxiety arising at the time from the quest to follow in the footsteps of the swashbuckling hero of Hellenism.[3]

But the European experience of scientific discovery, colonial rule and the 'civilising mission', suggestive though it is, has clear limits as a parallel to the age of Alexander: it is of the wrong world historical time. After all, it would be many centuries before India could be held from faraway Britain.[4] The world that emerged in the train of Alexander's meteoric careering across much of the South-West Asian landmass must be placed in a different context. But which? The Mauryan empire (321–185 BC), of which Aśoka was the third and most successful ruler, was founded by Chandragupta shortly after Alexander's campaign down the river Indus, but with its centre and capital much further east along the Ganges, at Pataliputra (modern Patna). It stands to reason that these events were somehow linked. The invasion may have changed the balance of power among the budding monarchical states in North India and thus indirectly facilitated the formation of the first large Indian empire. But very little information survives to put flesh on the bones of our historical speculations.[5] The inscriptions dating from the reign of Aśoka (269/8–233/2 BC), many of them carved into dressed rock surfaces, may seem rather reminiscent of the famous rock-cut inscriptions of the Persian Great King at Naqš-i Rustam and Behistun in Iran. 'I am Darius, the Great King, King of Kings, King of countries . . .'[6] Yet, it is the contemporary Hellenistic monarchies that occupy the horizon of the king Piyadassi, another of the names used by the Mauryan ruler. The

---

[2] William Jones had effectively sounded the clarion call for this search in the 1790s by establishing a chronological base-line for the Mauryan dynasty through the linking of its founder, Chandragupta, with the Sandrokottos known from Greek historians: Jones 1807: 219–20 (10th Anniversary Discourse, on Asiatick history, civil and natural). The fascinating process of subsequent discovery of inscriptions, their decipherment and connection to Aśoka (as well as the mentioning of some of Alexander's successors) can be followed in the *Journal of the Asiatic Society of Bengal* in the contributions of Prinsep 1837a; 1837b; 1838 and Turnour 1837 – at a time when even the most basic chronology was still uncertain. Cunningham (1877) assembled the accumulating stock of inscriptions into a corpus. Kejariwal 1988 for a history, though narrowly conceived, of these efforts.

[3] Tarn 1951 represents the culmination of the British quest for Alexander in India and Afghanistan.

[4] Manning 2010: 49–54; Bagnall 1997; Sherwin-White and Kuhrt 1993: ch. 6 for discussions of the limitations of the colonial parallel, suggested e.g. by Will 1985.

[5] Thapar 1997: 13–17; Ray 2007 for the significance of the preceding period of state-formation in North India.

[6] Pollock 2005: 416–17 (but also, and too hard it would seem, stressing differences in substance); Benveniste 1964: 140–6.

style of the edicts, moreover, where the 'beloved of the Gods' addresses himself to his subjects on many issues, does perhaps seem more closely related to the habit of Greek Hellenistic rulers of sending letters to subject communities.[7]

Achaemenid or Hellenic, this is the problem of Alexander himself. As Droysen observed in the work which defined the Hellenistic as a period in world history: 'Der Name Alexander bezeichnet das Ende einer Weltepoche, den Anfang einer neuen.'[8] More recently, the French historian Pierre Briant has taught us to think of Alexander as the 'last of the Achaemenids'.[9] To be sure, there is an element of provocation in this pronouncement and objections have been voiced. Military conquest did not leave the Persian infrastructure of power untouched and unscathed. The view of Alexander as Persianising is fundamentally one derived from later Greek sources and cannot be corroborated by 'indigenous' material.[10] But whether Alexander really had turned into an epigone of the Achaemenids is perhaps less significant than the presence of a discourse fearful that he would.

Granikos, Issos, Gaugamela, the string of brilliant victories scored over King Darius, left the Macedonian army with an even bigger problem on hand: how to hold on to the enormous prize. This really was a case of the smaller fish trying to swallow the bigger one. The new Greco-Macedonian rulers were acutely aware of the risk that, heavily outnumbered, they might 'drown' in the sea of subjects – as conquerors time and again would come to experience, most notably the first wave of Muslim Arab tribes and, later again, the Mongols.[11] Even so, finding ways to accommodate and co-opt powerful representatives of the conquered populations was imperative; government required the co-operation of such groups to function. Tensions, however, would inevitably accompany this process; it was a question about access to power, rank and wealth. Predictably, the attempts of Alexander to reach out to members of the defeated elite sparked discontent among the victors. Succeeding generations of Hellenised elites singled out a number of incidents of conflict between Alexander and his Macedonian nobles.

---

[7] Olivelle 2012; Hinüber 2010. Further Adrados 1984 (a combination of Persian and Greek influences).
[8] Droysen 2008 [1877], vol. 1: 3.
[9] Briant 1982: 330; 2009 and further 2003, based on the observation that, through his victory, Alexander took away not only Darius' realm, but also his historical identity; the figure of Darius was buried in the shadow left by the conqueror.
[10] Brosius 2003. Further discussion by Lane Fox 2007 and Wiemer 2007.
[11] Crone (forthcoming), introduction and ch. 8 for an analysis of the Abbasid revolution as a Persian take-over of the imperial caliphate from the Arab tribes.

In the narratives of the victorious campaigns composed by Greek historians, these episodes became imbued with emblematic status: the murder by Alexander of Kleitos, a prominent, battle-seasoned Macedonian hero, and the execution of the philosopher Kallisthenes, a nephew of none less than Aristotle.[12] Both had demonstratively criticised Alexander for taking on too much of the ceremonial of the Achaemenid court in trying to invite the former elite to participate in his rule, while neglecting the group to whom he really owed his success. Their deaths became symbols of the creeping megalomania of the young king; their myths served as a warning for the successors not to don too Persian a style of monarchy, but to stay true to their Greco-Macedonian aristocracies.[13] The conquerors, in short, strove to appropriate the Persian empire and give its model of rule a new inflection which would preserve their pre-eminence rather than allowing themselves to become absorbed within the pre-existing political culture.[14]

This was the defining feature of our period, the development of new models of universal empire arising from the margins of the Achaemenid world.[15] For lack of a better word, we may label this as an axial moment. The concept was brought to prominence by the German philosopher of history Karl Jaspers. To him the *Axenzeit* was the child of the work of thinkers across Eurasia such as Plato, Confucius and Gautama Buddha. Their thought had ushered in an intellectual revolution during the so-called classical centuries of antiquity which had seen a breakthrough to a more individual sense of the self, critical distance and reflexivity, and more universal types of thought. Civilised man as we have come to know him had been born.[16] In this form, however, the concept is rather difficult to manage and the contours of the epoch are hazy. Reflexivity and a sense of the self are not easily claimed as the children of any single period, nor is there any explicit connection between these culturally disparate founding figures. A group of historical sociologists who have taken their inspiration from Jaspers therefore also touch on the possibility of several

---

[12] These are key episodes in the classical Alexander histories, and in the modern: Arrian *Anabasis* IV, 8–9 (the murder of Kleitos); 10–14 (the Kallisthenes episode); Plutarch *Alexander* 50–2 and 53–5, to give only the most significant references; among the moderns, Bosworth 1996: ch. 4 (with verve and indignation). Quintus Curtius VIII, viii, 10–13 locates the discourse clearly in a context of the challenge of holding on to possessions dwarfing the previous Macedonian territories.

[13] Cf. the reassurance extended to the Macedonians ascribed to the founder of the Seleucid dynasty by Appian in his historical writings (App. *Syr.* 61 [my translation]): 'And I shall not impose on you the customs of the Persians, nor those of other people.'

[14] Strootman 2011: 81–3, Ma (forthcoming), Capdetrey 2008: 60 for the assertion of a Greco-Macedonian ruling class identity.

[15] Cf. Sherwin-White and Kuhrt 1993: 101–3.   [16] Jaspers 1955: part 1, chs. 1 and 5.

axial transformations.[17] By the same token, formation of large empires with universal aspirations makes the setting, the connection and the timing of parallel developments much more concrete and discernible. Hence the turning point constituted by the conquests of Alexander may fittingly be described as a key axial moment in the transformation of the ancient world from early civilised societies to the more complex and extensive versions developing in the last half-millennium or so before our era; it gave rise to two new cultures of universal imperial rule.[18]

UNIVERSAL KINGSHIP, AXIS OF THE WORLD

This result was firmly set in train when Seleucos, otherwise sporting the byname 'the victorious', felt compelled or saw it in his interest to cede the Greek conquests along the Indus to Chandragupta Maurya. In return, a matrimonial alliance was struck and the Macedonian ruler received 500 elephants to bring back west (*c.* 303 BC).[19] Across the length and breadth of the Hellenistic ecumene, elephants would wreak havoc on the battlefields and inspire awe among subjects in the coming centuries. Possession of the giant quadrupeds became a much coveted strategic and symbolic resource among Greco-Macedonian monarchs: an emblem of royalty.[20] Kingship was the main vehicle in the development of the new models of universalist rule. 'Euergetes', 'soter', to the qualities of the victor Hellenistic rulers added the roles of benefactor and saviour of men – and, not to forget, liberator of the Greeks.[21] The paternalist hue emanating from the grand pose struck by these monarchs was no less central to the model of kingship propagated by the Mauryas. *Dhamma*, the righteousness celebrated by Aśoka in his edicts, proclaimed a paternalist vision of social order, with deference and respect owing to parents and gods. In the Greek-language versions of the edicts, the key term was translated precisely as *eusebeia*.[22] The proud claim

[17] Arnason, Eisenstadt and Wittrock 2005: 8–9 and 17. Arnason 2005 for a critical discussion of Jaspers stressing the need for a more concrete sociological understanding of the Axial Age.

[18] Cf. Woolf 2009: 26–30 advocating a shift in emphasis from the classical, pre-imperial, periods of experiment and freedom idolised by Jaspers, to the elaboration and dissemination of universalist literary and religious cultures under the tutelage of the succeeding imperial monarchies.

[19] Strabo XV 2.9. The exact contents of the matrimonial arrangement, epigamia, mentioned by Strabo are unclear, see e.g. Thapar 1997: 17.

[20] Scullard 1974.

[21] Lund 1992: ch. 6 for an excellent survey of the ideals claimed by Hellenistic kingship.

[22] In addition to the 13th Major Rock Edict quoted above, a good example is Aśoka, 4th Major Rock Edict (trans. Thapar 1997: 251–2, with analysis on p. 147 emphasising paternalism and more generally ch. 5 and pp. 276–7). For the Greek edicts, Schlumberger *et al.* 1958; Schlumberger 1964; Pugliese Carratelli and Garbini 1964.

of the Mauryan emperor, that his order was now spreading far and wide by moral persuasiveness rather than military force, served as an example. Succeeding generations of Buddhist philosophers elaborated the Aśokan model into a theory of the *cakravartin*, the universal emperor turning the wheel of law. This wondrous lord of all the world would gain the submission of people by his upright, shining moral example. Recourse to arms would not be necessary.[23] Such ideas were less foreign to the belligerent Hellenistic world than one might have thought. One image popularised in theories of kingship was that of the queen among bees. Spoken of in the masculine format, the sting-less ruler of the beehive was often enough presented as a model that monarchs should strive to emulate. Him, by his very nature, his innate qualities, the swarms of subjects had an ardent desire to follow wherever he chose to reside or go.[24]

It is worth mentioning that culture power, in this sense, took centre stage in the famous and highly influential *Negara: The Theatre State in Nineteenth-Century Bali*. Incidentally based on a later avatar of Indic models of monarchy, Geertz's was a study of universal kingship. No monarch could ever hold effective power over all of the world, and the kings on Bali even less so than most. Nevertheless, claims to universal dominion were abundant across pre-colonial South East Asia. Co-existence of competing claims was not an obstacle, almost the opposite. If kings could not extend effective control over their rivals, they could aspire to staking out an impressive claim to embody the ideal of kingship better than any other. The world of kings was fiercely contentious. Through lavish display and elaborate rituals rulers sought to enhance the prestige of their courts and place them right at the centre of human society. If the reach of their government was limited, their fame would travel wider to make them an *axis mundi* or 'centre of centres' – the hub from which the spokes in the wheel of the world would protrude or the mark towards which all others would orient themselves in emulation.[25] But normally this competition between kings has involved a lot more than theatrical display. Royal rivalry over pre-eminence played

---

[23] See the discussion and translation by Strong (1983: 44–9; 201–4) of the second-century AD Buddhist text, written in Sanskrit, the *Aśokāvadāna*. Whether this ideal pre-dated Aśoka is doubtful. The textual tradition was only written down much later and it therefore seems more plausible that the claims of the Mauryan emperor came to inform this model as the tradition developed rather than the other way round.

[24] Xenophon *Cyropaedia* V 1, 24–6. This motif found a powerful reception in the Roman version of late Hellenistic literature and philosophy. Vergil made it a crucial part of the lead-up to his narration of the tale of Orpheus and Eurydice in the *Georgics* (IV, 197–218). Seneca included it in his Stoic tract on kingship, the *De Clementia* I 19, 2–3. The commentary (*ad loc.*) of Braund (2009) usefully collects classical references and some modern literature. Particularly of interest is Dahlmann 1954.

[25] Geertz 1980: 113–25 and 236–8.

itself out in several dimensions. War and the size of armies, conquest and the extent of subject territories, were, for most of history, of much greater import in deciding rank and status among rulers.

Hellenistic monarchs knew no prouder claim than having won a brilliant military victory; they governed over 'spear-won' land.[26] In a seminal article, Hans-Joachim Gehrke analysed Hellenistic kingship in terms of Weberian charisma. Rulers had to prove their worth, their exceptional ability on the battlefield, and by analogy, in other spheres of life as well: public pageantry and munificence, patronage of the arts, religious donations – the grand gesture. The need to add glory to the name made Hellenistic kings vulnerable. Their legitimacy rested on the shaky foundations of personal charisma. As a quality, charisma is born out of the exceptional. Failure, on the other hand, would break the spell of magic and immediately put the legitimacy of a ruler in question.[27] It is true that the organisation of the Hellenistic monarchies originally rested on an act of usurpation. When Alexander, with his usual excess, drank himself to death in Babylon in 323 BC, he left no heir behind, only a pregnant queen. An interim government of his trusted generals was put in place till the child would be born and then come of age. Meanwhile, the game of high politics was set for ruthless intrigue and brutal competition among the leaders of the Greco-Macedonian aristocracy. In the struggles of the ensuing years, no trick was too mean, no ruse left untried. Eventually, even the young king and his mother were swept away in the maelstrom of murder, deception and war which the fight to control the leaderless empire had unleashed. Five men, holding key parts of the empire as satraps, finally adopted the royal diadem, none of them strong enough to conquer all the others, the result an uneasy settlement and division of territories.[28] Tenuous at first, their hold on power was soon, as some of them fell out of the contest, consolidated into the dynastic regional monarchies of the Seleucids, the Antigonids and the Ptolemies. Around their courts developed an elaborate ritual grammar and formulaic language of kingship. This form of legitimisation and power, however, was anything but un-institutionalised.[29] Their royal authority

---

[26] The expression may be found in Diodorus Siculus XVII, 17, 2.

[27] Gehrke 1982. A similar argument was made by Pearson (1976) about the Mughal empire; it depended on the charisma of invincibility surrounding its rulers. The moment the Mughal emperors began to lose battles, their empire unravelled as people deserted. Most would now agree that this view underestimates the institutional supports of the Indian empire.

[28] Diodorus Siculus XX, 53; 106; 113, 5; XXI, 1–5. Will 1979–1982, for the basic modern narrative of Hellenistic political history.

[29] Weber 1995 for the development of an elaborate conventional and literary language of Hellenistic rulership. Ma in press and Manning 2010 for two recent succinct analyses stressing the institutional

was certainly both exceptional and numinous, but it was because they were presented as exemplary beings;[30] and the standard was defined by the historical myth of Alexander, the world conqueror.[31]

The highly adversarial nature of Hellenistic kingship is best understood in a Geertzian light. Intensely agonistic, the Greco-Macedonian rulers vied with each other about who could best step into the shoes of their heroic predecessor, embody the ideal of the universal ruler. Even if this activity fell (far) short of obliterating the other rivals, kings did their best to cut the most impressive and inspiring figure.[32] The Seleucid ruler (r. 223–187 BC) Antiochos III is a good example. From 212 to 204 he embarked on a grand campaign in the trail of Alexander, which mightily impressed his contemporaries, reasserting Seleucid hegemony deep into Central Asia. On his return, he then directed his energies towards extending his power across Asia Minor and Coele Syria. When the latter territory was conquered from the Ptolemies, he then adopted the title of 'Great King', 'Basileus Megas'.[33] A new Greco-Macedonian world ruler had announced his arrival. Claims could also move in the opposite direction. A victory scored in the preceding generation over the Seleucids, during the so-called Third Syrian War, was commemorated in like grandiloquent manner:

King Ptolemy the Great ... descended on his father's side from Herakles son of Zeus and on his mother's side from Dionysus son of Zeus ... marched into Asia ... Having secured control of all the territory within the Euphrates ... and of the Indian elephants, he crossed the river ... and having subdued Mesopotamia,

strengths of the major Hellenistic monarchies. Capdetrey 2007 straddles a middle course between Gehrke and the latter.
[30] Hellenistic kings were habitually likened to heroic mythological characters who had earned a position among the gods for their good deeds done towards humanity, and the mythologies of these characters were, in turn, calked on the exploits of Alexander. One philosopher, Euhemerus, even went so far as to describe Zeus, the royal god par excellence, as a human king who had won recognition and been elevated to Olympian divinity. See Diodorus Siculus VI, 1 with Bosworth 1999.
[31] Lane Fox 2011. On the iconic significance of Alexander's image for his successors, see further Stewart 1993 and Mørkholm 1991: 27.
[32] 'In declaring himself king, he was in the first place affirming and institutionalizing his power and making it hereditary; but the kingship of Antigonos was personal, not territorial or national ... The proclamation should not, then, be regarded as a claim specifically to supreme power over all of Alexander's empire. Neither should it be regarded as limited to particular territories ... none of them seems to have been ready to acknowledge definite and permanent boundaries to his area of rule ... it demonstrates that Antigonos acknowledged no definite limits to his power as king, which he attempted to enforce over Ptolemy in 306 and over Kassandros in 302.' Framing the question in Geertzian terms seems the obvious answer to attempts such as Billows (1990: 159–60) to circumscribe the contentious and agonistic nature of Hellenistic kingship. If rulers had to make do with less than Alexander's entire realm, they could at least strive for predominance.
[33] Ma 2000: 73 and 272–6. Polybios 11.34.16 comments on the *gloire* earned by Antiochos in the Hellenistic ecumene by his Eastern campaign.

Babylonia, Susiana, Persis, Media and all the remaining territory as far as Bactria . . .[34]

Genealogies were carefully crafted to inscribe the ruling dynasties into the divine mythology surrounding Alexander. Herakles and Dionysos, the two sons of the king of the Olympian gods Zeus and friends of man, had been assiduously cultivated by Alexander and his father Philip. Herakles was the Greek culture hero par excellence who had traversed the world to combat a medley of horrifying monsters, while Dionysos with the gift of wine offered release. Myths that Dionysos had brought the vine from Asia to Hellas were worked up under Alexander and his successors to mirror his route of conquests.[35] Royal power was prefigured in divine world dispensation; the dynasty represented an *axis mundi.*

Outside the battlefield, such statements were bolstered by the staging of grand and lavish spectacles.[36] Choreographed in a pictorial language mobilising both mythological motifs and the display of exuberant wealth, this pageantry was designed to add lustre to the ruling house and outshine rivalling courts. Several of these occasions became famous enough to earn inclusion in a Greek collection of miscellaneous antiquarian mirabilia half a millennium later.[37] By the same token, Hellenistic rulers erected monuments and showered public benefactions on sites which had acquired a Panhellenic status among the Greeks, such as Delphi, Athens and Rhodes. All these activities served to polish their credentials within the universalist tradition of kingship. It is remarkable testimony to the significance of this *agon* of the kings that the moment the Roman Republic entered the fray of Hellenistic power-politics, the step was conceived of in terms of a contest for world empire; and Roman generals would soon learn to compare themselves with Alexander. Long before Augustus could add Ptolemaic Egypt, by then the last remaining of the big Hellenistic monarchies, to his possessions, Polybios, the Greek historian (*c.* 200–118 BC), would marvel that Rome had established a new world hegemony and imposed its suzerainty on the oikoumene.[38] At the same time, the spectacular Roman successes against the Hellenistic kingdoms in the second century BC prompted the

---

[34] *Orientis Graecae Inscriptiones Selectae,* ed. Dittenberger, no. 54 (trans. from Austin 1981, no. 221). Strootman 2010 for an excellent analysis of the enduring universal ambitions of Hellenistic rulers based on Ptolemaic examples from the third century BC till the last incumbent of the dynasty, Queen Cleopatra, of the first century BC.

[35] Bosworth 1996: ch. 4.

[36] Much of the following examples conveniently collected by Gehrke 1982.

[37] Athenaeus, *Deipnosophistai* V, 193d–195f (with Murray 1996); V, 196a–203e (with Rice 1983).

[38] Polybios I, 1–4 (with commentary of Walbank 1957: 39–46). Further Walbank 2002: ch. 8 for the enduring ambition of the large Hellenistic monarchies to conquer 'the whole' of Alexander's empire.

Parthian dynasty to resurrect the Iranian traditions of universal empire in the face of a much weakened Seleucid realm. The scene was beginning to be set for the future confrontation of the Roman Alexander-like Caesars and the Arsakid Kings of Kings.[39]

THE FABRIC OF EMPIRE: COMPOSITE AND COSMOPOLITAN

However, even if the Hellenistic era may be seen as representing a new turn in the history of empire, the universalism of these rulers, as was the case with the Achaemenids before them, still had to embrace great cultural and regional diversity. Aśoka famously converted to Buddhism and patronised its monasteries. But, it is also clear that the *dhamma* he proclaimed was not a narrowly conceived Buddhist order. It preached tolerance among the different sects of the empire and was also addressed to the Brahmins. In the same vein, where in the north-west his power encountered the imperial cultures of the previous conquerors, the Persians and the Hellenes, his edicts have been found in both Aramaic- and Greek-language versions, instead of the predominant Prakrit.[40] Among the boasts of the victorious Ptolemaic descendant of Herakles and Dionysos we encountered above was the claim in old pharaonic fashion to have recovered and brought back 'all the sacred objects that were removed from Egypt by the Persians'[41] – the Greco-Macedonian ruler posing as champion of customary Egyptian religion. Both the Ptolemies and the Seleucids had to reach an accord with the powerful and well-entrenched temple elites of the ancient Near East, with all the authority of millennium-old traditions of religious worship to back them up. In the traditional temples of Egypt, Ptolemaic rulers appear depicted as Pharaohs in timeless conventional style and performing the sacred rites of the office.[42] Likewise, cuneiform chronicles show Seleucid rulers taking part in the age-old temple ceremonies of Babylonian kingship.[43] If this accommodation failed, temples and other powerful local institutions might serve as a rallying point for strong opposition against the monarchical regime and even rebellion.[44] The power of the aspiring universal kings was composite in a way of which the Ottomans, described by Kołodziejczyk in this volume, have become the standard in the

---

[39] Bang 2011a: 176–7. Fowler 2005: 140–3 in particular.

[40] Olivelle 2012; Thapar 1997: ch. 5; Schlumberger *et al.* 1958.

[41] *Orientis Graecae Inscriptiones Selectae*, ed. Dittenberger, no. 54 (trans. Austin 1981: 365).

[42] Hölbl 2001: 77–90, 102 and 257–85; Stanwick 2002.   [43] Kuhrt 1996; Sherwin-White 1987.

[44] A process of which the First Book of Maccabees presents a narrative, relating the successful rejection of their Seleucid rulers by a Jewish elite claiming the temple of Jerusalem as an alternative basis of power.

sociological literature.[45] Tolerance of the customs and respect for the institutions of conquered societies was usually articulated within an imperial
hierarchy. At the top, rulers promoted forms of culture transcending region:
Hellenism in the Greco-Macedonian case; in the Mauryan, Buddhism is a
likely candidate within the wider programme of *dhamma*.

To disseminate the vision of *dhamma*, officers were sent out from the
Mauryan court to represent the imperial order to the elites of the provinces.
In the same vein, the conversion of Aśoka to Buddhism and his sponsorship
of its monasteries may be seen as an attempt to align his empire with
a transregional network of powerful institutions. However, it must be
emphasised that the extant evidence is very scarce and it is difficult to
determine with certainty to what extent this actually happened. Later
Buddhist sources are likely to have exaggerated the significance of the
imperial alliance with Aśoka.[46] But from a sociological perspective, it is
easy to see what a network of monasteries could have brought to the
Mauryan empire: a group of privileged practitioners set off from the lay
majority by its embodiment of the religious ideal and unified across regions
by a set of core beliefs. There are the contours of a prospective imperial elite.
In this context it is notable that among the Aśokan edicts are instructions
to Buddhist monasteries about the religious canon as well as orders to weed
out schismatic members.[47] The polis, the Greek city-state, served as the
crucible in which the elite of the Greco-Macedonian conquest order was
forged. Kept to their allegiance, as we saw, by a Hellenising aristocracy
jealous of its position, the post-Alexander monarchs followed the example
set by him and continued to found new poleis. New royal capitals, massive
and sparkling like Alexandria in Egypt, Antioch in Syria or Seleucia in
Mesopotamia, advertised to the world the might of the Greco-Macedonian
lords and the attractions of entering into their service. Eye catching though
they are, these large cities were part of a wider urban 'sprawl'. Across

---

[45] Sherwin-White and Kuhrt 1993. Cf. Barkey 2008. Bang (2011b) discusses the character of such
   imperial composites in relation to the early-modern European composite state. In the former, the
   ruler and his government transcended the different communities, less so in the latter where each
   group or territory often was able to assert a strong degree of autonomy within the whole. In the same
   direction, on the Hellenistic monarchs, Ma 2003, though emphasising more strongly the cohesion of
   the imperial composites. But comparative experience holds out an analytical alternative, in the form
   of vast tributary empires, to the model of increasingly consolidated and penetrating state-power of
   the European absolutist state.
[46] Thapar 1981: 421–3, cautiously. Bailey and Mabbett 2003: 77–107 for a stronger view of the importance of Buddhism as a resource of power for the development of monarchy and empire in ancient
   India.
[47] Babra inscription and the so-called schism edict, translated in Thapar 1997: 261–2; Hultzsch 1925:
   159–64 and 171–4.

the Hellenistic realms a network of (smaller) Hellenic urban foundations was gradually created to fortify the order of rule.[48] Stripped to its bare bones, the classical city-state was a community of males of military age organised around a number of key public institutions. When created from contingents of veterans drawn from the armies of the Hellenistic rulers, this made the polis an excellent instrument of empire – and an avenue of social mobility. In the centuries after Alexander, myriad Greeks and Macedonians would seek to better their lot in life by enlisting as soldiers around the Hellenistic ecumene and eventually be settled on a new piece of land far from their place of birth.[49] Perhaps the most famous, certainly the most astonishing, of these Greek military colonies is the foundation on the river Oxus uncovered by modern archaeologists at Ai Khanoum in present-day Afghanistan.[50] Here was a city deep into Central Asia replete with Greek theatre and gymnasium which enabled life somewhat in the Hellenic Mediterranean manner to take place. On the heroon, the grave-shrine built inside the city for its founder Kineas, was inscribed: 'These wise sayings . . . are dedicated in the Holy Pytho. From there Klearchus copied them faithfully and put them up here in the far-shining precinct . . . ' The Holy Pytho was the oracular sanctuary of Apollo at Delphi, and following this proud announcement was listed a collection of Apollonian lore with ready instructions of moral philosophy for the Bactrian colonists. Whether or not the French master epigrapher Louis Robert was right in identifying Klearchus with the pupil of Aristotle, this is still tantalising evidence of mobility, not only of armies and people, but also of forms of knowledge.[51] Under the tutelage of the kings, Greek imperial civilisation was shaped by the transregional dissemination of the social rituals of the polis, such as the athletic contests of the gymnasium, and a literary culture based on poetry, rhetoric and philosophy. It was from this network of Hellenic communities that the Greco-Macedonian monarchs mostly recruited the members of their courts, their philoi or 'friends', to form a supra-local aristocracy.[52]

On the Indian side of our comparison, the inscriptions of Aśoka represent a new departure in more ways than one; they are also the first written texts from India which can be securely dated, and thus open the doors from a world dominated by oral transmission to one of literacy. The

---

[48] Surveyed in Fraser 1996; Cohen 1995 and 2006 and Mueller 2006.   [49] Shipley 2000: 54–8.
[50] Bernard 1973–87 (publication of excavations); Holt 1999 for an historical analysis. Further, the relevant contributions to Crib and Herrmann 2007.
[51] Robert 1968 (publication of the inscription followed by analysis).
[52] Herman 1997; Strootman 2011.

prevalence of variants of Prakrit in the edicts may be a sign that the Mauryan chancery was to some extent trying to promote a common transregional mode of communication. But this was still early days in the development of more overarching networks of power and communication in the process of Indian state-formation. Later Indian forms of script did derive from the orthography used in the Aśokan inscriptions, but the dialect would change as literacy became more firmly established.[53] In the long term, the development of a transregional medium would take place in Sanskrit. This happened as the language of the Vedas ceased to be the sole, and orally transmitted, possession of a group of religious and ritual specialists and moved decisively into the domain of court culture and writing in the centuries before and after the beginning of our era. Not unlike the post-Alexander Greek world, the dissemination and elaboration of Sanskrit took place in a context of several competing centres and dynasties, some of which even tried to inscribe themselves in the succession from the Mauryas, most notably the Guptas whose monumental boasts have been found chiselled into surfaces already dignified with the epigraphic remains of Aśoka. The two Sanskrit epics of the *Rāmāyana* and the *Mahābhārata* provided the canonical core of this literary culture. Grammar, learned allusion and studied elegance interlaced with arcane vocabulary were central values, the result a stable, classicising literary idiom seemingly place- and timeless. These and similar qualities have often enough been identified as key characteristics also of Hellenistic literature, as it developed under the patronage of the royal courts, and of the transregional language, *koine* or standard Greek which was the outcome.[54] It is therefore more than fitting that the literary culture of this 'wonderful structure; more perfect than the Greek, more copious than the Latin, and more exquisitely refined than either', as William Jones once famously declared about Sanskrit, has recently been described in terms of a cosmopolis.[55]

The cosmopolitan and the world of Alexander are inextricably linked in our intellectual tradition. Tarn, in a famous, but controversial British Academy lecture, ascribed to Alexander an idealistic ambition to unify

---

[53] Thapar 2002: 183; Olivelle 2012. Thapar (1981) and Seneviratne (1978) discussed the Mauryan empire in the context of 'early states'.

[54] Bing 1988; Pfeiffer 1968: 87–233; Fantuzzi and Hunter 2004; Weber 1993.

[55] Pollock 2006 (p. 68 on the Sakas putting up an inscription on the Junagarh rock, 'juxtaposed' to fourteen edicts of Aśoka; p. 239 on the Gupta's inscribing themselves on the Allahabad pillar of Aśoka). Quotation from William Jones 'Third Anniversary Discourse on the Hindus' (1807: 34). Pollock's is a pioneer study. His contrast between a peaceful, plural Sanskrit cosmopolis and a militaristic Latin one is unconvincing. The co-existence of several competing claims to universal lordship is neither particularly Indian nor Asian (cf. p. 252). As shown in this chapter, it is also a feature of the Hellenistic world.

mankind in common brotherhood.[56] In doing so, the Scottish historian drew on a rhetorical bravura exercise, dating to Roman times and attributed to the Greek philosopher Plutarch. This essay had playfully proclaimed Alexander to belong among the great philosophers. For while the Stoic Zeno had only written a utopian treatise on the cosmopolis, the young king had actually brought this programme into effect by conquest and his subsequent attempts to win the defeated Asians for his cause. Adoption of Persian forms of dress by the young king as well as his organisation of a massed wedding at Susa of Greco-Macedonian aristocrats and soldiers to Persian spouses were part of a philosophical quest harmoniously to unite humanity under a common set of laws and customs.[57] Of course, nothing of this idealistic dream had much to do with the historical Alexander;[58] nor did it have much to do with the austere Stoic doctrine inspired by the Cynic philosopher Diogenes.[59] But if Plutarch's Greco-Roman attempt to merge Alexander's imperial experience with Stoic thought makes for bad history and poor philosophy, it is all the better as sociology. Membership of Zeno's republic could only ever be achieved by a select few, the good and wise, while Diogenes' claim to be a cosmopolite signalled his independence of place and circumstance and ability to travel anywhere.[60] The unbounded exclusivity of the cosmopolitan principle is an excellent ideal-type through which to analyse the culture of imperial elites.

Within the Hellenistic world, the unbounded model set by Alexander was also mirrored in universalistic and encyclopaedic cultural claims. At the library of the famed Museum in Alexandria were said to be collected all the books in the world. Poets, geographers and other literati cultivated the marvellous, be it in the form of exquisite virtuoso composition, strange human customs or wonderful natural phenomena. Possession of these reflected the might, capacity and splendour of Hellenism.[61] Momigliano, the great polymath, once commented on the apparent lack of interest shown by Hellenic civilisation in its neighbours. Precious little was done to study the texts of the subjugated peoples, read them in the original, translate them and make them available in Greek language.[62] Here was no sustained move away from *curio-hunting* to the principles celebrated

---

[56] Tarn 1933; Toynbee 1969 for a classic and playful counter-factual version of Alexander's united humanity.

[57] Plutarch *On the Fortune of Alexander* 329a–330d.   [58] Badian 1958.

[59] Schofield 1991, appendix A. Baldry 1965: chs. 4–5 are still valuable.

[60] Diogenes Laertius VI, 63 (Diogenes: a cosmopolite); VII, 32–4; 121 (Zeno's exclusivist republic).

[61] Pfeiffer 1968: 134; Erskine 1995; Fraser 1972: ch. 6; Parker 2008: 33–53; Tybjerg 2003. Books 1–5 of Diodorus Siculus offer a good impression of this 'marvellous universalism'.

[62] Momigliano 1971.

by modern anthropology.[63] Arguably, Momigliano overstated the case. Cultural borrowings and transfer of knowledge often went unannounced and only left a tacit mark on, for example, notions of Hellenistic kingship. In the practical sphere, the Greeks are unlikely to have ignored 'indigenous' experience when it comes to fiscal information, agricultural techniques and other 'local knowledges'. But such processes of cultural mixing, high and low, nevertheless did surprisingly little to reorient the dominant currents within Greek imperial discourse. Science and literary scholarship were never harnessed, as they would later be by European colonial authorities, systematically to register and record subject societies and cultures.[64]

A good illustration of the issues at stake here is the translation of the Hebrew Bible into Greek, the Septuagint. An attempt to assert the status of this text, the second-century BC, pseudo-historical *Letter of Aristeas* originating from within the Alexandrine Jewish diaspora, refracts, like a prism, the cultural hierarchies of power in the Hellenistic world. In the letter, a fiction of royal patronage of the Ptolemies was invented for the production of the Greek translation. This project, it was claimed, had been instigated to enable the inclusion of the Jewish scriptures in the comprehensive royal library.[65] The implicit expectation, that to earn admission to 'world' literature Greek was necessary, is telling. Here we meet a Hellenising Jewish discourse asserting its status both within Judaism ('our new text bears the imprimatur of the king'), and within the hegemonic culture ('our ideas and customs are respectable and have a place within the cosmopolitan discourse'). That sort of claim, and cultural mixture, could work well enough for groups attempting to emulate aspects of Hellenic civilisation to carve out a position for themselves within the ruling order.[66] At the same time,

---

[63] The banner under which Malinowski (1922: 401) introduced his programme for a modern anthropology, based on field-work with the observer living for extended periods among the foreign peoples under study: 'Genuine scientific research differs from mere curio-hunting in that the latter runs after the quaint, singular and freakish – the craving for the sensational and the mania of collecting providing its twofold stimulus. Science on the other hand has to analyse and classify facts in order to place them in an organic whole.' See Stocking 1995: ch. 6.

[64] Cf. Woolf 2011: ch. 3. It may be possible to detect traces of some 'indigenous' influence, e.g. Egyptian mythological motifs subtly being absorbed by the Hellenistic poets of Alexandria as argued by Bing 1988: 128–39 and Stephens 2002 (to be read with Barbantani 2003), or even see the long tradition of Egyptian temple libraries as having inspired the Ptolemaic library in Alexandria, as suggested by Ryholt (forthcoming). Such phenomena of cultural mixture and appropriation should not be underestimated or ignored, Sherwin-White and Kuhrt (1993) are right to insist. Nevertheless, the Greek orientation remains the dominant outlook, so in general, Walbank 2002: ch. 5.

[65] *Letter of Aristeas* ch. 38, chs. 9–11 and 28–33. A standard edition of the Greek text is that of Pelletier (*Lettre d'Aristée à Philocrate*, Paris 1962); a modern English translation by Shutt is available in Charlesworth 1985: 12–34.

[66] Hunter 2011 for a basic discussion. Johnson 2004 is now fundamental on the role of 'pseudo'-historical literature in forging a Jewish identity within Hellenism. Honigman 2003: 114–18 seems

however, it is quite revealing that few, if any Hellenic authors outside the Jewish communities ever bothered much about this addition to the world of letters. It was, as Momigliano remarked, 'bad Greek'.[67] The situation resembles nothing so much as that now often commented upon under the Romans. In the eastern Mediterranean, Hellenistic society adjusted to the cultural impulses of the new imperial dispensation and absorbed some of its cultural practices while remaining stubbornly and assertively Greco-centric in its outlook.[68]

The cosmopolitan version of language based on canonical or classical models enabled, even invited, emulation by (ambitious and capacious) outsiders – it had a stable core, requiring education, and could thus be acquired independently of being born to the language – but also facilitated exclusion by its imposition of a demanding literary and philosophical idiom, command of which as a group only the elite could aspire to. In short, Hellenism, a badge of nobility, produced a cosmopolitan and trans-regional aristocratic culture tying together elite groups across culturally and linguistically very diverse regions. As such, like the courtly culture of Sanskrit, it seems like a particularly wide-reaching and successful example of the form of cultural integration which Ernest Gellner saw as characteristic of pre-industrial societies: a thin layer of laterally united elites presiding over a (peasant) majority of more insulated communities. This ideal-type, however, was paired with a vision of the different form of integration characteristic of nation-states which to some extent severed the transnational ties of elites to bind them closer together with the peasant majority inside the state.[69] But whereas the latter has been subject to extensive comparative analysis by historians of nationalism, the former has received much less discussion. Yet, it would seem like a promising field of comparative research for historians of pre-industrial societies.[70]

---

unnecessarily equivocal about the historicity of the myth invented for the translation of the Septuagint (why the need to 'salvage' a narrative loaded with so much obvious fabrication). Collins' (2000) argument, that the account of royal patronage given by the letter is essentially correct, inspires little confidence, at least with this reader.

[67] Momigliano 1971: 91.

[68] 'Becoming Roman, Staying Greek' as it was aptly phrased by Greg Woolf (1994).

[69] Gellner 1983, in particular ch. 2.

[70] An interesting recent attempt is Colvin 2011. Bang 2010 for an analysis of Roman imperial aristocratic culture informed by Gellner.

CHAPTER 4

The making of Oriental Rome: shaping the Trojan legend

Rolf Michael Schneider

In the history of cultures claims of universalism have been inflationary for millennia, notably in the fields of religion, philosophy and politics. Looking from this perspective on imperial Rome we are faced by a plethora of claims, statements and practices such as supreme military, matchless finances and unrivalled infrastructure, power of human resources and multi-ethnic cultures, global politics and universal imagery and architecture, boundless lands, flexible ideologies and adaptable religions. For the purpose of this chapter I am interested in three issues: (1) Rome's claim to dominate the world; (2) Rome's ambivalent habit to read Roman as an equivalent of 'world' and, at the same time, to focus intensively on the non-Roman; (3) the distinctive role of Roman imagery as a high-register narrative which globally and persistently refuelled the debate about what 'Roman' was. A good starting point for embarking on concepts of universalism in (early) imperial Rome are the *fasti*, an exceptional poem about the Roman festival calendar composed by the Augustan poet Ovid (43 BC – *c.* AD 17/18). Significant here is what the poet tells us about the *terminalia*, a festival celebrated on 23 February to worship the god Terminus. Towards the end he writes:

> Est via quae populum Laurentes ducit in agros,
> quondam Dardanio regna petita duci:
> illa lanigeri pecoris tibi, Termine, fibris
> sacra videt fieri sextus ab Urbe lapis.
> Gentibus est aliis tellus data limite certo,
> Romanae spatium est urbis et orbis idem.

My warm thanks to Peter Fibiger Bang and Dariusz Kołodziejczyk who asked me to contribute to this book. I thank my colleagues and friends in Pisa, Warsaw, Stanford, Tübingen, Kassel, Dresden, Munich, Berlin, Innsbruck, Leipzig, Cambridge and Pretoria for stimulating discussion when they invited me to give papers around this subject. And I thank my son Jeremy, Michael Squire and the two anonymous readers for good advice. For providing photographs I am indebted to Petra Cain (Leipzig), Mette Moltesen (Copenhagen), Alfons Neubauer (Munich) and R. R. Smith (Oxford), additionally to the Archäologisches Institut der Universität Köln – Forschungsarchiv für Antike Plastik (Cologne), the Ny Carlsberg Glyptotek (Copenhagen), the Trustees of the British Museum (London) and the Museum für Abgüsse Klassischer Bildwerke (Munich).

There is a road that takes people to the Laurentine fields,
to the kingdom once sought by the Dardanian chieftain (Aeneas):
on that road the sixth milestone from the City bears witness
to the sacrifice of a woolly sheep's entrails to you, Terminus.
To other people land may be given with a fixed limit.
But the space of the city of Rome and the world is one.[1]

With this statement Ovid addresses my first issue. Terminus was a Roman
god whose name literally means "boundary stone". He was the god worshipped to protect regional boundary markers but, in a wider sense, also to
keep vigil over Rome's cultivated universe, Vergil's famous *imperium sine
fine*.[2] For Ovid the city's claim to dominate the world was, in contrast to
the fixed limit of *externae gentes*, beyond debate as it followed Augustan cosmology and Roman sacrificial law. After all, the Roman Empire was never
ideologically conceived by its rulers and inhabitants as a territory within
fixed limits.[3] But the poet extends this ideology further when he links the
equation of *urbis* and *orbis* to another claim of Rome, her lineage from
Troy through Aeneas.[4] In doing so Ovid interweaves two main ideologies
of imperial Rome: the Trojan descent of the city and her right to have
possession of the world. Rome's purported ancestry from Troy highlights
my second issue. The poet grounds the above claims in Roman religion
and the city's legendary non-Roman origin. Integrating the non-Roman in
Rome marked a vital point in the debate about the city's fabled past. It was
a debate which commenced in Rome long ago, centuries before the period
of Augustus.[5] Here my third and key issue comes into play, the role of
Rome's universal imagery. I am especially curious about its role within the
global yet contradictory debate about what Roman and non-Roman essentially meant. Here I shall focus primarily on Roman portrayals of Asian
strangers.[6] I will show how they mediated and contributed to Rome's universalistic ideology of descending from Troy and ruling the world. What is
the wider context of these claims?

In the aftermath of the Persian Wars a powerful rhetoric surfaced in
Classical Athens and became a crucial factor in the political debate of
the West – the rhetoric of Orientalism. This rhetoric provided all the

---

[1] Ovid, *Fasti* 2.679–84 (ed. M. Robinson, Oxford 2010; with commentary). For the wider context of
this debate, see the excellent study of Whittaker 1994: 10–30.
[2] Vergil, *Aeneid* 1.279 (ed. R. A. B. Mynors, Oxford 1969); see below note 61.
[3] Whittaker 1994; Schneider 1997 (imagery of *urbs* et *orbs*).
[4] Horsfall 1987; Gruen 1990: 6–51; Rose 2008: 97–102; Dardenay 2010.   [5] Flaig 1999: 84–95.
[6] The Roman portrayals in question show only figures in Eastern Asian dress; hence, I call them
'Asians'. The more general (and loaded) notion 'Oriental' refers to all peoples of the East – inter alia
also Egyptians who, when depicted in Roman imagery at all, were shown in a different iconography.

ingredients needed to articulate universalistic claims, and steadily gained in importance. By the time of Cicero the terms *oriens* and *occidens* had become two metaphors with which to describe the world.[7] Cicero concluded that among the territorial powers of the East and the West the gods favoured Rome first, followed by Athens, Sparta and Rhodes, as all of them possessed parts of Europe, Asia and Africa. This is an unashamedly one-sided view of the world. Rome is labelled as the only superpower of both the eastern and the western parts of the world. Parthia and Egypt are not even credited with a mention. Such concentration of power in the West is based on a rhetoric of Orientalism which became, by the blessing of the gods, influential beyond the universe of ancient Rome. In recent times the challenging study of Edward Said has rekindled a wide controversy around the rhetoric of Orientalism.[8] My interest in the visual side of this rhetoric has shown me how much supposed dichotomies such as Occident and Orient, Roman and barbarian, friend and foe have biased the perception of today's politics.[9] It is necessary to overcome such dichotomies which have coloured the very fabric of Western thought both in writing and in imagery.[10] I only give one example. Despite the disparities between ancient and modern civilisations, both cultures have used clothing to distinguish between different cultural bodies. From antiquity to the present day, dress codes have played a key role in underpinning ideological contrasts between the peoples of the East and the West.[11] Yet, ironically, today's formal Western dress, long trousers and a long-sleeved jacket with a V-neck opening, follows not the classical tradition of Greece and Rome but the Asian style. This is obvious if we look at the bronze statue of a Parthian chieftain from the Iranian site Shami, usually dated to the first century BC or AD (fig. 4.1).[12]

In paving the way for a more nuanced reading of Rome's universalistic claims I want to show how, in my own field of ancient Greek and Roman art, imagery addresses and transforms Eastern cultures, and, in turn, is affected by them. But what are the qualities which distinguish the image from the text? Almost every text, regardless of whether it is told, sung or written, employs and stimulates a great variety of images oscillating between

---

[7] Cicero, *De natura deorum* 2.164–5 (ed. P. G. Walsh, Oxford 1997).

[8] Said 1978; Fisch 1984; Hentsch 1988; Shichiji 1991; Mackenzie 1995; Sardar 1999; Bohrer 2003; Wiesehöfer 2006; Varisco 2007; Warraq 2007; Parker 2008.

[9] Schneider 2007: 50–3 fig. 1.

[10] For Western categories of cultural asymmetries, Koselleck 1975. More open readings able to accept (ideological) ambiguities and contradictions, Hartog 1980; Stevens 1994: 64–7 (on C. G. Jung's concept of 'shadow'); Wiesehöfer 2006; Schneider 2007; Parker 2008; Hardie 2009; Heitz 2009; Woolf 2011.

[11] Flügel 1930; Eicher 1995. For Greek and Roman dress codes, Wallace-Hadrill 2008: 38–57.

[12] Mathiesen 1992: 166–7 no. 80; Invernizzi 2001: 230 colour plate; Landskron 2005: 95–6.

Fig. 4.1 Parthian chieftain wearing an Asian trouser-suit. Bronze (h. 1.94 m). From Shami (Khuzestan). First century BC/AD.

mental, verbal, physical, individual, collective, religious and ideological imaginations. Vice versa, the process of designing and reading images requires the faculty of language, although exceptions are possible. But, unlike a text, an image provides different qualities with which to stimulate social communication.[13] This is already inherent in the different ways images and texts are perceived. The reader normally needs the knowledge of grammar and vocabulary to understand a text whereas the viewer can get the 'picture' without the knowledge of iconographic conventions. The Western reader is trained to read the text from left to right and line by line. The viewer, however, cannot do the same with an image. Unlike reading, viewing creates not systematic but random patterns of eye movement.[14] Moreover, the reader knows, at least on a formal level, where the text starts and when it is at an end. The viewer, however, is at a loss if asked to do the same with an image. As a result, viewing an image is an infinite process despite the image's formal confines. This is one of the reasons why the viewer links with the image the quality of ambiguous subjective and collective readings. Such ambiguity, however, does not necessarily exclude the acknowledgment of intentional meaning. On the contrary, the intentional meaning of an image can be efficiently supported by a wide, even a contradictory spectrum of possible associations. The infinite process of viewing is linked to another distinctive quality of the image, its power to stimulate suggestiveness. An image can both catch the viewer's attention in a fraction of a second and stamp itself on his mind forever. Consequently, the image promotes per se more open, suggestive and diverse readings than the text. Owing to its distinct mediation of a reality, the image provides a differently coloured view on religious, social, emotional, ideological and universal issues than the text. With this in mind I return to Rome.

Imperial Rome was rife with non-Roman cultures. Rome used victories over non-Romans to legitimise imperial power. Rome claimed to rule the world. Rome integrated a wide range of different civilisations and ethnicities.[15] And Rome communicated with people beyond the *orbis Romanus*.[16] An empire of this diversity needed icons and rituals capable of being widely adopted.[17] One way Rome took to shape such icons was to

---

[13] Mitchell 1986; Smith 2002; Giuliani 2003: 9–19; 2006, 185–92; Squire 2009.
[14] Giuliani 2003: 27–9 figs. 1–2b.
[15] 'Foreignness' at Rome, Noy 2000. For Roman culture and the manifold debates about the notion of culture, Wallace-Hadrill 2008: 3–37.
[16] Recent studies on Rome's relations with non-Romans, Mattern 1999; Ferris 2000; Burns 2003; Woolf 2011.
[17] Similar Beard 1994: 185–7.

establish stereotyped images of non-Romans. The majority of these images portrayed non-Romans with two different Romanised dress codes, dividing more or less the peoples of the North and those of the East.[18] The most popular portrayal of a non-Roman was the Asian. The Roman portrayal of the Asian reflects primarily the ambiguous ways used by Rome to represent herself to a global public.

Two different but interrelated Roman stereotypes of the Asian can be identified. Both were introduced into Roman imagery under Augustus. One is the portrayal of the bearded Parthian. The other is the portrayal of the handsome Asian employed to represent every figure of the Asian East, mythical and historical alike. My focus is on the latter. Above all I am interested in the early imperial portrayals of handsome Trojan princes, Rome's alleged Oriental forefathers. Their portrayals address Rome's claim to rule the world in unprecedented sophistication. This leads me to a series of questions. By whom, how and when were the portrayals of the handsome Trojan conceptualised, set up and read in Rome? And how did their portrayals contribute to the making of Oriental Rome and her claim to universal power? Before I can pursue these questions, however, I need to outline the historical context in which the Roman imagery of the Asian Oriental took shape.

THE BEARDED PARTHIAN: PORTRAYING THE ENEMY

Official relations between Rome and Parthia started late, with a treaty of *amicitia* in 96 BC.[19] This situation changed when the Roman general Marcus Licinius Crassus attacked the Parthians in the winter of 55/54 BC. After the disastrous defeat of Crassus and the loss of his entire army in 53 BC, Caesar propagated the ideology of revenge on the Parthians, but did not initiate war.[20] In 20 BC, by exerting diplomatic and military pressure on Parthia, Augustus succeeded in recovering well over 100 Roman standards and thousands of captive Romans. Although it had been achieved through diplomacy, the so-called settlement of the Parthian question was marked in the public media of Rome as Augustus' greatest victory, as the final military legitimation of his new imperial rule.[21] Portrayals throughout

[18] For Roman imagery of (northern) non-Romans, Schneider 1992a; Zanker 2000: 410–19; Krierer 2004; Heitz 2009.
[19] Sonnabend 1986: 159–227; Campbell 1993: 213–28; Wheeler 2002; Brosius 2006: 92–101.
[20] See below note 83.
[21] Schneider 1986: 29–97, 114–20, 128–30; Sonnabend 1986: 197–221; Campbell 1993: 220–8; Rich 1998; Landskron 2005: 102–51; Rose 2005; Schneider 2007: 54–61, 70–5.

the Roman Empire propagated the Parthian settlement as the ultimate triumph of the Roman West over the peoples of the East, and as one of the greatest achievements of Augustan foreign policy. Consequently, Parthia constituted the only other enemy superpower next to Rome, and was perceived as such.[22]

The first Roman portrayals of the Parthian emerged in the aftermath of Rome's widely adopted self-aggrandisement.[23] The most famous example is the Prima Porta statue of Augustus found north of Rome in the villa of the emperor's wife Livia (fig. 4.2).[24] The statue can be dated around 17 BC. The two main figures on the richly decorated cuirass are depicted in the centre: a Parthian is presenting a Roman military standard to a military representative of Rome (fig. 4.3). The two interacting figures are surrounded by a circle of non-interacting figures highlighting geographic, cosmic and divine claims of imperial Rome. The two main figures, however, are portrayed in asymmetry. On the left, and larger in size, we see the cuirassed representative of Rome from a side view (probably Mars Ultor), extending his right hand as if to demand or receive the standard. On the right, the Parthian, smaller in size and largely viewed from the front, gazes up towards the Roman eagle.[25] This depiction is the most detailed portrayal of a bearded Parthian in Roman imagery. The Parthian is dressed in long trousers, a belted V-neck tunic with long sleeves and soft shoes. The dress and physiognomy of the Parthian became stereotypes deployed by Roman workshops to portray people of the Asian East generically.[26] Distinctively Parthian is the V-neck tunic, which is widely attested in Parthian imagery (fig. 4.1).[27]

THE HANDSOME ASIAN: PORTRAYING FRIEND AND FOE

More suggestive and ambiguous, however, is the portrayal of the handsome Asian. It was introduced into Roman imagery on the return of the Roman standards by the Parthians in 20 BC.[28] Initially shaped in Classical Athens around 520 BC, this image constituted the Greek stereotype of any

---

[22] For a comparison of the two superpowers, Howard-Johnston 1995; Wiesehöfer 2003, who is also discussing the ideological preconceptions of such a comparison; Schneider 2007: 54–61, 70–5.

[23] Potential portrayals of Parthians in Rome before the age of Augustus, Schneider 1998: 95.

[24] Boschung 1993: 179–81 no. 171 (bibliography); Wiesehöfer 2002; McEwan 2003: 250–75; Landskron 2005: 103–6 pl. 19; Bradley 2009a: 447–50.

[25] Rose (2005: 25–6), however, has proposed identifying the representative of Rome not as Mars Ultor, the Avenger (*opinio communis*) but as the goddess Roma because of the Attic helmet, the 'female' tufts of hair which escape from the helmet, the 'female' anatomy of the body and the dog.

[26] Schneider 2007: 54–60.   [27] See above note 12.

[28] Schneider 1986; Landskron 2005: 57–92; Schneider 2007: 60–80.

Fig. 4.2 Cuirass of a statue of Augustus (detail). White marble (h. 2.06 m). From the imperial villa of Livia at Prima Porta, north of Rome. *c.* 17 BC.

handsome youth from the Asian East (fig. 4.4).[29] Taken up by workshops first in Classical Italy and then in Augustan Rome it became the most

---

[29] Vos 1963; Raeck 1981: 10–66; Miller 1997; Ivantchik 2005 (who appropriately has questioned the close traditional reading of the Easterners as 'Scythians' portrayed on numerous Attic pots).

Fig. 4.3 Parthian presenting a Roman military standard to a representative of Rome.
Detail of the statue of Augustus (see fig. 4.2).

Fig. 4.4 Archer in Asian dress. Attic red-figure plate signed by the painter Epiktetos
(dm. 19.4 cm). From Vulci. *c.* 520 BC.

successful ancient icon of the Asian.[30] In contrast to the stereotype of the
bearded Parthian (fig. 4.3), the handsome Asian has a clean-shaven face
framed by long coiffeured hair and crowned by the Phrygian cap.[31] A typical Roman portrayal of the handsome Oriental is the painting of handsome
Mithras made around AD 170 for the Mithraeum of Marino near Rome
(fig. 4.5).[32] The god wears a double-belted tunic with long sleeves, a flow-
ing mantle, long trousers and soft shoes. In short, the handsome Asian
is distinguished by youthful beauty, rich dress and intensive colour. His

[30] Italic forerunners, Kossatz-Deissmann 1994: 181, 187–8 no. 57 pl. 120; Simon 2001: 154–62.
[31] For the Phrygian cap, see below notes 126 and 128.
[32] Vermaseren 1982; Ghini 1994; Mielsch 2001: 176–7 (dating).

Fig. 4.5 Mithras in Asian dress subdues the bull. Wall painting of the Mithraeum in Marino near Rome (h. 1.80 m, w. 2.50 m). Second half of the second century AD.

historical or rather mythical identity can be revealed through attributes, clothing and/or context. Such a visual stereotype made it possible to represent all the people of the Asian East as uniform and thus essentially the same: whether past or present, personifications of cities or territories as well as cosmic, mythical or divine figures, they could all be depicted by the same portrayal.

The ambiguity of the handsome Asian is clearly seen in Roman portrayals of Oriental cup-bearers, which often decorated the legs of marble tables in Roman villas.[33] A fine example is the marble figure found in the Casa del Camillo in Pompeii, and thus made before AD 79 (fig. 4.6).[34] The figure portrays a luxury-class slave from the Asian East: young, beautiful,

---

[33] Schneider 1992b; 2007: 61–2 fig. 11 (small stone figure of a Parthian servant with jug and wine ladle, found in Palmyra).

[34] Dwyer 1982: 64–5 pl. 21 fig. 80; Schneider 1992b: 303–4 fig. 5; Pugliesi Carratelli 1997: 540–64 (Casa del Camillo, VII.12.22–27, room 'e').

Fig. 4.6 Servant in Asian dress holding a wine ladle. Decor of a table leg. White marble (h. 0.74 m). From Pompeii, Casa del Camillo (VII.12.22–27, room "e"). *c.* AD 50–70.

clean-shaven and in Asian dress. The wine ladle in his left hand identifies him as a cup-bearer who is depicted in the act of waiting for orders. In an ode dedicated to Agrippa's steward Iccius in 25 BC, the Augustan poet Horace emphasised the appeal of exotic Asian cup-bearers to the Roman elite. The poet revels in the alluring prospect of wealth and a luxurious life-style when Iccius returns home after his victories over the Arabs, over the Parthians and perhaps even over the Chinese:

> What page from (Asian) court with scented locks
> will be set to offer you wine with a ladle?[35]

In Rome, the portrayal of the Asian cup-bearer with a wine ladle was closely related to that of the Trojan prince Ganymede, the most beautiful cup-bearer of all.[36] To highlight the (sexual) beauty of his body he was traditionally shown naked except for a short mantle and the Phrygian cap.[37] Just like the figures of Asian cup-bearers, marble sculptures of Ganymede often served in Roman villas as table legs.[38] The handsome Trojan prince is usually accompanied by a huge eagle, recalling his abduction to Olympus by Zeus and his eternal fate to serve wine to the gods. Zeus' Trojan cup-bearer was the mythical archetype of the historical slave cup-bearer from the Asian East. Both cup-bearers alike betoken the ability of the Roman elite to command all the resources of the empire in the endlessly enjoyable task of projecting and maintaining their rank.[39]

HANDSOME TROJANS AT SPERLONGA

More complex issues are at stake if we look at the stately villa at Sperlonga, situated on the Campanian coast about 70 miles south of Rome (fig. 4.7).[40] Here, in the seawater pool right at the large cavern's entrance, a great number of sculptural fragments were found.[41] Put together again they show an exceptional statue of Ganymede held in the clutches of Jupiter's huge eagle (fig. 4.8).[42] Made in the age of Augustus, it is the earliest known Roman portrayal of the handsome Trojan prince.[43] It is also the only

[35] Horace, *carmen* 1.29.7–8 (ed. F. von Klingner, Leipzig 1959): *puer quis ex aula capillis / ad cyathum statuetur unctis.*
[36] Sichtermann 1988; Schwarzenberg 2001/2; Turnheim 2004. Genealogy of Ganymede, Scheer 1997: 318.
[37] For a Trojan reading of the Phrygian cap, see below notes 126 and 128.
[38] Neudecker 1988: 46–7; Schneider 1992b. Handsome imperial slaves and cup-bearers wearing long hair and called Ganymede, Martial, *Epigrams* 9.16, 22, 25, 36, 103 (ed. D. R. Shackleton Bailey, Leipzig 1990); Cain 1993: 86–7.
[39] Bourdieu 1974: 159–201.
[40] For the villa, Iacopi 1963: 1–24; Neudecker 1988: 220–3; Cassieri 2000: 12–56.
[41] Iacopi 1963: 22 fig. 20; 114: 'fuori della grotta e della piscina circolare, all'imboccatura della prima'.
[42] Iacopi 1963: 22, 114–17; Schneider 1986: 154 note 1166 pl. 24; Andreae 1995: 115–34; Cassieri 2000: 145–7.
[43] The style of Ganymede has been disputed. For an Augustan dating, Schneider 1992b: 301; Andreae 1995: 116–24. For the traditional dating in the later first century AD, Iacopi 1963: 117; Cassieri 2000: 146–7.

Fig. 4.7 Cavern and artificial dining island of the stately villa at Sperlonga (reconstruction). Early first century AD.

Fig. 4.8 Statue of Ganymede in Asian dress held in the clutches of Jupiter's eagle.
Phrygian marble (h. 2.25 m). *c.* 20 BC–AD 10.

portrayal of Ganymede wearing Asian dress and the only one portrayed
larger than life and sculpted in exotic Phrygian (= Trojan) marble from
Anatolia.[44] The statue was erected above the entrance to the large cavern.
The latter was part of the villa's dining room set up on an artificial island
and built to face the cavern's entrance. The statue's plinth was specially

[44] See below notes 124 and 126.

Fig. 4.9 Original setting of Ganymede at Sperlonga erected above the cavern's entrance on a plinth specially fitted into the rock (reconstruction) about 20 m above sea level.

fitted into the rock, and so occupied a spectacular setting overlooking the sea (fig. 4.9).[45] For ultimate effect the back of the statue is fixed to a pillar, which is askew. This allows Ganymede to lean forwards at an angle of 7 degrees. Placing the weighty statue of Ganymede in this lofty height alone was a powerful demonstration of what Roman elite members were able to achieve. Giving every appearance of having arrived straight from Olympus, the statue was designed to combine privileged workmanship and setting with a new interpretation of Roman Orientalism. Ganymede here is not small but larger than life, he is displayed not indoors but as a landmark outside and appears not naked but in rich Trojan dress. And Ganymede here is made not of monochrome stone but of polychrome

---

[45] Andreae (1995: 118–23 figs. 56–63; 126–7, 142 fig. 87) and Cassieri (2000: 52–3) pinpointed this location *contra* the formerly suggested position to the right of the cavern's entrance (Neudecker 1988: 223).

Fig. 4.10 Cavern at Sperlonga with five marbles of the Augustan period (reconstruction):
(A) Homeric hero rescues his dead comrade, (B) Odysseus' fight against Scylla,
(c) Odysseus' blinding of Polyphemus, (D) Diomedes and Odysseus with the taken
Trojan Palladium, (E) Ganymede held in the clutches of Jupiter's eagle.

marble from his Phrygian homeland in Anatolia. In contrast the head and the left hand were carved separately in white marble and then attached to the body; originally the head may have been painted.[46]

The outstanding concept and context of the statue demanded wide-ranging readings. The statue is, in fact, the only known depiction of Ganymede as distinctively Trojan.[47] Placed to be seen from far away, the Trojan prince became the Roman villa's very signature. Thus he was irrevocably linked to four over-life-sized 'Trojan' marble groups arranged, around the time of Augustus, inside the cavern (fig. 4.10).[48] Staged between rocks and seawater the four marbles portrayed incidents selected from the

[46] For unknown reasons (different workshops and/or production dates?) style and proportions of Ganymede's head differ from the body. Note two further irregularities: (1) the head's findspot does not seem to be recorded; (2) both the head and its Phrygian cap are carved in white marble although the cap would have been made of Phrygian marble as is the body (this is the case with the statues of Asians found in the Basilica Paulli, see note 104).

[47] Roman portrayals of Trojans in Oriental dress, Grassinger 1999: 57–63, 207–9 nos. 34–40; Rose 2005: 34, 44.

[48] Conticello, Andreae and Bol 1974; Kunze 1996: 159–223 (dating); Andreae 1999: 177–223; 2001: pls. 98–102; Weis 2000; Squire 2009: 202–38.

epic cycle. Two of the marbles were placed opposite each other and next to the cavern's entrance: on the north side a group showing two Homeric heroes one of whom rescues the dead body of his comrade (the question of whether these are Greeks or Trojans is disputed); on the south side Diomedes' and Odysseus' theft of the sacred Palladium, the Trojan symbol of Rome's claim to eternal power. The Trojan Palladium was a small statue of an armed Athena which Aeneas in a competing version of the legend was said to have carried out of Troy and later to have brought to Latium and Rome.[49] The two other groups are colossal in size and portray Odysseus fighting two monsters. The one group showing Odysseus' blinding of Polyphemus was displayed in the cavern's back grotto as an allusion to the giant's own cave. The other group showing Odysseus' fight against Scylla's dreadful attack on his ship was placed right in the cavern's midst and was allusively surrounded by seawater. Loaded with the Augustan ideology of Rome's Trojan descent, the four sculptural dramas associated the fall of Troy with the rise of Rome. Transformed into three-dimensional marbles, the epic sculptures stimulated endless options of entertainment. Depending on the interest and sentiment of the viewer he could read the sculptures over and over again, debating the manifold relations between image and text, myth and history, heroes and men, narrative and ideology, style and technique, and the like. As a result, the owner(s) of the villa claimed that the epic cycle was part of the very history of Rome – and that the selected narratives in marble were shaped, staged and interpreted in a way only the Roman elite was able to accomplish. Hence, in Sperlonga the stories of Rome's alleged Trojan past stimulated the production of some of the most remarkable and meaningful visual narratives of the epic cycle. As a Trojan, Ganymede was a mythic forefather of the Romans and, especially, of the imperial Julian family. As an Asian servant on Olympus, however, he embodied the debt owed by Eastern cultures to the Roman elite. The statue at Sperlonga neatly unites in one and the same portrayal the paradoxical themes of nobility and servitude, Roman and Asian. This makes the Ganymede at Sperlonga a case in point, a potent visual manifesto of the universalistic claims with which Rome's elite propagated its heritage of and supremacy over Asia.[50] These claims were later taken up by Ilium, the Roman town near Troy. The city's mint struck coins with portraits of

[49] Dionysius of Halicarnassus, *Roman Antiquities* 1.68–69 (ed. V. Fromentin and J.-H. Sautel, Paris 1998); Pausanias, *Description of Greece* 2.23.5 (ed. D. Musti and M. Torelli, Milan 1986).

[50] The textual evidence, the intricacy of the marble narratives and their settings at Sperlonga do not support Bernhard Andreae's mono-causal reading of the villa as the property of the emperor Tiberius, and the sculptures as a mere manifesto of a supposed Tiberian ideology. To my mind the question of the ownership of the villa remains open; see Neudecker 1988: 221.

Fig. 4.11 Bust of a handsome youth in Asian dress. White marble (h. 0.93 m). Found 1898 south of the cavern's entrance at Sperlonga. Second quarter second century AD.

Hadrian, Marcus Aurelius and Commodus on the reverse but portrayals of Ganymede held by Zeus' eagle on the obverse.[51]

The ongoing interest in Troy at Sperlonga is shown by two almost identical marble busts of handsome Asians now in the Ny Carlsberg Glyptotek, Copenhagen (figs. 4.11 and 4.12).[52] The busts were found in 1898 immediately south of the cavern's entrance (fig. 4.7).[53] Next to their findspot

[51] Bellinger 1961: 47–63 nos. T136 (Hadrian), T149 (Marcus Aurelius), T186–T187 (Commodus), T209, T211, T213 (without an emperor's portrayal, second century AD).
[52] Patroni 1898; Spagnolis 1983; Fejfer 2005.
[53] For the findspot, Spagnolis 1983: 78: 'a Sperlonga furono rinvenuti, nel 1898, sul lato destro (guardando) della grotta di Tiberio'.

Fig. 4.12 Bust of a handsome youth in Asian dress. White marble (h. 0.95 m). Found 1898 together with the bust shown in fig. 4.11. Second quarter second century AD.

the remains of three brick columns had been unearthed, all facing the sea.[54] Originally the columns may have served as pedestals for the busts.[55] The evidence of at least three columns might indicate even a gallery of such busts. However, what are the facts? Both busts are larger than life, measuring 95 cm and 93 cm in height respectively. Both busts are unique as they show handsome Asians with beautiful long locks. Both wear a

---

[54] Spagnolis 1983: 78: 'poco discosto, dove furono trovati i busti, abbiamo rinvenuto le basi di tre colonne ben conservate, ma di materia laterizia. Erano, forse, dove poggiavano i busti.'
[55] (Freestanding) portrait busts, Fejfer 2008: 236–61.

Phrygian cap and a mantle only. And both busts can be dated stylistically around AD 140. Recently, Jane Fejfer recognised the implausibility of their conventional reading as Attis.[56] A more likely reading gains shape if we take the following issues into account: the specific iconography of the two Orientals, the function(s) of Roman busts, and the Trojan background of the marble groups displayed inside and on top of the cavern. Consequently, I suggest reading the two busts as portrayals of young handsome noble men in Trojan dress. Both busts are closely related to the statue of Trojan Ganymede (fig. 4.8), by their handsome faces, their beautiful locks and their Phrygian caps, and by their setting next to the cavern's entrance and their orientation towards the sea. Two different readings of the busts are equally sound, namely as Trojan princes *and* as Roman noble youths. The young sons of the highest-ranking Roman families used to present themselves in the Oriental costume of their Trojan forefathers when they participated in the Trojan games. The *lusus Troiae* was a mock battle on horseback which had been staged in the Circus Maximus throughout the Julio-Claudian period, from Augustus to Nero.[57] This reading might be supported by the dress of the two handsome youths as they are shown in a mantle but not in an Asian tunic with long sleeves. The two marble busts gave Rome's Trojan past a new Oriental face. This might also be true of a third head of a handsome Asian found in the villa, a marble herm which Bernhard Andreae believes portrays Iulus Ascanius.[58] From the mid second century onwards the viewer of the Trojan marbles at Sperlonga was confronted with a gallery of Roman busts portraying, from the retrospective point of historical narrative, young members of the Trojan-Roman elite in the dress code of the handsome Asian. As a result, his portrayal was made to coincide with the representations of both the princes of Troy and the *jeunesse dorée* of the Roman elite. Already by the time of Claudius (AD 41–54) long beautiful hair, originally a feature of handsome luxury-class slaves especially from the Asian East, can be found in portraits of young Roman males (fig. 4.13), who were for this very reason misguidedly taken for females.[59]

HANDSOME TROJANS IN ROME

Classical scholars have given little attention to the extent to which the portrayal of the handsome Asian was used to represent Rome's engagement

---

[56] Fejfer 2005: 192.   [57] Fuchs 1990; Fortuin 1996: 80, 83, 88–91, 161–75; see below note 134.

[58] Iacopi 1963: 126–9 figs. 122–4; Andreae 1995: 124–5 figs. 64–7, 127; Spannagel 1999: 100 pl. 11.

[59] Cain 1993: 80–8 pls. 43–6 (text fig. 13: 144 no. 23); Pollini 2004.

Fig. 4.13 Portrait of a handsome Roman male with a Nero-like coiffure and long locks. White marble (h. 0.24 m). Of unknown provenance. Second half first century AD.

with Eastern cultures. This theme runs through the imagery of the most distinguished monuments set up in the Augustan city, e.g. the Ara Pacis Augustae, the Forum Augustum and the Basilica (Aemilia) Paulli, which adorned the north-east side of the Roman forum (fig. 4.14). A key role in representing Rome's Oriental face was given to the Trojan prince Iulus Ascanius, the son of Aeneas. According to Augustan writers, Aeneas, the son of Aphrodite, had saved his father Anchises and his son Ascanius when he abandoned burning Troy and so contributed to Rome's foundation.[60] In the first book of the *Aeneid* Vergil renamed Ascanius in order to relate him by name to Augustus and the Julian family. The wider context of Ascanius' renaming is the not yet fulfilled prophecy made by Jupiter to Venus. Here Augustus' future mission to conquer and civilise the world is ingrained in Rome's Trojan past:

[60] Rome's making of the Trojan legend, Zanker 1988: 201–10; Gruen 1992: 6–51; Spannagel 1999: 162–77; Erskine 2001; Mavrogiannis 2003: 15–83; Hölkeskamp 2004: 201–4; Burzacchini 2005; Dench 2005: 248–53; Walter 2006; Dardenay 2010; Woolf 2011: 41–3.

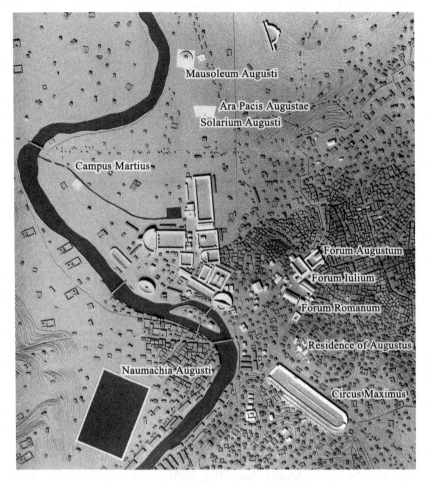

Fig. 4.14 Rome, model of the Augustan city (detail). AD 14.

His son Ascanius, whose surname is now Iulus,
Ilus it was, before the realm of Ilium (= Troy) fell ...
He shall build Alba Longa to be strong ...
Until one day Ilia (Rhea Silvia), a priestess and Trojan queen,
shall bear twin sons to Mars.
Romulus, then, gay in the coat of the tawny she-wolf which suckled him,
shall lead the people. He shall found the Mavortian walls (Rome)
and call his people Romans, after his name.

To Romans I set no boundary in space or time,
I have granted them dominion, and it has no end ...
From the fair seed of Troy there shall be born a Trojan Caesar (Augustus),

Fig. 4.15 Rome, Ara Pacis Augustae. Main entrance to the west. White marble
(about 11 × 10 m). 13–9 BC.

Iulius, his name derived from great Iulus. Shall his empire
reach to the ocean's limits, shall his fame end in the stars.
Holding the trophies taken from the Orient anxious no more (Venus)
because you once will welcome him into heaven.[61]

The Trojan Caesar to whom Jupiter granted *imperium sine fine* and who
will hold the *spolia Orientis* is none other than Augustus. To him Iulus
Ascanius had passed on the Trojan line. One of the first Roman portrayals showing Iulus Ascanius occurs on the frieze to the right of the
main entrance to the Ara Pacis Augustae, which was dedicated in 9 BC
(fig. 4.15).[62] Outstanding in the richness and subtlety of its sculpted marble body, the Ara Pacis Augustae portrays the chief concerns of the Augustan
order: Roman gods, sacrificial rituals, imperial processions, depictions of
religious symbols and the fecundity of nature as a metaphor of Augustus'

[61] Vergil, *Aeneid* 1.267–8, 271, 273–9, 286–90 (ed. Mynors): *at puer Ascanius, cui nunc cognomen Iulo /
additur (Ilus erat, dum res stetit Ilia regno) / ... et Longam multa vi muniet Albam. / ... donec regina
sacerdos / Marte gravis geminam partu dabit Ilia prolem. / inde lupae fulvo nutricis tegmine laetus /
Romulus excipiet gentem et Mavortia condet / moenia Romanosque suo de nomine dicet. / his ego nec
metas rerum nec tempora pono / imperium sine fine dedi ... / nascetur pulchra Troianus origine Caesar, /
imperium Oceano, famam qui terminet astris, / Iulius, a magno demissum nomen Iulo. / hunc tu olim
caelo spoliis Orientis onustum / accipies secura.*
[62] Simon 1967; Castriota 1995; Torelli 1999; La Rocca 2002; Pollini 2002; Rossini 2006.

Fig. 4.16 Aeneas, behind him Iulus Ascanius (to the major part extant). Marble relief to the right of the main entrance of the Ara Pacis Augustae (see fig. 4.15). 13–9 BC.

Golden Age.[63] Despite the fragmentary state of the frieze and different suggestions of identification, it is clear that the person who stands to the right of (that is, behind) Aeneas is his son Iulus Ascanius (fig. 4.16).[64] On the Ara Pacis Augustae, Iulus Ascanius is portrayed smaller than Aeneas

[63] Wallace-Hadrill 2004.
[64] Weinstock 1960: 57; Simon 1967: 23–4 figs. 24–25, *contra* Tracy 1989 'Venus' and Rose 2005 'Achates'.

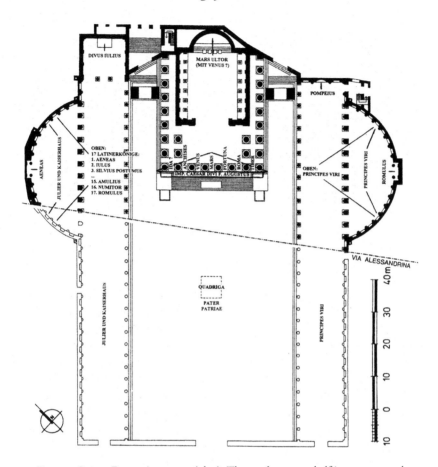

Fig. 4.17 Rome, Forum Augustum (plan). The south-western half is reconstructed
hypothetically (l. about 125 m, w. about 118 m). Dedicated 2 BC.

but as an almost grown man holding a shepherd's crook. In contrast to the
old-fashioned Roman toga of his father, the Trojan prince is depicted in
a long-sleeved tunic, a mantle and, perhaps, long trousers.[65] His eastern
origin would have been further coloured by the now lost paint of his Trojan
dress.[66]

However, the most influential portrayal of Iulus Ascanius was set up in
Augustus' forum, officially opened to the public in 2 BC (fig. 4.17).[67] Rome's

[65] The visible remains do not clarify if Iulus Ascanius was shown in trousers or not.
[66] Colour reconstruction: www.arapacis.it/mostre_ed_eventi/eventi/i_colori_di_augusto (17 April 2011).
[67] Zanker 1969; Kockel 1995; Spannagel 1999; La Rocca 2001; Haselberger and Humphrey 2006:
127–30, 183–90; Ungaro 2007; Geiger 2008; Meneghini 2009: 59–78.

Fig. 4.18 Romulus carrying a spear and military trophies. Adaptation of the colossal marble of Augustus' forum. Roman Aureus of Antoninus Pius (7.18 grammes).
AD 140–144.

first imperial forum was a completely enclosed space surrounded by walls measuring up to over 30 m in height. It transmitted the ideologies of the new imperial regime in outstanding architecture, imagery and workmanship. In the two flanking porticoes (fig. 4.22) a selection of over 100 marble statues portraying the most noble Romans were placed, hand-picked *summi* or *principes viri* of Rome's legendary past. Over-life in size these portrayals shaped a new political narrative with which to single out Augustus as the ultimate embodiment of the long history of Rome. The climax of this narrative was marked by two colossal sculptures that are considered to have portrayed the most important mythical ancestors of Rome. The two marbles were placed facing one another in the central niches of the Forum's two flanking exedras: to the south, a statue of Romulus carrying a spear and the military trophies of Rome's glorious past, the *spolia opima* (fig. 4.18);[68] to the north, a group of three Trojans, Aeneas carrying his father Anchises (out of Troy) and leading his son Iulus Ascanius by the hand (fig. 4.19). The two marbles have not survived. Their general appearance is, however, attested by more than 160 adaptations, not only in sculpture (fig. 4.21) but also on mosaics, wall paintings, coins (figs. 4.18 and 4.19),

---

[68] The military trophies carried by Romulus are the *spolia opima*: armour, arms, and other effects that an ancient Roman general had stripped from the body of an opposing commander slain in single, hand-to-hand combat; after Romulus that had happened only twice in Rome's history (Spannagel 1999: 136–54, 224–55).

Fig. 4.19 Aeneas carrying his father Anchises and leading his son Iulus Ascanius by the hand. Adaptation of the colossal marble of Augustus' forum. Roman Aureus of Antoninus Pius (7.3 grammes). AD 140–144.

gems and lamps.[69] After a thorough re-examination of the surviving evidence, Martin Spannagel was able to outline the iconographic concept of the two sculptures which are now lost.[70]

A good idea of the appearance of the Trojan group is provided by a marble relief in the Carian city of Aphrodisias (fig. 4.21).[71] Together with 179 similar marble reliefs depicting historical, mythical and cosmic narratives of Rome, the panel embellished the Sebasteion, Aphrodisias' exceptional sanctuary of the imperial cult. Laid out as a monumental road (some 14 × 90 m), the Sebasteion was flanked on each side by three-storeyed portico buildings (fig. 4.20). The upper two storeys served as large screens to show off the relief panels, ninety on each side. The processional cult complex of the Sebasteion was built around AD 20–60 and dedicated jointly to the city's Roman patron goddess Aphrodite and the Roman emperors. On the marble relief in Aphrodisias each of the three Trojans is given a different cultural body (fig. 4.21). Aeneas is depicted as a general in a historicised Hellenistic cuirass, only his old-fashioned beard identifying him as a mythical hero.[72] His father Anchises is shown in a mixture of foreign and Greco-Roman dress, namely trousers, tunic and mantle. But Aeneas' son, Iulus Ascanius, is dressed entirely in the Asian fashion.[73] The

---

[69] Spannagel 1999: 365–400.   [70] Spannagel 1999: 86–161.

[71] Smith 1987: 132–3 (location); Spannagel 1999: 371 no. A 17; Schneider 2007: 67–8 fig. 16.

[72] Type of cuirass, Laube 2006: 117.   [73] Barchiesi 2005: 301–2.

Fig. 4.20 Processional road of the imperial cult at Aphrodisias (reconstruction). The complex measures about 14 × 90 m. AD 20–60.

family group portraying the Westernised father, the Trojan grandfather and the Oriental son in dramatic action constitutes a most indicative icon of what Rome by genealogy and politics claimed to have achieved. The addition of Aeneas' mother Aphrodite serves to underline the unique bonds between Aphrodisias, Troy and Rome.[74]

Members of the elite inside and outside of Rome chose the traditional stereotype of the handsome Asian to portray the youngest Trojan forefathers of Rome, Iulus Ascanius and Ganymede. The same costume was worn by Rome's noble youth when it publicly performed the equestrian mock-battle of the Trojan games which had been (re-)invented by Augustus.[75] According to Vergil, the Trojan games had been set up by Aeneas to celebrate the rescue of his father Anchises from Troy.[76] Augustus made a calculated political move when he staged the battle in Rome, especially in the world's largest arena, the Circus Maximus. He gave the old Roman custom of obligation between father and son a new Trojan foundation. Father and son, however, followed two different role models. On the one side there were the two father figures, the Trojan Aeneas and his Roman descendant Augustus, who were always shown in Westernised dress. On the other

[74] Chaisemartin 2001.
[75] Suetonius, *Divus Augustus* 43.2 (J. M. Carter, Bristol 1982); see above note 57.
[76] Vergil, *Aeneid* 5.545–602 (ed. Mynors).

Fig. 4.21 Aeneas carrying his father Anchises and leading his son Iulus Ascanius by the hand (in the background Aphrodite). Adaptation of the colossal marble of Augustus' forum. Marble relief (h. about 1.6 m, w. about 1.6 m). From Aphrodisias, Sebasteion. AD 20–60.

side there were Trojan princes such as Iulus Ascanius, Ganymede and later Paris, as well as Rome's noble youth who were represented as handsome Asians. As a result, the Trojan East and the Roman West were brought together by the genealogical model of father and son. The new ideology of father and son culminated in Augustus' proclamation as *pater patriae* in 2 BC. In the widely distributed inscription of his *res gestae* Augustus comments:

Fig. 4.22 Rome, Forum Augustum and temple of Mars Ultor (reconstruction). The temple measures about l. 52 m, w. 40 m, h. 36 m. Dedicated 2 BC.

The senate and the equestrian order and the whole people of Rome gave me the title 'Father of the Fatherland'; and they determined to place an appropriate inscription in the vestibule to my house, in the Curia Iulia (the senate house), and beneath the quadriga which the senate had erected to me in (my) forum.[77]

Iulus became the Trojan prince on whom Rome's claim of imperial universalism depended. Together with his father Aeneas and later descendants of the legendary Trojan-Latin kings, Iulus was portrayed in a second marble statue set up in the northern exedra of Augustus' forum.[78] Here, Iulus was perhaps placed in the upper storey, above the colossal marble group showing Aeneas, Anchises and Iulus Ascanius (figs. 4.19 and 4.21). Although the statues of Rome's mythical ancestors are now lost, written and epigraphic evidence allows us to identify some of them, namely Aeneas, Iulus, Silvius Postumus, Amulius, Numitor and Romulus.

What is more, a third marble sculpture of Iulus Ascanius had been set up in Augustus' forum, in the pediment of the temple of Mars Ultor.[79] Here Mars was worshipped in the double role of both Avenger (*ultor*) and Rome's new father god (fig. 4.22).[80] Mars was the Roman god most closely associated with the mythical narratives of Rome's Oriental origin and her Italic pre-history. Already in Republican Rome he was supposed to

[77] *Res Gestae Divi Augusti* 35 (ed. P. A. Brunt and J. M. Moore, Oxford 1967).
[78] Spannagel 1999: 267–87 pl. 1.   [79] Ganzert 1996; 2000; Ungaro 2007.
[80] Spannagel 1999: 27 note 86 (*pater*); 60–78 (*ultor*).

Fig. 4.23 Pediment of the temple of Mars Ultor (detail). Sculptures from left to right: personification of the Palatine Hill or Mount Ida; Iulus Ascanius; Venus and Eros; Mars; Fortuna; Roma; personification of the river Tiber. Plaster cast of marble relief (h. 1.55 m, w. 1.22 m). *c.* AD 50. (The original relief decorates the garden façade of the Villa Medici in Rome.)

have impregnated Ilia or Rhea Silvia, a direct descendant of the House of Aeneas.[81] One could thus claim of Mars that he was the father of Romulus and Remus and, hence, a forefather of all Romans. At the same time Mars was regarded as one of the oldest gods of Rome. Together with Jupiter and Quirinus, an old local god later claimed to be the deified Romulus, he made up a kind of Capitoline 'Ur'-triad said to have been established in Archaic times.[82] The addition of Mars' Augustan cognomen *ultor* (avenger) referred to all the enemies plotting against Rome and her new emperor, with explicit reference to the murders of Caesar and to the Parthians.[83] The pediment of the temple to Mars provided a prominent place with which to stage another portrayal of Iulus Ascanius. It is handed down by a marble relief showing the temple's front including a detailed depiction of its pedimental sculptures (fig. 4.23).[84] The relief panel was made around AD 50 to adorn an unknown imperial monument. In the Renaissance it

[81] Spannagel 1999: 162–205; Käppel 2001. Augustan ideology of father and son, Hölscher 2009: 72–9.
[82] Scholz 1970; Beard, North and Price 1998a and b: I 14–16, II 5–7.
[83] Schneider 1986: 58–61; 63–7, 80–2; Spannagel 1999: 60–78; Rivière 2006: 40–2.
[84] Azevedo 1951: 37–8 no. 3; Hommel 1954: 22–30; Koeppel 1983: 98–101, 116; Siebler 1988: 173–82; Simon 1990: 140 fig. 174; Spannagel 1999: 123 note 224, 195, 203–4.

had been fixed high up in the garden façade of the Villa Medici in Rome.[85] According to this panel, seven colossal marble sculptures were arranged in the temple's pediment which created a large platform measuring more than 20 m in width.[86] The seven sculptures were composed not to interact with one another but to stand isolated, yet related to each other by their strict formal and semantic setting. Conventionally the sculptures are read from left to right: the personification of the Palatine Hill (or Mount Ida); then Romulus and Venus with Eros on her shoulder; the bearded father god, Mars Ultor, in the centre; then Fortuna (Redux), the goddess Roma and the personification of the river Tiber.[87] In my view of the seven sculptures Romulus is the one wrongly identified. This is evident if we follow the only description of the sculptures made in front of the normally inaccessible relief when it was in a much better state of preservation. About 130 years ago Friedrich von Matz described the figure later called for ideological reasons Romulus:

Anchises(?) dressed with a girded short(?)-sleeved chiton and a mantle (chlamys) [seated to the right]. He wears Phrygian trousers and the Phrygian cap. His right hand is casually rested on the shepherd's crook, with the left hand he is holding his head thoughtfully.[88]

The relief portrays a figure in Asian dress, with a shepherd's crook and without a beard. This excludes the traditional identification as young Romulus, and that of old Anchises.[89] On iconographic grounds only one reading makes sense, that of the Trojan prince Iulus Ascanius. As a consequence, we can now reconstruct a more coherent reading of the sculptures within Augustus' forum. The Julians were gathered at the north of the forum. In the northern exedra the colossal marble group showing Aeneas, Anchises and Iulus Ascanius were placed and, perhaps above them, the statues of Trojan-Latin kings including Aeneas and Iulus. In the northern half of the temple's pediment Venus, her Trojan grandchild Iulus Ascanius and the personification of the Palatine Hill or the Trojan Mount Ida were set. The Romans were grouped at the south of the forum. In the southern

[85] Simon 1990: 17 fig. 8, relief panel in the upper left corner.
[86] Kockel 1995: 458 fig. 121; Ganzert 1996: 196–200, Beilage 48a. The original pediment could have taken more than seven sculptures.
[87] Hölscher 1988: 378; Beard, North and Price 1998a: 1 200–1.
[88] Matz and Duhn 1881: 29, no. 3511: 'Anchises(?) im gegürteten Chiton mit kurzen(?) Ärmeln und Chlamys, [n.r. sitzend]: er trägt phrygische Hosen und die phrygische Mütze, die R. ruht nachlässig auf dem Hirtenstab, mit der L. stützt er nachdenklich den Kopf.'
[89] Spannagel 1999: 123 note 224.

Fig. 4.24 Tiberius and Livia sitting in the centre, above them Iulus Ascanius in Asian dress and Divus Augustus. Grand Camée de France. Agate (h. 31 cm, w. 26.5 cm). AD 23–24.

exedra Romulus (fig. 4.18) was placed. In the southern half of the pediment Fortuna, Roma and the personification of the river Tiber were to be seen. Mars, in the centre, is both the lover of Venus and the forefather of the Romans.

Another portrayal of Iulus Ascanius is shown on the Grand Camée de France, the largest surviving cameo from antiquity (fig. 4.24).[90] According

[90] Bernoulli 1886: 277–99; Megow 1987: 202–7 no. A 85; Giard 1998; Giuliani 2009.

Fig. 4.25 Divus Augustus and Iulus Ascanius in Asian dress. Detail from the Grand
Camée de France (see fig. 4.24).

to Luca Giuliani it was probably carved around AD 23/24. Made of exotic
sardonyx, the cameo was designed for exclusive use at Rome's imperial
court. It constitutes an outstanding political manifesto based on (disputed)
claims of the imperial succession. The cameo's narrative is divided into
three different panels arranged in vertical hierarchy. The Asian is the only
figure present in all three panels. The bottom panel is the smallest, and
the only one to be rigorously separated from the other two. It depicts the
edge of the world populated by defeated non-Romans from the East, the
West and the North. The middle panel is the largest. Clearly identifiable is
the seated couple in its centre, the emperor Tiberius and his mother Livia.
A handsome Asian crouches obediently at her feet. The middle panel
changes seamlessly into the upper panel. It shows a selection of deceased
members of the imperial family in cosmic space. The most prominent
of them is the deified Augustus. Portrayed at the highest point, in the
centre, he is placed above a large figure of a handsome Asian who seems to
carry him. The Oriental holds with both hands a celestial sphere, the very
symbol of Roman power (fig. 4.25).[91] Recently Luca Giuliani has re-read

[91] Schneider 1997.

the visual narrative of the cameo and re-established that the handsome Asian is no other than Iulus Ascanius. As one of the most venerated Trojan forefathers of the Julian family and Rome's people, he is the only plausible person in Asian dress to carry both the orb of the Roman emperor and Divus Augustus, the founder of imperial Rome.[92] But like Ganymede at Sperlonga, Iulus Ascanius is portrayed here in an ambiguous double role. As an Asian he is Augustus' obedient servant; but as a Trojan he is Rome's next of Eastern kin. This double role gets an even sharper edge by the figures of handsome Asians assembled submissively in the two panels below.

In the age of Augustus the politics of Rome's Oriental origins were profoundly reshaped. This is evident if we look at the new readings of the Trojan epics and the new portrayals showing Trojan princes as handsome Asians. Both became widely adopted symbols of Rome's universalistic ideologies. Rome claimed to be the only empire genuinely rooted in *oriens* and *occidens*. As a result, Rome could claim both the East and the West as her own, and as such her indisputable property. One of the most remarkable statements of this ideology is a grave epigram probably composed by Germanicus, the step-nephew of Augustus. Germanicus may have written the poem in Ilium, the city built next to the site of ancient Troy. He visited Troy in AD 18 on his tour of inspection through the Eastern provinces that ended with his unexpected death.[93] The epigram is addressed to the Trojan hero, Hector, who was killed by the Greek hero, Achilles:[94]

> Descendant of Mars, Hector, under the deep(est) earth
> (if you can but hear my words),
> breathe again, since an avenger has come to you as heir,
> who may forever enhance the fame of your fatherland.
> Behold! Renowned Ilium rises again, a race inhabits her
> inferior to you, Mars, but nevertheless a friend of Mars.
> Hector, tell Achilles that all the Myrmidons have perished
> and that Thessaly is under the sway of the great ancestors of Aeneas.[95]

---

[92] Giuliani 2009: 15–16, 26–7. Best illustration, Giard 1998: pl. VI.

[93] Ilium in the early empire, Rose 2002b.

[94] Hector's tomb, Erskine 2001: 109; Hertel 2003: 179–80.

[95] *Anthologia Latina* I 2, 708 (ed. F. Bücheler and A. Riese, Leipzig 1906): *Martia progenies, Hector, tellure sub ima / (Fas audire tamen si mea verba tibi) / respira, quoniam vindex tibi contigit heres, / qui patriae famam proferat usque tuae. / Ilios, en surgit rursum inclita, gens colit illam / te Marte inferior, Martis amica tamen. / Myrmidonas periisse omnes dic Hector Achilli, / Thessaliam et magnis esse sub Aeneadis.* Kroll 1917: 463; Pani 1975: 74–8; Braccesi 2006: 157–61. For a Greek(!) version of the epigram dedicated to either Germanicus or Hadrian, *Anthologia Graeca* 9.387 (ed. H. Beckby, Munich 1958).

Hector's avenger is none other than Rome, the city which ultimately avenges the devastation of Troy.[96] By tradition Hector was the son of the Trojan king Priam, a descendant of Tros, the mythical founder of Troy (and the father of handsome Ganymede; fig. 4.8). In the epigram, however, Hector's genealogy is radically changed. Here, he is made a direct descendant of Mars who too was worshipped as avenger in Rome, in his new temple built in Augustus' forum (figs. 4.17, 4.22).[97] Hector's newly acquired ancestry from Mars underpinned the fact that the Trojans and the Romans shared the same divine descent. Using the Augustan ideology of revenge, Rome revived the legendary power of Troy and achieved rule over Greece, Troy's arch-enemy, represented here by the descendants of Achilles: Myrmidons in Thessaly. Such claims emphasise once more the gripping quality of the portrayal of the handsome Asian that brought together two distinctive aspects of Rome's universalistic claims, her new global importance and her epic Trojan past.[98] The small Tabula Iliaca Capitolina made of marble in the age of Augustus highlights the Roman elite's interest in Hector's grave also in the city's imagery (fig. 4.26).[99] A large grave memorial to Hector is shown in the tablet's foreground on the lower left. It is prominently placed near another Roman icon of Troy set up in front of the city's gate, a copy of the famous marble of the three Trojans which adorned Augustus' forum.[100]

Statues of standing Asians with handsome faces open up further discourses in Rome's debate about her Trojan descent.[101] The first Roman sequence of these statues which follow the same compositional pattern was designed in the Augustan period and decorated the Basilica (Aemilia) Paulli.[102] The basilica, a two-storey building, was situated on the north-east side of the Roman forum, opposite the Basilica Iulia, in the very political heart of the city (fig. 4.27).[103] Since c. 1900, roughly 700 fragments of at least eighteen over-life-size statues of Asians in coloured marble measuring between 2.3 and 2.4 m in height have been found inside the basilica's nave (fig. 4.28).[104] Additionally, fragments of eighteen heads (fig. 4.29) and some

---

[96] The avenger is Rome not Augustus; *contra* Hertel 2003: 281.   [97] See above note 79.

[98] Vergil let Trojans appear in both Roman and Asian dress, Dench 2005: 276–7.

[99] Valenzuela Montenegro 2004: 26–149 (Hector's grave: 134–40); Spivey and Squire 2004: 122–3 fig. 205 (best illustration); Squire 2011.

[100] Spannagel 1999: 372–3 no. A 22.

[101] Schneider 1986: 98–138; Castella and Flutsch 1990: 18–30; Schneider 1998: 104–5; 2007: 72–5; Landwehr 2000: 74–83; Landskron 2005: 87–90; Bitterer 2007.

[102] Bauer 1993; Haselberger and Humphrey 2006: 169–73; Freyberger and Ertel 2007; Lipps 2011.

[103] Purcell 1995; Haselberger and Humphrey 2006: 163–82 (chapter by B. Frischer *et al.*); Hölscher 2006.

[104] Schneider 1986: 98–125; Bitterer 2007.

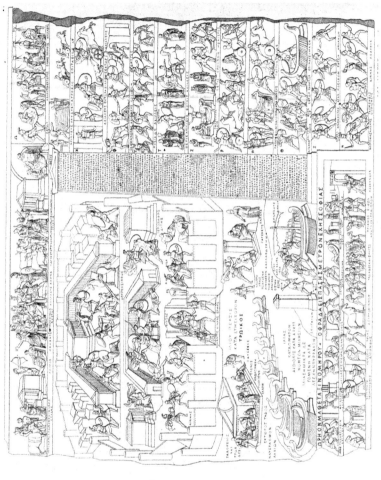

Fig. 4.26 Tabula Iliaca Capitolina showing selected portrayals and texts of the epic cycle (drawing). White marble (h. 25 cm, w. 30 cm). From a Roman villa at Le Frattocchie (via Appia) near Rome. *c.* 20 BC–AD 10.

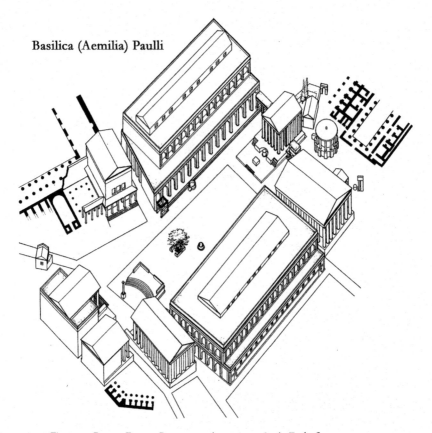

Basilica (Aemilia) Paulli

Fig. 4.27 Rome, Forum Romanum (reconstruction). Early first century AD.

hands have been unearthed.[105] The heads and the hands were separately carved in white marble and originally attached to the body as shown in the statue of Ganymede in Sperlonga (fig. 4.8). Hair and skin of the clean-shaven faces show intense traces of the original colouring (fig. 4.29).[106] The style of the statues and the heads, both worked to an exceptional finish, relates the Asians to the restoration of the Basilica Paulli after 14 BC when the building had partly burnt down. The renewed edifice stood out by design, decor, craftsmanship and coloured marble.[107] The statues are all shown in the same weighted stance and in an unusually rich Asian dress. The handsome faces are framed by long coiffeured hair with beautifully

---

[105] Bitterer 2007: 542–4 figs. 57–8 (heads); 545–6 fig. 62 (hand).   [106] Bitterer 2007: 543.
[107] Schneider 1986: 116–17; Bauer 1993: 185–6; Freyberger and Ertel 2007: 501–23; Lipps 2011.

Fig. 4.28 Torso of a handsome Asian (see fig. 30). Phrygian marble (h. 1.10 m). Found inside the Basilica Paulli in Rome. After 14 BC.

sculpted locks. After a thorough analysis of the basilica's architectural decoration Johannes Lipps has concluded that the statues originally stood in the upper storey inside the basilica's nave.[108]

---

[108] Lipps 2011; *contra* Freyberger and Ertel 2007: 513–18 (their new reconstruction of the basilica's architecture is under critical debate).

Fig. 4.29 Head of a handsome Asian showing rich traces of original colouring. White marble (h. 0.27 m). Found inside the Basilica Paulli in Rome. After 14 BC.

The sculptural evidence and the Roman imagery of the handsome Asian give us obvious clues as to how to reconstruct the statues' original pose. All show the same compositional pattern, a close correlation between the pose of their arms and their legs (fig. 4.30).[109] The arm over the weighted leg was stretched out sideways, then raised straight upwards and the hand again stretched out to the side. The arm over the non-weighted leg pointed diagonally downwards and then back to the body where the hand rested on the hip bone. Hence, the Oriental statues of the Basilica Paulli are shown in a pose of architectural support although they cannot hold actual weight.[110] The weighted stand and the purely virtual pose of acting as architectural support formed a highly ideologised portrayal of an Eastern servant: very handsome, lavishly dressed and richly coloured. It was a metaphor which soon became popular throughout Rome's empire, up to the third century

[109] Schneider 1986: 115–25; Schneider 1998: 108–10; Rose 2005: 62–3; Bitterer 2007: 545–50; *contra* Landwehr 2000: 75–6; Freyberger and Ertel 2007: 513–18.
[110] Figures composed to hold (architectural) weight without being able to do so in reality became popular in Roman wall painting around 40–20 BC; Strocka 2007.

Fig. 4.30 Handsome Asian from the Basilica Paulli shown in a pose as if supporting an architrave. Reconstruction based on surviving fragments.

Fig. 4.31 Handsome Asian shown in a pose as if supporting an architrave; to his right the decorated rim of a shield. Stone relief (h. 0.93 m) from the southern grave monument at Avenches (Switzerland). *c.* AD 40.

AD.[111] A striking parallel to the statues of the Basilica Paulli is the intact figure of an Asian servant from a little-known architectural relief which can be dated around AD 40 (fig. 4.31).[112] It once decorated a large exedra of a grave monument near Avenches.

[111] Hellenistic forerunners of this motif and its adaptations in Roman imagery, Schneider 1986: 98–138 nos. so 1–52; Landwehr 2000: 74–83 no. 110; Bitterer 2007: 546–9.
[112] Castella and Flutsch 1990: 25 fig. 9.

As the restoration of the Basilica Paulli in 14 BC was paid for by Augustus and friends of Lucius Aemilius Paullus, we may assume that the statues of the Asian servants also alluded to the so-called settlement of the Parthian question in 20 BC claimed to be Augustus' greatest foreign victory.[113] From the first century BC onwards, male figures of standing Asians acting as architectural supports could be related to both the Persians and the Parthians.[114] Following a standard set by Cicero, Augustan poets such as Vergil, Propertius, Horace and Ovid usually refer to the Parthians by the name of their historical ancestors, either Medes, Persians or Achaemenians.[115] The architect Vitruvius, who practised under Caesar and Augustus, confirms the political topicality of the standing Asian.[116] According to him, statues of Persians (*statuae Persicae*) in rich Persian dress and posed as if supporting architraves were widely set up in architecture for two reasons: to make the Eastern enemies tremble for fear of what Western bravery could achieve and to encourage the Western viewer to remain ready to defend freedom. Vitruvius' statement is loaded by universal claims and ideologies of Orientalism.

A further reading of the basilica's Asian statues is suggested by Pliny the Elder. Around AD 70 he listed among the most magnificent buildings of the world three edifices in Rome: the Forum Augustum, Vespasian's Templum Pacis and the Basilica Paulli. Pliny gave the Basilica Paulli special praise for its columns and Asian statues which he called *Phryges*.[117] The ethnic term *Phryx* oscillated in early imperial texts between opposite poles such as Phrygian (Asian) slave, hero and god. Predominant among Roman authors, however, was the use of *Phryx* as synonym for *Troianus*, a reading already established in Greek texts of the fifth century BC.[118] Thus Pliny links the famous *Phryges* of the basilica to the Trojan origin of Rome. Pliny's interpretation may be further supported by the juxtaposition with the long frieze, which decorated the nave of the Augustan basilica. The frieze portrays episodes of Rome's legendary history, namely selected narratives

---

[113] Financing the Augustan basilica: Dio Cassius, *Roman History* 54.24.3 (ed. E. Cary, London 1917); Schneider 1986: 116 note 796. Freyberger and Ertel 2007: 513–14 misunderstood the complex formal and semantic blueprint of the Asian statues found in the basilica as they refer to them simply as 'barbarians' and 'Parthians'.

[114] Schneider 2007: 70–5.   [115] Schneider 2007: 70 with note 91.

[116] Vitruvius, *De architectura* 1.1.6 (ed. C. Fensterbusch, Darmstadt 1964).

[117] Pliny the Elder, *Naturalis historia* (ed. J. André, R. Bloch and A. Rouveret, Paris 1981) 36.102: *basilicam Pauli columnis et* [*sic*] *Phrygibus mirabilem (est)*. The traditional reading *columnis e Phrygibus* is wrong, Schneider 1986: 120–5.

[118] Pani 1975: 74; Schneider 1986: 123; Hall 1988 (Greek tradition); Wilhelm 1988; Rose 2002a: 332; Dench 2005: 248.

regarding the city's ancestors, Aeneas and Romulus.[119] In short, Ganymede at Sperlonga (fig. 4.8), Iulus Ascanius in Augustus' forum (figs. 4.19 and 4.21) and on the Grand Camée (figs. 4.24 and 4.25) and the *Phryges* of the Basilica Paulli, all employ the imagery of the handsome Asian to convey the same ideological paradox: Rome's universalistic claims to an Eastern descent and to unconditional servitude owed to her by the people of the East.

In this context the new staging of coloured marble acquired significant readings (figs. 4.8 and 4.28).[120] The over-life-size statues of the Asians were worked in coloured marble for the first time. Only the most expensive stones were used, mostly Phrygian marble, but occasionally also Numidian marble.[121] As the quarries of the two marbles were situated in distant provinces (map 6) and required a large-scale infrastructure to be transported to Rome, the polychromes became a distinctive symbol of the city's global power, constituting a new coloured map of the Roman Empire.[122] Additionally, their exotic colour and high polish gave the Asian body an intensity and meaning unprecedented in ancient art.[123] The polychrome Orientals granted the Asian East a new presence in Rome as coloured embodiments of Eastern dress, attitude and luxury. The favoured use of Phrygian marble to portray the Trojan prince Ganymede at Sperlonga and the *Phryges* of the Basilica Paulli in Rome stimulated further readings. From Augustus onwards this marble became known as either *Phryx* or *Phrygius*, i.e. after the home of both Troy and Rome.[124] The Asians were made of and represented by 'Trojan' marble which was quarried in their Phrygian homeland. This ideology of origin, colour and power increased as most of the polychrome quarries became imperial property under Augustus. Now they began to produce coloured marble on a large scale for the first time. The polychrome Asians represented spoils never before seen in Rome. The display of such spoils would have reminded the viewer of the triumphal procession.[125] Embedded in Rome's sacrificial laws, this ritual was a compelling demonstration of Rome's claim to rule the world and her manifold

[119] Schneider 1986: 118; Kränzle 1994; Freyberger and Ertel 2007: 502–8.

[120] Schneider 1986: 139–60; 2001; 2002. Roman concepts of colour: Bradley 2009a; 2009b.

[121] Schneider 1986: 115–17, 200 nos. SO 1–22; Bitterer 2007. At least one of the sculptures, however, is made in Numidian marble.

[122] Wittke, Olshausen and Szydlak 2007: 84.

[123] Polishing, Schneider 1999: 934. Greek sculptures of Asians coloured by paint, Wünsche 2011, 222–61.

[124] Schneider 1986: 140–1.

[125] Östenberg 2003; Itgenshorst 2005; Beard 2007; Hölkeskamp 2010. For the staging of statues of (acclaiming?) Parthians on top of the arch erected after 20 BC in the Roman forum to commemorate the settlement of the Parthian question, Rich 1998: 97–115; Rose 2005: 28–36.

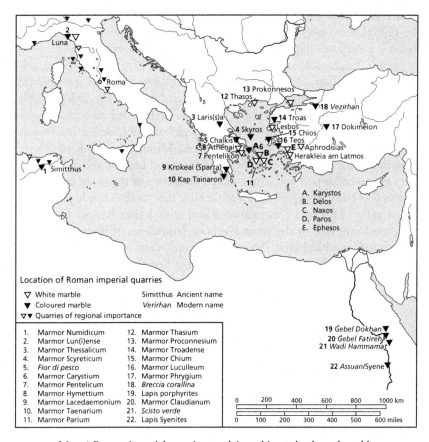

Map 6 Roman imperial quarries supplying white and coloured marble

relationships to non-Roman cultures. By this ritual, foreign people and things were declared the property of Rome.

Trojan was not only the Phrygian marble but also the Phrygian cap, an essential of the Eastern dress.[126] As noted earlier, Trojan and Phrygian had been used as synonyms ever since the fifth century BC.[127] The Roman satirist Juvenal who wrote in the earlier second century AD, however, is the first to call the Asian headgear a Phrygian cap. He describes the *Phrygia bucca tiara* as part of the dress of the flamboyantly foreign Galli, the self-castrated attendants of the Mater Magna. In Rome the goddess' Asian origin was

---

[126] Hinz 1974: 790–2; Seiterle 1985; Schneider 1986: 123–4; Rose 2005: 34–5.   [127] Hall 1988.

closely associated with Troy.[128] A military version of the Phrygian cap was
the Phrygian helmet. On coins struck in Republican Rome the goddess
Roma is sometimes depicted with a Phrygian helmet, evidently an allusion
to Rome's Trojan descent.[129] Later in history the Phrygian cap served new
masters in the West. Most famous became the *bonnet rouge* of the Jacobins
in the French Revolution, the equally liked and dreaded cap of liberty.[130]

Mater Magna sheds more light on Rome's self-styled association with
Troy. In 205/204 BC, driven by the city's global ambitions, a non-iconic
cult stone of Cybele was stolen from Asia Minor and taken to Rome.
Here the goddess was renamed Magna Mater and became the first foreign
deity ever worshipped within the sacred boundary of the inner city.[131] Her
temple was built on top of the Palatine Hill, next to the temple of Victory
(fig. 4.32).[132] This was a unique location, with Mater Magna becoming
integrated into one of the most symbolic landscapes of Rome, the heart
of the city's mythical past. There was Rome's very origin, the legendary
urbs quadrata, which included an Iron Age hut that was constantly re-
built and declared to represent Romulus' first home. Augustus chose the
area adjacent to the city's beginnings and the two ancient temples for
his own residence. But next to his house he had erected a new temple
which he dedicated to his patron Apollo Palatinus in 28 BC (fig. 4.14).[133]
In doing so Augustus presented himself not merely as an Apolline but
as a rather solar (and Oriental) ruler, since Apollo Palatinus was closely
associated with Sol. The location on the south-western part of Mons
Palatinus offered Augustus and the gods around him a perfect panorama of
the Circus Maximus where 'the most spectacular "Phrygian" component
of Roman spectacles', the *lusus Troiae*, was staged.[134] Such a view of the
Circus from the Palatine Hill can be found on several Roman imperial coins.
An extremely fine specimen is a Sestertius issued by Caracalla in AD 213

---

[128] Iuvenalis, *Saturae* 6.513–516 (ed. J. Willis, Stuttgart 1997): *semivir (sc. Gallus) . . . plebeia et Phrygia
vestitur bucca tiara*. For the Galli, Graillot 1912: 287–319; Beard 1994: 164–5, 173–83; Roller 1998;
Rose 2002a: 332–4. For *semivir*, Vergil, *Aeneid* 4.215; 9.614–20; 12.99 (ed. Mynors). Roller 1998:
129.

[129] Crawford 1974: nos. 19.2, 21.1, 22.1, 24.1, 26.4, 27.5, 41.1, 98A.3, 102.2b–c, 269.1, 288.1, 464.3b; Rose
2002a: 331–2 fig. 3.

[130] Wrigley 1997.

[131] Wiseman 1984; Wilhelm 1988; Gruen 1990: 5–33; Simon 1990: 146–51; Beard 1994; Burton 1996;
Takács 1996; Beard, North and Price 1998a and b: I 164–6, II 43–9; Roller 1999: 261–343; Takács
1999; Bremmer 2004: 557–66.

[132] Pensabene 1996; 2004; Haselberger and Humphrey 2006: 34–49.

[133] Tomei 2004; Balensiefen 2009; Zink and Piening 2009.

[134] For an excellent analysis, Barchiesi 2009: 170–88 (quote p. 187).

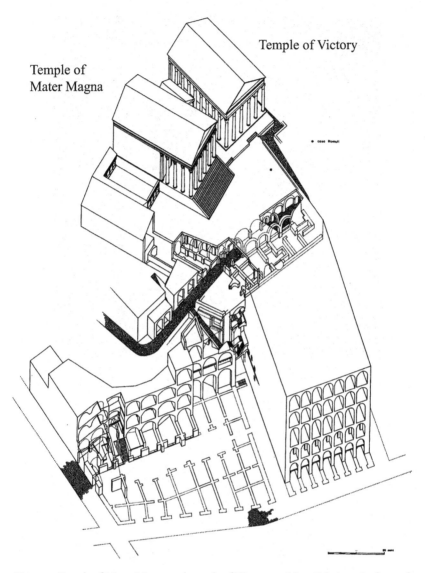

Fig. 4.32 Temple of Mater Magna and temple of Victory on Mons Palatinus. In front of
Mater Magna's temple is a large terrace raised on multi-storey vaults (reconstruction).
After III BC.

Fig. 4.33 View on the Circus Maximus from the imperial palaces on Mons Palatinus.
Roman Sestertius of Caracalla (27.45 grammes). AD 213.

(fig. 4.33).[135] The Circus Maximus itself was a very solar space as it housed an old temple of Sol and, since 10/9 BC, a spectacular Egyptian obelisk taken at Augustus' behest from Heliopolis and dedicated by him to Sol.[136] Around the second half of the first century BC, writers increasingly propagated the concept of the purported origin of Mater Magna from Mount Ida near Troy. Her full title was now *Mater Deum Magna Idaea*, the great Idaean foremother of all gods, also of Rome.[137] It is worth noting that the Great Trojan Mother of the gods was Rome's sole major deity to be distinguished by a mural crown. In effect, an Asian goddess had become the patron goddess of Rome.[138]

---

[135] Photo: www.acsearch.info/record.html?id=469593 (16 September 2011) [= Numismatica Ars Classica, Auction 59 lot 1053, 4 April 2011]. Beck, Bol and Bückling 2005: 723–4 no. 338 (R. M. Schneider). For pictorial narratives of the Roman circus, Bergmann 2008.

[136] Schneider 2004: 161–6; Barchiesi 2009: 183–8.

[137] Degrassi 1963: 129, 435 (Fasti Praenestini, 10 April); see also Cicero, *Cato Maior de senectute* 45 (ed. M. Winterbottom, Oxford 1994); Livy, *Ab urbe condita* 29.10.5; 29.14.5 (ed. R. S. Conway and C. F. Walters, Oxford 1934); Ovid, *Fasti* 4.263–4 (ed. E. Fantham, Cambridge 1998).

[138] Kaiser 1968. For the mural crown in Roman elite portraiture, Sande 1985.

ROMANISM – ORIENTALISM – UNIVERSALISM

The Greeks had themselves been deeply engaged in Oriental cultures early on.[139] Roman elite members, however, went a step further. They gave the old civilisations of the East a new visibility and material reality modelled to fit Rome's ideological claims of imperial universalism.[140] The most influential icon of this ideology was the portrayal of the handsome Asian which became, from the Augustan period onwards, a core element of Rome's globally adopted imagery.[141] His portrayal enjoyed long-standing popularity with Roman emperors and members of the Roman and non-Roman elite, and later on also with worshippers of Eastern deities, especially of Attis and Mithras.[142] The handsome Asian gained further significance through his ambiguous iconography. His portrayal was chosen not only to represent Rome's Trojan descent but also to mark subjugation and servitude; at the same time it was coloured by desirable beauty and all the connotations of 'Trojan' marble. More than any other portrayal of a non-Roman, the handsome Asian was integrated into all areas of Roman life, even into the most eminent political, religious and domestic sites.

The ambiguity of the handsome Asian has caused modern scholars many methodological headaches. A striking example is the ongoing dispute over the identity of the images of two children in foreign dress, one on the south frieze, the other on the north frieze of the marble walls enclosing the Ara Pacis Augustae (figs. 4.34 and 4.35). Both children are shown taking part in the procession of selected members of the imperial family.[143] Two opposing readings have dominated the scholarly debate. The children portray either the two Augustan princes Gaius and Lucius Caesar in the costume of the Trojan games, or two of the Parthian or rather Armenian princes who lived as hostages at the imperial court.[144] On iconographic grounds both readings can stand – and precisely this solves the problem. The foreign clothing of the two children, whether we interpret them as Gaius and Lucius Caesar in Trojan costume or as two Parthian/Armenian princes in Eastern dress, marks the Asian East as a core theme within the stately procession depicted

---

[139] Hartog 1980; Hall 1989; Burkert 1992; 2003; Dihle 1994; Miller 1997; Parker 2008.

[140] Ball 2000; Parker 2008. For significant differences in staging Oriental civilisations such as Egypt and Asia in Rome: Schneider 2004; 2007: 78–9; Beck, Bol and Bückling 2005: 305–450, 611–752.

[141] Landskron 2005: 57–92.

[142] Gordon 1996; 2001; Clauss 2001; Lancellotti 2002; Price 2003; Bremmer 2004.

[143] Simon 1967: 18, 21 pls. 14, 17, 19–21; Rose 1990; 2005: 38–44.

[144] Trojan games: see above note 57. Parthian/Armenian princes in Rome: Sonnabend 1986: 221–2, 254–60; Nedergaard 1988; Spawforth 1994: 242; Rose 2005. Further engagements between Romans and Parthians, Krumeich 2001: 88–92.

Fig. 4.34 Male child with non-Roman coiffure and in foreign dress. North frieze of the
Ara Pacis Augustae (see fig. 4.15). 13–9 BC.

on the Ara Pacis Augustae.[145] Our modern tendency to categorise neatly
may prove a hindrance here. Today's scholars prefer to keep notions such
as Roman and non-Roman, Occident and Orient, friend and foe distinct.
These dichotomies, based as they are on a modern Hegelian reading of the
bipolarity of force and counterforce, fail to fuse such supposed political
and cultural opposites. The Romans, however, were not hampered by such

---

[145] Rose (2005: 38–44) argues that the two boys are portrayed as foreign princes, the one on the south
frieze of Oriental, the one on the north frieze of northern descent. Together they will represent the
new peace achieved under Augustus in the East and the West.

Fig. 4.35 Male child with non-Roman coiffure and in foreign dress. South frieze of the Ara Pacis Augustae (see fig. 4.15). 13–9 BC.

distinctions. On the contrary, they promoted ambiguous readings and allowed them to stand as they were.

It was this open and ambiguous reading which made the portrayal of the handsome Asian such a global success, and a ground-breaking point of reference for Rome's universalistic claims. His portrayal points to a conceptual overlap between seemingly contradictory categories such as Roman and Oriental, friend and foe.[146] As a result, even young Roman noblemen

---

[146] Schneider 2007. For recent discussions on Carl Schmitt's political-theological reading of friend and foe, Meier 1994; Palaver 1998.

could be portrayed as handsome Asians wearing the costume of the Trojan games (figs. 4.11 and 4.12). Concepts of such adaptability were mediated mainly in imagery, beyond the written narrative and beyond a modern concept of history predominantly structured by dates and events. Thus the portrayal of the handsome Asian helps us to identify some of the contradictory and ambivalent issues of universalistic politics which otherwise seem to escape the framework of annalistic history.[147] Consequently, for Rome, the Asian forefather and the Asian enemy were not, I argue, two mutually exclusive poles. On the contrary, the discourse around them was one of the contexts in which the Roman elite defined their claims of universal power. For the elite of imperial Rome, the concept of Romanism was synonymous with the world. A non-Roman could well become Roman, while at the same time retaining his own cultural affiliations.[148] In the constantly shifting debate on the Roman and the Foreign, Mary Beard has rightly placed the contradictory Roman representation of Mater Magna's Orientalised cult.[149] The different readings of the role of Asians in early imperial Rome, ranging from the city's venerated Trojan forefathers to the Parthians as her worst enemy, effectively amounted to different claims and conflicting counterclaims on how Romanness was to be defined.

The concept of Roman citizenship reflects a similar political practice. In contrast to modern societies, Roman citizenship characterised not primarily a specific ethnic and/or national status but a universal rank which was defined mainly in legal and political terms.[150] Recently, Andrew Wallace-Hadrill emphasised the ambiguity and permeability of Roman citizenship in the imperial period.[151] The definition of what Roman was can be described as an ongoing process of absorption and disengagement, a process driven by the political, religious, social and economic interests of Rome. For the Greeks living under Roman rule, Greg Woolf has captured these dynamics in the neat phrase 'becoming Roman, staying Greek'.[152]

---

[147] It would, however, be helpful to scrutinise Greek and Latin texts for similar contradictory readings (and they are plenty) when they focus on Troy and Eastern cultures.
[148] Recent debates about concepts of Romanisation and Romanism: Hingley 2005: 14–48; Roth 2007: 9–39; Wallace-Hadrill 2008: 9–27.
[149] Beard 1994: 166–7, 183–7.
[150] Sherwin-White 1973; Balsdon 1979; Dench 2005: 93–151; Wolff 2007; Wallace-Hadrill 2008: 41, 443–7, 451–3. Gruen (1992) offers a rather vague reading of Rome's *national* identity. He focuses mainly on notions such as origin, tradition, religion, culture, civic life, politics, ideology, values, adaptation, Trojan, Greek, (Phil-)Hellenism, etc. but there is little on a debate about how he would define a 'national' identity of Rome.
[151] Wallace-Hadrill 2008: 445–7.   [152] Woolf 1994.

Rome was the only ancient culture to make the foreigner in her imagery so popular, so political – and so universal.[153] This is especially true of the handsome Asian. He was transformed into a very Roman icon with which imperial Rome claimed Asian descent and, simultaneously, supremacy over the cultures of the East and the West. It is the pragmatic, flexible and ambivalent use of this icon that reflects significant aspects of Rome's ideology of universalism shaped by Roman elite members in the age of Augustus. I argue that conflicting readings such as those around the handsome Asian contributed to the continuation of the Roman Empire up to Late Antiquity, and ultimately to Rome's control over so many non-Roman cultures.[154] The appropriation, stimulation and propagation of such ambiguous readings were key features of Rome's universalistic politics.[155] With her universal claim to have the Asian as both forefather and enemy, Augustan Rome had reinvented for herself a new Oriental identity – and enthused a contradictory reading of Orientalism that has reached beyond the confines of popular ideologies of today. However, it was the reinterpretation of the Trojan legend in imperial Rome that has gradually become a universal point of reference. Since the Renaissance, aristocratic families of Western descent have legitimised their inflationary claims of global religious, political and imperial power by relating themselves to Rome's glorified past and, especially, her famed Asian forefathers.[156]

---

[153] Nuanced view on 'Roman identity', Hingley 2005.
[154] Contradictory readings of Rome's 'Oriental' imagery remained popular in Late Antiquity, especially in the Christian narrative of the Three Kings, Schneider 2006.
[155] Another key feature is the ambiguous reading of the Roman emperor as both man and god, Clauss 1999; Gradel 2002; Hallett 2005: 223–70.
[156] Yates 1975; Tanner 1993.

CHAPTER 5

Pseudo-Aristotelian politics and theology in universal Islam

Garth Fowden

When Islam burst on the world in the 630s, it came as both religion and empire. It measured itself, instinctively, against the far-flung creeds of Judaism and Christianity, and against Iran and Rome, the mightiest states in its vicinity.[1] Although the Qur'ān was revealed specifically to Arabs and in Arabic (so that they could no longer claim they had not been warned[2]), while translation was not on the agenda, there was no serious impediment to wider acceptance of the religion of 'submission'. After all it was the One God, 'Lord of all beings/worlds',[3] who had chosen to speak, and if he had done so in Arabic not Middle Persian, Aramaic, Greek or Latin, that could not be for purposes of exclusion. Early Islam offered, in short, the prospect of a universal religious, social and political identity and community, bearing in mind always, of course, the relativity of ancient 'universalisms'.[4] Even Alexander had succeeded in reaching the uttermost ends, heights and depths of this world more in his Legend than in historical reality.[5]

Reality turned out hard for the Islamic caliphate too, in all its dimensions. On the politico-military level, significant loss of territory already occurred during the last two Umayyad decades, notably in North Africa,[6] while after the Abbasids took over in 750 the Umayyads kept control of Spain. By the first decades of the tenth century the Baghdad caliphate was in turn collapsing. On the social level, disputes over caliphal succession and political legitimacy had bitterly divided the community already from the reign of the fourth caliph ʿAlī (656–661). The Umayyads, who ruled by might, never could suppress the Alids, who insisted on family

---

[1] Qur'ān 2.111–17, 120; 30.2–3. This is a revised, extended version of the article published, under the same title, in Darbandi and Zournatzi 2008: 65–81. I would like to thank Cristina D'Ancona for detailed comments and a stream of offprints; Antonis Kaldellis for illuminating discussions of some of this material; Irene Noel-Baker for dispelling many obscurities of expression; also Nadia al-Baghdadi, Miklós Maróth and Adam Ziółkowski for kindly providing various Central European publications.
[2] Qur'ān 13.37, 26.192–200, 46.12.   [3] Qur'ān 1.2.   [4] Fowden 1993: 12–14.
[5] Jouanno 2002.   [6] Blankinship 1994: 230–6.

right, kinship to the Prophet. In time, such divisions took on theological dimensions, hence the rise of heresy to afflict Islam no less than it already had Christianity (as the Qur'ān tirelessly points out).

Despite this rapid subversion of Islam's prospects for religious, social and political universality, there emerged in the tenth century a powerful commonwealth of Muslim states – Samanids, Buyids, Fatimids, Umayyads and other lesser players. Right across the commonwealth there were, despite all the schisms and wars, unmistakable common denominators: the Qur'ān, obviously; reverence for Muḥammad and the first four, 'rightly guided' caliphs; basic legal concepts; the mosque; and at least that minimal sense of community which is imposed by awareness of 'the other', here in the sense of Jews, Christians or Mazdeans living in the very midst of Islam. There was also the possibility for intellectuals and artists to pursue their vocations without being overpowered by the multiplying sectarian and political divisions, and even profit by the multiplicity of patrons they threw up. My concern here is mainly with the philosophers of Islam, who were the category of intellectual least constrained by conventional religious affiliations, freest in their ways of thought, and most likely actually to live out in real life, or at least in their heads, the promise of universalism Islam could offer. One thinks for example of al-Fārābī and his synthesis of Plato, Aristotle, the Alexandrian philosophy of later antiquity, and the Qur'ān into a universal science (*ilm al-kullī*) of metaphysics which studies what is common to all things: being, unity, God.[7]

The philosophers were much abetted in this pursuit of universalism by their preference, among the Greeks, for Aristotle, who offered them an encyclopaedic survey of human knowledge as well as a model, in his logical works, for thought and argumentation. Among the first of his treatises to be translated into Arabic, towards the end of the eighth century, was the *Topics* on techniques of disputation, together with the *Physics* on the nature of the natural world.[8] The *Metaphysics* also attracted a lot of interest during the ninth and tenth centuries,[9] but could not satisfy those who, beyond acquiring knowledge about beings and their causes, wished to investigate the ultimate cause which stands at the origin of everything – for the simple reason that, by definition, Aristotle's universe has no beginning in time, but is in eternal movement. (Hence his rather colourless 'unmoved mover'.) It is easy to see how, in such situations, a demand might arise for an analysis, on Aristotle's high authority, of subjects on which the historical

---

[7] Martini Bonadeo and Ferrari 2005: 400–9, 427–8.
[8] Gutas 1998: 61–74.   [9] Bertolacci 2005: 270–1.

Aristotle had refrained from pronouncing. It is this demand which lies at the origins of the phenomenon of pseudo-Aristotelianism, to which the present article is dedicated. I am not proposing that pseudo-Aristotelianism is central to our understanding of Islamic universalism in its mainstream manifestations. But it is a major and much neglected symptom of the caliphal elite's desire to create as comprehensive as possible an account of the world it ruled, its causes and its potentialities.

Open the standard Oxford English translation of Aristotle's complete works, revised in 1984, at the Contents, and you will see that, of 2,465 pages of text, no fewer than 484 – roughly one fifth – are taken up by titles whose 'authenticity has been seriously doubted' or whose 'spuriousness has never been seriously contested', as the editor has it. In earlier times there were far larger quantities of suspect Aristotle in circulation. Some of these works were among his most influential, in Arabic and Latin as well as Greek – the *Secret of Secrets*, for example, or the *Theology of Aristotle*, to both of which the present chapter pays particular attention. Although these Arabic and Latin versions might derive in one way or another from Greek sources, these were not necessarily by Aristotle, and anyway the Arabic translators often added extra matter of Iranian or Indian provenance or their own devising. The authentic works, whether done into Latin directly from the Greek or by way of Syriac and Arabic, were rendered either more or less literally. By contrast, those pseudo-Aristotelian treatises which reached Europe from the East intimately reflected the tastes and preoccupations of the inhabitants of the caliphate – who were, of course, far from being uniformly Muslim.

As it happens, the very first Aristotelian text rendered into Arabic appears to have been a largely spurious one, though modern scholars speculate about fragments of genuine Aristotle it may have contained. Conventional wisdom holds that the second Abbasid caliph, al-Manṣūr, inaugurated the translation movement by commissioning versions of various Greek, Persian and Syriac books including some of Aristotle's logical treatises.[10] Al-Manṣūr reigned from AD 754 to 775. The Aristotle translations must have been executed in the very first years of his rule, if they really were done either by the famous Iranian scholar-administrator Ibn al-Muqaffaʿ, who was put to death *c.* 756, or conceivably by his son who was also dead by 760.[11] Our source for Ibn al-Muqaffaʿ's involvement is a report

---

[10] Gutas 1998: 29–32.
[11] Ess 1991–7: 2.27; D'Ancona 2005c: 202 (reading 'al-Manṣūr' for 'al-Maʾmūn').

by the hugely learned tenth-century Baghdadi bibliophile Ibn al-Nadīm. The same writer records something else, which has been found far less interesting, namely that:

Sālim, surnamed Abū'l-ʿAlāʾ, was the secretary of [the caliph] Hishām b. ʿAbd al-Malik... He was one of the best stylists and most eloquent (speakers). He translated (*naqala*) the *Letters of Aristotle to Alexander,* (or) they were translated for him (*nuqila lahu*) and he made corrections (*aṣlaḥa*).[12]

In other words, Muslims' familiarity with Aristotle goes back at least to the closing decades of the Umayyad dynasty: Hishām reigned from 724 to 743, and Sālim also served his successor al-Walīd II (743–744).[13] Our almost complete neglect of this fact[14] reflects anachronistic concern with the authentic Aristotle to the exclusion of pseudo-Aristotle, to whom the *Letters* indubitably belonged. Nobody in the eighth century had the means to make this distinction which seems so crucial to us. Readers happily accepted as genuine Aristotle a version of a correspondence mentioned by various Greek and Latin authorities,[15] and also known, to a limited extent, from pseudo-Callisthenes' popular and imaginative Greek *Alexander Romance,* a product, as it seems, of the third century AD[16] and eventually translated into a spectrum of other languages, including Arabic.[17]

Some or all of the Aristotle–Alexander correspondence translated – presumably from Greek – under Sālim's supervision may have survived in a collection of sixteen letters addressed mainly by Aristotle to Alexander, but also containing two letters from Alexander to Aristotle and three letters exchanged between Aristotle and Alexander's father Philip. The correspondence is preserved in two early fourteenth-century Arabic manuscripts in Istanbul, first noticed in the 1930s. It was published spasmodically and

---

[12] Ibn al-Nadīm, *Kitāb al-fihrist* 131. For my translation of this rather compressed text I have been guided by the paraphrase in ʿAbbās 1988: 30–1. (The translation by Dodge (1970: 257–8) reads 'Epistle' incorrectly.) Evidently Ibn al-Nadīm had seen a manuscript under this title attributed to Sālim, but suspected it could not have been translated by him in person because, unlike most translators from the Greek at this early date, his name was not Christian. As Hishām's secretary he will though have employed men fluent in Greek: Fowden 2004: 269–70. Judging from the section-heading and immediately adjacent entries, Ibn al-Nadīm's concluding observation that 'there is a collection of about 100 folios of his letters' refers not to Aristotle's letters to Alexander, but to Sālim's work as caliphal secretary, the remnants of which are collected by ʿAbbās 1988: 303–19.

[13] Fowden 2004: 262–3.

[14] Cf. Gutas 1998: 23–4 (glancing allusions to the *Letters*); Leder 1999: 26 (Aristotle–Alexander correspondence enters Arabic with (much later) *Sirr al-asrār*, on which see below); Dakhlia 2002: 1192 n. 5, 1199 (Islamic political thought begins with Ibn al-Muqaffaʿ). An exception is ʿAbbās 1988: 31.

[15] Plezia 1977: 13–14, 16–18, 28, 30–1.   [16] Jouanno 2002: 26–8.

[17] On the Arabic version, see Doufikar-Aerts 2003.

in fragments, and printed as a whole for the first time only in 2006.[18] The collection apparently lacks its original title; we may call it, neutrally, the 'Alexander file'. What it conveys – partly through transitional passages between the items of correspondence – is an episodic narrative of Alexander's career, along with a summary education in the art of governance, military tactics, ethics, cosmology and metaphysics, reminding us that in Islam it was no less essential to the political thinker than to the theologian to know what God is.[19] The value of studying philosophy is strongly emphasized in the opening sections. That any of the letters substantially derive from authentic Aristotelian writings is on balance doubtful;[20] but at least one of them, translated from the *De mundo* also addressed to Alexander, had certainly circulated as 'Aristotle' long before Islam.[21]

As for the 'corrections' Sālim made to his original, they apparently ran to sizable insertions, if we may judge from the Alexander file. These insertions included, for example, the version of the *De mundo* therein contained, if it really was based on the Syriac translation rather than the Greek;[22] there are also passages that reflect the Muslim Arab milieu, and others variously related to the Sasanian sphere.[23] In fact, the cultural stratigraphy of these

---

[18] Ed. Maróth 2006 (Arabic text with English introduction, separately paginated). The Arabic text of the letters ends on p. 133. On the structure and history of the collection, and its lack of an original title, see Grignaschi 1967: 215–23; also Gutas 2009, who provides a useful breakdown of the correspondence's constituent parts, and some criticism of Maróth's edition.

[19] On Islamic political thought as an outgrowth of metaphysics, see Crone 2004: 169–70.

[20] Carlier 1980; Weil 1985.

[21] Maróth 2006: 108–30 (Arabic). Cf. Besnier 2003; Raven 2003. Another compendium that includes the *De mundo* is the seventh-century Syriac ms. B.L. Add. 14658, embracing logic, physics and ethics but not politics: Hugonnard-Roche 2004: 108–11, 119. Among Greek references to the Alexander–Aristotle correspondence, the one most likely to allude to some form of the original from which the Arabic Alexander file was translated is John Philoponus (d. *c.* 570), *In categorias* p. 3: αἱ ἐπιστολαὶ ἢ ὅσα ἐρωτηθεὶς ὑπὸ Ἀλεξάνδρου τοῦ Μακεδόνος περί τε βασιλείας καὶ ὅπως δεῖ τὰς ἀποικίας ποιεῖσθαι γεγράφηκε ('the letters, or what he [Aristotle] wrote – when asked by Alexander the Macedonian – on kingship and how to found colonies'). The context is a conventional discussion of how to categorize Aristotle's works. Philoponus is the only ancient authority known to have stated that these lost but apparently genuine writings were actively solicited by Alexander (cf. Plezia 1977: 10–11), while the Alexander file supplies (i.e. invents) the actual letter of request: Maróth 2006: 85–7 (Arabic). The letter from Aristotle which follows, often known as the *Risāla fī siyāsat al-mudun* or *Letter on policy towards the cities* (Maróth 2006: 88–101 (Arabic)) may in some way derive from the *On kingship*, about which, though, we know very little: see Ross's meagre collection of testimonia and fragments; also Laurenti 2003: 380–1 (authenticity), 460–2.

[22] Grignaschi 1996: 109–13; Maróth 2006: 81–3 (Introduction). Note, though, that the abridged Arabic version of the *De mundo* in ms. Istanbul, Köprülü 1608, appears to be both the oldest, and based on the Greek: Raven 2003: 482.

[23] Grignaschi 1975, with Maróth's criticisms, 2006: 67–71 (Introduction); Grignaschi 1996: 109–11; Shaked 1984: 41–9. Gutas (2009: 65) suggests that the *Letters* may have been transmitted from Greek to Arabic via Middle Persian.

texts is extremely complex, and since one of its elements derives from an East Roman military manual (the so-called *Strategikon* of Maurice) composed between about 592 and 610,[24] it may be that the Greek original emerged, or indeed was still in course of formation, as late as the seventh or even early eighth century.[25] But however long it took the Alexander file to reach the point at which Sālim could impart something like its present form by overseeing a process of translation and editing, there is no doubt that an exceptional person in his privileged position, and resident in Syria, could by the second quarter of the eighth century have acquired more than a smattering of both Greek and Iranian culture.[26] We should perhaps imagine the culturally eclectic but linguistically Greek original being finalized in Syria,[27] though that need not exclude an earlier, more purely Hellenic phase.[28]

The Alexander file, whose at least partially Umayyad date is perhaps confirmed by the fact that Ibn al-Muqaffaʿ quoted two of the letters it contained,[29] has for us a double interest. On the one hand, it rather reminds us of the 'phantom inscription' that survives only in its impress on the earth where the stone that bore it once fell. Just as what had been monumental incised letters with their play of light and shade are reduced to a dim reverse image to be read off the soil by archaeologists, so in the Arabic Alexander file we glimpse aspects of the sixth- and early seventh-century Greek world otherwise mostly lost to us. Justinian the Davidic and Christian emperor cedes ground to Alexander the ancient philosopher-king, whose familiarity is attested by the popularity of the *Alexander Romance*;[30] military and

---

[24] Grignaschi 1975: 39–50, 198–221; cf. Dennis 1981: 16.   [25] Grignaschi 1975: 49–52, 62.

[26] On the late Umayyad intermingling of Hellenism and Iranism, especially in Syria, see Fowden 2004: 296–302. For a possible specific source for Sālim's knowledge of the Sasanians, see 2004: 218. Sālim was a *mawlā*, and it has been thought he was Iranian (Grignaschi 1965–6: 12, 25; Latham 1983: 161; Fowden 2004: 262; Bladel 2004: 155–6); but Ibn al-Nadīm, *Kitāb al-fihrist* 305, is not evidence for that, *pace* Zakeri 2004: 188–9.

[27] Cf. Manzalaoui 1974: 218, and Maróth 2006: 76 (Introduction).

[28] Gutas (2009: 65–6) raises the possibility that the connecting narratives, and therefore the ultimate form of the work, are to be attributed to Sālim.

[29] Ibn al-Muqaffaʿ: Boyce 1968: 27–9. Alexander file: Maróth 2006: 102–5 (Arabic; French translation Grignaschi 1965–6: 63–6). Unfortunately, Ibn al-Muqaffaʿ's lost Arabic translation of the *Letter of Tansar* is preserved only in an inflated thirteenth-century retrotranslation into Persian. But the fact that he and Sālim were contemporaries who both frequented the court milieu (in which there had been some continuity despite the change of dynasty) encourages one to suppose Ibn al-Muqaffaʿ knew Sālim's *Letters*, and that the Alexander file, since it contains (albeit in elaborated form) the letters Ibn al-Muqaffaʿ quotes, may therefore in some way reflect Sālim's compilation. Both Grignaschi (1965–6: 16–21) and Maróth (2006: 71–3 (Introduction)) argue for the Alexander file's priority to Ibn al-Muqaffaʿ. For another allusion to something like the Alexander file in a mid-eighth-century source, see Grignaschi 1975: 52–3, on al-Masʿūdī, *Murūj al-dhahab* §558.

[30] Compare A. Kaldellis's recent disinterment of a whole circle of intellectual dissenters from the Justinianic vision, among them John Lydos with his interest in constitutional or republican ideals

political theory are reunited after their unnatural separation by fifth- and sixth-century emperors who had resided at Constantinople and left war to their generals;[31] and Iran is woven skilfully into a seamless fabric reflecting – especially as viewed from Syria – a reality our Greek sources cannot deny, but plainly resent.[32] Above all, Hellenism and Iranism appear as the natural antecedents, not the vanquished antithesis, of an Umayyad – and increasingly Muslim – civilization.

But besides illuminating the world in which it emerged, and allowing early Muslims to discuss the proper use of absolute power with the authority – and neutrality – of a distant past, the Alexander file also points forward to the genre of so-called *Fürstenspiegel* or 'Mirrors for princes', manuals of advice for rulers, which had been anticipated already in the Greek world[33] but became especially popular in later Islam.[34] In particular, the beginning of its longest section, *Al-siyāsatu'l-ʿāmmīya – Policy toward the Common People*[35] – is elaborated in the opening discourse of the famous *Sirr al-asrār* or *Secret of Secrets*, a voluminous manual for princes again addressed by Aristotle to Alexander. Though some of its disparate parts existed earlier, the *Secret* seems to have come together *c.* 950–987. It was eventually translated into both Persian (which will have helped it spread in the Indian world too) and Ottoman Turkish.[36] The *Secret* differs from the Alexander file in that it ranges more widely if not necessarily deeply, while excluding the narrative element. Besides politics and military affairs it embraces almost encyclopaedic discussions of medicine (including diet and personal hygiene), physiognomy, magic, astrology, alchemy and other subjects vital for the prince to know about if he is to meet the Platonic

of government: Kaldellis 1999; 2004ab; 2005ab. Alexander was also seen as an eschatological ruler yet to come, or identified by some with Heraclius: Reinink 2002.

[31] Kaldellis 2004b: 66; cf. O'Meara 2003: 174–7, on the coverage of both military and political theory in the anonymous and fragmentary dialogue *On political science*, perhaps an implicit criticism of Justinian.

[32] Cf. Kaldellis 2004b: 120–8.

[33] Cf. Justinianic advisers like Agapetos the deacon of Haghia Sophia or the anonymous author of the dialogue *On political science*. On the *Alexander Romance* as a type of *Fürstenspiegel*, see Jouanno 2002: 191–6. Hadot (1972) on *Fürstenspiegel* moves straight from East Rome to the Latin West without the slightest reference to the Islamic development of the genre, typifying the traditional approach to which the present chapter offers an alternative.

[34] Crone 2004: 148–64.

[35] Cf. Netton 1997. The treatise is summarized by Latham (1983: 157–61) in such a way as to illustrate the appropriateness of the title.

[36] On the Badawī edition and the English translation by Ali, see the primary sources (pp. 147–8). On two more recent editions see Bladel 2004: 151 n. 1. Cf. also Zonta 2003: 648–51; Forster 2006: 1–112, esp. 11–19 (date), 39–41 and 108–11 (genre: *Fürstenspiegel* and encyclopaedia), 44–7 (Persian and Turkish translations). On the relationship with *Al-siyāsatu 'l-ʿāmmīya* see Manzalaoui 1974: 156–7, 241–2; Bladel 2004: 154–5, 162; Forster 2006: 56 n. 298.

ideal that he 'truly possess expert knowledge' (although this ideal is not explicitly invoked by the *Secret*).[37] But these things are also of concern to the rest of mankind as well.[38] The prince is portrayed as one who must aspire not just to expert but to universal knowledge, without which he can hardly expect to control his subjects.[39] The ultimate application of such knowledge may, as appears at the end and culmination of the *Secret*, be the Hermetic science of manufacturing magical talismans; but the key to everything is the exercise of reason – even talismans are but the exploitation of a law of nature, namely that 'to every physical category corresponds a higher category'.[40] 'O Alexander', declares Aristotle near the beginning of the *Secret*,

now I will tell thee a short maxim which alone would have sufficed even if I had not told thee others. O Alexander, reason is the head of policy . . . It is the chief of all praiseworthy things, and the fountainhead of all glories.[41]

In other words the *Secret* is no mere accumulation of technical and (pseudo-)scientific knowledge, but is founded on philosophical concepts and intended, indeed, as an introduction to a philosophical way of life. 'He who abstains from little gains much' is one of the fundamental principles of Aristotle's advice to his royal master.[42]

The universal perspective was of course already implicit in the epistles addressed by Aristotle the most erudite of all philosophers to Alexander the world-conqueror; but in the *Secret of Secrets* the idea really takes on flesh and blood. At one point Aristotle goes so far as to present Alexander with a precursor of the academic handout, the so-called 'Circle of Political Wisdom', which he describes as 'the essence of this book':

I have invented for thee a diagram according to wisdom, philosophy and law. It is eight-sided and will inform thee of everything that is in the world. It comprehends the government of the world and comprises all the classes of the people, and the form of justice required for each of them. I have divided this figure according

---

[37] Plato, *Politicus* 293c, *Euthydemus* 291cd.

[38] This point is underlined at *Sirr al-asrār* 100 (trans. Ali 205).

[39] Cf. the Syriac inscription allegedly found in an old royal tomb ('I . . . acquired the extreme knowledge of creation'): *Sirr al-asrār* 165 (trans. Ali 261); also Murray 1978: 119–22.

[40] *Sirr al-asrār* 156–68 (trans. Ali 252–63), esp. 156 for the quotation (trans. Ali 254) and 166–7 (trans. Ali 262; Hermes Trismegistus).

[41] *Sirr al-asrār* 75 (trans. Ali 182).

[42] *Sirr al-asrār* 79 (trans. Ali 186). The most theoretical philosophical section comes at 129–34 (trans. Ali 227–32), an account of intellect (*'aql*), universal soul, matter and body. Forster (2006: 74) sees this as beside the point in a political treatise; but if scientific knowledge is power, so is spiritual knowledge or gnosis: cf. pp. 144–5, below, on the Imam Khomeini.

to the divisions of the heavenly spheres: each division corresponds to a class (of people).[43]

Clearly this universalist dimension is an important reason why the *Secret* became so enormously popular: it contained something for almost everyone, in convenient summary form.[44] In its Latin translations, as the *Secretum secretorum*, it was one of the most widely read books of the European Middle Ages.[45] But the Arabic original also did well,[46] and was surely helped to do so, in a Muslim commonwealth no longer dominated by men of Arab birth and culture, by the space it gave to Iranian – particularly Sasanian – wisdom, literature and institutions.[47] This Iranian dimension is already there in the Alexander file, but much less conspicuously. The Alexander file's strong narrative strand tends to foreground the political and cultural clash between Hellenism and Iranism, as when Alexander writes to Darius:

From Alexander, who is devoted to religion and is striving to support justice, who rejects the might of tyranny and defends manliness, who aspires to take after (his) Roman (*Rūm*) ancestors and the virtuous among the Iranians, to Darius the leader of the Iranians, who rules over them without having the right to do so, who has turned religion into defence serving his kingship, his meditation serving his stomach, his mind serving his senses.[48]

And although there is a lot of Sasanian material woven into the Alexander file's fabric,[49] it no more treats Iran as a cultural equal than does, say, the sixth-century East Roman historian Agathias, for all his undeniable interest in the subject. For an Arabic writer who puts Iran centre-stage we have to turn to one who is himself an Iranian, namely Ibn al-Muqaffaʿ in his almost contemporary *Book of Kalīla and Dimna*, another early 'Mirror for

---

[43] *Sirr al-asrār* 126 (trans. Ali 226). Cf. Manzalaoui 1974: 160: 'The belief... in "correspondences" between three entities, the individual man or "microcosm", the universe or "macrocosm", and the state or "body politic", made it possible to attach both philosophical concepts, and practical rules of, for example, hygiene, to a treatise in the form of a *Fürstenspiegel*.' The *Secret* was neither the first nor the last text in which either Alexander himself was held to have catalysed encyclopaedism (Pliny, *Naturalis historia* 8.17.43–4, also referring to Aristotle), or else the Romance took on encyclopaedic dimensions (Sawyer 1996: 135).
[44] A point emphasized at 117 (trans. Ali 219).
[45] Murray 1978: 120; Williams 2003; Forster 2006: 127–9.   [46] Forster 2006: 12–14, 30, 37, 47.
[47] E.g. *Sirr al-asrār* 73 (trans. Ali 180), on kings' generosity and avarice (cf. Shaked 1984: 41–9); *Sirr al-asrār* 126–7 (trans. Ali 226), the 'Circle of Political Wisdom', identified as Sasanian by Ibn Khaldūn, *Muqaddima* 1.64–5 (trans. Rosenthal 80–1) (cf. Forster 2006: 62 n. 336); and *Sirr al-asrār* 140–2 (trans. Ali 240–1), the story of the Jew and the Zoroastrian (cf. Forster 2006: 76–8). See further Bladel 2004: 151–72.
[48] Maróth 2006: 47 (Arabic), 47 (Introduction; translation slightly emended).
[49] See above note 23.

princes'.[50] Here we see the Greek and Iranian tributaries to the Muslim mind just beginning to unite their flow, a process which has advanced much further by the time we get to the *Secret*.[51]

Despite occasional Qur'ānic phraseology,[52] sometimes plainly interpolated, neither the Alexander file nor the *Secret* is religious in tone to the point of invoking scripture apodeictically. Nor, on the other hand, are they secular, since they constantly invoke God; and this neutrality was another reason why they circulated widely – at least, the *Secret* did – without falling foul of Islam's vivid sectarianism. It also permitted the *Secret* to pass in reasonably faithful translations[53] to the Christian world of the Latin West. Instead of depending on scripture for their arguments, Alexander and Aristotle cultivated a distinctive and personal aura of authority. The Greeks and Romans had already depicted Alexander as a philosopher of sorts, and collected his wise sayings. Jews and Christians went so far as to make him a monotheist. Muslim writers adapted this approach to their own purposes.[54] The Qur'ān presented Dhū 'l-Qarnayn as something of a prophet, preaching to the peoples of the West.[55] By the mid eighth century at the latest, this mysterious figure was understood to be none other than Alexander;[56] and the prophetic view of Alexander's career had been much developed by the time of the Persian poet Neẓāmī Ganjavī (1141–1209).[57] In the *Secret*, Aristotle reminds him that 'the king whom God has chosen to rule over his people . . . is like a god' to the extent that he fosters justice.[58]

As for Aristotle himself, the *Secret*'s preface speaks of him as

outstanding for his majesty of character, his pleasing way of life and his godly learning. For this reason many learned men number him among the prophets. I have seen in numerous histories of the Greeks that God vouchsafed him this revelation: 'Indeed, you are more deserving to be called an angel than a man' . . . There are different traditions about his death. It is contended by some . . . that he was lifted up to heaven in a column of light. By following his good advice and obeying

---

[50] On the Middle Persian version from which the Arabic was translated, see Niehoff-Panagiotidis 2003: 14–19.

[51] *Sirr al-asrār* 86, 97, 107 (trans. Ali 193, 204, 212), invoking the sages of India, Rome and Iran, but especially of Greece. For further background, see Capezzone 2004: 149–54. There is a subtle analysis of the *Secret*'s wide-ranging debts to Greek erudition in Manzalaoui 1974: 194–238.

[52] Alexander file: Maróth 2006: 47 (Arabic: Alexander exhorts Darius to 'command right and forbid wrong'; cf. Qur'ān 3.104, 110, 114), 78 (Arabic: cf. Introduction 60–1); Grignaschi (1975: 198–221) finds only occasional and dim echoes.

[53] See e.g. Forster 2006: 123.   [54] Grignaschi 1993: 206–21; Doufikar-Aerts 2003: 82–117.

[55] Qur'ān 18.84–8.   [56] Nagel 1978: esp. 76–7; Bladel 2007: 65; cf. Abbott 1957–72: 1.50–6.

[57] Hanaway 1998; Blois 1998.

[58] *Sirr al-asrār* 125 (trans. Ali 224); also, on the king's manifestation of God's true sovereignty, 165 (trans. Ali 261).

his commands, Alexander achieved his famous conquests of cities and countries, and ruled supreme in the regions of the earth far and wide.[59]

Rather than conferring on his teachings the credentials of dogma, this religious-sounding vocabulary was simply the most widely understood code the author disposed of in order to underline Aristotle's exceptional intellectual and spiritual authority, which Alexander translated into universal political omnipotence as well. It represents a perfectly natural development from the already very high Roman and late Greek view of Aristotle: Cicero placed him next after Plato; John of Damascus accused his opponents, the 'Jacobites' who rejected the definition of Christ's nature propounded at the Council of Chalcedon in 451, of treating him as the Thirteenth Apostle; while the eighth-century Syriac-speaking monk David bar Paulos declared that 'None in any age was wise like he.'[60] Covering all conceivable knowledge,[61] his writings were insured against Christian or Muslim prejudice by being earlier than both New Testament and Qur'ān, and derived from observation and reasoning, not the gift of any angel, even if Aristotle himself had something angelic about him.

From the sixth century the *corpus Aristotelicum* began to be transferred into Syriac, and from the 750s into Arabic. The Arabic-speaking world both assimilated and remoulded this authentic Aristotle according to its own criteria. The *Politics* was apparently ignored,[62] perhaps because it failed unambiguously to endorse the monarchic ideal (despite the author's approval of monarchy if advised by a true philosopher, i.e. himself, in *On Kingship*);[63] but starting *c.* 830 and continuing through the tenth century, sustained attention was given to the *Metaphysics*. Book Lambda, where Aristotle finally gets to his doctrine of the ultimate cause, the unmoved mover, was translated about six times.[64]

Soon after the first *Metaphysics* translation, and drawing on it, there emerged another classic of pseudo-Aristotelianism, the so-called *Theology of Aristotle* compiled *c.* 840 in the circle of the first serious Arabic philosopher, al-Kindī (d. *c.* 866). The *Theology*, only parts of which survive, brought together translated and edited texts by, but not attributed to,

[59] *Sirr al-asrār* 67–8 (trans. Ali 176). 'Aristotle' underlines his sole responsibility for Alexander's victories at 152–3, 163, 164 (trans. Ali 250, 259, 260). On the Greek background of the passage quoted, see Manzalaoui 1974: 189–91.

[60] Cicero, *De finibus* 5.3.7; John of Damascus, *Contra Jacobitas* 10; David Bar Paulos translated by Brock 1984: v.25.

[61] Hadot 2002: 193.   [62] Pellegrin 2003: 199.

[63] Miller 1995: 191–3. On *On kingship* see above note 21.

[64] Martin 1989; Martini Bonadeo 2003; Bertolacci 2005: especially 244–5, 270–3, on the popularity of Book Lambda.

the late Platonist philosophers Plotinus (205–270) and Proclus (412–485) –
and perhaps others too – in a sort of metaphysics handbook designed
to complete the task Aristotle had only partially discharged in his own
Metaphysics.[65] Discussion of the nature of God, notoriously depicted by
the Qur'ān in terms alternately anthropomorphic and transcendent,[66] had
recently gained impetus and indeed political resonance from the clash
between strictly scripturalist theologians like Ibn Ḥanbal (780–855) and
the Muʿtazilites who, forcefully backed up by the caliph al-Maʾmūn (813–
833), used reason to probe the modes of divinity.[67] Al-Maʾmūn was even
said to have seen Aristotle in a dream and been reassured by the great sage
as to the validity of personal, rational judgment (*raʾy*).[68] The surviving parts
of the *Theology* in fact concentrate mainly on the soul. What they do say
about God amounts to a re-reading of Plotinus' and (to a lesser extent)
Proclus' One in the light of scripture so that, for example, God – rather
than just Intellect – is imagined to be a conscious creator and providential
supervisor of all being, rather than a sublimely unaware emanator of it.[69]
The *Theology* preserves, nevertheless, much of Plotinus' apophaticism, his
belief that it is not possible to describe the One; and accordingly it eschews
talk of God's attributes. It thereby implicitly takes sides against the scrip-
turalists, who had found in the Qur'ān no fewer than ninety-nine different
descriptive names for Allāh.[70]

If the Alexander file and the *Secret* addressed themselves to a historical
reality that had evolved far beyond the historical Aristotle's *Politics* and
the Greek *polis*, the *Theology* somewhat similarly (and self-confessedly[71])
aimed to complete the *Metaphysics*. In both cases the authentic Aristotle
is being not just re-read as in the still-influential Alexandrian commentary
tradition,[72] but extended to meet the demands imposed by the late antique
world of universal monotheisms such as Christianity or Islam, and universal
states such as Rome, Iran and, above all, the caliphate.

---

[65] D'Ancona 2005c: 203–10; D'Ancona and Taylor 2003 (on the Proclus texts only). For the current
editions and translations, see primary sources (below). Note that the title *Theology of Aristotle* is
usually employed to denote only the Plotinus extracts. On the more comprehensive – if strictly
speaking hypothetical – *Theology* which preceded or accompanied the formation of the Plotinian
Theology, see D'Ancona and Taylor 2003: 625–9. For a brief comparison of Plotinus' and Proclus'
theology see D'Ancona 2005a: 29–30.

[66] Anthropomorphic: 5.64, 7.54, 20.5, 23.27. Transcendent: 42.11 ('There is no other thing like him').

[67] For the controversies under al-Maʾmūn and his successors, see e.g. Zilio-Grandi 2005: 145–7.

[68] Gutas 1998: 96–104.

[69] *Theology of Aristotle*: Adamson 2002: 151–5. Plotinus: 5.8.7.1–16 (and, on the Arabic version,
D'Ancona 2003b). Proclus, *Commentarium in Platonis Parmenidem* 953–61.

[70] Adamson 2002: index s.v. 'God'. On Allāh's 'most beautiful names', see Qur'ān 7.180, 17.110, 20.8.

[71] See the Preface 3–7 (trans. Lewis 486–8).   [72] Ferrari 2005: 360–1.

Let us... mention now... what we wish to explain in this book of ours, namely universal knowledge (*'ilm kullī*), which is a subject by which we complete the whole of our philosophy,

as Aristotle is made to say in the *Theology*.[73] By the standards of the age, this was at times done with some skill, since it is by no means clear that even the alertest minds – al-Fārābī (d. 950/51), for instance, or Ibn Sīnā (d. 1037) – could tell the difference, at least as regards the *Theology*, between Aristotelian doctrine and what we (not they) call pseudo-Aristotelian.[74] For the classical Islamic thinkers of the ninth and tenth centuries, Aristotle had become the completest possible mind and the universal authority (alongside the Qurʾān) even in theology. He no longer necessarily needed Alexander's support: the *Theology* too is addressed to a prince, but to al-Kindī's courtly pupil Aḥmad b. al-Muʿtaṣim, not the mythical Macedonian.

Had princes been pseudo-Aristotle's only readers, the remarkable expansion and dissemination of both theological and secular learning achieved by this literature might never have occurred. In fact there was a much wider audience in the shape of the growing administrative class charged with governing the vast Abbasid empire, and the various smaller states into which it disintegrated during the tenth century.[75] In Latin translation, both the *Secret of Secrets* (*Secretum secretorum*) and excerpts from the Proclan section of the *Theology* (*Liber de causis*) were then lapped up in the West too from the twelfth century onwards, thanks to the rise of secular education which not only met growing administrative needs but also stimulated the more rational theology of scholasticism.[76] In fact, the Arabic pseudo-Aristotelica are still often studied mainly as background to the extraordinary popularity of the Latin translations and the vernacular versions they spawned. But on the present occasion what interests us is pseudo-Aristotle's fortune in Islam.

---

[73] *Theology of Aristotle* 5–6 (trans. Lewis 487; also [as here] Adamson 29).

[74] D'Ancona 2003a: 98–103.

[75] Gutas 1998: 107–16; cf. Murray 1978: 121–4. This wide dissemination of pseudo-Aristotelian political thought, and a certain immunity to censure conferred by its supposedly pre-Islamic date, gave it an advantage over the less approachable but undeniably contemporary political writings of such as al-Fārābī, well discussed by Crone (2004: 167–8, 170–87, 193–6), who gives virtually nothing on pseudo-Aristotle. In any case, there was no demand for systematic political philosophy under an absolutist regime. The authors of 'Mirrors for princes' sought not to change the polity but to provide moral antidotes to the corruption that beset any prince as the price of power: an admirable realism, well illustrated by Aristotle when he responds to Alexander's enquiry whether he should execute the Iranian nobles: Maróth 2006: 102–5 (Arabic; French trans. Grignaschi 1965–6: 63–6); *Sirr al-asrār* 68–9 (trans. Ali 177).

[76] Murray 1978: 121–4, 218–27. *Secretum secretorum*: above n. 43. *Liber de causis*: D'Ancona and Taylor 2003.

A few brief indications about the later phases of this story must suffice, since this is as yet largely unexplored territory.

If al-Kindī's extracts from Proclus' (that is, pseudo-Aristotle's) *Elements of Theology* enjoyed huge success among the Latins, very few manuscripts of the original Arabic version survive, and research has so far shown only relatively limited use of it by Arabic philosophers after al-Kindī.[77] Its brevity, clarity and division into brief logical propositions and proofs general enough to be applicable in various situations will have given it the air of being just a schematic summary of the Arabic Plotinus (that is, pseudo-Aristotle) *in usum scholarum*, a guide to that text's much more personal explorations of the soul's search for reality. The fact that al-Fārābī and Ibn Sīnā had made no explicit reference to the Proclus extracts did not help either. The Plotinus translations offered, by contrast, an enjoyable challenge. Al-Fārābī quotes them, and Ibn Sīnā even wrote a commentary. Most influential in the long term, though, was al-Suhrawardī, the Iranian sage put to death in 1191 at Saladin's behest because he held – tactlessly, given Crusader pressures in the region – that God can raise up prophets whenever he sees fit (i.e. even after Muḥammad).[78] Al-Suhrawardī's so-called 'illuminationist' philosophy was in part inspired by the Arabic version of Plotinus' *Ennead* 4.8.1 on the experience of shedding the body and beholding 'the sublime light high in that divine place' – though, realizing al-Kindī's 'Aristotle' could not possibly have said this, al-Suhrawardī reattributed the idea to Plato.[79] Illuminationism was systematized by Mullā Ṣadrā (d. 1640) and other representatives of the seventeenth-century Iṣfahānian renaissance, and is still today influential in the schools of Qom where the Iranian clerical elite is formed.

Besides his reverence for Greek philosophy, al-Suhrawardī also felt a strong romantic attachment to the spiritual culture of pre-Islamic Iran, and in particular to the legendary monarch and ascetic Kay Khusraw, whom he elevated to the status of a prophet of light alongside Zarathustra himself.[80] Recent investigation of two large seventeenth-century composite manuscripts from Iṣfahān has shown how, beside al-Suhrawardī himself, later illuminationists also read both the *Secret of Secrets* and the *Theology of Aristotle* (the Plotinus section).[81] Their political – and more general philosophical – conceptions were therefore a mixture of Iranism and

[77] D'Ancona and Taylor 2003: 636–40.   [78] Walbridge 2005: esp. 217 on prophets.
[79] Al-Suhrawardī, *Ḥikmat al-ishrāq* §171 (trans. Corbin 155), alluding to *Theology of Aristotle* 22 (trans. Lewis 225). Plotinus himself made no reference to light in this passage; but cf. e.g. 5.3.17.28–30 (not included in the *Theology*).
[80] Corbin 1971–2: 2.96–104.   [81] Endress 2001: esp. 46 no. 46, 48 no. 54.

Hellenism, as well as the fundamentals of the Islamic tradition. All three tributary streams tended to reinforce the notion – congenial to the Safavids – that the ruler is God's vicegerent on earth. The dynasty's founder, Shah Ismāʿīl (1501–24), claimed to be the reincarnation of both Kay Khusraw and Alexander as well as Muḥammad.[82]

More recent Iranian regimes have emphasized the glories either of the Achaemenids and Sasanians (the so-called Pahlavi dynasty) or of Islam, without wanting to mix them. But the revolution of 1979 owed a not very widely understood debt to illuminationism as well, and through it to Greek philosophy, including pseudo-Aristotle. During the earlier part of his life spent as student and then teacher at Qom, the Imam Khomeini took an at that time unfashionable interest in the mystical and gnostic rather than just the more legalistic aspects of the Muslim tradition, and so became a – not uncritical – reader of the *Theology of Aristotle*. Khomeini's thought was overwhelmingly dominated by Mullā Ṣadrā. 'Mullā Ṣadrā! Who will make you understand who Mullā Ṣadrā is?', exclaimed Khomeini in one of his courses. 'He managed to resolve problems about the resurrection that had defeated even Ibn Sīnā.' Though Khomeini acknowledged Ibn Sīnā's great intellectual acuity, he declared 'his errors in metaphysics [to be] extremely numerous', and his Greek philosophy of little value to those who truly seek God. Real wisdom and light come from the Qurʾān and the traditions, mediated by such as Mullā Ṣadrā – 'Muslim wisdom and gnosis do not come from Greece or the Greeks.' To convince oneself of this, according to Khomeini, one need only compare on the one hand 'the books and writings of the world's great philosophers – though their knowledge too comes from the source of revelation – ... [books] of which the most elevated and subtle is perhaps the *Theology* ... of Aristotle', with on the other hand 'the perceptions present in the pure religion of Islam and in the great Muslim sages and gnostics'. 'To derive, then, all wisdom from Greece, and to deem the Muslim sages followers of Greek wisdom', is to reveal one's ignorance both of the books of the Muslim sages and, at the same time, of the contents of 'the Holy Book and the traditions of the Infallibles'. 'If it were not for the Qurʾān, the gateway to knowledge of God would be forever closed. Greek philosophy is something quite different, which' – Khomeini concedes – 'is of great value in its own way. It proceeds by argument, but one does not in that way acquire knowledge. The Prophet's mission wrought a great change in the domain of knowledge. The arid philosophies of the Greeks ... which had and still have their merits, have

[82] Babayan 2002: xxviii–xxx.

been transformed for the contemplative masters into an effective gnosis and true contemplation.'[83]

Whatever it loses in comparison with the luminaries of Islamic gnosis, the *Theology of Aristotle* is still studied in Iran and treated with reverence, though even in the schools of Qom it is now understood that its doctrines are those of Plotinus not Aristotle.[84] Nor is it the only symptom of the continuing stimulus offered by Greek thought. The revolution put into practice a new political concept, that of the *vilāyat-i faqīh*, the governance or guardianship of the jurist.[85] In its absoluteness, this concept takes us back not just to the early centuries of Islam we have been looking at, but behind that – via al-Fārābī's *Principles of the opinions of the people of the excellent city* – to the Platonic ideal of the philosopher-king.[86] Yet there is no necessary contradiction between revolution in the name of Islam and the illumination that had its roots in the Greeks, for the Imam Khomeini could not have led the revolution so successfully had he not first been immersed in and disciplined by the philosophy of, above all, Mullā Ṣadrā.[87] Hence the invocation of Plato's and Plotinus' influence already on the first page of a recent study of Khomeini's political thought and action.[88] Indeed, given the authority and influence enjoyed by those who have received the traditional religious education, it would be reasonable to claim that Iran is the only place in the world today whose public doctrine is based on a reading – however selective – of Greek philosophy very much in the spirit in which it was read in the latest phase of the ancient tradition, in Alexandria, taking account of the adjustments which have had to be made, and were already being made then, in order to reconcile the sages of antiquity with the doctrines of scriptural monotheism.

Illuminationism also fertilized universalist currents of thought at the Indian and supposedly Sunni court of the Mughal emperor Akbar (1556–1605), who backed an eclectic religion emphasizing reason and light (see also the discussion by Koch in this volume).[89] Admittedly Shi'ism

---

[83] Extracts translated by Bonaud 1997: 49–50.
[84] I am indebted for information about the *Theology* in contemporary Iran to Professors Mohammad Fanaei Eshkevari (Qom), Mahmoud Binaye Motlagh (Iṣfahān) and Mahdi Ghavam Safari (Tehran), whom I met at a conference on Plato and al-Suhrawardī held in Athens in February 2006.
[85] Algar 1985: 25–166; Moin 1999: 225–6, 294–7, and further references in the index s.v. 'velayat-e faqih'; Martin 2000: 160–3, 170.
[86] Martin 2000: 32 n. 16, 35 n. 29, 162; O'Meara 2003: 191–3 on al-Fārābī.
[87] Martin 2000: 41, 45–7, 153–4, 170, 202–3 ('a subtle unseen authority behind the visible jurisprudential one').
[88] Martin 2000: ix. O'Meara (2003) breaks new ground in describing the political dimension of late Platonism and tracing its influence – but only as far as al-Fārābī.
[89] Corbin 1971–2: 2.353–8; 4.28–9, 58; Ahmad 1965.

influenced Akbar, and notably his successor Jahangir, alongside Sunnism.[90] Additionally, the need to reconcile India's Hindus provided a pressing political motive for credal flexibility. But the Sunni world had not grown entirely immune to philosophy, even after the orthodox Hanbalite reaction sealed by the career of Ibn Taymīya (d. 1328).[91] Since my concern has mainly been with the interaction between the cultural worlds of Greece, Arabia and Iran, I would like to conclude by glancing at the Turks, who as intruders into all three were well placed to bring about a synthesis of the universalist elements in their thought worlds (discussed by Kołodziejczyk below), which (as we have seen) tended to associate political omnipotence ('Alexander') with intellectual omniscience ('Aristotle') and a positive attitude towards human rationality and, therefore, human diversity – since experience teaches that there is more than one way to the truth.

Consider, for example, the library of Mehmet II, the conqueror of Constantinople.[92] It almost goes without saying that this collection included the pseudo-Aristotelian *Secret of Secrets*; it may also have contained the Alexander file. Ibn Sīnā and al-Suhrawardī were there too, and a Greek translation of Thomas Aquinas's *Summa contra Gentiles*, copied by one of Mehmet's court scribes with illuminated decorations in the Ottoman style.[93] By far the best surviving manuscript of the *Theology of Aristotle* was copied at Edirne in 1459[94] – if not for Mehmet II himself, then for someone close to his eclectic circle. And what remained of the Platonist Gemistos Plethon's collection of *Magical Oracles Transmitted by the Magi of Zoroaster* – after the Greek Patriarch had burned it – was translated into Arabic *c.* 1462 in this same milieu,[95] whose horizons embraced Latin Europe (or at least Italy) and West Asia, not just the eastern Mediterranean, and also the ancient world as well as the revealed religions of Christ and Muḥammad. Mehmet was keen to attract eminent Iranian scholars to his court, since they were considered among the most learned of their

---

[90] Ansari 1965: 380b; Schimmel 1993: 327b.   [91] Gutas 1998: 166–72.

[92] Raby and Tanindi 1993: esp. 49, 62, 78–9, 150–1, 172–3, 178–9; Gutas 1998: 174–5; Rogers 2009. For the availability in Bayazit II's library, which included his father's, of a wide selection of works in or translated from Persian and Greek as well as Arabic and Turkish, see Maróth 2002: esp. 120–1 (the manuscripts of the Alexander file), 127, 128 (*Sirr al-asrār*), 130–1; also Maróth 2004.

[93] Raby 1983: 20, 29 and fig. 42. Aquinas's criticism of Ibn Sīnā and Ibn Rushd (Averroes) will have attracted Mehmet, who organized a disputation aimed at sustaining al-Ghazālī against his philosophical critics: Gutas 1998: 174.

[94] The colophon is printed in Badawī's edition p. (50). Mehmet was intermittently resident at Edirne during 1459: Babinger 1978: 162, 172–3. My thanks to Dimitri Gutas for help with Aya Sofya 2457.

[95] *Pace* Gutas (1998: 174), there is no evidence that the Plethon translation was done at Mehmet's personal initiative: see the carefully worded discussion by Nicolet and Tardieu (1980: 55).

age;[96] while on his western flank the Aristotelian Cretan convert to Rome, George Trapezuntius, flattered him for his commitment to Aristotelianism, and notoriously proposed he assume universal rule over Christians as well as Muslims.[97] Had Mehmet not been unavailable to meet him when he visited Istanbul for that very purpose, the new Alexander[98] might have found his Aristotle, and a correspondence might have ensued in which the Latin world's revived appreciation of Greek philosophy would have been put at the service of a renascent, rational, militarily vigorous and credally tolerant Islam (always of course within the limits of the politically possible).

As for us, our aspirations are different. As Jocelyne Dakhlia recently put it, 'to discover today, in Islam, *endogenous* formulations of political universalism and an a-religious understanding of good government, should not be seen as just one more accessory piece of knowledge'.[99]

PRIMARY SOURCES (SELECTED)[100]

Agapetus, *Ekthesis* = R. Riedinger (ed.) (1995), *Agapetos Diakonos: Der Fürstenspiegel für Kaiser Iustinianos* (Athens).
Aristotle, Περὶ βασιλείας (*On Kingship*) = W. D. Ross (ed.) (1955), *Aristotelis fragmenta selecta* (Oxford), 61–2.
Ibn Khaldūn, *Muqaddima* = E. Quatremère (ed.) (1858), *Prolégomènes d'Ebn-Khaldoun* (Paris). English trans. F. Rosenthal (1967) [2nd edn], *Ibn Khaldûn, The Muqaddimah: An Introduction to History* (Princeton).
Ibn al-Nadīm, *Kitāb al-fihrist* = R. Tajaddud (ed.) (1971), *Kitāb al-fihrist li 'l-Nadīm* (Tehran). English trans. B. Dodge (1970), *The Fihrist of al-Nadīm* (New York).
John of Damascus, *Contra Jacobitas* = B. Kotter (ed.) (1969–), *Die Schriften des Johannes von Damaskos* (Berlin), vol. iv, 99–153.
John Philoponus, *In Categorias* = A. Busse (ed.) (1898), *Philoponi (olim Ammonii) In Aristotelis Categorias Commentarium* (Berlin).
al-Masʿūdī, *Murūj al-dhahab* = C. Barbier de Meynard and J.-B. Pavet de Courteille (eds.), revised by C. Pellat (1966–79), *Masʿūdī: Les prairies d'or* (Beirut). French trans. C. Barbier de Meynard and J.-B. Pavet de Courteille (eds.), revised by C. Pellat (1962–), *Masʿūdī: Les prairies d'or* (Paris).
On political science = C. M. Mazzucchi (ed.) (2002), *Menae patricii cum Thomae referendario de scientia politica dialogus* (Milan) [revised edition].
Plotinus, *Enneades* = P. Henry and H.-R. Schwyzer (eds.) (1964–83), *Plotini opera* (Oxford) [editio minor].

---

[96] Babinger 1978: 490–2; İnalcık 1973: 166–7; Rogers 2009.
[97] Monfasani 1976: 131–6, 184–94.   [98] Babinger 1978: 499–500; Raby 1983: 18–19.
[99] Dakhlia 2002: 1206.   [100] For secondary sources, see General Bibliography.

Proclus, *Commentarium in Platonis Parmenidem* = V. Cousin (ed.) (1864), *Procli philosophi platonici opera inedita* (Paris), vol. III, 617–1244.

Sirr al-asrār = ʿA. Badawī (ed.) (1954), *Al-uṣūl al-yūnānīya li-ʾl-naẓariyāt al-siyāsīya fī ʾl-islām* (Cairo) [paginated in two sequences; all references are to the text section], 65–171. English trans. I. Ali (ed. A. S. Fulton), in R. Steele (ed.) (1920), *Opera hactenus inedita Rogeri Baconi*, fasc. V: *Secretum secretorum* (Oxford), 176–266, here adopted in varying degrees. Ali based his translation on a selection of manuscripts – listed at p. 176 – which yielded a text not always identical with Badawī's.

Al-Suhrawardī, *Ḥikmat al-ishrāq* = H. Corbin (1952), *Shihâbbadîn Yaḥyâ Sohrawardî, Œuvres philosophiques et mystiques (Opera metaphysica et mystica* 2) (Tehran and Paris). French trans. H. Corbin (1986), *Shihâboddîn Yaḥya Sohravardî: Le livre de la sagesse orientale* (Paris).

Theology of Aristotle. Plotinus extracts = ʿA. Badawī (ed.) (1966) [2nd edn], *Aflūṭīn ʿinda ʾl-ʿarab* (Cairo), 3–164. English trans. G. Lewis, in P. Henry and H.-R. Schwyzer (eds.) (1951–73), *Plotini opera* (Paris) [editio maior], vol. II, 37–488. Proclus extracts = (1) O. Bardenhewer (ed.) (1882), *Die pseudo-aristotelische Schrift Ueber das reine Gute bekannt unter dem Namen Liber de causis* (Freiburg im Breisgau), 58–118. (2) ʿA. Badawī (ed.) (1955), *Al-aflāṭūnīya al-muḥdatha ʿinda ʾl-ʿarab* (Cairo), 1–33. (3) G. Endress (ed.) (1973), *Proclus arabus: Zwanzig Abschnitte aus der Institutio theologica in arabischer Übersetzung* (Beirut).

CHAPTER 6

The Christian imperial tradition – Greek and Latin

Dimiter Angelov and Judith Herrin

What difference did Christianity make to ancient Mediterranean empires? Did the change in official religion reduce or increase the powers of an autocrat? Modern scholars have traditionally considered the Christian religion to have brought restrictions, at least in comparison with ancient Mediterranean monarchies and pre-Christian Germanic kingdoms. Adherence to Christian law and its practical implementation in the world became criteria for political legitimacy.[1] The role of the church in inaugurating rulers and the widespread popularity of Old Testament models of charismatic kingship (invoked, for example, in imperial coronation prayers and acclamations) could compromise ideas of autocracy and dynastic succession to the throne.[2] In the Byzantine Christian mindset, rule by divine right meant that an emperor who gained God's approbation might lose it if he turned into a tyrant – an interpretation which was opposed to arbitrary rule. A monastic *florilegium* circulating widely in Byzantium furnished the Pauline words favouring obedience to the ruler, 'there is no authority unless it has been instituted by God' (Romans 13:1), with the revealing addition that 'God appoints and removes emperors'.[3]

The impact of Christianity on medieval rulership was, of course, complex and varied across geographical areas and time periods. What interests us here is the narrower problem of the historical linkage of Christianity with empire, imperialism and political universalism during the Middle Ages. This relationship proved surprisingly symbiotic and was marked by

[1] Kern 1939: 40–50, 69–79, 97–117. Cf. Bloch 1973: 33.

[2] See the Byzantine coronation prayer in the *Euchologion* (*Book of Prayer*) in use in the eighth century: Goar 1730: 726–7; translated in Dagron 2003: 58. For the prayers at the coronation of the western emperors, see Elze 1960: 13, 18–19, 20, 24; Kantorowicz 1957: 81 (the acclamation of Louis the Pious). For the coronation of kings, see the *ordo* for the crowning of the Frankish king Louis the Stammerer in 877 in Boretius and Krause 1883–97: II, 461–2. See the discussion of the role of the Old Testament in Byzantium by Dagron 2003: 48–53, esp. 50: 'In Byzantium, the Old Testament had a constitutional value.' Cf. Schramm 1968–71: IV, pt 1, 127–32.

[3] *Melissa* (tenth or eleventh century), in J. P. Migne (ed.), *Patrologiae cursus completus, series graeca*, 161 vols. (Paris, 1857–66), vol. 136, col. 1000D.

the adoption and adaptation of ancient ideas and ritual and the working out of specifically Christian notions of empire. A hierarchical institution with a wide local network of bishoprics, the Christian church proved equally capable of supporting and undermining empire-building in the Middle Ages. In the medieval East and West Christian imperialism evolved separately, but also concurrently and with some interesting points of convergence. By the tenth century AD the rulers of the two medieval empires – Byzantium (the resilient Roman empire in the East whose existence spans the entire Middle Ages) and the medieval western empire revived in 800 – vied with each other for recognition as the sole legitimate successor to *imperium Romanum* and each claimed an all-important status in the international arena. The rival emperors shared common symbols and insignia of power, notably the crown, orb and sceptre, and special imperial costume, such as purple-dyed garments and red boots.[4] A comparison of Christianity's role in shaping the identity of the two empires brings to the fore similar experiences as well as differences, the latter being shaped by patterns of the reception of the late Roman heritage, divergent politics and varying strategies of empire-building.

A brief comparative outline of the main characteristics of the two medieval empires will assist in examining their specifically Christian aspect. By its very origin Byzantium had an advantage and a head-start over its western counterpart. It had a fixed capital, the city of Constantinople, and a fixed court which was a powerful magnet for individual talent and ambition. The role of Constantinople as a symbolic centre of empire can hardly be overestimated. The city of New Rome, officially inaugurated in 330, was designed to overshadow Rome on the Tiber with its majestic secular and ecclesiastical buildings and other material statements of imperial stature, such as the Egyptian obelisk the emperor Theodosius I set up in 390 in the Hippodrome. In true Roman fashion the obelisk symbolised the emperor's victories and the submission of non-Roman enemies. A centralised tax-gathering state, Byzantium was capable, at least during its heyday, of generating speedily substantial monetary revenues to meet military and court expenditure.[5] Byzantium's budgetary capacity was unmatched by any western European power until 1204 when the

---

[4] On the crown and the orb, see notes 26 and 28 below. On the use of purple-dyed garments and red boots, see Reinhold 1970, and many images of Carolingian monarchs wearing purple cloaks and red boots (e.g. Lothar I's Gospel Book of 849–851). On the sceptre as an imperial insigne, see Kazhdan, 'Scepter', in Kazhdan 1991: III, 1849. On the West, see, for example, the Golden Bull of 1356 in Fritz 1972: 83, line 22.

[5] See in general Hendy 1985.

armies of the Fourth Crusade captured Constantinople, and the restored Byzantine empire in 1261 remained a fragmented and weak state. Its monetised economy was supported by the continual minting of coins in gold, silver and bronze; indeed, Byzantium was the only medieval power to issue gold currency between the eighth and the thirteenth centuries.[6] Coins also served as tools of propaganda with an extensive geographical and social outreach.

The imperial educational establishment, which trained successive generations of students to fill posts in the civil service, came to terms early on with the new religion. In the late fourth century St Basil of Caesarea, one of the fathers of the Greek church, advised young men to read the classics selectively, and from this time on pre-Christian texts formed the basis of education at all levels (primary, secondary and higher) in schools in different localities.[7] The ancient curriculum of the seven liberal arts, the basis of the structure of Byzantine secondary education, was taught by private and public salaried teachers. School curricula transmitted ancient Greek knowledge (but very little Latin after the sixth century) to medieval Christian pupils continuously until the fall of the Byzantine empire. Notably, in early and middle Byzantium (330–1204) bishops and patriarchs were often recruited from among the ranks of the educated laity. For example, the high civil servants Tarasios (784–806), Nikephoros (806–815) and Photios (858–867, 877–886) were elevated to the patriarchate of Constantinople during critical times of theological controversy and missionary competition with the papacy.[8] All three men left a deep imprint on the doctrines and expanding influence of the Byzantine church in eastern Europe. Alongside state-sponsored education in secular subjects, the church maintained its own schools centred on the patriarchate and concerned mainly with scriptural studies. The church gained an increasing importance as patron of higher education from the late eleventh century onward.[9]

Finally, imperial and ecclesiastical power was closely intertwined in Byzantium. This linkage was institutional as much as physical: the Great Palace and the patriarchate were situated next to each other near the acropolis of ancient Byzantium. The emperor exercised a much tighter grip over the institutions of the church than elsewhere in the medieval West: he appointed and invested the patriarch of Constantinople and was entitled to convene and preside over church councils and levy taxes on ecclesiastical

---

[6] Lopez 1951; Spufford 1988: 19–20, 169–86.   [7] Lemerle 1986; Herrin 1987.

[8] Lemerle 1986, 146–54 for Nikephoros and Tarasios. On Photios see Dvornik 1948 and 1970.

[9] Browning 1975; Constantinides 1982.

property.[10] In 325 Constantine I, assuming the role of a most Christian emperor, summoned and presided over the first universal council of the church at Nicaea, issuing imperial laws to reinforce theological definitions. As Constantinople's founder, later recognised as a saint, Constantine set an imperial model for emulation. Imperial interventions in theological controversies and other doctrinal matters were not infrequent in Byzantium's history. Iconoclasm in the eighth and early ninth centuries and the politically motivated unions with the papacy of 1274 and 1438–9 are well-known examples.

As a political formation, the medieval western empire was quite unlike Byzantium in its lack of a fixed capital and a centralised taxation system. In the fourth and most of the fifth centuries the late Roman emperors held sway over parts of western Europe, although they usually resided in Milan or Ravenna. Rome was left to old senatorial families often at loggerheads with the Christian community under its bishop. In 476 the last Roman emperor in the West was deposed by Germanic warriors and the imperial office was discontinued. For more than three centuries thereafter Latin Christendom knew no imperial politics, with the notable exception of Italy, including the city of Rome, which reverted to Byzantine control under the emperor Justinian I (527–565) along with other dispersed territories in the western Mediterranean. The revival of the empire occurred under special historical circumstances. In 800 Pope Leo III took the initiative to endow the king of the Franks Charlemagne (768–814) – a victorious military leader and a proven political ally of the papacy – with an imperial title and thus invoked a new level of authority. In the Christmas Day ceremony at St Peter's he arranged for the king to be crowned and acclaimed with the title of *imperator augustus*.

A new imperial polity was born destined to rival the millennial existence of Byzantium. Its conventional name is 'The Holy Roman Empire', although the designation is misleading with regard to the medieval phase of its existence. The Frankish concept of empire at the time of Charlemagne was not Rome-centred, even though an association with the imperial past of Rome and Italy was at times sought (for example, the palatine chapel of Charlemagne in Aachen was modelled on Justinian's church of S. Vitale in Ravenna). The 'Romanisation' of the empire in official ideology and more permanent involvement in politics in Italy took place only in the tenth and eleventh centuries.[11] The adjective 'holy' was permanently

[10] Dagron 2003: 282–312, with a bibliography and critical assessment on the lengthy scholarly discussion of the concept of caesaropapism; Drake 2007.
[11] Nelson 1988: 230–2; Barraclough 1950: 15–16; McKitterick 2008: 169, 339.

added to 'empire' during the reign of the emperor Frederick I Barbarossa
(r. 1152–90, emperor since 1155) under the influence of the rediscovery of
Roman law.[12] In 1254 the empire became 'holy' and 'Roman', while from
the middle of the fifteenth century until its dissolution in 1806 it bore
the name 'Holy Roman Empire of the German Nation'.[13] Charlemagne's
empire was no unitary state; it consisted of separate regions maintaining
distinct local legal traditions, while his itinerant court moved from palace
to palace throughout the year. The construction of the palace complex at
Aachen did not lead to the permanent establishment of an imperial capital and remained a unique attempt. In later centuries Aachen was a holy
place of royal inauguration and burial rather than an imperial capital like
Constantinople.

Medieval western emperors after Charlemagne may be described as 'feudal' overlords ruling over a loosely held territory shifting according to military success. Attempts at setting up a centralised tax administration, no
matter how well conceived, failed to take hold.[14] In the late Middle Ages,
in contrast to the centralisation of the French and English pre-national
monarchies, the western emperors presided over a patchwork of lordships
and semi-independent towns in central Europe. The few regalian rights
of the emperor were mostly related to the imperial cities in Germany.[15]
Partly due to the absence of a bureaucratic tradition, education in the
western empire differed in its nature and function from that in Byzantium.
Charlemagne's court attracted scholars from as far away as York and northern Spain, yet the Carolingian schools were monastic rather than secular
and taught an almost exclusively Christian curriculum.[16] In the period of
the emergence of the universities (a corporate institution unknown in the
same form in Byzantium), the western emperors seized the opportunity to
become patrons of these educational establishments. Their motivation was
understandably practical. A sign of the high authority of Roman law and
Romanitas in Frederick I Barbarossa's eyes was the charter of privileges he
issued in 1155 on behalf of the nascent University of Bologna, a centre of the
revival of Roman law.[17] In 1224 his grandson Frederick II Hohenstaufen
(r. 1212–50, emperor since 1220) founded the University of Naples primarily
as a centre for legal studies in the expectation that he would be able to
recruit trained civil servants. However his hopes were never fulfilled.[18]

The link between the idea of empire and Rome lured many an emperor
into the fractious politics of the Italian peninsula and further weakened

---

[12] Benson 1982: 362–3; Barraclough 1950: 19.   [13] Offler 1965: 218–19, with further references.
[14] Bulst 1989.   [15] Offler 1965: 227–8.   [16] McKitterick 1989: 90–126, 211–70; Sullivan 1995.
[17] Benson 1982: 360–4.   [18] Abulafia 1992: 163, 210.

efforts at creating a seamless state. In the thirteenth century the emperor Frederick II Hohenstaufen – a ruler who pursued grandest ambitions of Roman revival – divided his time between Germany and Italy and fought a prolonged, ultimately losing battle against the Lombard League, an alliance of northern Italian city-states supported by the papacy. Frederick II's itinerant court has aptly been called 'a government by remote control', while his treasury relied mostly on the income derived from the well-administered kingdom of Sicily, which he inherited from his Norman mother.[19] From the tenth until the first half of the thirteenth century the western emperors were of German rather than Frankish origin (the Ottonian, Salian, Guelf and Hohenstaufen families). After 1040 the title *rex Romanorum* was bestowed on the heir to the empire, indicating that he would be the next emperor.[20] However, the king of the Romans was able to attain the rank of emperor only after gaining the approval of the pope, who anointed and crowned him in Rome. As we will see, the ceremony was not a mere formality, but underlay the political and ideological ambitions of the medieval papacy. Frederick II's reign marked a turning point in the history of the western empire – the last major attempt at uniting Germany and Italy in an imperial context and the last significant confrontation between an emperor and the papacy. Afterwards the empire evolved into an elective and essentially central European monarchy. The electoral procedure set up by the Golden Bull of 1356 removed any vestige of papal involvement in making and unmaking emperors. The seven electors were German princes and archbishops; the coronation of 'the King of the Romans and Emperor-Elect' was to be performed in Aachen. The last Holy Roman Emperor to be crowned in Rome was Frederick III in 1452, one year before Byzantium's fall to the Ottomans.

I   CHRISTIAN EMPERORS AND THE ROMAN IMAGERY OF POWER

Christianity proved generally tolerant towards ancient Roman imperial symbols, many of which entered the ideological repertory of the Christian emperors. The new religion dealt with those symbols and with ancient power imagery in three distinct ways. It tolerated the carryover of most of them into the Middle Ages, refashioned some to fit the new religion and abolished only those with compromising pagan associations. When the emperor Constantine I (306–337) became a supporter of Christianity in 312, the Roman empire had already been established for centuries. The

---

[19] Abulafia 1992: 321–39.   [20] Buchner 1963; Barraclough 1950: 16.

Roman emperor was *divi filius* ('son of the divine one'), venerated under various forms in a state-sponsored religious cult in his lifetime and often deified after his death. Since the times of Augustus rulers had borne the title of *pontifex maximus* previously reserved for the highest priest in Rome. Initially the Christian emperors made use of this title, although it was soon abolished by a law of the emperor Gratian (375–383) because of its pagan connotation. Revealingly, however, medieval popes and Latin bishops continued to style themselves occasionally as 'Christian pontiffs' – a sign of the characteristically papal tendency to absorb imperial symbols.[21] The adjective 'divine' was commonly used in Byzantine chancery documents with reference to the emperor and the empire, although it no longer carried the same religious and cultic overtones.[22] The biographer and panegyrist of Constantine I, the Arian bishop of Caesarea Eusebius, took a first important stride towards the explication of the link between the Christian God and the Roman emperor. In an imperial panegyric written in 336 to commemorate thirty years of Constantine's accession, Eusebius wrote that the empire was modelled after God's eternal kingdom. 'Outfitted in the likeness of the kingdom of heaven', the emperor was said 'to pilot affairs below with an upward gaze, to steer by the archetypal form'. Monotheism and monarchy were presented as two closely related concepts and Christianity as the ideal religion for the empire.[23] The political theology of Eusebius was no great innovation, but represented the Christian adaptation of antique Neoplatonic and Neopythagorean political philosophy.[24] His views became a tenet and a commonplace in Byzantine imperial rhetoric throughout the centuries, and were rarely expressed again with the same fullness and subtlety.

The monarchical royal insignia, which increasingly entered the Roman imperial court during the third century and marked a move away from the republican ideal of the *princeps* as a first among equals, proved appealing to the Christian emperors. The pagan emperor Diocletian (284–305), one of the great Christian persecutors, is reported to have taken to wearing a purple robe and a diadem which had been an attribute of Hellenistic kings. He required his subjects to prostrate themselves in his presence or kiss the hem of his robe (*adoratio, proskynesis*).[25] The diadem was to become

---

[21] Kazhdan, 'Pontifex', in Kazhdan 1991: III, 1696, with further references.
[22] See, for example, the references gathered by Hunger 1964: 47–75.
[23] Eusebius 1976: ch. 3, 87.   [24] O'Meara 2003: 145–51. Dvornik 1966: II, 612–22.
[25] Corcoran 2006: 43, with further references. See the reservation of Alföldi 1970: 6–25, according to whom the sources intentionally portrayed Diocletian as an Oriental despot, whereas many of the monarchical insignia had already appeared earlier at the Roman court.

one of the crowns worn by the medieval Byzantine emperors. Starting from the reign of their Christian predecessor Constantine I, it assumed a permanent place in imperial iconography on late Roman and Byzantine coins (sometimes set above the emperor's military helmet).[26]

Another attribute adopted from the Roman emperors and subsequently Christianised was the cross-bearing orb or *globus cruciger*. A symbol of universalist rule, the globe was advertised on Roman imperial coins since the first century AD.[27] The addition of the cross occurred in the Christian empire. Coins struck from the reign of the eastern emperor Theodosius II (408–450) onward depict the ruler holding in his hand the cross-bearing orb.[28] The orb became an ubiquitous symbol of Byzantine imperial rule; its symbolism was apparent and sometimes commented upon. In the sixth century Procopius of Caesarea interpreted the *globus cruciger* held by Justinian I in his famous equestrian statue set on a column in the porticoed square of the Augustaeum (between the Great Palace and the church of St Sophia) as signifying his dominion 'over earth and sea'.[29] When in his imaginary travelogue drawn from authentic sources and dating to the middle of the fourteenth century Sir John Mandeville referred to the fall of the 'golden apple' from Justinian's statue, he interpreted its absence as a 'token that the Emperor has lost a great part of his lordship'.[30] From Byzantium the *globus cruciger* entered also the symbolic repertory of the medieval emperors. While in the eastern empire it may or may not have been a material object, the orb was a real insigne in the West from the beginning of the eleventh century onward.[31]

The ceremony of the triumph and victory ideology represent another case of a Roman imperial ritual being carried over into the medieval imperial setting. The late Roman empire and Byzantium (at times of both minor and great successes on the battlefield) witnessed a flurry of triumphal celebrations on the streets of Constantinople and in the Hippodrome.

---

[26] The diadem is first seen on the coins of Constantine. See Sickel 1905; Deér 1950; Grierson 1968: 80–4; 1973: 127–30; on other types of crown worn in Byzantium, see Kazhdan, 'Modiolos', in Kazhdan 1991: II, 1387–8; McCormick and Kazhdan, 'Crown', in Kazhdan 1991: I, 554–5.

[27] Alföldi 1970: 235–8.

[28] Grierson 1968: 84–6; 1973: 131–3; Grierson and Mays 1992: 75; Papamastorakis 2005.

[29] Procopius, *Buildings*, 1.ii.11 in Dewing 1940.

[30] *The Travels of Sir John Mandeville* in Moseley 1983: 46. The globe had been repaired in 1317 during the reign of Andronikos II Palaiologos (1282–1328). See Nikephoros Gregoras, *Byzantina historia* in Schopen 1829–55: I, 275–7.

[31] Ullmann (1955: 254, n. 3) and Schramm (1958: 24–7, 61–3) have dated the first instance of a western emperor being handed the *globus cruciger* to 1014 (the coronation of Emperor Henry II). The Golden Bull of 1356 mentions the orb as a real object. See Fritz 1972: 83, line 22. On the issue of the existence of imperial orbs in Byzantium, see the contrary opinions of Deér 1961: 70–124 and Grierson 1968: 86; 1999: 73.

This ancient ceremony now featured the novel element of thanksgiving and litanies performed in the church.[32] Under Christian influence the pagan image of the goddess Victory, traditionally depicted on Roman imperial coins, was gradually transformed into a winged angel on Byzantine numismatic issues.[33] Imperial triumphs continued to be celebrated as late as the thirteenth century: Frederick II Hohenstaufen organised an extravagant ceremony in Cremona marking his victory over the Lombard League in 1237;[34] the Byzantine emperor Michael VIII Palaiologos staged a triumph in 1281 after defeating an invading Angevin army at the battle of Berat.[35]

Medieval emperors adopted Roman imperial insignia and ceremonies also without readjusting them to Christian sensitivities. A symbol of Jupiter, the eagle, served as the military standard of the Roman legions. Jupiter's eagle-headed sceptre, the *scipio eburneus*, was displayed on Roman imperial coins and hence on Byzantine numismatic issues struck between the late sixth and the early eighth centuries as well as on western imperial coins of the late tenth and the eleventh century. The imperial eagle was ubiquitous in the coinage of the Hohenstaufen emperors Frederick I and Frederick II.[36] The transformation of the single-headed into a double-headed eagle was a gradual process taking place simultaneously across the Mediterranean and Europe, in which it is difficult to trace mutual influences. The double-headed eagle was of ancient Near Eastern origin; it resurfaced as a royal symbol of the Seljuk sultans and Turkoman emirs on coins and stone reliefs during the twelfth and thirteenth centuries.[37] In the twelfth century it is found on Byzantine sculpture and textiles, becoming an imperial symbol from the thirteenth century onward.[38] At about the same time the double-headed eagle made its way as a royal symbol in the empire of Frederick II. It was officially adopted by Emperor Sigismund (1410–37; king of Hungary since 1387; crowned emperor in 1433) on his seals and became an enduring

---

[32] McCormick 1986: 100–11.   [33] Grierson and Mays 1992: 81–2.

[34] Abulafia 1992: 303–4. The captured *carroccio* of the Lombard League (an ox-drawn cart bearing saints' relics and sacred banners used in battle) was paraded. It was drawn by an elephant from the emperor's menagerie on top of which the emperor's pennant was unfurled.

[35] Angelov 2007: 43, 46.

[36] Grierson 1968: 88. On the western empire, see the online exhibition of the Department of Coins and Medals at the Fitzwilliam Museum, Cambridge: www.fitzmuseum.cam.ac.uk/gallery/eaglesoncoins/eagles_3.html (accessed 25 July 2008).

[37] Spengler and Sayles 1996: 87–90 (coin of Imad al-Din Zengi II, r. 1170–97); Redford 2004: 397, with further bibliography.

[38] Chotzakoglou 1996; Grierson 1999: 85–6, with further references; Lampros 1909. Late Byzantine coins rarely depict a double-headed eagle; it appears more commonly elsewhere: for example, as decoration on the emperor's hassock and as an embroidered image on the garments of the highest-ranking imperial dignitaries.

symbol of Habsburg imperialism.[39] Later in the second half of the fifteenth century the double-headed eagle also emerged as an emblem of the Russian monarchy.[40]

An ancient ritual with imperial overtones carried over into the Middle Ages was that of prostration before the ruler (*proskynesis*, *adoratio*). Also of ancient Near Eastern origin, this gesture of complete submission before authority was known at the court of the pre-Christian Roman emperors.[41] Hence the ritual entered Byzantium where it could take a variety of forms, from full prostration before the emperor to a kiss on his foot or knee, a genuflection, a bow or a simple greeting. The tenth-century *Book of Ceremonies* is replete with reference to ritual *proskynesis* without elaborating on its actual expression.[42] The fourteenth-century Byzantine ceremonial book of Pseudo-Kodinos describes an annual ceremony each Easter when the holders of court titles along with the Genoese *podestà* presented themselves at the palace, kissing the right foot, right hand and right cheek of the emperor.[43] A form of *proskynesis* was also practised in the medieval West, although – and this is significant – the ceremony was characteristic of papal rather than imperial ceremony. The report by the Royal Frankish Annals that Pope Leo III 'adored' Charlemagne after crowning him in 800 remains a unique case and mirrors Byzantine coronation ceremonial, according to which, at least in the tenth century, each imperial dignitary performed *proskynesis* by kissing the knees of the newly crowned emperor. Rather, in the medieval West it was normally the pope who expected the emperor to kiss his feet during the imperial coronation.[44] A history stretching back to late antiquity justified this common gesture of respect and humility before the successors of St Peter. It is understandable that a Greek observer attending the Council of Ferrara-Florence in 1438–9 considered the ritual as being foreign and unacceptable to Byzantine taste. The patriarch of Constantinople Joseph II refused to disembark in Italy until a compromise had been agreed.[45]

[39] Hye 1973.
[40] A double-headed eagle of Byzantine design was adopted on the seals of the Grand Prince of Moscow Ivan III (1462–1505) who in 1472 married Zoe Palaiologina, niece of the late Byzantine emperor. See Obolensky 1971: 364. The immediate inspiration may have come, however, from the seals of the Habsburgs. See Alef 1966.
[41] Alföldi 1970: 45–79.
[42] In general see McCormick, 'Proskynesis', in Kazhdan 1991: III, 1738–9. On the *Book of Ceremonies*, see Guilland 1967: 144–50.
[43] Verpeaux 1966: 234–7.
[44] On the Byzantine coronation ceremony in the tenth century see n. 67 below. On the ritual kissing of the pope's feet see Eichmann 1942: I, 155, 189–90; Ullmann 1955: 146–7, 257, 316.
[45] Laurent 1971: 226, 230, 232, 340, 500.

Since Byzantium enjoyed uninterrupted political continuity with antiquity it was able to inherit Roman imperial symbols that never became known in the West. Consider the *mappa*, a white kerchief tossed as a signal for the beginning of the circus games on the Hippodrome. The *mappa* was originally a badge of consular authority and became an imperial attribute by the sixth century.[46] By the eighth century the *mappa* was transformed into *akakia* (lit. 'without guile'), a pouch full of dust used in ceremonial and shown in pictorial representations of the emperor.[47] According to the commonest interpretation, the *akakia* was a symbol of imperial humility, mortality and subordination to Christ. The fourteenth-century ceremonial book of Pseudo-Kodinos interprets the pouch as showing that the emperor 'does not boast because of the exalted status of his imperial office'.[48] The *mappa-akakia* exemplifies the Byzantine adoption of a Roman secular insigne and its Christianisation over time.

Byzantium's special role in the reception and preservation of the political imagery of empire meant that Constantinople was seen in the eyes of neighbouring or faraway rulers as an authentic repository of symbols of regal or imperial status. In the early Middle Ages the barbarian chieftains and princes who had settled on former imperial territories legitimated their rule through late Roman and Byzantine symbols of power. A few examples of this trend may suffice. The Vandal kings of northern Africa displayed on their coins the Roman figure of Victory.[49] The first extant gold coin-medallion of the Bulgarian rulers portrays the pagan khan Omurtag (816–832) dressed in Byzantine imperial costume and holding a cross-topped sceptre and *akakia*.[50] Charlemagne's chancery adopted from Constantinople the custom of authenticating certain documents by hanging lead seals from them.[51] The western emperor Otto III (r. 983–1002, emperor since 996) received both eastern and western influence, from his mother, the Byzantine princess Theophano, and from the Carolingians. In May 1000 he discovered and opened the tomb of Charlemagne with great reverence and insisted that he should be buried beside him at Aachen.[52]

Byzantium exploited to the utmost the political capital of its uninterrupted imperial continuity and exclusivity. Until the very end of the empire the Byzantine rulers insisted on being the sole legitimate bearers of the title

---

[46] Coins and other artistic media depict the emperor holding it in his hand. See Grierson 1973: 86–7; Grabar 1936: 12, 75.
[47] Grierson 1973: 133; Dagron 2007.   [48] Verpeaux 1966: 201–2.   [49] McCormick 1986: 265.
[50] Jordanov 1976; Oberländer-Târnoveanu 2005. Cf. Georganteli and Cook 2006: 31.
[51] McCormick 1987: 216, with further discussion.
[52] Arnold 1997: 81–90; Görich 1998; Althoff 2003: 102.

of Roman emperors.[53] Diplomatic usages expressed and buttressed this imperial theory. The protocol for official correspondence in the tenth-century *Book of Ceremonies* shows an elaborate notion of a 'family of kings' under the tutelage of the Byzantine emperor. Foreign rulers were referred to as being the emperor's friends and allies, sons or brothers. The adoption of Christianity from Byzantium mattered in this system of 'diplomatic kinship'. Thus, throughout the Middle Ages the rulers of the neighbouring Orthodox Bulgarians were always considered to be the emperor's sons.[54]

Byzantine royal insignia and court titles were invaluable diplomatic tools by which emperors shared their own sense of imperial status with their allies. In the middle of the tenth century the most important insignia were guarded from indiscriminate dissemination outside of the empire's borders. The emperor Constantine VII Porphyrogenitus (913–959) advised his son and heir to the throne to beware of 'the greediness' of the barbarians, whose requests for crowns, imperial vestments and purple-born princesses were to be politely turned down.[55] Yet imperial insignia, including crowns, could be granted selectively to foreign rulers to underline the theoretical suzerainty of the empire. In the sixth century, Armenian satraps were exceptionally permitted to wear the imperial fibula and red boots.[56] Crowns were sent to the Hungarians rulers. The one with portraits of Constantine IX Monomachos, Zoe and Theodora with dancing women may have been looted from Constantinople in 1204; but the crown of St Stephen with portraits of Michael VII Doukas and Hungarian king Geza I was sent from Constantinople between 1074 and 1077 to mark an important marriage alliance.[57] In 1188 the emperor Isaac II Angelos sent to Saladin, sultan of Egypt and a Byzantine ally at the time, imperial vestments and a golden crown, so that he would be 'rightfully a king, with my assistance and God willing'. The evidence from a western source may be exaggerated, yet the idea of power delegation by diplomatic gifts of insignia corresponds to real imperial practices.[58] The granting of court titles to foreign rulers also underscored a sense of imperial superiority. Thus, the title and insignia of an imperial *patricius* were sent as gifts to

---

[53] See Ullmann 1975 regarding an episode during the negotiations for the Union of Ferrara-Florence (1438–9).

[54] Dölger 1953a and b; Ostrogorsky 1956–7.

[55] Constantine Porphyrogenitus, *De administrando imperio*, in Moravcsik 1967: 67–77. Liudprand of Cremona, an ambassador of the western emperor Otto I at the Byzantine court in 968, found his purple garments confiscated at the border of the empire.

[56] Mango 2002: 62.

[57] McCormick and Kazhdan in Kazhdan 1991 (cf. note 26 above). The crown of St Stephen is currently housed in the Hungarian Parliament in Budapest.

[58] Brand 1962: 171.

secure an alliance with Arichis, the Lombard ruler of Salerno in 787.[59] According to a fourteenth-century legend, the emperor Constantine I had rewarded the ruler of the Russians with the court office of *epi tes trapezes* ('attendant at the imperial table') and for this reason the Byzantine emperors could still be considered ranking higher than the Grand Prince of Muscovy.[60] Byzantium made a more frequent and spectacular diplomatic use of its imperial status than the western emperors, who, at least until 1000, had their eyes fixed on Constantinople as an imperial model worth imitating and borrowing from.

2 CHRISTIAN INAUGURATION CEREMONIES

One of the unique ways which enabled the bishops of the Christian church to mould the medieval imperial office was the leading role they played in imperial inauguration ceremony. A variety of symbolic and quasi-legalistic acts and gestures constituted this ceremony, of which coronation was just a single element. The form and political implication of the emperor's ritual inauguration in the church differed substantially in the medieval East and West.[61] The constitutive element in the ceremony of accession of the Christian Roman emperors during the fourth century was their acclamation by representatives of the army and the senate, a surrogate and ritualised 'election.'[62] The emperor's crowning with a torque performed by an army officer, the *campiductor*, normally accompanied the acclamation, and it was usual for soldiers to elevate the acclaimed ruler on a shield.[63] Military torque-crowning is highly unusual when seen in the context of the later development of royal inaugural ceremonial in the Middle Ages; it was not performed by a bishop as would become the norm, nor did it take place in a church context. The patriarch of Constantinople became involved only gradually in inaugural ceremonies. In 457 when the Theodosian dynasty came to an end, the powerful head of the army Aspar, a Gothic general, picked Leo I (457–474), a previously obscure military figure, to be the next

---

[59] Herrin 1987: 424–5.
[60] Nikephoros Gregoras, *Byzantina historia* in Schopen 1829–55: I, 239. For further evidence and discussion see Vasiliev 1932, esp. 353–4.
[61] For a critical comparison of the inauguration ceremonies in the early Middle Ages, see Nelson 1986b.
[62] Jones 1964: I, 321ff.
[63] The custom is usually thought to be of Germanic origin. See Ensslin 1942; McCormick, 'Shield-Raising', in Kazhdan 1991: III, 1888; Walter 1975: 162–3. Raising on a shield as a part of imperial inauguration ritual is attested from the reign of Julian (361–363) until that of Phokas (602–610). It reappears as a standard part of imperial coronation ritual in the Nicaean and the Palaiologan periods (1204–1463).

emperor. In the Hebdomon palace situated in the immediate vicinity of Constantinople, Leo was acclaimed by representatives of the army and a torque was placed on his head. The patriarch is mentioned as being present both at this ceremony and at the ensuing triumphal entry (*adventus*) of the emperor into the capital, but his role at the time appears to have fallen short of performing a coronation.[64]

The patriarch assumed a more prominent position during the accession of the emperor Anastasios I in 491. The protocol in the *Book of Ceremonies* shows that the patriarch said a prayer for the new ruler, invested him with imperial robes and then crowned him with the imperial diadem.[65] The act of coronation took place in the imperial box of the Hippodrome, which had replaced the Hebdomon as the main ceremonial grounds. On this occasion, the coronation by the patriarch followed after Anastasios had been raised on a shield, acclaimed and crowned with a torque by the *campiductor*. The patriarch's act was secondary in sequence and importance, and it was not performed in a church setting. Yet it was a first step with long-term consequences. In the middle of the seventh century the patriarch's coronation of the emperor was permanently transferred to the ambo of the church of St Sophia. From this time onward until the end of the Byzantine empire the patriarch of Constantinople was charged with crowning the senior emperor in a religious setting.

Even when coronations were conducted in the church of St Sophia, however, the ceremonies continued to feature the non-liturgical acclamations of the emperor, a central inauguration rite.[66] The two surviving ceremonial books dating to the tenth and the fourteenth centuries record an interesting testimony. The tenth-century coronation of the senior emperor by the patriarch was followed by the acclamation performed by the crowd inside the church and by *proskynesis* – imperial dignitaries would each come and kiss the knees of the enthroned emperor.[67] The more detailed account in the fourteenth-century ceremonial book describes the acclamation as occurring at the porticoed square of the Augustaeum, where the acclaimers, representatives of the populace of Constantinople, gathered to

---

[64] On the basis of a close reading of the protocol incorporated into the tenth-century *Book of Ceremonies*, Dagron (2003: 60–5 (esp. 63), 80–3 (with further bibliography)) has argued against the traditional view that this is the first attested case of a coronation performed by the patriarch.

[65] See the protocol in Constantine Porphyrogenitus, *De cerimoniis* in Reiske 1829: 423.11–15, where the diadem is referred to as a *stephanos dialithos*. Cf. Dagron 2003: 67.

[66] Dagron (2003: 82) justly considers the coronation ceremony in the year 641 (the accession of Constans II, a child emperor) in St Sophia as a decisive moment in the evolution of the ritual.

[67] On this enigmatically brief model coronation, see Dagron 2003: 54ff. For the text see *De cerimoniis* in Reiske 1829: I, 191–6.

witness the emperor being raised on a shield near the entrance to the Great Palace; afterwards the ecclesiastical ceremony was conducted in St Sophia.[68] A notable element of the inaugural ceremonies influenced by the church was the inclusion of an imperial statement of orthodoxy – first attested at the accession of Anastasios I in 491 – in the form of a declaration signed by the emperor prior to his coronation by the patriarch.[69] The requirement for a pre-coronation statement of orthodoxy was an attempt by the church to seize the opportunity of an ecclesiastical ceremony to try and prevent imperial heresy. For example, the coronation of Emperor Leo III in 717 could be performed only after he made a statement of orthodoxy.[70] This must be set against the recent revival of Monotheletism under Emperor Philippikos (711–713) but it proved to be quite ineffective. When Leo III learned that some bishops and advisors considered that icons led people into idolatry, he had religious images banned and thus plunged the empire into a policy of iconoclasm.

Unlike Byzantium, the ceremonial inauguration of the western emperors was closely bound from the very outset with the papacy and religious ritual. Rather than being a routine ceremony, often performed by a docile churchman, the coronation and anointment of the emperor had a constitutive import, which was enhanced by medieval popes into the power of conferring the imperial title. In a way, the popes followed in the footsteps of early medieval bishops who had developed a rite of royal anointing based on Old Testament models. (The Book of Kings describes ancient Jewish rulers as being divinely anointed with kingship both metaphorically and physically.) First attested among the Visigoths in 672, royal anointing – the ritual of unction with holy oil performed by the senior bishop of the kingdom – became the act of elevation and inauguration to regal power.[71] As a divine mystery, the ritual naturally became subject to multiple interpretations. For example, circles close to kings and emperors were able to argue that royal anointing bestowed on secular potentates a sacral and quasi-priestly aura.[72]

Most importantly, the ceremony gave great powers to those bishops who performed the sacramental ritual, which in the case of the western emperor meant the pope. Before Charlemagne's coronation Pope Stephen

---

[68] Verpeaux 1966: 255–6.   [69] Theophanes 1883: 136. See Charanis 1939: 10; Haarer 2006: 2, 127.

[70] Theophanes 1883: 390.

[71] See Nelson 1986a: 247–57, esp. 253–4, and Nelson 1986b: 264–6. Anointing was more important than the transfer of royal insignia through coronation.

[72] Ullmann 1955: 154–6. It was commonly believed in late medieval England and France that the royal touch had magical curing powers. See Bloch 1973: 38–51 and *passim*.

II had sanctioned the Carolingian usurpation of regal power from the Merovingian dynasty by undertaking a risky journey in 754 to the land of the Franks and anointing Pepin, Charlemagne's father, and his entire family. This act of royal anointing was accompanied by Pepin's oath of friendship and fidelity to the pope.[73] In the course of the ninth century the popes gradually but persistently asserted their sole right to authorise the crowning and anointing of emperors. Pope Leo III's imperial coronation of Charlemagne in 800 bore the marks of an experiment, and contemporary sources report it briefly and with a sense of surprise. Charlemagne himself crowned his son Louis the Pious emperor in 813, and Louis the Pious his son Lothar I in 816. The two coronations were influenced by the Byzantine custom of a father-emperor crowning his son as a junior co-emperor. Yet the popes refused to tolerate this practice. In 816 Pope Stephen IV travelled to Rheims to re-crown and anoint Louis the Pious. In 823 Lothar I himself felt the need to travel to St Peter's to receive the imperial crown from the pope's hands. Notably in 850 Lothar I sent his son Louis II to be crowned and anointed in Rome.[74] Thenceforward the medieval papacy held tenaciously to its right of conferring the imperial insignia and anointing the emperor as well as arbitrating between candidate emperors. Pope Innocent III (1198–1216), one of the strongest medieval popes and a canon lawyer, stated in a decretal that the pope possessed the special right to examine and, if necessary, reject the elected western emperor who came to Rome to be crowned and anointed.[75] Imperial legitimacy was acquired solely through the ceremony in St Peter's. Herein lay the most significant difference between imperial inauguration ritual in the western empire and Byzantium.

It is illuminating to examine the procedure for imperial coronation described in the official papal protocol used during the twelfth century (the so-called *Ordo* C).[76] Upon his arrival at St Peter's the emperor-elect would kiss the pope's feet as a sign of submission and veneration (a ritual derived, as we saw, from the ancient *proskynesis*). Then the emperor-elect would promise under oath to be faithful to the pope and his successors as well as to serve as a protector and defender of the holy Roman church (an oath of subordination not dissimilar to Pepin's of 754). The pope would examine the emperor by a series of questions and answers, in which the

---

[73] Herrin 1987: 370–9; in addition the two parties were bound together in an alliance of spiritual fatherhood, *compaternitas*.
[74] See the analysis of these events in Ullmann 1955: 143–8, 157–66.
[75] See Weiland 1896: 505–6. Partial translation can be found in Tierney 1964: 133–4.
[76] Published in Eichmann 1942: I, 169–80; Elze 1960: 35–47; analysis in Ullmann 1955: 257–61.

emperor would agree to be 'the son of the church' and the pope would informally adopt him by spreading his mantle around him, while the latter would kiss the pope's chest. There would be further examination of the emperor-elect modelled on that of a bishop, which would include a confession of faith. As the ceremony moved towards its culmination, a cardinal bishop would anoint the emperor's right arm and his chest and the pope would hand over the imperial insignia: the ring, the sword and the crown. The setting is that of a mass accompanied with the antiphonal singing of liturgical acclamation (*laudes*). The entire ceremony is imbued with papal hierocratic spirit: the kissing of the pope's feet, the sworn promise of fidelity, and the ritual adoption of the emperor by the pope.[77]

Another ritual conceived in the very same vein is the groom service to the pope (*officium stratoris*). It re-enacted the honour which Constantine I rendered to Pope Sylvester according to the *Donation of Constantine*, a spurious document traditionally dated by scholars to the second half of the eighth century, which justified, among other things, the papal entitlement to use imperial insignia and the crown in particular.[78] The Frankish king Pepin is said to have performed *officium stratoris* in 754 when he met Pope Stephen II at the time of his anointing. *Officium stratoris* to the pope was sometimes performed in a coronation context, although it was not a part of any official *ordo*, as well as during encounters between emperors and popes.[79]

Ecclesiastical rituals with remarkably close western parallels entered late Byzantine coronation ceremonial, yet the differences from the West are instructive. Royal anointing appeared in Byzantium centuries after its invention. The ritual is incontrovertibly attested for the period after 1204, and it is probable that it was introduced under Latin influence after the capture of Constantinople.[80] Another innovation was the clause added to the confession of faith of the emperor which he traditionally signed before his coronation; the emperor declared himself 'to be a faithful and genuine son and servant of the holy church and, in addition, to be its

---

[77] The ritual adoption was dropped in *Ordo* D composed at the time of Pope Innocent III, while the other two elements persisted. See the text in Eichmann 1942: 1, 259–65, and commentary, 265–307.

[78] Notable in the vast bibliography on the *Donation* is Fuhrmann 1966; Huyghebaert 1979. Cf. Fried 2007, for a recent attempt at a revisionist interpretation and a reprinted Latin text. For an English translation see Edwards 2003.

[79] Ullmann 1955: 56, 59, 160. Before his coronation Frederick I Barbarossa served as the pope's groom in Sutri outside Rome, see Fuhrmann 1986: 143–4.

[80] This is the well-argued opinion of Ostrogorsky 1955: esp. 246–52. Cf. Dagron 2003: 275–6. Nicol (1976: 37–52) has pointed to evidence that the ceremony was practised in the twelfth century. See Macrides 1992. The question of when anointing was introduced remains open due to the ambiguity of the available evidence.

defender (*defensor*) and vindicator'.[81] The solemn promise of the emperor-
son of the church is reminiscent of western coronation ceremonial (especially the ritual adoption of the emperor by the pope in *Ordo* C). Even
with the new additions, however, the Byzantine coronation ceremony
lacked a constitutive significance. The official promissory document shows
that in the fourteenth century the emperor bore the imperial title already
before being crowned by the patriarch. In different words, obtaining the
Byzantine imperial office never came to depend on the patriarch's approval
and sanction.[82] The innovations in coronation ceremonial mattered most
in the rich field of political discussion and hierocratic theory that emerged
in the late Byzantine period.[83]

3   EMPIRE BUILDING AND CHRISTIAN INSTITUTIONS

Solidifying the loyalty of bishops was immensely important for the two
medieval empires which by ideology, and often in practice, aspired to
rule large and diverse territories. 'The head bishops' of the empires, the
patriarch of Constantinople and the pope of Rome, did not share the same
status and function. As noted, the emperor always appointed the patriarch
of Constantinople, whom he tended to view as a state functionary. Indeed
the emperors had helped elevate the rank of the patriarch of Constantinople
in the initial formative years of the Christian empire. Unlike other episcopal
sees, Constantinople had no history of being an apostolic foundation.[84] In
381 Emperor Theodosius I and in 451 Marcian and Pulcheria successfully
insisted on the promotion of the see of Constantinople, New Rome, to a
status equal to Old Rome. In this way the bishop of the imperial capital
not only was raised to the same authority as the pope, but also was made
superior to the eastern patriarchates of Antioch, Alexandria and Jerusalem.
The pentarchy of the five great sees could claim to represent the entire
oikoumene as the final arbiter of doctrine, but it was the emperor who
presided at universal councils and exercised a high degree of control over
them all, and thus over the entire Christian structure. In alliance with the
bishop of Constantinople, rulers like Justinian in the mid sixth century
took the lead in imposing theological definitions on the whole body of

---

[81] Verpeaux 1966: 253–4. The introduction of this clause has been dated to the first half of the fourteenth
century by Angelov 2007: 411–12.
[82] See Franz Dölger's perceptive comments on Charanis 1941 in *Byzantinische Zeitschrift*, 43 (1950),
146–7.
[83] Angelov 2007: 384–92, 413–14.
[84] The legend of the Apostle Andrew being the founder of the see of Constantinople is late. See
Dvornik 1958.

Christian believers. He removed Pope Vigilius from Rome, imprisoned him in Constantinople and forced him to sign the acts of the fifth ecumenical council.

By contrast, the papacy had a long history of independent-mindedness. In the early Middle Ages, after Justinian I's reconquest of Rome, the popes found themselves sharing power with a Byzantine governor in the city. They claimed the power to ordain all bishops in the West and developed their own court with a permanent staff, maintaining an efficient administration and keeping excellent records of negotiations. Some of them took up leadership in the city and ruled over the papal lands, especially because Rome's geographical distance from Constantinople (and Constantinople's own military preoccupations) meant that imperial protection against foreign invaders was not always forthcoming. In organising the defences of the city against the Lombards, Pope Gregory I (590–604) proved himself a masterful administrator.[85] Relations with the church in the East were traditionally uneasy because of frequent imperial doctrinal interventions which the popes did not recognise. Iconoclasm marked the decisive shift when eighth-century popes turned for help and protection to the Franks. The recently anointed Frankish king Pepin acted as papal ally when he ceded to the papacy the former Byzantine territories in central Italy (that is, the corridor connecting Rome and Ravenna) which he had taken by conquest. Ecclesiastical rule replaced imperial government at the heart of the ancient empire. The papacy acquired an added reason to press for its universalist claims in western Europe.

A fundamental problem of the early medieval papacy (before and after Charlemagne's imperial coronation) was the unclear procedure of papal election. In theory the electors were 'the clergy and people' of Rome, which led to free interpretations. Many elections were contested as aristocratic factions in the city of Rome jostled for control over the papal office and its resources. The western emperor could claim the right to participate in elections (he, too, was nominally a Roman), while the popes needed protection against their own internal political enemies and Saracen incursions.[86] In the tenth century the Ottonian emperors made determined efforts to win control over Rome. In 961 Otto I entered the city to support the position of Pope John XII, who anointed him as emperor in 962, and although he was drawn back to problems back in Germany, his son Otto II was crowned emperor in Rome at Christmas 967, and Otto III received the imperial crown in 996.[87]

---

[85] Markus 1997.   [86] See in general Noble 1995.   [87] Arnold 1997: 84–9.

The eleventh century marks a decisive shift in the powers and ambitions of the papacy. It was a period of comprehensive reform. The college of cardinals was founded in 1059 and hence the election of the pope was freed from secular intervention, notably that of the emperor. The *Donation of Constantine* was actively used by the papacy at the time, also in disputes with the Byzantine emperors, to assert Petrine primacy. The papal court took on more regal appearance: the pope wore a crown in addition to the tiara, a scarlet mantle and red shoes.[88] He required feudal oaths of loyalty and led armies, famously Leo IX against the Normans of Sicily and southern Italy. Thus the papacy increasingly saw itself as a mirror image of the imperial office.

No lasting power sharing between popes and emperors could be established in the course of the eleventh and twelfth and the first half of the thirteenth centuries. For example, Gregory VII (1073–85), the strongest reformist pope who opposed simony and lay investiture in the empire, excommunicated Emperor Henry IV in 1076 in an attempt to dethrone him, and, despite the latter's famous act of penance at Canossa, provoked civil war in the empire.[89] Frederick II was excommunicated several times; as excommunication proved an ineffectual tool, the council of Lyons in 1245 convoked by Pope Innocent IV declared the emperor deposed from his office, although the latter had been holding the imperial crown for twenty-five years.[90] The problematic relationship between papacy and empire became the central subject of political debate in the later Middle Ages. Each claimed to be universalist, enjoying supremacy over the other. While rival theories were ardently defended by pro-papal and pro-imperial authors, in reality political struggles weakened the power and prestige of both.[91]

By contrast the relations between emperor and patriarch in Byzantium were generally a source of strength for the empire. The relationship was clearly unequal, although it was not antagonistic. A common idea repeatedly articulated throughout the centuries was that of symphony or cooperation between imperial and priestly power, which is voiced, for example, in the preface of Justinian's Sixth Novel.[92] The cooperation can be seen working in practice in the way imperial and patriarchal powers combined their efforts in missions to convert the leaders of non-Christian peoples, such as those in the Balkans (Bulgaria) and later in Russia.

In the West the church took a more independent role in missionary activity, from Gregory I's mission to England in the late sixth century,

[88] Ullmann 1955: 310–43.   [89] Fuhrmann 1986: 58–69; Arnold 1997: 98–100.
[90] Abulafia 1992: 372–4.   [91] Black 1992: 42–84.
[92] See Angelov 2007: 360–1, with further references.

and much of the work of conversion was done by individual holy men, such as Boniface and Anskar. Emperors promoted this pattern, setting up monasteries and bishoprics beyond imperial territory, such as Magdeburg established by Otto I, to further the Christianisation of unknown territory, with a clear sense of subordination to Rome.[93]

The relationship between the emperors and the network of bishoprics on imperial territory presents a different aspect of the institutional role of the church; this relationship was a source of strength for empire-building both in the East and in the West. Christian bishops enjoyed long tenure (they were canonically elected for life) which enabled them to strike roots in local society in ways in which the transient agents of secular authority could not.[94] Hence they were a factor of local power which the imperial government could not ignore and sought to integrate to the maximum possible extent.

In Byzantium the loyalty of ecclesiastics to the emperor was secured in various formal and less formal ways. Canon 84 of the Holy Apostles, which was never recognised in the West, decreed that whoever insulted a king or a ruler should suffer punishment. If the offender was a layman, he was to be excommunicated; if he was an ecclesiastic, he was to be deposed. Thus, insulting the emperor became a punishable offence in the church. The emperor lacked the legal prerogative to elect or ordain bishops, in contrast to his right to pick and invest the patriarch. The custom was that the permanent synod at the patriarchate of Constantinople would elect three candidates, from among whom the patriarch chose the future metropolitan. When in the tenth century the emperor Nikephoros II Phokas (963–969) decided that no ordination of metropolitan bishops (bishops presiding over larger districts to whom the 'simple' bishops were subordinated) should take place unless confirmed by the emperor, the church took the first opportunity to repeal this uncanonical ordinance.[95] However, emperors sought and managed to influence the elections in unofficial ways. In the late eleventh and the twelfth centuries many of the metropolitan bishops were seasoned members of the Constantinopolitan elite recruited from the patriarchal school or the patriarchal bureaucracy. All newly elected bishops were required to present themselves to the emperor and deliver a prayer on his behalf. Furthermore, an agreement of 1380–2 between the patriarchate and the emperor John V Palaiologos (1341–91) stipulated that every new bishop was to make an official promise of fidelity to the emperor. The

---

[93] Dvornik 1970; Reuter 1991: 162–4; Sullivan 1994.
[94] Herrin 1975: 258–9; von Falkenhausen 1997; Rapp 2005: 41–55, 242–89.
[95] Dagron 2003: 310 and n. 106.

emperor was given the right to impose a veto on any of the three candidates proposed to the patriarch for metropolitan election.[96]

The pattern of the relationship between emperors and bishops in the western empire was shaped by the salient characteristics of Charlemagne's political formation. Due to the lack of a strong central bureaucracy, Charlemagne and later western emperors relied heavily on bishops as chief administrative agents in the royal government. Bishops and abbots were given the right to exercise royal justice, and could be granted the control of counties. Upon their investiture by the emperor, the bishops did homage and took an oath of obedience. In return, episcopal churches and imperial monasteries were freed from royal taxation. The imperial church thus benefited economically from being the backbone of royal government.[97]

The emperors' internal ecclesiastical policies were rarely contested by the papacy until the eleventh century, when a series of reformist popes (ironically some of them Germans and initially promoted by the Salian emperors) were elected to the see of St Peter. Following Pope Gregory VII (1073–85) they sought to put into practice their legalistic and ideological claims of ecclesiastical authority in the West. The main accusation against the emperors was their flagrant breach of the canons when they invested a bishop with his staff and ring, the symbols of pastoral authority.[98] Uncanonical simoniac practices (the purchase of ecclesiastical office for money) also provoked the ire of the reformers. The papal-led movement for the eradication of lay investiture and simony led to severe confrontations with emperors and resulted in a compromise solution at the Concordat of Worms in 1122. Bishops were to be chosen by the clergy in the emperor's presence, with the emperor being consulted only in the case of contested elections. Ecclesiastical superiors invested the bishops with the ring and the staff, while the emperors were to invest him with secular privileges and lands, for which bishops were to do homage.[99] Although a concession, the concordat served the main interests of imperial authority. Direct imperial control over the bishoprics was transformed into an indirect one; the emperor could still bring his influence to bear on episcopal elections and use bishops as instruments of government.

In a way, the Carolingian system of an imperial church was never abolished. In the later Middle Ages leading bishops in Germany acted as territorial princes and were involved in choosing the king and emperor-elect

---

[96] See Laurent 1955. Cf. Angelov 2007: 356–7, for a further discussion.
[97] Reuter 1991: 195–9.
[98] Southern 1970: 173–88; Fuhrmann 1986: 33–5; Reuter 1991: 278–86.
[99] Fuhrmann 1986: 92–5; Arnold 1997: 100–3.

of the Romans. According to the Golden Bull of 1356, the archbishops of Mainz, Trier and Cologne were part of the college which was to elect the emperor. Thus the church still continued to maintain an effective constitutional role in the western empire, although it was bishops rather than the pope who exerted influence on the office of the Holy Roman Emperor.

4 IMPERIAL ESCHATOLOGY

The influence of Christianity on medieval imperialism was not limited to ceremonies, institutions and the adaptation and enrichment of ancient symbols of state. Christianity itself fuelled ideas of empire and political universalism through aspects of its teaching about the end of the world. Political eschatology is especially important because of its wide appeal to all levels of society (most prophetic and eschatological texts were composed in lower registers of Greek and Latin) and its ability to shape and stir mass imagination.

Medieval eschatological writings in both East and West were made up of diverse texts reflecting the perspectives and agendas of different authors and time periods. There was much disagreement as to when the end days would come (whether in the year of the Lord one thousand, six thousand of the World or some other time), and the problem was complicated further because of the existence of diverse chronological systems. Central to medieval apocalyptic thought was the Book of Revelation. However, from the point of view of political eschatology, most significant was chapter two of the Book of Daniel and specifically the dream vision of the Babylonian king Nebuchadnezzar (Daniel 2:27–43): the king sees a statue with a gold head, silver chest and arms, bronze middle and thighs, and iron and clay feet which 'a stone cut out not by human hand' breaks and then grows into a great mountain filling the entire earth. According to Daniel's interpretation of the dream, the various parts of the statue were four great kingdoms which would rise in succession, starting with Nebuchadnezzar's golden reign, while the stone which destroys the last kingdom would inaugurate a fifth one which 'will stand forever'. In the Christian apocalyptic tradition Daniel's interpretation of Nebuchadnezzar's dream was closely linked with Christ's Second Coming. The fourth and last of the great empires, which would persist until the end of time, was seen as imperial Rome. The empire thus became part of God's scheme for human salvation. Byzantine authors consistently saw their own empire as Daniel's fourth kingdom.[100] Prophetic eschatological works in Byzantium and

---

[100] Podskalsky 1972.

the West (such as the apocalypse of Pseudo-Methodius, composed in Syriac in the seventh century and subsequently translated into Greek and Latin) interwove into this scheme of salvation the legend of a last Roman emperor, who would inflict a decisive defeat on his enemies and would then surrender his crown to God, ushering in the brief reign of Antichrist.[101] Another eschatological interpretation, which emerged in the Greek East starting with Eusebius in the early fourth century, was that Byzantium was Christ's universal and eternal kingdom on earth, that is, the empire was identified with the fifth extra-historical empire.[102] In the mid ninth century, during an embassy to the kingdom of the Khazars on the Volga river, the Byzantine diplomat and missionary Constantine the Philosopher, the Apostle to the Slavs, later known as St Cyril, was asked why the Roman empire still remained in existence. He is reported to have answered by referring to the Book of Daniel that their empire was not really 'the Roman, but Christ's' eternal kingdom.[103]

The medieval West also knew the eschatological identification of their empire with the fourth great kingdom which would usher in Christ's Second Coming. This interpretation was propagated by various authors, lay and ecclesiastical, during the reigns of the late Carolingian, Ottonian and Hohenstaufen emperors.[104] In the influential apocalyptic scheme of the Calabrian mystic Joachim of Fiore (*c.* 1135–1202) and his followers, ideas about the rise of a last world emperor outlived the Middle Ages, persisting until the seventeenth century.[105] It has been suggested that Charlemagne's imperial coronation may have been timed to coincide with the expected arrival of the year 6000 calculated in accordance with an early medieval chronological system from the beginning of the world. The imminence of the end days would have spurred the elevation of an emperor at a time when the imperial office in Byzantium was considered to have lapsed.[106] Political eschatology played a role even in the idea of Moscow's imperial destiny. When in the early sixteenth century the monk Philotheus of Pskov

---

[101] Alexander 1985: 151ff.

[102] Podskalsky 1972: 11–12 and 16–19. Interestingly, in the late medieval West, Ptolemy of Lucca, a disciple of Thomas Aquinas, saw Christ's extra-historical kingdom as the Christian church. This opinion may be seen as a reflection of the characteristically Augustinian universalist view of Christendom. See Ptolemy of Lucca, *On the Government of Rulers* 3, 10 in Blythe 1997: 176. Cf. 3, 12–13 in 1997: 182–3.

[103] Kantor 1983: 53.

[104] Ullmann 1955: 236–7; Kantorowicz 1957: 292–3 and n. 39 with further bibliography; Larner 1980: 24–5; Classen 1982: 401; Nelson 1988: 234; Arnold 2003: 273–4.

[105] Reeves 1961.

[106] See the chronological and historical arguments of Landes 1988: esp. 196–203. According to the apocryphal *Epistle of Barnabas*, the end of the world was to come at the year 6000.

first declared that Moscow was the Third Rome which had risen on the ashes of the two fallen ones, he did so in an apocalyptic context – the third Rome was a 'prelude to the kingdom to which there shall be no end'.[107]

CONCLUSION

In general, the question posed at the opening of this chapter has been answered positively. Christianity and the organisation of the church served to consolidate medieval empires, more so in the East than in the West. Christian belief proved able to strengthen the medieval empires both politically and ideologically. During the reign of the first Christian emperor Constantine I an effective effort at accommodation between empire and religion can be observed. Constantine and his successors in the fourth and the fifth centuries adapted many of the symbols of empire to a more Christian interpretation, although Christianity only exercised a haphazard influence. Constantine's biographer, Eusebius, formulated an imperial political theology and eschatology which became very influential in the Greek East. Throughout the Middle Ages, both in the East and in the West, hopes for other-worldly salvation could be related to the fate of empires and the rise of emperors. Another important sign of Christian influence on empire at the ideological level was the religious act of imperial inauguration – right from the start in the West and evolving gradually in this direction in Byzantium.

Byzantium played a special and important role in maintaining alive and enriching Roman imperial traditions. The eastern empire remained an authentic repository of imperial symbols of state in the eyes of foreign powers, especially during the early Middle Ages. Medieval rulers with imperial and humbler ambitions eagerly sought to import these symbols from Byzantium. Cross-fertilisation could go both ways, however, as witnessed by the adoption of royal anointing.

The main difference in the impact of Christianity on the two medieval empires was the powerful role of the papacy in the creation and conferral of the western imperial title. Indeed the bishop of Rome saw himself as the heir to Roman imperial rights and insignia. In this way the papacy became a third medieval 'empire', an empire more notional than real, which maintained an uneasy coexistence with the other two. While the papacy played a strong part in both creating and weakening the western

---

[107] Obolensky 1971: 366. This doctrine, however, was never endorsed by the Russian state at the time. See Meyendorff 1981: 274.

empire, there was no equivalent development in the East. Byzantium's fatal weakness in its last centuries was due not to confrontations with churchmen, but mainly to aristocratic infighting and invading foreign powers. Yet the imperial heritage of Byzantium was just as strong and long-lasting as the Roman traditions of the West. In their transformed Christian guise, Roman imperial patterns of rule proved viable well into the modern era and in the long run inspired modern imitators, such as Napoleon and nineteenth-century Russian tsars.

CHAPTER 7

Khan, caliph, tsar and imperator: the multiple identities of the Ottoman sultan

Dariusz Kołodziejczyk

From the beginnings of the Ottoman state around 1300, both its official chroniclers and foreign observers stressed its Islamic identity. Osman, the dynastic founder, was presented as an exemplary Muslim warrior – a *gazi*, who owed his triumph and conquests to the religious enthusiasm of his own and his followers. This view, based on the late medieval Ottoman literary tradition, was perpetuated in twentieth-century historiography by a prominent European scholar, Paul Wittek.[1]

For Christian Europe, the Muslim 'Turk' long played the role of 'the most familiar enemy', both admired and dreaded. According to a modern anthropologist, early modern Europeans 'organized' their neighbouring world by attributing to the Ottoman realm all the features of an imaginary *Gegenwelt*.[2] The recent career of Samuel Huntington's bestseller *The Clash of Civilizations* shows that such a bipolar image still resonates forcefully within Western political discourse. Authors who stress parallels and shared symbols between the Christian and Muslim worlds, even though their views are deemed 'politically correct', can hardly compete with the popular impact enjoyed by the like of Huntington or Oriana Fallaci.

In fact, within the entourage of the first Ottoman rulers we find numerous Christians who could hardly be suspected of sharing the ideals of Jihad. The heterogeneous nature of the Ottoman ruling class in the fourteenth and early fifteenth centuries, studied by Heath Lowry, led him to challenge the *gazi* theory and to describe the early Ottoman state as a 'predatory confederacy' wherein the elites of conquered lands were subsumed rather than destroyed.[3]

---

[1] Wittek 1938.   [2] Harbsmeier 1994: 123–69.

[3] Lowry 2003: 5–94 and 131–43, esp. 57 and 90. Admittedly, in his more recent study Lowry concedes that, driven by polemical fervour, he might have overemphasized the role of booty and slaves and underestimated genuine religious feelings as the motivating factor of many an Ottoman warrior; see Lowry 2008: 9, n. 28. The image proposed by Lowry in his book from 2003 is somewhat uncritically

The Ottoman conquest of Constantinople, in 1453, posed a further challenge to the Ottoman sultan's Islamic self-image. Even though Mehmed II did his best to convert the Byzantine capital into a model Muslim city, he could hardly resist the siren call of the ancient empire, founded centuries before the birth of Prophet Muḥammad. The sultan's infatuation with the Byzantine past is best reflected by his adoption of a new title: 'the ruler of the two seas and the two continents' (referring to the Black Sea, the Mediterranean, Europe and Asia).[4] The Conqueror's great grandson, Süleyman the Magnificent, used to arrange solemn parades consciously modelled on ancient Roman triumphs and commissioned his court architect, Sinan, to construct a mosque that would equal the splendour of the famous Byzantine church of Hagia Sophia.[5]

Yet, at the same historical juncture, the impressive Ottoman conquests in Asia and Africa, obtained in the early sixteenth century, reinforced the sultan's Islamic identity. With the acquisition of Damascus (1516), Cairo (1517) and Baghdad (1534), three centres of Muslim learning and former seats of caliphate were included into the Ottoman realm. The sultan's name came to be invoked in the sermons (*khutbe*) pronounced during the Friday prayer in the most holy Muslim cities: Mecca, Medina and Jerusalem. The influx of graduates of religious colleges from the Arab lands, who looked for career opportunities in the Ottoman capital, and the need to legitimize the sultan's reign among his new Muslim subjects, led to a conscious 'Islamization' or 're-Islamization' of Ottoman laws.[6]

Moreover, the fervent military and ideological confrontation between the Ottomans and the Safavids, who introduced Shi'ism as the official religion in Iran, prompted the sixteenth-century Ottoman rulers to stress their Sunni Muslim orthodoxy more strongly than their predecessors had done. The German term *Konfessionalisierung*, coined by Heinz Schilling and referring to the enforcement of confessional and social discipline in

---

accepted by Karen Barkey in her otherwise valuable sociological study of Ottoman imperial statecraft. Barkey seems to under-rate the role of Islam in the early Ottoman state and presents Ottoman rulers as quasi-modern 'rational' managers who manipulated with religion almost at will, alternatively invoking or ignoring Islamic slogans in order to gain support from one social group without alienating the other; cf. Barkey 2008: esp. 27, 32 (a polemic with Colin Imber who, in turn, seems to overemphasize the role of the Islamic law in the Ottoman politics), 99 and 105. Although the present author shares the admiration for the pragmatism and tolerance of early Ottoman rulers, by presenting them as religiously indifferent one risks ignoring the psychological realities that influenced the behaviour of medieval and early modern humans; nor is one able satisfactorily to explain the fact that many a sultan composed intimate religious poetry or even contemplated (like Murad II in 1444) adopting the ascetic life of a dervish.

[4] Cf. Kafadar 1995: 152.   [5] Cf. Necipoğlu 1989: 407–9; Günay 1998: 52.
[6] See İnalcık 1992; cf. Kafadar 1995: 153–4.

early modern states of Protestant and Catholic Europe, seems equally useful if applied to early modern states of the Muslim Middle East.

Heath Lowry may be right in regarding the Ottoman conquest of the heartlands of the Islamic world in 1516–17 as 'a major fault line in the history of the six hundred year polity'.[7] Karen Barkey concurs that a decisive shift from multi-religiosity towards the Sunni Islamic orthodoxy occurred in the Ottoman collective identity in the sixteenth century, resulting in the construction of 'the other' and the rise of more rigid boundaries between Muslims and non-Muslims, redefined as rulers and ruled, respectively.[8] Still, even if after the conquest of the Arab, predominantly Muslim, lands the Ottoman rulers became less tolerant and less pragmatic, they could not lose from sight millions of their subjects who remained non-Muslims and whose alienation would be undesirable and dangerous. The sultan's manifestation of power, reflected in institutions, art and political language, was intended for both his Muslim and non-Muslim subjects. Likewise, in their international diplomacy and external propaganda, the Ottomans addressed not only Muslims, but Christians as well. The latter were expected to tremble before the sultan's military might, but also to acknowledge his symbolic and legal right to universal rule. This chapter focuses on some aspects of the Ottoman self-image reflected in the sultan's official titles.

SULTAN, KHAN, SHAH AND CALIPH

In their official documents, Ottoman rulers adopted multiple titles which reflected different Middle Eastern and Central Asian traditions, Islamic as well as pre-Islamic. Paradoxically, the Arabic term *sultan*, most commonly used today in reference to the Ottoman ruler, was the least prestigious as it could refer to any sovereign Muslim ruler. Nevertheless, it was extensively used along with other titles and the solemn inscription *as-sultan ibnu's-sultan* ('the sultan, son of the sultan') figured on Ottoman coins.

Although the Ottomans could not claim Genghisid descent, the Turco-Mongolian title of khan (*han*) figured prominently in their documents, solemn inscriptions, and most notably the official monogram (*tughra*) that served to legitimize documents issued on behalf of the sultan.[9] Used along with its Turkic variant, khakan (*hakan*), the title stressed

[7] Lowry 2008: 7.

[8] Barkey 2008: 63–4 and 71–2. Invoking the terminology developed in social sciences by Ronald Burt, Barkey defines the early Ottoman rulers as successful brokers between heterogeneous socio-ethno-religious groups and ascribes their political success to their flexibility and pragmatism; see 2008: 45.

[9] For the inscriptions of Ottoman *tughras*, see Umur 1980.

the Ottoman ruler's imperial ambitions and his claim to dominate the vast steppe area extending from the Black Sea to Central Asia. The Ottomans in fact controlled western parts of the former Ilkhanid empire and reduced the Crimean khans, the last ruling Genghisids who claimed the heritage of the Golden Horde, to vassalage. The appeal and prestige of the Genghisid dynasty was so great that in the seventeenth century Ottoman statesmen seriously regarded the Crimean Girays as potential successors of the Ottoman dynasty in the case of the latter's extinction or deposal.[10]

Another title, commonly encountered in the *tughra*s, was the Persian pre-Islamic title of shah (*şah*). Its more solemn variant, padishah (*padişah*), was perhaps the favourite title of Ottoman rulers. It was almost exclusively reserved for the Ottoman emperor, as the Ottoman chancery rarely and unwillingly addressed foreign monarchs as padishahs. The Habsburg emperors were consequently denied this title and addressed merely as the 'kings of Vienna' (*Beç kıralı*). Even the Treaty of Zsitvatorok (1606), long regarded by historians as the turning point in the relations between Istanbul and Vienna, did not bring the Habsburgs a formal recognition as peers from the side of the Ottoman chancery.[11] Similarly, the Spanish Habsburgs, the Ottoman archrivals in the Mediterranean, were addressed merely as 'the kings of Spain' (*İspanya kıralı*).[12] Only the French kings, valued in Istanbul as trusted allies against the Habsburgs, were granted the title of padishah, first in the correspondence of grand viziers, and from the 1540s in the letters issued on behalf of Ottoman sultans.[13] Requests of other European monarchs, even those of a friendly disposition towards the Porte, to be treated as equals and titled as padishahs were openly rejected or ignored.[14]

---

[10] İnalcık 1965: 1113.   [11] Köhbach 1992. On this issue, see also below.

[12] Admittedly, a document of the Hispano-Ottoman armistice of 1581, published by Susan Skilliter, refers to Murad III and Philip II as 'the two padishahs' (*iki padişahlar*), but its copy extant in the British Library is a bilingual draft (Italian and Ottoman Turkish), negotiated between an Ottoman second vizier and a Spanish ambassador. A formal instrument, corroborated by the Ottoman chancery, would probably have looked different and employed another terminology; see Skilliter 1971: 492–4 and 501; the document is also discussed in Kołodziejczyk 2000: 47–9. Still, at least Siyavush Pasha, the Ottoman second vizier who negotiated the draft of 1581, consistently treated the Ottoman and Spanish monarchs as peers. In 1583, having advanced to the post of grand vizier, he commissioned an illuminated manuscript, whose miniatures have been recently studied by Baki Tezcan. Tezcan persuasively identifies two kings, one Muslim and one Christian, depicted in a miniature, with Murad III and Philip II; the rulers are depicted in full symmetry and at the same size, in contrast to the Ottoman iconographic tradition where the figure of the sultan is usually larger than any other figure; see Tezcan 2011. For another variation of this pattern, see the discussion by Ebba Koch of Mughal–Safavid relations in the following chapter of this volume.

[13] Köhbach 1992: 224, n. 5.

[14] For instance, a Polish envoy dispatched to Istanbul in 1597 was instructed to demand that the sultan address the king as a 'padishah' (Pol. *patysza*); the request did not bring any visible result in the ensuing correspondence between Istanbul and Warsaw; see Kołodziejczyk 2000: 127.

In their relations with Muslim rulers, the Ottomans were no more disposed to treat their correspondents as peers. The Persian shahs were commonly labelled as Shi'ite heretics and usurpers, especially during frequent Safavid–Ottoman wars, which were accompanied by persecutions of Shi'ites in the Ottoman realms. Other Muslim rulers, such as the khans and emirs of Central Asia or the sultans of Acheh (in Sumatra), typically asked for Ottoman military assistance against common enemies – respectively Persian and Portuguese – and readily accepted a subordinate position as Ottoman clients. The greatest challenge came from India, whose rulers, the Great Mughals, reigned over territories comparable to if not exceeding in size and population the ones controlled by the Ottoman sultans. Moreover, the Mughals were Sunni Muslims, who could compete with the Ottomans as patrons for all the Muslims of the Indian Ocean and even claim the right of patronage over Mecca. An Ottoman admiral, Sidi Ali Reis, left a fascinating account of his adventures and travels in the Indian Ocean and India, where he was solemnly received at the Mughal court in Delhi. Upon hearing the admiral's description of Sultan Süleyman's might, Emperor Humayun reportedly commented that the Ottoman ruler was 'surely the only man worthy to bear the title of padishah . . . he alone and no one else in all the world'.[15] Yet, when reading this report one must keep in mind that, firstly, by boasting of his diplomatic skills in extolling his patron's position, the author tried to appease Süleyman's expected wrath related to the fact that the admiral had lost his fleet and returned to Istanbul empty handed; secondly, Humayun had recently returned to Delhi, after numerous years in exile, and was too busy quelling domestic rebellion to challenge the distant Ottoman rival. Already Humayun's son and successor, Akbar, had infuriated Murad III by sending alms to Mecca without having consulted the Ottoman sultan first.[16] In the seventeenth century, especially during the reign of Aurangzeb, the conflict between Istanbul and Delhi regarding the leadership of the Sunni Muslim world was even more tense. When Süleyman II asserted the Ottoman primacy over all Muslim monarchs in his letter addressed to Aurangzeb in 1689, the incensed Great Mughal refused to send a return embassy to Istanbul.[17]

This Ottoman–Mughal conflict was closely related to the issue of another title, namely that of caliph. The Ottomans did not descend from the Prophet's tribe, the Quraish, and this sole fact nullified their claim to the caliphate in the eyes of more rigid Sunni scholars. A later legend, according

---

[15] Sidi Ali Reis 1975: 53; cf. Farooqi 1989: 16.   [16] Farooqi 1989: 118.
[17] Farooqi 1989: 65–9 and 201.

to which the last Abbasid caliph at the Mamluk court willingly relin-
quished his title in favour of Sultan Selim I after the latter's conquest of
Syria and Egypt, in 1517, has proved spurious.[18] Nevertheless, a number of
prominent early modern Muslim lawyers within and outside the Ottoman
empire, including Süleyman's grand vizier, Lutfi Pasha, and famous mufti,
Ebu's-su'ud, asserted the Ottoman sultan's title to the caliphate and his
claim to rule over the whole Muslim world. The claim was strengthened
by the Ottoman sultans' control over the Muslim holy cities of Mecca,
Medina and Jerusalem, and their victories against the infidels that continued until the seventeenth century.[19] Paradoxically, the Ottoman claim to
the caliphate found widest international recognition in the last 150 years
of the empire's existence. In 1774, Russian diplomats softened Istanbul's
resistance to the idea of granting independence to the Crimean khanate (in
fact the move facilitated its annexation to Russia that followed in 1783)
by assuring the sultan that his spiritual prerogatives as the caliph would
remain in force with regard to its Muslim inhabitants. Other European
powers followed this pattern, even as late as the twentieth century. In 1912,
after Italy annexed Tripolitania, the Ottoman sultan retained the formal
right to appoint the chief justice (*cadi*) of Tripoli. The popularity of the
Ottoman sultan-caliph simultaneously rose among the Muslims of Asia
and Africa, both inhabitants of former Ottoman provinces annexed by
colonial powers (e.g., French Algeria), and foreign Muslims whose own
states had been reduced by European colonialism (e.g., British India or
Russian Turkestan).[20] During the First World War, a weekly newspaper
bearing the name *al-Jihad* (*El Dschihad*) was published in Berlin by the
German authorities. Addressed to Muslim prisoners of war originating
from the British, French and Russian armies, it summoned them to join
the holy struggle against the infidels under the standard of the Ottoman
sultan-caliph, hand in hand with his German allies.[21]

On the ideological level, the sultan claimed his authority, not just over
the Sunni Muslims, but over all mankind. This claim is reflected by
the inscription engraved over the portal of the Süleymaniye Mosque in

[18] Farooqi (1989), 181–3 and 208–9, n. 47. This legend was already current in the seventeenth century
and further popularized by Ignatius Mouradgea D'Ohsson, an Armenian dragoman in Swedish
service, in his book published a century later. Even though spurious, it proved useful in legitimizing
the Ottoman claims both at home and abroad.
[19] İnalcık 1993: 78–80; Imber 1997: 104–6; Karateke 2005: 26–31.
[20] For an authoritative study of the late Ottoman state ideology and the use of panislamism as an
effective tool in domestic and foreign policy, see Deringil 1998.
[21] The newspaper was published in two language versions, Arabic and Russian, in the years 1915–18.
Later on, a Tatar version was issued as well.

Istanbul, referring to Sultan Süleyman as 'the caliph, resplendent with Divine Glory, who performs the command of the Hidden Book and executes its decrees in [all] regions of the inhabited quarter [i.e., inhabited portion of the earth]'.[22] The effectiveness of such propaganda is proven by the fact that in the following century similar wording was used in reference to the Ottoman ruler by the Crimean khan, who wanted to intimidate his Christian neighbours by extolling the power of his patron. In the peace instrument of Khan Islam III Giray, sent to the Polish king in 1649, the Ottoman sultan is referred to as 'the prosperous padishah of the inhabited portion of the earth' (*sa'adetlü padişah-i rub'-i meskun*).[23] The cosmic dimension of the sultan's rule is further reflected by his titles *sahib-kıran* ('the lord of the fortunate [planetary] conjunction') and *hüdavendigâr* ('lord' or 'creator of the world'; interestingly enough, the same title was used in reference to God).

The sultan's imaginary rule extended far beyond the actual reach of Ottoman troops and even beyond the borders that the Ottomans had themselves formally acknowledged and demarcated. When, after the Ottoman–Polish war of 1672–6 was formally concluded with a peace in 1678, the commissioners from both sides worked out a formal line of demarcation in 1680, the Ottoman Turkish version of the protocol contained a telling preamble that invoked the omnipotence of God and alluded to the temporary character of all human borders. It followed with an Arabic saying (*hadith*) of Prophet Muḥammad, promising that sooner or later all the lands of unbelievers would be open to the Muslim warriors.[24] In sum, though the document deals with borders, one should not treat them too seriously since only God may hand out kingdoms to the rulers in this world.[25]

CAESAR, TSAR, BASILEUS AND IMPERATOR

Having enumerated the major titles of the Ottoman ruler deriving from the Central Asian and Near Eastern traditions, one may focus now on

---

[22] See Imber 1997: 75; for the original text in Ottoman Turkish, see Çulpan 1970: 293–4 and ill. 1.

[23] See Kołodziejczyk 2011: 960 and 962 (English translation).

[24] سيفتح عليكم الامصار ('[and] the cities [of unbelievers] will be open to you'); see Kołodziejczyk 2004: pt 1, 454 and 495 (English translation).

[25] The preamble, entered in a copy intended for an Ottoman domestic audience, is conspicuously missing in another copy which was given to the Polish commissioners. The reason for its absence in the second copy is clear: although the demarcation formally crowned the Ottoman–Polish reconciliation, the preamble still referred to the 'giaours' in offensive language and announced that the victorious march of Islam would never cease. For a further analysis of the Ottoman attitude towards their frontiers with the infidels, see Kołodziejczyk 2012.

the aspects of his identity that can be labelled as Greco-Roman. One of the titles of the Ottoman ruler was 'the sultan of the sultans of the East and the West' (*sultan-i selatin-i şark ve garb*).²⁶ Eastern and Western traditions were typically mixed in the Ottoman political vocabulary and symbolically united in the person of Alexander the Great (*İskender Du'l-karneyn*, lit. 'Alexander, lord of two horns'), the ruler and warrior with whom the Ottoman sultans liked to compare themselves.²⁷ Two other great ancient heroes of the West and the East, Caesar (*Kayser*) and Cyrus²⁸ (*Kisra*, i.e., Khosru, Khusraw or Chosroes), figured no less prominently in the Ottoman symbolic pantheon. In their megalomania, the Ottomans even placed themselves above the former two heroes. In the sixteenth century, the great mufti Ebu's-su'ud referred to Sultan Süleyman as 'Chosroes of Chosroeses' and 'Caesar of Caesars', and even 'the breaker of Caesars' and 'the one who casts dust in the faces of Chosroes and Caesar'.²⁹ In 1623, in the treaty instrument ('*ahdname*) sent by Sultan Mustafa I to King Sigismund III Vasa of Poland, the sultan referred to 'our court, the refuge of sultans and the seat of felicity which feeds the lips of the Caesars of the epoch and is thronged by the mouths of the Khusraws of the age' (*dergah-i selatin-penah ve bargah-i sa'adet-destgahımız ki mukıt-ı şifah-i Kayasire-i zaman ve müzdaham-i hayat-i Ekasire-i devrandır*).³⁰

In 1538, the Ottoman troops, headed in person by Sultan Süleyman, conquered the Moldavian fortress of Tighina, which was duly renamed as Bender. In the memorial inscription, left by the conquerors in the fortress and preserved until today, Süleyman refers to himself as 'the shah of Baghdad and Iraq, the Caesar of Rome and the sultan of Egypt' (*şeh-i Bagdad ve 'Iraq kayser-i Rum Mısra sultanım*).³¹ The triple identity of the Ottoman sultan is also expressed in the *intitulatio* of Sultan Ahmed I (r. 1603–17), who referred to himself as 'the lord of the fortunate conjuction of [i.e., ruling over] the Roman, Persian, and Arab kingdoms' (*sahib-kıran-i memalik-i Rum ve 'Acem ve 'Arab*),³² whereas Sultan Mehmed IV (r. 1648–87) referred to himself as 'the one who issues orders to the Roman,

---

²⁶ Kołodziejczyk 2000: 329 and 339 (English translation).

²⁷ On the eve of his conquest of Cairo in 1517, Selim I announced in his letter sent to the last Mamluk sultan Tumanbay: 'I shall become the possessor of the East and West, like Alexander the Great'; see Karateke 2005: 25.

²⁸ The Arabic term *Kisra*, identical with the Persian-Ottoman *Hüsrev*, derived from the Achaemenid king Cyrus the Great (d. 529 BC) but with time began to refer to any Persian king; it was often associated with the last powerful Sasanid king, Khusraw the Just (d. AD 579).

²⁹ Imber 1997: 75.

³⁰ Kołodziejczyk 2000: 390 and 396 (English translation). The terms *Kayasire* and *Ekasire* are Arabic plurals of *Kayser* and *Kisra*, respectively.

³¹ Guboglu 1958: 133 and 167 (facsimile 8).

³² Kołodziejczyk 2000: 329 and 339 (English translation).

Arab, and Persian kingdoms' (*ferman-ferma-yi memalik-i Rum ve 'Arab ve 'Acem*).[33]

In his *Monetary History of the Ottoman Empire*, Şevket Pamuk observes the striking Ottoman conservatism reflected in preserving local pre-Ottoman currency systems in the newly conquered territories. Hence, while the silver *akçe*, originally patterned on the Byzantine *asper*, dominated in Rumelia and western Anatolia, in Syria, Egypt and Yemen the Ottomans continued to mint a local silver coin named *medin* or *para*, and in the former Safavid lands in Iraq, Transcaucasia and eastern Anatolia the standard currency remained the silver *şahi*, although in 1555 it was officially renamed as *padişahi*, to distinguish it from the Persian Safavid coin.[34] Probably not by accident, the three large zones of the *akçe, para* and *şahi* roughly coincided with 'the Roman, Arab and Persian kingdoms' enumerated in the formal *intitulatio* of Ottoman sultans.

It is well known that Turkish newcomers to Asia Minor adopted the Byzantine term *Rom/Rum* while referring to their own states – first the Seljuk and then the Ottoman sultanates. Turkish bureaucrats and soldiers, sent to rule over Egypt and Arabia in the sixteenth to eighteenth centuries, were invariably referred to as 'Romans' (Arabic plural *Arwam*) by the local Arab historiographers. In the Indian Mughal chronicles, the Ottoman sultan was likewise referred to as the 'Roman emperor' by such titles as *khawandkar-i Rum* ('the lord of Rome'), *sultan-i Rum* ('the sultan of Rome') or *qaiser-i Rum*.[35] The last term – *qaiser* or *kayser* – is especially telling as it derived from Julius Caesar and had been used by the Roman and Byzantine emperors. The title *kayser-i Rum* ('Caesar of Rome'), assumed by Mehmed II after the conquest of Constantinople, became an integral part of his and his descendants' *intitulatio*.[36]

A scholar studying the Ottoman rule over non-Muslims, especially in the Balkans, still encounters highly emotional attitudes towards the Ottoman past, embedded in the nineteenth- and twentieth-century national historiographies. The notion of the 'Turkish yoke', still omnipresent in the collective imagination of many a Balkan nation, implies that for over 600 years of its existence the Ottoman state was regarded as alien and hostile by its Christian subjects.[37] Yet, in their theory and political practice, the Ottomans carefully exploited imperial ideology aiming to appease and win

---

[33] Kołodziejczyk 2000: 477 and 483 (English translation).
[34] Pamuk 2004: 89–104 and esp. map 1. Pamuk distinguishes further monetary zones within the empire such as the Crimean, Tunisian and Persian Gulf ones, where the common units were the Crimean *akçe*, the *nasri* and the *lari*, respectively, but these zones were of lesser size and importance.
[35] Farooqi 1989: 200.   [36] İnalcık 1991: 979.
[37] Some of the arguments and examples quoted below are treated more extensively in Kołodziejczyk 2006.

the loyalty of their new subjects, both Muslim and non-Muslim. To quote Antony Black: 'Ottoman ideology oscillated between the concept of the Sultan as emperor ruling over diverse peoples and faiths and the concept of him as Caliph of Muslims.'[38] According to Black, balancing between Islamic rectitude and a more pragmatic, patrimonial system which enabled different cultural groups to coexist peaceably was characteristic of other Islamic empires as well, for instance the Indian Mughals, to mention only one prominent example.[39] In similar fashion, Karen Barkey sees a lasting controversy between the early Ottoman version of Islam, promoted by the Sufi orders, which was 'open, syncretic, and tolerance based', and the later scripturalism that called for a strict application of the Shari'a and was gradually espoused by the Ottoman administration in the sixteenth and seventeenth centuries.[40] Ottoman tolerance, it is worthwhile emphasizing, unfolded in a context of empire and hierarchical submission (cf. our comments in the opening chapter).

Having entered the Balkans, the Ottomans encountered the Slavic title of tsar (Cyrillic *цар*), first used by Slavic writers in reference to Byzantine emperors and then adopted by a number of Bulgarian and Serbian monarchs.[41] As in the case of the Latin *Caesar* or the Greek Καίσαρας, the Slavic title *C[es]ar* derived from Julius Caesar and referred to an emperor. Hence, no wonder that the Ottoman chancery, which issued numerous documents in Serbian in the fifteenth and early sixteenth centuries, adopted the Slavic term for the Ottoman ruler. Ottoman documents composed in Serbian, issued on behalf of Mehmed II, Bayezid II and Selim I, typically referred to the sultan as 'the great and mighty tsar'.[42]

More importantly, the sultans were referred to as tsars by their Christian Slavic subjects. Few early texts by Bulgarian Orthodox clergymen, containing references to their Ottoman rulers, have survived to our days.[43] Typically, these are just margin notes, written by copiers or readers of

[38] Black 2001: 271.   [39] Black 2001: 350.

[40] Barkey 2008: 163. An especially puritanical version of Islam was promoted in the seventeenth century by the Kadızadeli movement, whose prominent representative, Vani Mehmed Efendi, exerted much influence on the Ottoman domestic as well as foreign policy in the second half of the seventeenth century.

[41] Cf. Grala 1996: 158–60.

[42] Köhbach 1992: 232; the expressions *veliki car, silni car* or *veliki i silni car* can be found in numerous documents of Mehmed II, Bayezid II and Selim I, composed in Serbian and preserved in the originals in the State Historical Archives in Dubrovnik; see Stojanović 1934: 241–71, 284–342, 386–93; some of these documents have been published in French translation in Bojović 1987; for the Serbian *intitulatio* of Sultan Selim I, preserved in his ferman sent in 1514 to Dubrovnik [Ragusa], see also Elezović 1932: 6–7 (a facsimile is provided).

[43] Kacunov 1996; Načev and Fermandžiev 1984.

religious manuscripts. In 1476 a Bulgarian priest, Stefan, characterized Mehmed II as 'the ill-fated, bad-tempered and greedy Judas tsar Mehmed Beg, whose glory ascended to heaven but who will not escape descending to hell'.[44] Selim II was described, not unexpectedly, as 'tsar Selim, a bloodthirsty lustful wine-drinker'.[45] Yet, other notes are neutral (e.g., 'in the days of the Turkish tsar, Sultan Ibrahim'[46]) or even laudatory. In 1469, the deacon Vladislav (known as Vladislav Gramatik) dated his manuscript 'in the days of the great and autocratic Muslim tsar, the emir Mehmed Beg'.[47] Though hardly enthusiastic towards Ottoman rule, the Bulgarian writers – at least some of them – apparently got accustomed to their Ottoman sovereigns and no longer treated the sultans as alien usurpers and newcomers.

On the eve of the Ottoman conquest, the most common Greek monarchic title of the Byzantine emperor was not *Kaisar* (Καίσαρ) but *basileus* (βασιλεύς). In analogy to the use of the title *car* in his documents composed in Serbian, Sultan Bayezid II adopted the title βασιλεύς in his documents issued in Greek.[48] The practice was continued by Selim I and Süleyman, as is evidenced by their documents in Greek addressed to the Venetian doges.[49] It is worth noting that in the following centuries Greek writers referred to their Ottoman Muslim rulers with the very same title. Synadinos, a seventeenth-century Orthodox priest from Serres, accused his Greek compatriots that, owing to their sins, the imperial crown of Constantine had been taken by strangers,[50] but nonetheless he referred to the Ottoman sultans with the Greek royal title of βασιλεύς, thus giving them a kind of legitimacy.[51] In his memoirs, Synadinos deplored the assassination of Osman II (1622), describing him as a young and promising ruler,[52] and highly praised the latter's younger brother, Murad IV, known for his strict measures against corruption. The Greek priest recorded the outburst of

---

[44] 'В дните на злочестивия и злонравия, и ненаситния Юда Мехмед-бег цар, който се въздвигна до небесата, и който ще се снизи в ада': Načev and Fermandžiev 1984: 61.

[45] 'Писах в дните на царя Селима, кръвник, блудник, винопийца': Načev and Fermandžiev 1984: 24.

[46] 'В дните на турския цар, султан Ибрахим': Načev and Fermandžiev 1984: 76.

[47] 'В дните на великия и самодържавен цар мюсюлмански амир Мехмед бег': Načev and Fermandžiev 1984: 60.

[48] Köhbach 1992: 233; Miklosich and Müller 1865: 310, 320, 325, 331–2, 337–8, 344, 350, 353, 355–7; Lefort 1981: 15–16, 100 and 108. On the incorporation of former members of the Byzantine aristocracy into the Ottoman court and their cultural influence, visible during the reigns of Mehmed II and Bayezid II, see the chapter entitled 'The last phase of Ottoman syncretism – the subsumption of members of the Byzanto-Balkan aristocracy into the Ottoman ruling elite' in Lowry 2003: 115–30.

[49] Miklosich and Müller 1865: 359–64; cf. Pedani Fabris 1994: 44–5 and 69 (nos. 163, 165, 250).

[50] Synadinos 1996: 56–7.   [51] Synadinos 1996: 43.   [52] Synadinos 1996: 84–5.

common joy and solemn celebrations after Murad IV had taken Erevan in 1634[53] and mourned the sultan's death in 1640, admitting that he could not imagine anyone fit to replace such a perfect king.[54]

To quote Benjamin Braude and Bernard Lewis: 'some Greek writers of the late eighteenth century [and apparently earlier centuries as well: DK] were more sympathetic to Ottoman rule than are their descendants today'.[55] This opinion seems equally valid for other Greek Orthodox Balkan nations and their early modern ancestors: the Bulgarians, Serbs and even Romanians.[56] In 1935, Nicolae Iorga, a great Romanian historian, published his seminal study *Byzance après Byzance*. Its title suggested a continuity between the Byzantine and Ottoman empires, but in fact Iorga denied the Turks any credit as state builders, treating them merely as alien usurpers who benefited from the ready imperial infrastructure left by the Greeks. The actual subject of Iorga's study was the Greek Orthodox church after 1453, treated by the author as the sole civilizing factor in early modern south-eastern Europe, operating in a hostile and corrupt Islamic milieu. In fact, it might be observed that the Greek patriarchate often closely cooperated with the Porte, benefiting from its support against the Latin church, and largely facilitated the legitimization of Ottoman rule among the Orthodox Christians. Over 200 years before Iorga, who denied the Ottomans any legitimacy, his compatriot Radu Popescu, a Wallachian chronicler, argued that the Ottomans rightfully inherited Constantinople, recalling their alleged kinship with a medieval Byzantine dynasty – the Komneni.[57] The argument was not new as already in the early sixteenth century a Greek author, Theodore Spandounes (Spandugnino), had invoked Mehmed II's claim to the Komnenian lineage.[58]

It is sometimes forgotten that Roman Catholics, most notably Italians, Albanians and Southern Slavs from Dalmatia and Bosnia, also constituted a group of Ottoman subjects, not numerous but visible and quite prominent. Italian residents of Pera and Galata actively participated in trade and some of them served in the Ottoman chancery as clerks and translators. In the fifteenth and early sixteenth centuries, a number of original documents of

[53] Synadinos 1996: 116–17.   [54] Synadinos 1996: 94–5.
[55] See the 'Introduction' to Braude and Lewis 1982: 1–34, esp. 17.
[56] Admittedly, mainstream Romanian historiography has presented the Ottoman rule in the Balkans in a much more favourable light than the historiographies of neighbouring countries. The difference was not entirely detached from political circumstances. Following the rising crisis in Romanian–Soviet relations, after 1965 the communist regime in Bucharest allowed Romanian historians to abandon the dismissive view of the Ottoman past then obligatory in Marxist eastern Europe and adopt a more balanced stand, intended to improve Bucharest's relations with Ankara; see the summarizing article by Maxim 2001, esp. 207–8.
[57] Popescu Vornicul 1963: 6–7.   [58] Cf. Karateke 2005: 24.

Ottoman sultans were composed in Latin and Italian and their protocol was clearly modelled on Western and/or ancient formulas. In the instrument of peace, sent in 1489 by Sultan Bayezid II to the Polish king and provided with an Arabic-script imperial *tughra*, the sender titled himself as *Dei gratia Asie, Grecie etc. Imperator Maximus*. In the following instrument from 1494, the same ruler titled himself as *Dei gratia Imperator ambarum terrarum, Asiae atque Europae et marium Magnus Sultanus* ('by the grace of God the emperor of the two continents, Asia and Europe, and of the [two] seas, the great sultan'), and in the instrument from 1502, composed in Italian, as *Dei gracia Grande Imperator Asie atque Europe et marium etc.*[59] The conquests of Selim I are fairly reflected in the *intitulatio*, contained in his instrument of peace sent to the Polish king in 1519: *Per la Divina favente clementia Grande Imperator di Constantinopoli, di Asia, Europa, Persia, Soria et Egipto et Arabia et de li mari etc.*[60]

However, as already mentioned, the very same impressive conquests of Selim I and his successor, Süleyman the Magnificent, encouraged the Ottomans to adopt a more rigid and less tolerant Islamic stand towards the 'infidels': the sultan's Christian subjects as well as Christian foreign rulers. Imperial rule took on a more elevated and firmly hierarchical expression. The shift was symbolized by the discontinuity in the use of 'infidel' languages and scripts by the sultan's chancery. Victor Ménage established that, as of 1525, the Ottoman chancery ceased to issue documents in scripts other than Arabic.[61] Such documents were still issued by Ottoman provincial chanceries on behalf of local governors, but no longer by the imperial chancery on behalf of the sultan.[62] Although the sultan's letters sent to foreign rulers continued to be provided with translations in Latin, Italian, German or Polish, such translations were not legitimized with the sultan's monogram (*tughra*), which was appended exclusively to Arabic-script originals. As the titles of tsar, basileus and imperator had previously been used to refer to the sultan exclusively in his Cyrillic-, Greek- and Latin-script documents, with the passing of time the Ottomans apparently forgot that

---

[59] Kołodziejczyk 2000: 200, 202 and 210.   [60] Kołodziejczyk 2000: 218.

[61] Ménage attributed the reform to Mustafa Celâlzade, a secretary of the Ottoman grand vizier, Ibrahim Pasha, who had served under his patron in Egypt and returned to Istanbul in 1525 to assume the post of the *re'isü'l-küttab*; see Ménage 1985: 301; Ménage's discovery has been confirmed by the present author on the basis of additional evidence from the Polish archives; cf. Kołodziejczyk 2000: 35–6.

[62] Admittedly, Süleyman's letter, dated 13 November 1529, in which the sultan notifies the Venetian doge, Andrea Gritti, of the Ottoman victorious campaign against the Habsburgs, is issued in Greek; nonetheless, after 1525 such documents seem to have been extremely rare; on Süleyman's Greek letter from 1529, already mentioned in note 49 above, preserved in the original provided with the *tughra*, see Miklosich and Müller 1865: 361–4; Pedani Fabris 1994: 69; 1998: 190 (no. 12).

these titles had once been adopted by their own rulers. This obliviousness
explains the fact that, in the following decades, the Ottomans began to use
these titles liberally in reference to foreign rulers, who were simultaneously
denied the status of padishah. Halil İnalcık convincingly argues that the
title *sar* or *çar*, with which the Ottoman sultans addressed 'Moscovian
kings' in their Arabic-script letters in Ottoman Turkish (e.g. *Moskov kıralı
sar* in a letter from Selim II to Ivan the Terrible), 'did not mean Caesar or
emperor at that time' to the Ottomans.[63]

In analogy, Markus Köhbach argues that the Ottoman initial consent
to address the Habsburg emperor as *çasar* and no longer as *kıral* ('king'),
stipulated by the Treaty of Zsitvatorok (1606) and long celebrated as the
symbolic victory of the Habsburgs, did not reflect a genuine change in the
Porte's attitude towards the Christian rival and had no lasting impact. As
the Ottoman chancery clerks were aware that the term *çasar*, adopted into
Ottoman Turkish from the Hungarian *császár* (Caesar), was equivalent to
the title *kayser* used by the Ottoman sultan, in the ensuing correspondence
with Vienna they chose instead to address the Habsburg ruler by the term
imperator alias *imperador*, which had already been used by Sultan Suleyman
in his correspondence with Ferdinand I beginning in 1559. The solution
was ideal as it satisfied both sides: the Habsburg chancery in Vienna readily
accepted the Latin term *imperator* as fully equivalent to Hungarian *császár*
or German *Kaiser*, whereas in the Ottoman vocabulary the term *imperator*
had by that time lost its association with the sultan so its attribution to an
infidel ruler, regarded as inferior, did not infringe the padishah's dignity.[64]
Such pragmatic manipulation of the formal titles applied to one's own
versus foreign rulers was used with equal skill in Europe, the Middle
East and the Far East and served to maintain the façade of one's own
symbolic superiority, at least in the eyes of one's domestic audience. Below
in Chapters 8 and 10 both Koch and Rawski offer discussion of further
examples of this practice involving the strategic extension of courtesies and

---

[63] İnalcık 1993/1986: 383.
[64] Köhbach 1992. Although Köhbach persuasively argues that, unlike the term *çasar*, the term *imperador/imperator* was not 'ideologically loaded' (*nicht ideologisch besetzt*) in the Ottoman political vocabulary of the time, one should not forget that the latter title continued to be used in reference to the Ottoman sultan in official translations prepared by the Ottoman chancery. For instance, in the Latin translation of the Ottoman Turkish instrument of the Karlowitz Treaty, prepared by the chief Ottoman dragoman, Alexander Mavrocordatos, and given to the Polish envoy at the congress, Sultan Mustafa II is referred to as *Augustissimus, Potentissimus, Amplissimus Imperator*; for the translation, authorized by Mavrocordatos with his own hand, see Warsaw, Archiwum Główne Akt Dawnych, Archiwum Koronne Warszawskie, Dział turecki, karton 78, teczka 503, no. 833. The original Ottoman Turkish instrument is published in Kołodziejczyk 2000: 587–98.

toleration of a measure of independent behaviour as long as it did not openly challenge the imperial majesty.[65]

The title of imperator returned to the sultan's own *intitulatio* in the nineteenth century, when the Ottomans accepted French as the language of international diplomacy. But the political circumstances had now changed dramatically. Everywhere the Ottomans were on the retreat and could not anymore set their own terms for diplomatic relations, as they had been wont to. Modernization became an urgent problem, a matter of survival in the face of an advancing European imperialism. The title of imperator, therefore, no longer reflected the sultan's aspirations to universal rule but rather his wish to become eligible to the Concert of Europe and receive equal recognition among the other sovereigns by assuming the monarchic title already in use in Russia and Austria, and later on to be adopted in France (1804 and again 1852), Germany (1871), and even, with reservations, England (Queen Victoria's assumption of the title of Empress of India, but *not* of Britain, in 1877, cf. the discussions in Chapter 1 above, and further by Haldén in Chapter 12 below).[66]

THE OTTOMAN SULTAN AS KING SOLOMON

The Porte's inconsistent efforts to accommodate its non-Muslim population by invoking their pre-Ottoman and non-Muslim traditions and titles always remained subject to ideological challenge from its European neighbours and were increasingly frustrated by the rising appeal which Christian rulers, especially the Russian tsars, began to enjoy among the Ottomans' Christian subjects as the nineteenth century drew nearer. The absence of

[65] According to Ronald Toby: 'in order for a symbolic ordering of the countries of the world to be useful, it need not necessarily be consistent with all other beliefs held by the "operators" of the system or by the perceivers of the system; on the contrary, it may be precisely *because* certain "facts" or data of "objective reality" are uncomfortable or inconvenient to the maintenance of a desired or needed self-image and self-perception that peoples construct alternate realities in the symbolic systems of their world, of the world that they can control; certain aspects of that reality can then be masked, others highlighted, to create and preserve a desired image'; see Toby 1991: 201–2. The symbolic competition between Qing China, Tokugawa Japan and Chosŏn Korea, which all claimed to be the most legitimate representatives of the Confucian world order, is discussed by Rawski in Chapter 10.

[66] Already in the project of an Ottoman–Polish treaty from 1790, drafted in Istanbul in two language versions, the Ottoman Turkish title *şevketlü kudretlü padişah-i Al-i 'Osman Sultan Selim-i Salis hazretleri* is rendered in the French version as *Sa Hautesse Impériale Sultan Sélim III Han, Empereur des Ottomans*; see Kołodziejczyk 2000: 644 and 649. Significantly, the annex to the treaty stressed the need to restore the European equilibrium (French version: *l'équilibre de l'Europe*; Ottoman Turkish version: *Avrupa mevazinesi*) which had been violated by Russia; see 2000: 654 and 657.

such a foreign challenge facilitated the legitimization of Ottoman rule among the Jewish dwellers of the empire, by far the most successful legitimizing of the sultan's rule among his non-Muslim subjects. One must not forget that many Jews had found a safe haven in the Ottoman domains after having experienced and escaped persecutions in Christian Europe. In the sixteenth century, Rabbi Yosef Caro referred to the Ottoman sultan as 'our lord the king, may his splendor rise aloft'.[67] His contemporary, Rabbi Mosheh Almosnino, wrote about 'our great master Sultan Süleyman, may his memory live forever'.[68] Sultan Süleyman was also the first Ottoman ruler in whose honour a special poem was written in Hebrew by an Istanbuli poet, Shelomoh ben Mazal-Tov.[69] Süleyman's very name (Süleyman < Solomon) reflected the appeal of the ancient Jewish king, regarded as the archetypal just ruler in the Jewish and Christian as well as the Muslim traditions. In the rabbinic responsa, studied by Minna Rozen and Aryeh Shmuelevitz, the Ottoman state is often referred to as 'the gracious Kingdom' or – with a significant possessive pronoun – 'our Kingdom'.[70] It is perhaps not an accident that, during Süleyman's reign, Hebron (Halilü'r-Rahman in Arabic) was entered in the sultan's *intitulatio* as the forth holy city along with Mecca, Medina and Jerusalem, though admittedly it was no longer listed in the *intitulatios* of his successors.[71] After all, Jews and Arabs (and hence all the Muslims) could claim common biblical ancestry descending from Abraham/Ibrahim, through Sarah and Isaac and through Hagar and Ishmael, respectively, so Abraham's tomb in Hebron was equally venerated by the faithful of both religions.

TYRANT OR EMPEROR? THE OTTOMAN SULTAN IN EUROPEAN EYES

The last question to be briefly examined in the present chapter is the reception of the sultan's imperial claims outside the Ottoman empire, precisely in early modern Christian Europe. Predictably, the most familiar

---

[67] Rozen 2002: 20.   [68] Rozen 2002: 42.   [69] Rozen 2002: 43.

[70] Shmuelevitz 1984: 33. Karateke proposes to distinguish between 'normative legitimacy' which the sultan enjoyed in the eyes of his Muslim subjects and 'tolerated legitimacy' which he could expect from the side of his non-Muslim subjects; cf. Karateke 2005: 33–4. Yet, the enthusiastic praise of some Jewish authors and even some fragments of Synadinos' memoirs (see above) suggest that at times a sultan might have enjoyed more than 'tolerated' legitimacy in the eyes of at least some of his non-Muslim subjects.

[71] Hebron is listed in Süleyman's *'ahdnames* from 1553 and 1559, sent to King Sigismund II Augustus of Poland and Emperor Ferdinand I, respectively; see Kołodziejczyk 2000: 235; and Schaendlinger 1983: 1, 60. Admittedly, Hebron also figures in the *intitulatio* of Murad IV contained in his *'ahdname* sent to Poland in 1634, but, unlike Murad's earlier instrument from 1623 and the instruments of his successors from 1640 and 1667, Murad's *'ahdname* from 1634 was closely patterned in form and contents on the instruments of Sultan Süleyman; see Kołodziejczyk 2000: 138 and 449.

case to the present author is the Polish-Lithuanian Commonwealth. In the Polish noble republican opinion, the autocratic and imperial ambitions of Ottoman sultans perfectly fitted the image of Oriental tyranny. Common distrust towards tyranny, be it Oriental or Western, was injected into noblemen's minds both at home and in school, in Jesuit colleges where, unlike in Jesuit colleges in Habsburg Spain or Austria, Cicero was among the most favoured assigned readings. In fact, in the contest for the most dreadful foreign ruler the sultans had strong rivals, most notably the Habsburg emperors, the French kings and the Russian tsars, who all, one or more times, tried to secure the Polish throne for themselves or their relatives and were suspected – not without reason – of the desire to replace the noble republican *libertas* with the *absolutum dominium*.[72] Mirroring Campanella's contest between a Habsburg and an Ottoman universal empire, discussed in the opening chapter above, contemporary Polish political language used the title of emperor only about two foreign monarchs: the 'Christian emperor' (*cesarz chrześcijański*) in Vienna and the 'Turkish emperor' (*cesarz turecki*) in Istanbul. As we see, the only differentiating qualifier was the adjective, which in both cases referred to the given emperor's religious rather then national identity.[73]

One should expect that the sultan's claim to the Roman imperial heritage, easily accepted by Arab and Indian Muslims, would be less readily acknowledged within Christian Europe, with her own pretensions to the Roman tradition and her 'own', Christian and Habsburg, Holy Roman Empire. Yet, at least the Polish royal chancery had no inhibitions to title the Ottoman sultan as *Imperator* or *Caesar Turcarum*.[74]

To be sure, cultural prejudice regarding 'the Oriental tyranny' was not absent. A fascinating example of political demagogy is furnished by a parliamentary speech delivered in 1646 during the conflict between the Polish king, Vladislaus IV Vasa, and the nobility assembled in the Diet. Criticizing the royal plans to support Venice in its war against the Porte, one Polish noble deputy claimed that even a victory over the Turk and a conquest of Constantinople would be harmful to the Commonwealth. According to the speaker, King Vladislaus treated the Turkish war as his private enterprise, so it was unlikely that he would share his spoils with

---

[72] Cf. Kołodziejczyk 2009: 12.

[73] In the given context, the Polish adjective *turecki* ('Turkish') referred to religious rather than ethnic identity; in analogy, a conversion to Islam was referred to in early modern Polish as *poturczenie* ('one's becoming a Turk').

[74] For the expression *Caesar Turcarum*, admittedly less common than *Imperator* or *Imperator Turcarum*, see the royal instruments of peace sent to the Porte in 1554 and 1577; Kołodziejczyk 2000: 243 and 279.

the Republic. And even if he did so, argued the deputy, how different were these peoples (i.e., the Ottoman subjects) from the Poles! Accustomed to slavery, after their admission to the Republic, they would bow easily before the throne, thus gaining royal favour. 'As for us – he concluded – we would share the fate of the [ancient] Macedonians, who led to war as free people would have returned as slaves if not for the death of Alexander.'[75]

Comparing the Polish king to Alexander, the deputy was very far from extolling him. In fact, it was Alexander who symbolized the infatuation with the Oriental despotism that was regarded as so dangerous for ancient Greco-Roman (and contemporary Polish) republican virtues. Paradoxically, the scornful allusion to the servility of Ottoman subjects in the Balkans was largely directed against the same Greeks whom the author praised as ancient republicans. In consolation, one should note that Polish noble writers, who styled themselves as Catos and Brutuses, were equally scornful when commenting on the servility of contemporary Frenchmen and Germans towards their absolutist monarchs.

CONCLUSION

The survival of the Ottoman state for over 600 years would be unthinkable without its legitimization in the eyes of its subjects. The Ottoman propaganda, presenting the sultan as a pious, just and ever-victorious ruler, was addressed primarily to his Muslim subjects with no regard to their ethnic origin. At the same moment, the Ottomans could not ignore their non-Muslim subjects, whose consent – at least partial and temporary – to the sultan's rule was crucial for the empire's stability and wellbeing. Moreover, the Ottoman involvement in European diplomacy in search of Christian allies against the Habsburgs, and later against Russia, required a more subtle and nuanced language in foreign policy than the language of political Jihad. The adoption of foreign titles, belonging to pre-Muslim or non-Muslim traditions, such as *kayser, tsar, basileus* or *imperator,* can be regarded as a conscious effort to appease non-Muslim subjects and gain the recognition of far from always hostile European elites. Still, the inconsistent and halfhearted use of these titles by the Ottoman chancery demonstrates that the Ottoman flexibility and pragmatism, admirable at certain periods, was severely limited by the Sunni Muslim religious rigidity and cultural exclusiveness, demonstrated until the very end of the empire. Ottoman

[75] The speech of Jerzy Ponętowski, a deputy from Czernichów (Černihiv in the Ukraine), is summarized and partially quoted *in extenso* in Szajnocha 1877: 118.

tolerance was always articulated in a context of imperial hierarchy and sub-jection. On the other hand, one might presume that even the most open and 'liberal' policy, no matter how attractive in the eyes of a present-day reader, would hardly have been effective to save the Ottoman 'state-project' in the era of ascending nationalisms.[76]

[76] For a similar conclusion that invokes 'the inescapable trajectory from empire to nation-state', see Barkey 2008: 27; cf. also Murphey 2009: 93–4.

CHAPTER 8

How the Mughal pādshāhs *referenced Iran in their visual construction of universal rule*

Ebba Koch

In March 1594 Akbar (r. 1556–1605), the third ruler of the Mughal dynasty, sent a letter to Shah 'Abbas of Iran (r. 1587–1629) in which he made a fundamental statement about Mughal universalism and Mughal kingship. The Mughal emperor admonished the Persian king because of his intolerance in religious matters and expressed the opinion that his own stance towards different religions and cultures gave him the right to rule over them all. Since the letter has been neglected in the discussion of Akbar's ideology of kingship it will be worthwhile to quote the relevant passages verbatim, at least as the historian Abu'l Fazl penned them in the third volume of his *Akbarnāma* (1590–5):

As in the rules of sovereignty and the religion of humanity, concord is preferable to opposition and peace better than war, and especially as it has been our disposition from the beginning of our attaining discretion to this day not to pay attention to differences of religion and variety of manners and to regard the tribes of mankind as the servants of God, we have endeavoured to regulate mankind in general.

... The sections of mankind, who are a Divine deposit and treasure, must be regarded with the glance of affection, and efforts must be made to conciliate their hearts. It must be considered that the Divine mercy attaches itself to every form of creed, and supreme exertions must be made to bring oneself into the every vernal flower-garden of 'Peace with all'. The increase of one's good fortune must always be kept in full view, for the eternal God is bounteous to all souls and conditions of men. Hence it is fitting that kings, who are the shadow of Divinity, should not cast away this principle. For, the Creator has given this sublime order (that of kings) for the discipline and guardianship of all mankind, so that they may watch over the honour and reputation of every class. Men do not knowingly and intentionally make mistakes in worldly affairs, which are unsubstantial and pass away, why then should they be negligent in the affairs of faith and religion, which

I thank the Austrian Science Fund (FWF) for a grant to support my project 'The Palaces and Gardens of Shah Jahan (r. 1628–58)' (Project No. P 21480-G21) which I carry out as a senior researcher of the Institute of Iranian Studies of the Austrian Academy of Sciences (2009–12). The project includes the study of Mughal court culture and enabled me to prepare this chapter for publication.

are permanent and everlasting? In fine, the position of every sect comes under one of two categories. Either it is in possession of Truth, and in that case one should seek direction from it and accept its views. Or it is in the wrong, and then it is unfortunate and suffering from disease of ignorance, and is a subject for pitying kindness, and not for harshness and reproach. One must exercise wide toleration and knock at the door of inspection, for in this way will the veil be removed from the wide extent of spiritualities and temporalities, and there will be ample life and fortune... Patience and endurance must ever be one's companions, for the maintenance of permanent dominion depends thereon.[1]

Akbar's letter was written in reply to a letter which Shah ʿAbbas had sent in 1590–1 with the ambassador Yadgar Sultan Rumlu (also called Shamlu) and in which, after extensive honorifics, he reminded the Mughal *pādshāh* of the good relations between the Safavids and the Mughals and reproached him for not having congratulated him upon his accession and for not having written at all since then, despite the support which Shah Tahmasp had given to his father Humayun when in exile in Iran.[2] It took Akbar four years to answer and to make clear that the days when the Mughals felt indebted towards the Safavids were over and that he was superior to rulers like Shah ʿAbbas because they accepted only one religion and acted merely within one culture while his tolerance gave him – Akbar – the moral authority to take care of all mankind and thus he was a true universal king.

It is a typical phenomenon in the articulation of Mughal kingship that the thoughts of Babur, of Humayun and especially of Akbar were taken up and expressed in allegory and symbolic images by Jahangir (r. 1605–27), and in turn by Shah Jahan (r. 1628–58). Art became an indispensable instrument for the Mughal emperors in their ideological formulations as world rulers. Mughal art was fed by heterogeneous sources. Thus universalized, it had a transcultural value and was in turn able to speak to a universal audience.[3]

---

[1] Abu'l Fazl 1979: III, 1008–14. See also his *Mukātabāt-i ʿAllāmi* (Abu'l Fazl 1998: 93–101). I earlier drew attention to this letter in Koch 2002: 23. Akbar's letter was what Mitchell (2009: 185) described in his discussion of kingly correspondence as *fathnama* ('victory letter'), informing the *shāh* about his recent victories and conquests. Typical is that advice about rule is included; but exceptional is Akbar's position about the acceptance of all religions and all cultures. Lefèvre (2010) does not refer to this correspondence though it sets a precedent to the correspondence between Shah ʿAbbas and Jahangir which she discusses at 35–6. Her perceptive analysis of Mughal and Iranian relations focuses on the Timurid connection, circulation of elites and state *mercantili*.

[2] The letter has been published by Nava'i (1974: 331–43) and was discussed by Mitchell (2009: 184). I thank Colin P. Mitchell for explaining the letter to me, and Dr Yunus Jaffery for translating it. Abridged versions of the correspondence between Akbar and Shah ʿAbbas are given in Islam 1979–82: I, 123–39. See also Islam 1970: 56–67.

[3] I have several times discussed the problem of Mughal allegory and the use of European techniques to construct it, most recently in Koch 2010.

A well-known allegory of Jahangir explores in visual terms the idea of moral superiority over other rulers which Akbar had addressed in his letter to Shah ʿAbbas. The painting which is today in the Freer Gallery, Washington DC shows Jahangir giving preference to a Sufi *shaikh*, identified as Shaikh Husain Chishti of Ajmer,[4] over the rulers of the world, among them an unidentified Ottoman sultan, and James I of England (fig. 8.1).[5]

The inscription in the four cartouches above and below the picture tells us that

The *pādshāh* (emperor) is an image (*sūrat*) and the inner meaning (*maʿanī*) of God (Allah)

[Namely] Shah Nur al-Din, the Light of the Faith, Jahangir, the World-seizer, son of Akbar *pādshāh* (emperor)

Although in [the domain of material] form (*sūrat*) the kings (*shāh-ān*) stand before him, in the [inner, the] spiritual domain (*maʿanī*) he regards only the dervishes.

It is significant that the painter Bichitr is allowed to include himself with a self-portrait in the gathering, as the creator of the image (*sūrat*).

What the image and text convey is that the universal ruler, 'the World-Seizer', looks beyond worldly affairs to the spiritual realm which gives him supreme authority over other kings.

But the claim to universalism (meaning pertaining to the whole world, to all mankind) could be modified, especially when it served *Realpolitik*. Akbar takes a different stand towards another of his contemporaries, namely Philip II of Spain (r. 1556–98), in his letter of 1582. Two years earlier Philip II had also become king of Portugal, and was represented by a viceroy at Goa which bordered on Mughal territory. Akbar writes:

We are, with the whole power of our mind, earnestly striving to establish and strengthen the bonds of love, harmony and union among the population, but above all with the exalted family [*ṭāʾifat*, literally tribe] of princes [*sulṭāns*], who enjoy the noblest of distinctions in consequence of a greater (share of the) divine favour, and especially with that illustrious representative of dominion, recipient of divine illumination and propagator of the Christian religion, who needs not to be praised or made known [= Philip]; (and this decision is) on account of our propinquity, the claims whereof are well established among mighty potentates, and acknowledged to be the chief condition for amicable relations.[6]

[4] Asher 2004: 181.
[5] The painting has often been reproduced and discussed, since the classical studies by Ettinghausen (1961a, caption of pl. 14 and 1961b).
[6] Rehatsek 1887. Abu'l Fazl 1998: 8–12. Although in the collection compiled by Abu'l Fazl the letter is addressed to 'the wise men of the Franks', it is clear that it was meant for the king of Portugal. For a discussion of the addressee and the different editions see Maclagan 1990: 44 n. 57. Similar words of Akbar are recorded by Monserrate (1993: 182).

Fig. 8.1 Bichitr, Jahangir preferring a Sufi *shaikh* to the rulers of the world, *c.* 1625.

Since Akbar was trying to win Philip II for an alliance against the Ottomans[7] he does not claim supreme authority and his tone is quite different from his condescending advice in his letter to Shah 'Abbas. He treated Philip on equal terms as 'recipient of divine illumination' and was concerned to establish them both as equal members of the universal family of the kings of the world.

From the above it follows that the social and political position of the ruler may be as important if not more important than his religion, his ethnicity or his cultural background and this paves the way for a sharing of identities, ideologies and symbols.

For a ruler 'to regulate mankind in general' is a tall order – even in Mughal propagandistic terms. In order to meet the challenge to address such a heterogeneous audience, not only within the empire but also beyond and across space and time, the Mughals developed what one would describe in modern terms as a multiple identity.

If we try to be more specific we note that the areas of particular relevance for the Mughals were Central Asia, the country of their origin; India, over which they ruled; and Iran, their immediate neighbour and rival and also a place of reference with regard to culture and ideas of kingship.[8] Moreover, a good part of the Mughal ruling elite came from Iran. Lastly there was Europe, the newly emerging power of the West. The Europeans kept coming, bringing with them trade, politics, ideas about religion and, most importantly for the Mughals, art.[9]

What interests us, especially in the context of this chapter, is how the Mughals referred to Persian ideas in their representation of rulers and how they expressed this in their arts.

Here we have to make an important distinction between, on the one hand, contemporary Iran ruled by the Safavids, in whose regard the Mughals were motivated by *Realpolitik* and rivalry, and on the other hand with ancient Iran, and its mythical and historical kings and heroes from a distant past – here the Mughals sought authority and legitimation through ideological construction. It will emerge that one had a bearing on the other.

The Safavids, descendants of the Sufi *shaikh* Safi al-Din (d. 1334), were the immediate neighbours and rivals of the Mughal dynasty and represented

---

[7] For Mughal–Ottoman relations, see Farooqi 1989.   [8] See below, note 41.

[9] One wonders about China. The relations between Mughal India and China are as yet not sufficiently explored. In the area of the arts, Chinese porcelain was valued, collected, and displayed in the Mughal *chīnī khāna* ('china room'), a type of wall decoration made of registers of niches meant to hold porcelain objects and vessels. Several blue and white dishes are preserved which bear inscriptions of Jahangir, Shah Jahan and Aurangzeb. See Pal *et al.* 1989: 166–9.

with them and the Ottomans the three superpowers of the Islamic world. But as *shāh*s of Iran, the Safavids were much more: they were the direct heirs of the ancient kings of Persia – both mythical and historical – who had been absorbed by Islam as model rulers and exemplary kings. It is well known that Firdausi's *Shahname* was an obligatory reference book at the courts of the Islamic world which identified with Persianate culture. The ancient Persian kings, especially the Sasanians, also appear as exemplary figures in the *adab* literature, a genre which gives advice to rulers in the manner of *Fürstenspiegel* or mirrors for princes. In classical works of this type such as the *Siyāsatnāma* of Nizām al-Mulk (d. 1092), Anusharwan, that is the Sasanian king Khusrau I (r. 531–579) appears as a paragon of justice.[10] Also, Persian was after Arabic the second language of the Islamic world and Persianate culture underpinned the life of the ruling elite both at the courts and in the cities.[11]

The Mughals came into direct contact with Iran in 1543, when the second Mughal emperor Humayun lost the newly conquered territories in Hindustan to his Afghan rival Sher Shah Suri and had to take refuge with Shah Tahmasp (r. 1524–76). With this began the precarious interaction of the Mughals with the Safavids, and it was also an incentive for Humayun to redefine himself as Mughal *pādshāh* in Persian terms. The distinctly eccentric Humayun began to enrich the Mughal myth of kingship which he had commenced to build up in India with borrowings from ancient Persian concepts. This trend was further explored under Akbar. It was expressed in visual terms by Jahangir, and was continued and enriched by Shah Jahan. Persian ideas became important components in the construction of Mughal universalism. Most distinct is perhaps the concept of divinely illuminated rule.

Badāuni, the critical voice of Akbar's court, tells us that when Humayun was in Mashhad in 1544, having fled from India, a pilgrim whispered into his ear

'So! you are again laying claim to omnipotence!' This was a reference to the circumstance that Humayun used generally in Bangala [Bengal] to cast a veil over his crown, and when he removed it the people used to say, Light has shined forth![12]

Humayun associated himself thus with Indian and Iranian practices of sun rulership and with the old Iranian concept of the divine effulgence *khwarena* (Arabic *farr*) of the king which were not forgotten in Islamic

---

[10] Nizām al-Mulk 1891–3: 35–6; 1893: 51–2. See also Fowden in this volume. Also, I would like to thank Garth Fowden for reading this chapter and making several suggestions to improve its English.
[11] Fragner 1999.   [12] Badāuni 1973: I, 573. This and the following passage rely on Koch 2002.

times.[13] The connection was made through Persepolis, which was visited throughout the centuries by rulers who associated themselves with the Persian idea of kingship. They left inscriptions there, beginning with the Sasanians and they were followed by many *sultāns* and *shāhs*.[14] The learned theologian, poet and moralist Davani, for instance, who visited Persepolis in 1476 with Sultan Khalil, the son of the Turcoman ruler Uzun Hasan, claims that the mythical Persian king Jamshid (according to him taken by some historians to be Solomon), after having constructed Persepolis,

had caused a golden throne studded with shining jewels, to be placed on the columns... and sat on it in state. At sunrise he ordered the throne to be turned towards the Sun, and the eyes of the onlookers were dazzled by the brilliancy. Saying that they beheld two suns, one in the sky and the other on earth, they knelt down... and thenceforth he was surnamed Jamshid, his name being Jam and shid meaning 'Sun'.[15]

Back in India, Humayun must have thought of the legendary carpets and throne of the Sasanian Khusraus when he designed a large cosmological carpet of concentric rings in which his court had to sit according to origin and rank, with the emperor 'like the Sun' in the circle in the middle of the planetary rings.[16]

Akbar's chief ideologue (as Richard Eaton has famously called him) and programme writer Abu'l Fazl elaborated on Humayun's associations with sun and light rulership which were reinforced with Mongol concepts of kingship begotten by light; and with the neoplatonically infused light mysticism (theory of *ishrāq* – illuminationism) of the Persian philosopher Shihab al-Din Suhrawardī (executed in Aleppo in 1191), who argued that all existence is a reflection of God's brilliant blinding light.[17] Illumination occurs in degrees, and Akbar was declared to be more illumined than others, and thus he was the master of the age.[18] Fusing these ideas with Indian concepts and practices, Akbar appeared at sunrise like a traditional Indian king or a Hindu deity for public viewing (*darshan*) and his subjects prostrated themselves before him. He even went so far as to pray to the

---

[13] On *farr* see Soudavar 2003.   [14] Melikian-Chirvani 1971.
[15] Minorsky 1940: 150–1. See also Koch 2002: 21 and Mitchell 2009: 122.
[16] Khwāndamīr 1940: Persian text 110–12, translation 80–1; see also Necipoğlu 1993: 313–14. In a paper entitled 'Cosmic Kingship', presented with Claire Sotinel on 24 April 2009 in Rome at the conference 'Tributary Empires – Comparative Histories', organized by Peter Fibiger Bang for the EU sponsored network *Tributary Empires Compared: Romans, Mughals and Ottomans in the Pre-Industrial World from Antiquity till the Transition to Modernity* (COST Action 36), I attempted a digital reconstruction and explanation of Humayun's cosmic carpet.
[17] On Mughal light rulership and its sources see Asher 2004; also Skelton 1988.
[18] See also the discussion of illuminationism and its impact on Akbar by Fowden in this volume.

sun, as his heavenly counterpart so it seems, enraging his Muslim orthodox critics.[19]

Jahangir and Shah Jahan elaborated further on Mughal sun rulership and the Persian connection. These ideas were given a stunning pictorial expression in the celebrated political allegories of Jahangir (I have mentioned already the one of *Jahangir prefering a Sufi shaikh over the kings of the world*). Another of these allegorical paintings, *Jahangir receiving Shah ʿAbbas*, also at the Freer Gallery, takes up the Persian issue (fig. 8.2).[20] It is again the image of a virtual meeting, as we would describe it today, because in real life Jahangir never met his Persian rival. Both rulers sit on a bench; Jahangir's divine aura is expressed by a halo while Shah ʿAbbas is shown in a deferential posture. Both are attended by two eminent Mughal courtiers, Asaf Khan, and Khan-i ʿAlam. The latter knew Shah ʿAbbas in person because Jahangir had sent him in 1613 as ambassador to the Persian court. Luxury objects, namely an Italian table and ewer, a small Chinese porcelain cup, a Venetian glass and a clockwork statuette of Diana on a stag from Augsburg, celebrate the universal patronage of Jahangir. The inscription reads:

> When Shah Jahangir and Shah ʿAbbas
> two young and brave kings and both shadows of God
> seize with joy the cup of Jam[shid]
> and sit together in majesty (*daulat*)
> the world flourishes through their justice
> and the people of the world are at peace
> When friend (*yār*) and brother (*barādar*) are worthy of each other,
> O God, may they enjoy the fruits of each other's good fortune.

The words describe the Persian *shāh* as the equal of the Mughal *pādshāh*, whereas the image is more flattering for Jahangir who adopts a superior and condescending attitude towards his rival. It becomes clear that the visual representation makes a different statement than the text. Image and text send opposite messages to the viewer and reader and this dialectic gives us a full insight into the ambivalent attitude of the Mughals towards the Safavids. Also Shah Abbas spoke, at least around this time, of Jahangir as his brother and was interested in friendly connections, as we learn from the scholar and Mughal court official ʿAbdul Latif ʿAbbasi (died 1638–39) who was put in charge to receive the Persian envoys Zainul Beg, Aqa Beg and Muhib Ali Beg at the tomb of Akbar at Sikandra, Agra in 1621.[21]

---

[19] Badāuni 1973: II, 336; cf. Monserrate 1993: 184.

[20] The basic discussion of the painting is again by Ettinghausen (1961a: caption of pl. 13).

[21] Abdul Latif wrote an account about the visit which is found in the collection of his Persian letters, generally called Ruqʿat-i ʿAbdul Latif, now in the library of the Asiatic Society of Bengal, Calcutta Collection No. 364. For a translation see Desai 1999.

Fig. 8.2 Jahangir entertains Shah ʿAbbas of Iran in an imaginary meeting, 1618–22.

In any case, in both ways Jahangir brings up, like Akbar in his letter to Philip II, the image of kings as members of a universal family of rulers. As brother of Shah ʿAbbas, he can claim to be equal heir to the ancient Persian kings, here evoked by the legendary cup of Jamshid in which the world could be seen. Jamshid was, as Firdausi tells us, one of the first mythical kings of Iran (and mankind) whose justice brought peace to the world and who, as we have seen, was believed to have founded Persepolis, the quintessential place of enactment of the Persian idea of universal empire.

While in the image presented above the reference to Iranian kingship is expressed in the pictorial representation itself (to the Safavid *shāh* of contemporary Iran) as well as in writing (to ancient Iran), the next alle-gorical painting I am going to discuss speaks to us in almost purely visual terms. It is only discreetly accompanied by tiny explanatory scribbles. This is the much-reproduced and much-discussed painting by Abu'l Hasan, to whom Jahangir gave the title Nadir al-Zaman ('the wonder of the age') because he was one of the luminaries in the emperor's atelier. Around 1618, Abu'l Hasan painted what Jerry Losty declared to be 'one of the greatest of political pictures from any culture',[22] an imaginary meeting between his imperial patron and Shah ʿAbbas, which had occurred in a dream of Jahangir as one of the inscriptions on the painting tells us (fig. 8.3).[23] The two rival emperors are shown embracing each other in the aura of an immense halo composed of a radiant sun and a crescent moon supported by two Europeanizing *putti*. Sumathi Ramaswamy has aptly summarized the research on the painting:

Numerous commentators have noted that not only is Jahangir painted lighter and brighter than his dark-complexioned rival (alerting us to the prevalence of a non-European/pre-colonial racial economy at work), but he is also bigger than the Shah, who appears frail and meek, his arms unable to grasp the majesty of the great man he seeks to embrace. On the other hand, 'the attitude of the Mughal emperor is that of a great monarch generously patronizing an inferior rival'.[24] This impression is further strengthened by the fact that Jahangir is made to stand on a large lion while his Persian rival's feet rest on a smaller lamb.[25]

This is the proverbial lion and lamb of Isaiah, adopted by the Mughals in a European form, to give a visual expression to the effect of the ruler's justice,

[22] Losty 1991: 81.
[23] The historical backdrop was the growing tension between the two courts, especially over the valuable frontier town of Qandahar, finally captured by the Safavids in 1622, soon after this painting was completed: Okada 1992: 54–5, 170–5.
[24] Das 1978: 217 (thus quoted by Ramaswamy).
[25] Ramaswamy 2007 with further literature, starting with the pioneering study of Ettinghausen 1961a: caption of pl. 12, besides which see especially Skelton 1988.

Fig. 8.3 Abu'l Hasan, Jahangir's dream of a visit of Shah ʿAbbas of Iran, 1618–22.

for which existed similar metaphors in the Islamic tradition.[26] Justice was the first and foremost legitimation of Islamic, if not 'Oriental' rulership.

The animals on which the two emperors are made to stand are placed in turn on the upper half of a terrestrial globe on which are clearly delineated and named the territories of the two rulers.[27] Jahangir appropriated the globe, the latest device of European cartographical science, as symbol of his universal rule and it became a leitmotif of his portraits, where he appears standing on globes and holding globes, as world-holder, as the world king.[28]

Jahangir and his theorists and artists fully recognized the potential of European scientific achievements as well as techniques of allegorical construction for the purposes of articulating Mughal kingship. They ingeniously appropriated them to illustrate their own political concepts. Science and metaphor appear on the same level of pictorial reality.[29]

Another example is Abu'l Hasan's *Jahangir shooting at the head of Malik Anbar* (fig. 8.4), the commander of Ahmadnagar, whom in the real world Jahangir could not vanquish. It represents yet another visual expression of the emperor's wishful thinking. Jahangir stands on a terrestrial globe which contains beasts pacified by his justice, spreading out from India into Iran and China. The globe is supported by a bull which in turn stands on a fish, according to Islamic cosmology.[30] In defiance of all Western cartographic conventions, the European scientific instrument has been manipulated to move India into the centre, in alignment with the equatorial axis.[31] In the context of our discussion of Iranian–Mughal connections, I would like to draw special attention to the chain of justice which features prominently in the painting. It is suspended between the globe and the lance on which Malik Anbar's head is stuck. The chain of justice, here reinforced symbolically by a scale attached to it, is an ancient symbol of rulership which can be traced back to the Achaemenids and Sasanians.

[26] Koch 2001: 1–11, 112–29; 2006; see also Skelton 1988.
[27] See Koch 2009: 330–3; 2011a.   [28] Ramaswamy 2007: 755; see also Koch 2009: 330–3; 2011a.
[29] This relates to what the French sociologist of science Bruno Latour (2007) has described as a hybrid system when he questions the definitions of modernity. On this point see also Koch 2009: 335.
[30] Koch 2009: 330. For a basic discussion of the painting see Leach 1995: cat. no. 3.25, though she ignores the meaning of the bull standing on the fish. The concept of Jahangir's painting shows great affinity with the Discworld of the fantasy writer Terry Pratchett: his Discworld stands on four elephants which in turn stand on a tortoise. One of my anonymous readers informed me that there might be indeed an Indian connection, though Pratchett seems to have derived the idea not from Islamic cosmological concepts but 'from early modern European reports of Indian/Hindoo beliefs. See for instance John Locke, *An Essay Concerning Human Understanding* (1690): 13.19: "Had the poor Indian philosopher (who imagined that the earth also wanted something to bear it up) but thought of this word substance, he needed not to have been at the trouble to find an elephant to support it, and a tortoise to support his elephant: the word substance would have done it effectually".'
[31] I have analysed this globe in Koch 2009: 330–8; 2011a.

Fig. 8.4 Abu'l Hasan, Jahangir standing on a terrestrial globe supported by the cosmic bull and the world fish shooting at the head of his enemy Malik 'Anbar.

Herakleides of Kyme, who wrote shortly before the fall of the Achaemenid empire, included in his ethnographic account of *Persian Things* a small anecdote about the king from the land of frankincense that this ruler had a chain attached to the window of his palace which made it possible for the subjects to appeal directly to the king:

There is a window in the topmost part of the palace to which is attached a chain. Whoever believes to have been judged unjustly pulls that chain and in this way moves the window, and when the king notices it, he calls the person in and pronounces justice himself.[32]

The memory of the chain of justice was kept alive in the Islamic *adab* literature, where it famously became an emblem of the Sasanian king Anusharwan, to whom we have already referred as the proverbial paragon of just rulers. Nizām al-Mulk informs us about its working in his *Siyāsatnāma*:

In consequence Anusharwan ordered a chain to be made to which should be attached bells and which could be reached by the hand of a child of seven years. [This measure was undertaken] so that any victim of injustice coming to the court would not have to depend on the intervention of the chamberlains. When the chain was shaken, the bells would sound, Anusharwan would hear it, and give justice to the plaintiff. And so it happened.[33]

The rulers of India activated the justice device at times. King Harsa (r. 1089–1101) put up bells of justice at the gate of his palace in Kashmir which are described poetically in the *Rajatarangini*, the Sanskrit chronicle of the kings of Kashmir:

879. At the palace gate (*siṁhadvāra*) he hung up great bells in all four directions, to be informed by their sound of those who had come with the desire of making representations.

880. And when he had once heard their plaintive speech, he fulfilled their desire [as quickly] as the cloud in the rainy season [fulfils] that of the Cātaka birds.[34]

Also Ibn Battuta describes the chain of justice which Sultan Shams al-Din Iltutmish (r. 1210–36) put up between two marble statues of lions on towers at the gate of his palace at Delhi.[35]

---

[32] Haberkorn 1940: 66. This fragment of Herakleides of Kyme is preserved in Athenaeus, *The Deipnosophistae* Book 12, 517b (translation by the author) and analysed imprecisely by Haberkorn 1940: 66. I thank Peter Fibiger Bang for helpful discussion of this passage with me.

[33] Nizām al-Mulk 1891–3: 52.

[34] Kalhaṇa 1991: vol. 1, book 7, verse 879. I thank Joachim Deppert for referring me to this passage.

[35] Ibn Battūta 1993: iii, 630.

Jahangir would not fail to make the most of such a spectacular device. He himself tells us in his autobiography that after his accession he put up a chain at the *jharōka-i darshan*, his viewing window on the outer wall of the Agra palace:

After my accession, the first command issued by me was to have a chain of justice hung, so that if those charged with administering the courts were slack or negligent in rendering justice to the downtrodden, those who have suffered injustice could have recourse to the chain and pull it so that the sound would cause awareness. It is set up as follows. I ordered a chain to be made of pure gold, thirty ells in length, with sixty bells. It weighs four Hindustani mounds, which is thirty-two Persian mounds. One end is attached to the crenellations of the Shah Tower of the Agra citadel, and the other end is stretched to the bank of the river and affixed to a stone post erected there.[36]

The chain of justice appears in several of Jahangir's paintings (fig. 8.4).[37] We also find it in the symbolic imagery of his son Shah Jahan, where, in depictions of *darbar* scenes, it is placed right under the *jharōka-i khāṣṣ-u-ʿāmm* of the public audience hall in which he appeared before his court. We learn from Shah Jahan's early historian Qazwini that 'it laughed with many mouths [= chain openings] at the justice of Anusharwan', in other words that Shah Jahan's justice put that of the Persian paragon of justice Anusharwan to shame.[38]

There are many more spectacular and unique Mughal references to revivals and performances of, and depictions of ancient ideas, practices and institutions of Persian kingship. In their acceptance of the cultural and religious diversity of their subjects the Mughals can be compared to the Achaemenids.[39] They had themselves represented as royal hunters, who, like the Achaemenids and the Sasanians, confronted their prey in direct combat.[40] Shah Jahan recreated the multi-pillared halls of Persepolis in his audience halls,[41] where Nauruz, the Persian New Year, was merged with Julus, his accession day, and celebrated as one of the great Mughal court festivals. Hardly anywhere else in the Persianate world was it celebrated with such splendour. Moreover, the favourite wives of Jahangir and Shah Jahan were from an Iranian family and, altogether, a great part of the Mughal nobility and administrators of the empire came from Iran. Also Iranian

[36] Jahangir 1999: 24.   [37] Jahangir 1999: 25, 165; Koch 2001: fig. 0.1; Skelton 1988.
[38] Koch 2001: 127; Beach, Koch and Thackston 1997: 137, 168, 191.
[39] On the laissez-faire approach of the Achaemenids see Fowden 1993: 19–22.
[40] See Beach *et al.* 1997: 188. On the Mughal hunt in general see Koch 1998.
[41] Koch 2001: 229–54; 2011b.

artists and poets flocked to the Mughal court.[42] Shah Jahan's Iranian poets created the *sabq-i Hindi*, the Indian style of Persian poetry.[43]

CONCLUSION

In their ideological construction of universal empire the Mughals laid claims to the Safavid position and appropriated the mythical Iranian past. With their broad outlook, inspired artistic patronage and sense of glamorous performance it is they who emerge in this synergetic project as the true heirs of mythical ancient Persian kingship. Of course, this was but one facet in the concept of Mughal universal rule which they expressed in their use of the globe with India represented at its centre.

[42] See e.g. Haneda 1997; Dadvar 1999; Barzegar 2000; Lefèvre 2010 with further literature.

[43] The *sabq-i Hindi* has lately received more attention. See e.g. Losensky 1998: 3–7, 40–2, 198–202; it was also the subject of the conference 'Persian Literature in Multilingual India: Genres, Contexts, Styles', organized by Francesca Orsini (SOAS), Stefano Pellò (Venice) and Christine van Ruymbeke (Cambridge) at the University of Cambridge, 16–18 June 2008.

CHAPTER 9

Ideologies of state building in Vijayanagara and post-Vijayanagara south India: some reflections

Velcheru Narayana Rao and Sanjay Subrahmanyam

> In the said city of Belur [Velur] the emperor of Bisnaga [Vijayanagara] who was called Ramarraja had his court . . . So great was his power that the kings of Bengal, Sind and Cambay, who are powerful kings, were tributaries of the empire; [and] of him many authors have written rather variously, giving him the title of king and not of emperor. I do not doubt that in the beginning it may have been a kingdom, but it is said that he has always been known through all of the Orient as emperor, just as that of Germany was known in Europe and the whole world.
>
> Jacques de Coutre, *Vida de Jaques de Couttre* (1640).[1]

I

Indian historiography of the medieval and early modern periods (say, *c.* 700 to 1700) has long suffered from a curious – conventional but nonetheless enigmatic – divide that separates the southern from the northern part of the subcontinent.[2] This old convention was certainly strengthened and somewhat transformed in the colonial period; and it is related in part to the different sets of materials that historians use, as well as to the division of labour between distinct schools of historical writing from about 1900. The divide was based in large measure on the idea that northern India was dominated by Muslim states, as distinct from a 'Hindu' south, and that the two could not be reconciled – a view that fitted well with the inherent prejudices of colonial-period writers.[3] Further, the writing of the histories of the Delhi sultanate, its successors and eventually the Mughal empire has largely, though not exclusively, been based on materials in Persian, while the history of the south has been based on regional language and

---

[1] Coutre 1991: 246.
[2] See Kulke 1997: 46–7, which is one of the rare attempts to grapple with a problem posed squarely a decade earlier in Subrahmanyam 1986.
[3] Cf. the historiographical survey in Stein 1989; and compare Thapar 2002.

Sanskrit materials, in the form both of inscriptions and of other texts. This has meant sets of competences that were usually not intersecting between those working north and south of the Vindhya mountains, the conventional dividing point between north and south. It was rare to find a historian who felt comfortable dealing with both northern and southern Indian history in these middle centuries, whereas historians both of ancient India and of the colonial period seemed more easily to straddle the divide. For the India of the ancient period was thought to be unified somehow by Sanskrit (what some have called the 'Sanskrit cosmopolis'),[4] while the English-language archives of the colonial period also allowed historians of many different persuasions to generalize constantly at the level of the whole subcontinent.

This chapter is concerned with a set of states which help us to question these easy divisions, both temporal and spatial. The Vijayanagara or Karnataka state, which transformed itself in a matter of two generations from its creation into an imperial structure, was founded sometime towards the middle of the fourteenth century in an area that lies between the north and the south – the so-called Deccan. The location of its capital city lay not in the fertile deltas of the east coast but in a relatively rugged area on the banks of the river Tungabhadra as it made its way from the Western Ghats to the eastern coastal plain. The career of the Vijayanagara empire is somewhat atypical when compared to many other states of the period, for it consisted not of the more-or-less continuous rule of a single male lineage (as happened with the Cholas, the Bahmanids or the Mughals), but of a succession of different lineages, which nevertheless saw themselves as preserving a form of continuity in rulership. In this respect, it corresponds most closely to the Delhi sultanate, where several lineages – Mamluks or 'Slave Dynasty' (already a complex case), Khaljis, Tughluqs, Sayyids and Lodis – follow one another while still preserving a notion of continuous rule.[5] In the Vijayanagara case, the earliest formation, namely that of the Sangama clan, seems to derive from the preceding south-western kingdom of the Hoysalas, who are best remembered for having built spectacular and intricate temples in sites such as Belur (not to be confused with Velur) and Halebid.[6] However, even if we are unable to identify the links precisely, some retrospective materials quite clearly suggest that the early history of the Sangamas was also tied up to the Kakatiya dynasty to the north-east (around the region of Warrangal), and even – perhaps more indirectly – to

[4] Pollock 1996.   [5] See Jackson 1999; Kumar 2007.
[6] Materials for this early period have been brought together in Filliozat 1973; for a recent reconsideration of this period, also see Wagoner 2000.

the Delhi sultanate which had begun expanding into the region in the late thirteenth century.

Sangama rule was followed by that of a second, relatively short-lived but powerful dynasty, in the latter half of the fifteenth century, one of whose rulers – Saluva Narasimha (d. 1491) – was seen as sufficiently important that Portuguese writers still used a distorted form of his name 'Narsinga' as an equivalent for the whole kingdom in the sixteenth century. After his death, his lineage was unable to cling to power for long, and was eventually replaced by the third Vijayanagara dynasty, that of the Tuluvas – who came from the Indian west coast. Tuluva rule, founded by the warlord Narasa Nayaka, is seen by most historians of Vijayanagara as the moment when the empire reached its greatest territorial extent as well as the height of its effective power, but it lasted less than a century.[7] By about 1570, following a major defeat at the hands of rival powers from the northern fringes of the kingdom, the Tuluva rulers were replaced in a familiar pattern by a lineage of warlords with whom they had intermarried, namely the Aravidus from the Telugu country. It is this fourth lineage then which presides over the last century of the so-called 'Vijayanagara period', during which the empire shrinks back into a rump-state, so that eventually, by about 1650, the Aravidu rulers were in control of no more than a small principality in the Chandragiri hills not far from the emergent colonial port-city of Madras.

This is potentially a confusing history then, involving several lineages, but also at least one major shift of political centre, from the initial capital at Vijayanagara to a later (post-1570) set of intermittent capitals, which also corresponds roughly to a transition between imperial consolidation and a period when a set of compact regional states had emerged under the carapace of Vijayanagara authority. These latter are the so-called Nayaka states which we shall discuss in a subsequent part of this chapter, and they numbered at least five. To the far west was the Ikkeri state, ruled over from a centre in the Western Ghats, while the south-west was dominated after about 1600 by the Wodeyar lineage at Mysore. To the east along the Coromandel coast lay – from north to south – the Nayaka states of Senji, Tanjavur and Madurai, each with a different life-span. Senji, the shortest lived, emerged in about 1570, was extinguished in 1649 by the forces of the sultanate of Bijapur, and then eventually fell under Maratha control for a brief period. Tanjavur, which like Madurai emerged around 1530, for its part managed to survive as late as 1673, while Madurai was the last to be overrun,

[7] On this transition of the early sixteenth century, see Subrahmanyam 2000.

in 1736. This complex set of chronologies further muddies what are in any event not very limpid historiographical waters. Perhaps this explains why few historians have attempted to venture to analyse these states seriously since the 1920s and 1930s, when a set of conventional monographs was first produced on them by historians associated with the University of Madras.

It is to these historians one normally turns for an understanding of the bedrock on which the English-language historiography is built. To be sure, we can find some primitive steps taken already in the nineteenth century by colonial administrators such as Colin Mackenzie and Mark Wilks, who were attempting to show how the Muslim rulers (such as Tipu Sultan or the Nawwab of Arcot), whom the English East India Company defeated or subjugated in order to gain its control of the region, were mere usurpers.[8] A significant intermediate moment is also marked by Robert Sewell, whose book *A Forgotten Empire*, published in 1900, tried to revive the 'forgotten' rule of Vijayanagara in an intervention that was based on a combination of epigraphy and translated Portuguese texts from the sixteenth century. Sewell began his work with the following words, before developing his thesis of Vijayanagara as 'a Hindu bulwark against Muhammadan conquest':

In the year 1336 A.D., during the reign of Edward III of England, there occurred in India an event which almost instantaneously changed the political condition of the entire south. With that date the volume of ancient history in that tract closes and the modern begins. It is the epoch of transition from the Old to the New. This event was the foundation of the city and kingdom of Vijayanagar.[9]

In the next half-century, scholars very largely associated with the University of Madras attempted to flesh out the picture produced by Sewell, while also casting their net wider for materials. One of major figures in this respect was Nelatur Venkataramanayya, whose *Studies in the Third Dynasty of Vijayanagara* is an important attempt to describe the political and fiscal structure of sixteenth-century Vijayanagara rule, possibly drawing inspiration from the work of K. A. Nilakantha Sastri on the earlier Chola dynasty.[10] The main thrust here was to produce a systematic listing of the appropriate fiscal and administrative categories that operated from the imperial treasury down to the level of the individual village. A corresponding work based largely on Kannada materials was that of B. A. Saletore, who also attempted in his two-volume study *Social and Political Life in the Vijayanagara Empire (A.D. 1346–A.D. 1646)* (1934) to cover a far larger temporal sweep. A third, more

---

[8] See the posthumously published work, Mackenzie 1844.   [9] Sewell 1972: 1.
[10] Venkataramanayya 1935; also Venkataramanayya 1933.

eccentric, attempt at understanding Aravidu times based largely on Portuguese, Italian and Latin sources was that of the Spanish Jesuit H. Heras in
his *The Aravidu Dynasty of Vijayanagara*.[11] It is significant that none of these
writers concerned himself in any substantial way with ideological questions,
or with understanding the manner in which the Vijayanagara empire or
its Nayaka successors were conceived of in terms of any form of internal
political theory. The same remained largely true for writers who began to
treat the period once again in the 1960s and 1970s, notably Burton Stein
and Noboru Karashima. At one level, these two writers represent opposed
poles in the historiography, with the Chicago-trained Stein espousing an
approach that appears to derive from historical anthropology (notably the
use of the 'segmentary state' model), while Karashima preferred a conventional set of Marxist categories, seeking to fit Vijayanagara into a received
framework of 'feudalism' (though suggesting intriguing and – alas – unexplored parallels with 'the Tokugawa feudalism of Japan'). However, what
was remarkable was that neither sought any more than their predecessors
to discover what might have constituted the deeper ideological premises
of these states. In Karashima's case, this may be explained in part through
his single-minded recourse to inscriptional materials as the only reliable
'factual' basis for any study of the period, although it is unclear whether
this is a case of cause or effect.[12] In the case of Stein, despite the common
view that he devoted great attention to ideological matters, the explicit
reflections we find from him on the question are only three: first, an early
formulation suggesting that classical Indian notions of universal rulership
(the idea of the *cakravartin*, for example) are still at work here; second,
an analysis of one particular ritual performance, that of the Mahanavami
festival in the capital city; and, finally, a later rejection of any suggestion
that the Vijayanagara kingdom was a bulwark of 'Hindu' rulership holding
steadfast against Muslim incursions from the north. The last, as we can
see, is a negative statement, denying another formulation, rather than one
with marked positive content.

Thus, we may conclude this introductory section by pointing to the
relative poverty of writings regarding Vijayanagara and post-Vijayanagara
ideology, even within the narrow and admittedly unsatisfactory terms of
Weberian 'legitimation theory'.[13] The only exceptions that exist to our
knowledge may be found in some work for late eighteenth-century Mysore,

[11] Heras 1927; Saletore 1934.   [12] Karashima 1992; also Karashima 1999.
[13] For a rare attempt within the Weberian framework to deal with an aspect of Vijayanagara ideology as
both the 'gross manipulation of religious institutions' by the state, and reflecting 'the most intricate
and mutual relations between *ksatra* and *ksetra*', see Kulke 1993a.

and in our own earlier work on the Nayakas – something of a voice in the wilderness – entitled *Symbols of Substance*.[14] This is in some contrast with the case of other parts of India in the same period. We may point to the long debate in the Mughal literature, for example, regarding the status of the so-called Turco-Mongol theory of kingship, the discussion by the late John Richards regarding the 'formulation of imperial authority' under Akbar and Jahangir, and S. A. A. Rizvi's discussion of intellectual currents in the court and period of Akbar, with a particular focus on the figure of Abu'l Fazl.[15] Most recently, the work by Muzaffar Alam on *The Languages of Political Islam in India* takes this debate to a new level of sophistication, drawing on political treatises and chronicles, as well as poetry and Sufi literature, to show the struggle between various conflicting social elements to define an appropriate ideology (or set of ideologies) for rule in northern India between about 1200 and 1700.[16] We shall argue below that by similarly taking a wider view of the historical materials in the Vijayanagara and post-Vijayanagara cases, we can advance our understanding of the ideological currents that were present in these states as well as the conflicts between them. To set out our case schematically, we shall argue that in the first half of the sixteenth century, during the rule of the Tuluva dynast Krishnadevaraya (r. 1509–29), a particular ideological formulation was proposed to resolve the problem of the relationship between imperial centre and outlying regions. Then, with the emergence of the Nayaka kingdoms, this point of view was set aside and another formulation emerged, which was perhaps seen as more appropriate for the compact regional kingdoms that the Nayakas in fact ruled over. Both these approaches may have sought referents in the materials that were available from classical India, but we can also see them as representing approaches to near-universal problems of centralization and decentralization, which obviously take us not only into northern India but to a larger sphere of comparative reflection. It is also important to note that both the problems posed and the solutions chosen were specific to the period at hand, rather than simply rehashing debates that had been conducted in Indian courts and states a millennium before.

II

At the heart of our argument is the idea of the transition from an imperial structure to a set of compact regional kingdoms. Before proceeding

---

[14] Narayana Rao, Shulman and Subrahmanyam 1992.
[15] Richards 1978; and earlier Rizvi 1975.   [16] Alam 2004.

further, we may stop to reassure ourselves that Vijayanagara was indeed an 'empire'.[17] We are aware that notions of levels, and even multiple layers, of rulership existed in the Vijayanagara state by the middle years of the fifteenth century. In other words, there was a ruler at the centre – the great western capital city that had been founded in about 1340 – who disposed of the title of 'Raya' or 'Maharaya', but who also had other 'rajas' under his domination in the far-flung regions that extended by the 1430s as far as the Kaveri delta to the south-east. Anthony Pagden has recently reflected in his *Peoples and Empires* on what might define an empire, and this is a useful starting point for our purposes. He notes that 'ultimately it would be size which separated empires from mere kingdoms and principalities', and also notes that 'empires have . . . embraced peoples who have held a wide variety of different customs and beliefs, and often spoken an equally large number of different languages'. All of these clearly fit the Vijayanagara case after its first wave of major expansion, which meant that by 1400 it had penetrated deep into the Tamil country. These rulers saw themselves in grandiose terms as above other monarchs, but were also consistently perceived in this way by visitors to their court, such as 'Abdur Razzaq Samarqandi from Herat, who – as representative of Timur's son Shahrukh – knew something about imperial structures.[18] The use of titles such as 'sultan over Hindu kings' (*hindūrāyasuratrāṇa*), or 'establisher of Muslim kings' (*yavanarājyasthāpanâcārya*), testifies amply to such claims.[19] In the sixteenth century, Portuguese chroniclers who sought to depict the grandeur of Vijayanagara always used the conventional metaphor that this ruler had 'forty crowned kings as his vassals'.

What problems did ruling over such a vast empire – which in the early sixteenth century stretched from coast to coast, and went down more than half the length of the Indian peninsula – present in ideological terms? Empires may be conquered by force but are ultimately held together by an ideology. To quote Pagden again, 'in the case of the Roman empire, this ideology was that of "civilization," the lure of a more desirable, more comfortable, and infinitely richer way of life. In the case of the Spanish, French, and British empires, it was this too, now reinforced by differing brands of Christianity. In the case of the Ottomans it was [Sunni] Islam, and in the case of the Soviet Union, Marxism.'[20]

---

[17] For a brief reflection on this problem, also see Morrison 2001.
[18] 'Kamaluddin Abdul-Razzaq Samarqandi: Mission to Calicut and Vijayanagar', in Thackston 1989: 299–321.
[19] Wagoner 1996.   [20] Pagden 2001: xxi.

What then was the ideology that answered this need for Vijayanagara? The studies that have looked into the modes of revenue-collection and military arrangements (including the so-called *amara-nāyankara* system) at best explain the mechanics of imperial administration. Stein's theory of ritual kingship and his idea that rituals such as *mahānavami* which were attended by all the subordinate rulers of the empire had a certain potential to explain the imperial ideology is worth some consideration. Stein argued that 'this annual, royal rite was probably the most important ceremony that occurred in the city during its two centuries as a great capital, and [that] it serves as a means of understanding the relationship among some of the key structures of the royal centre'.[21] Further, while these rituals were conducted by the king on a lavish scale in his capital city, they could to some extent have had an 'integrative' function. However, one has the impression that Stein's reading of this ritual is strongly influenced by what *navarātri* had become in the later Wodeyar kingdom of Mysore, which was a relatively compact state. A serious issue of scale remains unanswered. Similarly, John Fritz, George Michell, Anna Dallapiccola and others have given us an elaborate description of the capital city of Vijayanagara, which was divided according to them into two centres, the sacred and the royal.[22] They also indicate that the Ramachandra temple in the urban centre had a powerful ritual role in the city. Together Stein and Fritz *et al.* give us an elaborate explanation to suggest that the imperial level of kingship in Vijayanagara was sustained by rituals alone. Granted that rituals such as these had a powerful visual impact in demonstrating the glory of the empire to those who were invited to attend it, they would still lack the power to convince us that by themselves they carried an ideological charge that was sufficient to influence the vast population of the empire. Ideological enactments that require a physical attendance at the centre of power may thus be effective with respect to the upper echelons of the elite, but we need to consider the problem of spatial spread in an empire, precisely because it is an empire and not a compact kingdom.[23]

One of the areas that had largely been left out of consideration by nearly all the earlier scholars of Vijayanagara was its literary production. We know that the kings of Vijayanagara encouraged and patronized poets. In particular the emperor Krishnadevaraya in the early sixteenth century

---

[21] Stein 1989: 37; also see the far more extensive, and explicitly Hocartian, discussion in Stein 1980: 384–92. Here, Stein extensively and approvingly cites Hocart 1970, for his 'attention to the symbolically integrative character of the temple and the city' (390).

[22] Fritz, Michell and Nagaraja Rao 1984; Dallapiccola and Zingel-Avé Lallemant 1985.

[23] For an earlier critique of Stein's views, see Subrahmanyam 1997b.

had a galaxy of poets around him such as Allasani Peddanna, whose work *Manucaritramu* is widely considered to be the greatest *kāvya* narrative poem in Telugu literature. In addition, the emperor himself wrote one of the greatest *kāvya* poems in Telugu literature, entitled the *Āmuktamālyada*. If the Mughals cultivated the culture of patronizing artists to paint miniatures, a practice which then became an important symbol of imperial culture, the Vijayanagara kings above all patronized poets. However, unlike a painting which sits uniquely and cannot easily be circulated or duplicated, a well-crafted narrative poem has a high degree of popular circulation.[24] Telugu court-narrative is composed with the patron king as the listener. The poet addresses his patron in mellifluous language at the beginning and the end of each chapter. Furthermore, he takes a whole chapter at the beginning of his poem to tell how his patron came to commission him to write the poem for him. The context is so beautifully described that the readers of the poem remember the verses and recite them for the sheer aesthetic joy they get out of it. In addition, the poet also describes the family history of the patron beginning from the earliest ancestors.

Such extensive prefatory verses, placing the duo of poet and patron at the heart of the matter, are unique in South Asia to Telugu literature, and became a staple of all courtly poetry in Telugu. *Kāvya* poems were thus read by the elite over a vast area of the empire, which offered a wide distribution network. Verses from the poems were memorized and recited among cultured people, and if you could not read verses, you were not included in such groups that determined the boundaries of proper culture. A person who was not properly educated to appreciate courtly poetry was often not seen as fit to be a head of a village, a chief of an army unit or even an accountant – not to speak of such high positions as the head of a fortress. In addition, there was a belief that a person who received the dedication of a poem kept his good name alive in the memory of people, which hence bought him a passage to heaven. It was also believed that a poem received in dedication was like a son who helped the father to ascend to higher worlds after death by performing proper funerary rituals. There are seven kinds of actions that lead a person to heaven, all of which are called his 'sons' – building a temple (*devâlaya*), constructing a water tank (*taṭāka*), instituting a Brahmin village (*agrahāra*), growing a garden (*vana*), establishing an endowment (*nidhi*), receiving a poem in dedication (*kriti*) and, of course, literally giving birth to a son (*putra*). Among these, the poem

---

[24] On texts that circulated as a part of imperial ideological affirmation, also see (for the case of Qing China and the Kangxi emperor) Mair 1985.

was seen as the one act that never died. Temples collapse, water tanks dry
up and so on, but a poem lives as long as the sun, the moon and the stars
shine. With beliefs such as these around a poem in circulation during and
after Krishnadevaraya's time, it was no wonder that the kings believed that
literature was the most ideally suited vehicle for creating, and propagating,
an ideology. So, let us look into the courtly literary production of the
Krishnadevaraya period, to explore evidence towards shaping an ideology
for the empire.

One of the things poets do for a patron king is to invent a mythological
origin for his family. Traditionally, ancient royal families originated from
either the Sun or the Moon. In the two great classical Sanskrit epics, the
hero of the *Rāmāyaṇa* comes from the Solar dynasty, while the heroes
of the *Mahābhārata* emanate from the Moon. Using the family origin of
either of the celestial bodies has been a time-honoured strategy of kings
with imperial aspirations. Krishnadevaraya's court poet Allasani Peddanna
obliges his patron by doing this for him.[25] According to Peddanna, the
dynasty goes like this. It begins with the Moon, a male figure in Hindu
mythology, whose son is Atri, who in turn gives birth to Budha. Budha's
son is Turvasu, and this is where mythology ends and almost seamlessly
history begins. The Turvasu family becomes the Tulu family, the family
into which Krishnadevaraya is born. The poet begins the description of
the Tulu family with King Timmaraya. To quote the words of Peddanna,

The mighty Timma, the greatest of the lords of the earth, relieved
the ancient tortoise, the mighty mountains, the king of snakes,
the elephants that stood in each direction and the old boar
of their burdens, and held the earth secure on the pedestal of his strong arms.
His fame spread all the way to the sky while his enemies were humbled to serve.
They bent their heads and stood by his side as he wielded his scorching power.[26]

Let us note that Krishnadevaraya's court poet takes care to state that
the king was the bearer of the burden of the earth, similar to *ādisesa*,
the primeval snake; *ādivarāha*, the primeval boar; *kūrma*, the tortoise;
or the *ashṭa-dig-gajas*, the eight elephants of the directions. Later on, after
a few more verses describing the other members of the dynasty, the poet
states that Krishnadevaraya was born sharing an aspect of Vishnu. This
section concludes after a series of stunningly beautiful verses describing
Krishnadevaraya's successful military campaigns, his charitable qualities
and his love of poetry.

---

[25] On Peddanna, also see Narayana Rao and Shulman 2002: 241–51, and Shulman 2001: 323–50.
[26] Peddanna 1966: ch. 1, v. 23 (our translation from Telugu).

Descriptions of emperors' families and conquests are not new. The great imperial poet Kalidasa from the Gupta period, a thousand-odd years before Krishnadevaraya, wrote about the Raghu dynasty as a family of kings who ruled the earth encircled by oceans, and whose chariots travelled all the way to heaven. Conquering the eight directions of the earth (*digvijaya*) is what a great emperor is supposed to do in order to establish his sovereignty (*sārvabhaumatva*) over the other kings by demanding subordination and tributes from them to symbolize it. Vedic sacrifices that kings boasted of included rituals such as *asvamedha*, where the king lets a horse loose to roam free all over the earth. Any king who finds the horse walking over his territory has only two choices: allow it go unobstructed, thus symbolically accepting the suzerainty of the king over his territory, or stop the horse and fight a battle with him.

A king according to this imaginary is the *kshatriya* warrior who protects *dharma*, or righteous conduct. He is guided by the *śāstras* (the code of laws) and the Brahmins who interpret them. In effect the king does not make laws, he only executes them. They are already laid out in the *śāstras* and do not change from king to king. So a conquering king does not, in principle, change anything. He operates as a new executive in place of the old one, upholding *dharma*. Then why do kings still want to conquer other kings? Because it is the *dharma* of a king to make himself the ruler of all the land, rendering every other king his subordinate. A kingdom as defined in this culture is one that is available to anybody who can conquer it. Since the earth needs a conqueror, a king has to establish himself as the ruler of the entire earth and make her, according to another metaphor, his consort. The conquering king is not perceived as an aggressor. The concept of aggression does not occur in this scheme of things: a perfect ideology crafted for an empire builder. Every school child recites the names of the six great emperors of India: Harishchandra, Nala, Purukutsa, Pururava, Sagara and Kartavirya, who are certainly mythological, but also in a sense 'real' enough.

In medieval India, the concept of empire and the idea of an emperor were hence deeply embedded in mythology and literature and were a part of received knowledge. Whereas, in Europe, an imperial imagination had to develop over a period of time beginning from an unassuming Latin word *imperium*, in India it was ready at hand for an aspiring king from early on. For clear evidence that Krishnadevaraya adopted this ideology for his kingship, we do not need to look any further than the king's own narrative poem *Āmuktamālyada*, in which the king borrows Peddanna's description of the king's family and incorporates it in the prefatory chapter of his own poem. In effect this indicates that Krishnadevaraya adopted the concept of kingship Peddanna had promulgated. In addition, Krishnadevaraya produced his own version of an imperial ideology in the so-called *rājanīti* section of his *Āmuktamālyada*, where the reigning king, Yamuna, who is leaving the kingdom as a renouncer, instructs and advises the incoming king.[27] The advice is the most elaborately detailed policy to run an empire.

One item in this rather long advice deserves our attention and is related to the support of Brahmins. Krishnadevaraya recommends posting Brahmins as commanders of forts, *durga*, and in fact this practical advice is corroborated by studies of the prosopography of the notables of the empire in that time.[28]

> Make trustworthy Brahmins
> the commanders of your forts
> and give them just enough troops,
> to protect these strongholds,
> lest they become too threatening.
>   (Verse 207)

Brahmins, in this view, have certain clear advantages over non-Brahmins, in that they do not make a living off the land and therefore do not have an emotional attachment to it. They are freely mobile, living off their scholarship or other skills they individually acquire. The normative function of Brahmins is to legitimize a king by elevating him to the status of a classical warrior-ruler, a *kshatriya*. They are more secure in this position than by wanting to be kings themselves. Krishnadevaraya clearly wanted to plug into this normative system by elevating Brahmins, which in turn elevated him. This is a clear deviation from the policy adopted by the earlier Kakatiya kingdom, where the military leaders, or Nayakas, were chiefly drawn from communities who were rooted in the land they lived on and entertained strong aspirations to be kings themselves. In the end they fought among themselves and this may have contributed to the collapse of the Kakatiya kingdom. Apparently from his experience of the nature of such castes, Krishnadevaraya, who himself came from a Tulu land, at a distance from the land over which he actually gained military control, promoted his support of Brahmins. To quote again from his *rājanīti*:

---

[27] For a detailed examination of these materials, see Narayana Rao, Shulman and Subrahmanyam 2004.
[28] Talbot 2001.

The king will often benefit by putting a Brahmin in charge,
for he knows both the laws of Manu and his own *dharma*.
And from fear of being mocked
by Kshatriyas and Sudras,
he will stand up to all difficulties.

(Verse 217)

This policy is not just pragmatic; it is made with a critical and strategic understanding of how to build an empire which includes different regions, castes and languages, each holding inherent centrifugal tendencies. The support of a trans-regional caste such as Brahmins who hold allegiance to a pan-Indian ideology of the *varṇa*-order as defined in the *śāstras* is crucial for a king aspiring to build an empire. This policy need not be confined to the oft-repeated nationalist formulation that Krishnadevaraya was building a 'Hindu' bastion in opposition to the advancing Muslim power from the north of the Krishna river. The *varṇa*-order Krishnadevaraya articulated was more secular than is apparent on the surface. Though deeply rooted in the religious traditions of Vaishnavism and truly devoted to the god Vishnu in his personal life, as well as in the role of the king, Krishnadevaraya was still very eclectic in his political policies and followed shrewd practices dictated by *Realpolitik*. He was no enemy of any kingdom on the basis of religion alone. He was in fact more friendly with the Muslim rulers to his north and west when it was expedient than with the Hindu Gajapatis to the east, in Orissa.

A second and equally pragmatic choice in promoting an imperial ideology was related to the choice of a court language. Krishnadevaraya was acutely aware that he ruled over a multilingual empire, and he published his inscriptions in multiple languages – Sanskrit, Kannada, Tamil and Telugu. A few decades before him, it was still possible to use Sanskrit as a court language and achieve the necessary royal status, as well as the trans-regional legitimacy needed for an empire. But political culture had changed by the sixteenth century and there were now regional languages that had achieved a literary status of their own. Local chiefs who were upwardly mobile preferred using their own languages as a matter of prestige. Sanskrit still had a place of course, but it did not possess the same legitimizing power it once had.[29] For a ruler who came from a small area, Tulunad on the west coast, and who spoke Tulu – a language that does not even have a script of its own – Krishnadevaraya was linguistically neutral, and free from any emotional attachment to one major language or the other. Being totally neutral, he

---

[29] For the long-term evolution of Sanskrit, see Pollock 2006.

seems to have made a pragmatic decision in choosing Telugu as the royal language. Telugu chiefs were at this time the most powerful, and the most widespread across the several regions of his empire, and Telugu speakers were possibly a majority among his subjects. Even in doing so, he enlisted the support of Vishnu himself in announcing that choice.

The situation that led the king to compose his magnum opus – *Āmukatmālyada* – in Telugu is worth looking into in some detail to understand Krishnadevaraya's choice of language. The king describes in the prefatory chapter to the book that, while he was on his way to a military expedition, he happened to stay in the grounds of the temple of Andhra Mahavishnu in Srikakulam in the Krishna district of present-day Andhra Pradesh, when, during the early hours of the night, the god Vishnu, along with his two wives Wealth and Earth, came to him in a dream and, after introducing himself and his wives, asked him to write a poem in Telugu. The god already knew that Krishnadevaraya had written many books in Sanskrit, and thought therefore that Telugu could not be beyond his reach. Vishnu went on, raising the question of language himself:

> Why Telugu?
> The country is Telugu, and I am
> a Telugu lord,
> and Telugu is sweet.
> You know when you speak the language
> to all those kings who come to serve you.
> Among the languages of the land,
> Telugu is best.

It is very significant that the imperial ideology of Krishnadevaraya survived his demise with enhanced popularity in the popular imagination – though not in the policies and practices of kings who inherited the empire. A large body of legends were soon in oral circulation about the emperor, his military campaigns, his literary glory with a galaxy of poets seated around him (also metaphorically called the *ashta-dig-gajas*, the eight cardinal elephants that support the earth) in his royal assembly hall called the *bhuvana vijaya* – the conquest of the earth – and the constant play of literary competitions between his own poets and visiting poets. Krishnadevaraya is called the emperor of both the battlefield and the field of letters, *sāhitī-samarāṅgaṇa-cakravarti*. Several *kaifiyat*-texts or local histories that Colin Mackenzie and his assistants collected in the early nineteenth century begin their narrative with words such as 'When, in the beginning, Krishnadevaraya was ruling', as if civilization and the process of settlement began with the rule of this great king.

The story of royal ideology in south India takes a sharp new turn, how-ever, during the reign of the Nayaka kings of Madurai and Tanjavur. During this period the dominant depiction is one where the king *is* Vishnu, the god himself. The equation of god and king had significant implications for the ideology of rulership, as we will elaborate below. Let us remember that in the ideology of Krishnadevaraya, the king was not himself Vishnu; he was only sharing an aspect of Vishnu in ruling the earth under the prescriptions of the ancient laws given by Manu. In this imaginary, the Brahmin makes the king a *kshatriya* warrior and the king in turn confirms the other's status as a Brahmin. Their mutual ideological dependence is the structure on which the entire system sustains itself. This is the well-known dual hierarchy of Brahmana and Kshatriya that Louis Dumont writes about, albeit in a more elaborate and considerably modified form.[30] But, when the king becomes god himself, the dual hierarchy collapses. Everyone in the kingdom, including the Brahmins, now by definition is a servant of the king, because no one is superior to god (cf. the discus-sion of pope, patriarch and emperors by Angelov and Herrin, Chapter 6 above).

The potential of this ideology is briefly hinted at even during Krish-nadevaraya's time, by one of his court poets, Nandi Timmanna, in his *Pārijātâpaharaṇamu* (the story of Krishna stealing the Parijata plant from Indra's garden to please his demanding wife Satyabhama). In the customary preface to his *kāvya* poem, Nandi Timmanna describes Krishnadevaraya, making him an incarnation of Krishna himself. Here is a section of the poem suggesting the identity:

> Because as a cowherd, he [Krishna] could not sit on a throne,
> he [Krishnadevaraya] was to take his place, radiant, on a throne.
> Because he made love to the wives of other cowherds,
> he was to act as a brother towards all women not his own.
> Because he lost Mathura to the demon Jarasandha,
> he was to take by force the fortresses of his enemies.
> Because he had greedily stolen Indra's Parijata tree,
> he was to wipe out that blemish with his charity.
> Because all these faults had to be his when born
> before as Krishna, he has returned so as to remove them.
> He is Krishna descended again, who has taken on a form
> that receives utmost honour from everyone in the world:
> the son of Narasaraya, Krishnaraya, lord of the earth.[31]

---

[30] Dumont 1970.   [31] Timmanna 1978: ch. 1, v. 17 (our translation from Telugu).

There is no evidence, however, that Krishnadevaraya encouraged the god-king concept of rulership beyond this isolated occurrence. However, as we shall see below, during the Nayaka period that followed Krishnadevaraya's rule, this ideology went on to reach its fullest potential.

III

As we have noted above, the Nayaka kingdoms emerged in the decades following Krishnadevaraya's death, and consolidated themselves over the latter half of the sixteenth century. In what follows, our focus will be largely limited to two of these kingdoms, namely Tanjavur and Madurai, since the Senji case is far more poorly documented and difficult to discern in its internal logic. We have argued at length elsewhere that the social basis of rulership in these states was somewhat different from what had obtained in Vijayanagara, and that a prominent role was played by castes such as the Balija Naidus – who occupied a curious place in between the older warrior and merchant roles (while often claiming proudly to be Shudras). The Nayaka rulers rarely presented themselves, in any of the quite elaborate materials they produced and patronized, as active warriors and conquerors in the mould of Krishnadevaraya. Rather, they drew upon a set of elements that might at first sight appear to be internally contradictory – but which eventually yielded up a complex ideological statement.

Put schematically, we might say that the Nayaka ideology of rulership draws upon four elements. The *first* of these is a claim that kingship is based strongly on ties to the accumulation of liquid resources in an economy that is overflowing with cash and intimately tied to commerce and artisanal production. To be sure, the Nayaka states are small in relation to the great empire from which they have sprung, but this also means that they are 'managed' in a way that is more akin to an estate than an imperial polity. Nayaka rulers deploy revenue-farmers, oversee the trade in ports, buy shares in ships trading across the Bay of Bengal, accumulate resources, and, instead of using them in the traditional mode to hand out grants to temples and Brahmins (*devadāna* and *brahmadeya*), spend lavishly in a manner that is meant to proclaim defiantly their own 'spendthrift' cult of enjoyment (*bhoga*). This in turn is linked to great public rituals of feeding, the so-called *annadāna*, and a strong drive to present the ruler as an aesthetic and erotically charged figure, exemplifying the virtues of *vīraśriṅgāra*, what we have elsewhere termed a heroism not of the battlefield but of the bedroom. Even the Jesuits, sourly observing the functioning of these kingdoms from their own Counter-Reformation standpoint, were aware of some of these new facts of Nayaka political economy. Thus the following Jesuit description with regard to Madurai's seventeenth-century ruler Chokkanatha Nayaka:

The young king Chokkanatha came from Madura to Trichinopoly and gave a public banquet to the poor, who hastened in thousands from all the neighbouring countries. A vast plain, situated on the banks of the Kaveri, formed the dining hall. The plates of the country, that is to say banana leaves, were arranged in several rows. From distance to distance rose heaps of rice, around which were prepared diverse condiments, according to Indian custom. Bands of men and women were entrusted with the distribution of food to the guests, each seated before his plate in diverse parallel files. At the commencement of the repast, the prince arrived on horseback surrounded by his court. He proceeded along the space between the rows and was pleased to see the poor starving people eat.[32]

A *second* aspect that stems from this first one is the Nayaka claim that earlier ascriptive models, notably the *varna*-based social order we have remarked upon above, cannot be seen any more as the appropriate ways of holding together polities. Rather, the world that the Nayakas inhabit is one of tricksters and 'self-made' men, devious and often ruthless, a world that comes depicted to us in such works as the *Annadānamahānātakamu*, a parodic play from seventeenth-century Tanjavur, which casts a complex glance at the scramble for resources amongst competing groups in the Nayaka state. Texts from this period thus feel the right to state confidently and cynically:

> Never mind if he is born in a low caste,
> never mind if he is timid,
> never mind if he is son of a whore.
> If he has money, he is king.

The *third* crucial element of Nayaka rule is the claim that king and god have somehow merged, once again breaking down the distinctions that were still operative in the time of Krishnadevaraya. This is not a wholly unique or unprecedented claim, for we may find traces of it elsewhere, notably in the medieval 'Indianized' kingdoms of South East Asia (where it appears much attenuated as a form of 'apotheosis') and more recently in nineteenth- and twentieth-century Nepal.[33] However, there is something paradoxical about the process; the reduction in scale from the grandeur of empire to the more

[32] Narayana Rao, Shulman and Subrahmanyam 1992: 70–1.
[33] For a reconsideration of the problem in South East Asia, see Kulke 1993b. For Nepal, see Burghart 1987.

modest scale of the regional kingdom thus has produced a curious inflation in royal claims rather than a depletion. It is with the Nayakas that we find claims such as these, in a courtly *kāvya* concerning the Tanjavur Nayaka Raghunatha in the seventeenth century:

> Those who enshrine Raghunatha, the splendid son of
> Achyutendra, in their hearts as [the god] Raghunatha [Rama]
> Himself, visibly present, have the joy
> Of ultimate bliss.

An echo of this merging of king and god can be glimpsed in the description by the Venetian adventurer Nicolò Manucci of the end of the Tanjavur dynasty in 1673. Manucci, who probably derived his information from Jesuits residing in south India, wrote of how Vijayaraghava Nayaka 'was so full of haughtiness and vainglory that he wanted to imitate one of his gods called Quisina [Krishna], of whom it was said in their Scriptures, that he had the same number of wives'.[34] The bizarre manner in which the Nayaka chose to end his life, preferring death to negotiation with the Nayakas of Madurai, seemed to Manucci to offer further confirmation of this rather particular mindset.

And *finally*, the Nayaka ideological structure is based on an ever greater emphasis on *Realpolitik*, the 'secular' vision that is embodied in the tradition of *nīti* texts on statecraft, which may find its counterpart in the *akhlāq* texts that Muzaffar Alam has studied in the Mughal context. The growing importance of these *nīti* texts is stressed in a verse such as this one, from a collection by Madiki Singana that was widely read:

> In the training of horses and elephants,
> while doing the king's work,
> when making peace or fighting a war,
> in affairs of trade,
> or of cultivating land,
> and even when thinking of *moksha*,
> without looking into the mirror called *nīti*,
> can anyone find the best course of action –
> even Brahma himself?[35]

It is possible, as we have argued at greater length elsewhere, to bring out these complex elements of Nayaka ideology in relation to a whole series

---

[34] Manucci 1990: III, 100. This passage does not appear in the Portuguese text in the Biblioteca Nazionale Marciana, Venice, Codex Zanetti, It. 44 (= 8299), 433–5, and seems to derive from the other Manucci manuscript at the Staatsbibliothek zu Berlin.

[35] Singana 1970 (our translation from Telugu).

of materials, whether textual or visual, often produced by members of the group of *karanams*, scribes and literati who resided in small towns and cities of the Nayaka world.[36] The anonymous chronicle of the rulers of the Tanjavur kingdom, the *Tañjāvūrī āndhra rājula caritra*, probably written (or at least completed) in Madurai in the early eighteenth century, is an excellent example of the shift in perspective that the Nayakas embody, as set out by a *karanam* author. Its description of how the Nayaka kingdoms emerged, through a complex political interplay between region and imperial centre, is itself a masterpiece of Machiavellian realism, where the illusion of loyalty rather than rebellion is what permits Visvanatha Nayaka to hive off a kingdom in Madurai in about 1530. In this text, as the Tanjavur Nayaka state eventually works its way through the full cycle of formation, maturity, collapse and an eventual attempt at revival (in the 1670s, centring on the figure of the pretender Chengamaladasa), the typical Nayaka actors – including manipulative figures of would-be kingmakers like Rayasam Venkanna – crowd the pages, portraying a world that is rather far removed from the far more sober imperial ideal of Krishnadevaraya's time. The same vision comes to be confirmed to us in a host of other writings, from both the courtly and the more popular milieux. Interestingly, though the dominant language continues to be Telugu, the Nayaka rulers also promote a flourishing polyglossia, which survives in some form into the eighteenth century.

The Nayaka ideology was bound to be contested by others, especially on account of the starkly antinomian and transgressive elements that it embodied. We see this in the context of the eighteenth century, when the Maratha dynasty of the Bhonsles seized power in Tanjavur, and installed a state that, though similar in size to that of the Nayakas, returned to conservative elements of a far more *dharma*-oriented kingship. The referents here are both classical, as seen in the revival of ersatz *dharmaśāstra* texts such as Tryambaka's *Strīdharmapaddhatī* and perhaps also in terms of the Maratha reappropriation of the legacy of Vijayanagara as they saw it from the perspective of the Deccan.[37] Ironically, it was the Maratha rulers, such as the pious and ineffective Sarabhoji II, who then came to epitomize the last gasp of 'traditional' Hindu kingship to colonial writers in the nineteenth and twentieth centuries. The Nayaka interlude had meanwhile passed somewhat into oblivion. We can thus see this as the process of the reinvention of what traditional kingship in India was, stripping it of its

---

[36] Narayana Rao, Shulman and Subrahmanyam 2001.
[37] See the discussion in Subrahmanyam 1995.

secular and commercial concerns, and reinserting it into a deeply *dharma*-oriented context which – as we have argued – can only be a very partial view of the ideological resources that states in medieval and early modern south India in fact had at their disposal.

IV

A last troubling question remains, which we must seek here to address, even if briefly. Is the transition we have seen, from the mature Vijayanagara ideology as expressed in the time of Krishnadevaraya to the later position taken by the Nayakas, to be regarded as more-or-less inevitable? In other words, could the mutual dissolution of god and king into one another have equally been sustained in a proper 'imperial' context? The answer to the symmetrically opposed question has already been given by us in our brief review of Maratha-period Tanjavur: a strong and traditionally *dharma*-oriented kingship was always possible, with a clear separation between ruler and divinity, even in a compact regional kingdom. Yet how does one explain the shift between one set of ideological supports and another, or the preference (if indeed it is a preference) for this position over that one?

The usual view that one finds in the social sciences depends very much on the notion of the 'efficiency' of ideology. An example of this may be found in a discussion of Angkor, where the modern-day historian tells us that in the late twelfth century, during the reign of Jayavarman VII, 'the people, exhausted by the burden which the Hindu apotheosis of the ruler and its later Buddhist forms placed upon them, turned to the Ceylonese Theravāda Buddhism'.[38] This formulation, within a more-or-less Weberian conceptualization of ideology-as-legitimation, suggests that different ideologies of state-building compete within a field, and that one or the other of them triumphs if there is a proper fit with the reigning circumstances, or an intersection between the 'supply and demand of ideology', as it were. As another writer, analysing the Aztec empire within a neo-Marxist framework, has recently asserted, 'dominant ideologies were specifically tailored and selectively deployed in ancient empires to win the support of strategically important groups', though the same historian also proposes that 'it is probably unrealistic to expect that whole empires could be integrated by a single dominant ideology'.[39]

We should return here, if only briefly, to the larger Indian context. The situation we have described above in south India does provide an interesting

[38] Kulke 1993b: 375–6.   [39] Brumfiel 2001: 310.

comparison with what obtained in Mughal India, the rulers of which were the exact contemporaries of the Nayakas. It is clear that the Mughal rulers never themselves sought divine status, and even the claim that Akbar sought an 'infallibility decree' from the juriconsults of his empire (made famous by F. W. Buckler) is no longer admitted by serious historians.[40] There is no doubt a host of reasons for this reticence, but we are aware above all that such a position could not seriously be contemplated in an empire where a significant point of ideological reference was still provided by Sunni Islam. On the other hand, the Mughals could and did claim a status that elevated them above run-of-the-mill humans, by claiming to be the 'Shadow of God' on earth, or by using other illuminationist rhetoric. Less developed in the historiography, but also of importance, are Mughal claims that members of the lineage possessed extraordinary powers or *karāmāt*; this is a claim that persists well into the later decades of the eighteenth century.[41] Even if not divine, there was certainly a serious claim made by members of the Timurid line (or *nasl-i Timuriyya*) to being 'thaumaturgical'.

The Mughals were, of course, aware that in a neighbouring state, namely Safavid Iran, a ruler had in the early sixteenth century made far taller claims. This was Shah Isma'il (d. 1524), who had deployed a very extreme form of Shi'i ideology in support of his own claims to divine kingship. But such claims soon proved impossible to sustain, and it has been shown that his son Shah Tahmasp moved away from this position to a far more orthodox Shi'i one, where royal power did not attempt to extend its claims too far into spiritual domains.[42] The history of the two and a quarter centuries of Safavid rule in Iran is that of a move then from heterodoxy to orthodoxy, a taming of the forces of 'extremism' into a form of Imami Shi'ism that is recognizable even today. In a sense, it is the opposite of what we have seen in the transition from Vijayanagara to the Nayakas.

The obvious question that such a contrast begs is whether the broadly 'Hindu' context of south India is once more responsible for what we observe. Let us clarify: what the Nayakas claim is not only far more than what we see in either Mughal India or Safavid Iran, but also a more affirmative claim than the general process of 'imperial apotheosis'.[43] For the Nayakas made this claim not as a possibility to be asserted after death, but to be enacted while they were living; the version that the *Tañjāvūrī āndhra rājula caritra* presents of the demise of Vijayaraghava Nayaka (the

[40] Buckler 1924.   [41] Alam and Subrahmanyam 2006.   [42] See Babayan 2002.
[43] The distinction between 'imperial apotheosis' and the worship of living rulers may be found in Price 1987.

only one of the Tanjavur Nayaka line to die in battle, in 1673) takes this only a step further by suggesting that, at the very moment of his death, his body was seen entering the temple of Vishnu at Srirangam and becoming one with the god. The late Richard Burghart, who addressed a parallel problem for the Gorkha kingdom of Nepal, attempted to downplay the significance of the issue. To be sure, he argued, 'the King of Nepal saw himself as a divine actor in his realm. He considered himself to be an embodiment of the universal god Vishnu and his palace was known as a temple.' But was this really of any import? After all, wrote Burghart, 'he acted in a universe which was populated by a proverbial thirty-three million gods', and he added that 'the implication of the king's divinity in Hindu society was rather different from those societies in which an absolute distinction is posited between the one true god and humankind'.[44] Burghart here seems to lose sight of the fundamental distinction between what he himself calls a 'universal god' such as Vishnu, and minor divinities (*devas*) of the pantheon, and falls into a misreading of the Indian tradition. Moreover, if the claim to divinity was so easy to make, it is remarkable that the rulers who preceded the Nayakas did not do so.

We ourselves have no simple answer to propose to this puzzle. We shall hence offer only two elements that may help. The first of these relates to a problem with which we began this chapter, namely the very weak character of lineage continuity in the Vijayanagara case, and the fact that what we see as the imperial family in fact consists of four separate patrilineages, with contested junctions between them. Can it be that this under-developed aspect of Vijayanagara rule, which meant that the gradient between mere warlords and the status of 'Raya' was a low one, discouraged even the Tuluvas from pushing their claims too far? It is interesting after all to note that, with the Nayakas, the dynastic model becomes far more stable, and far more invested in a single male lineage. A second element would link the Nayakas' ideological moves with the new political economy that emerged under their rule, which enabled them perhaps to dream of liberating themselves from the cycle of land-grants and alienation that had characterized earlier Vijayanagara practices. For if, on the one hand, the king was a god, the relationship to god also came to evolve into a far more transactional mode, the tone of which is captured by the *padam* songs of the Nayaka-period poets. It is a mode from which, as we have noted, the rulers of the eighteenth century (like the Marathas) recoiled, preferring

[44] Burghart 1987: 237.

to recreate a form where they gave away a very large proportion of their resources to the support of 'traditional' institutions such as *brahmadeya*. Ironically, it may have been this very tactic that left them sufficiently depleted of resources that they were unable to resist the military advances of the new rulers of south India, the debonair gentlemen of the East India Company.

CHAPTER 10

Sons of Heaven: the Qing appropriation of the Chinese model of universal empire

Evelyn S. Rawski

Because the founders of the Qing dynasty (1644–1911) were a conquest group originating outside the Great Wall of China, their political pronouncements constitute an interesting point from which to examine the notions underlying the Confucian model of universal rule, based on the Mandate of Heaven.[1] Even though the Mandate of Heaven did not specify ethnic qualifications for rule, its universalism was challenged by other Confucian discourses, most notably one which divided the world into a civilized core region of Chinese speakers, surrounded by peoples of inferior cultural attainment. The Qing followed earlier conquest rulers in formulating a rebuttal of the ethnic issue to claim the Mandate and rule China from a Confucian structure of legitimacy.[2] That is, they drew on a framework for political legitimacy that had been widely disseminated to other states that were situated within the Chinese cultural sphere in East Asia.

Tracing the history of the Mandate of Heaven concept and its related model of an idealized world order, expressed through the tributary system, we see how successive regimes in Korea and Japan appropriated these expressions of Confucian universalism. By the early seventeenth century, when Qing rulers created a Chinese-style dynastic state, Korean and Japanese regimes used elements of the Confucian heritage to refute Qing claims to Confucian hegemony, specifically to challenge Qing attempts to claim the Mandate. Their efforts to create alternative world orders is itself an eloquent testimony to the power of the Chinese model of universal rule, just as the new Korean and Japanese self-images that were created in the seventeenth century helped to shape the nation-states that would emerge in modern times.

[1] The Jurchen ruled the Later Jin state from 1616 to 1636, when the name of their ethnic group was changed to 'Manchu', and the state was renamed the Qing. I have tried to use the historically correct terminology in this chapter. To place the Chinese, Japanese and Korean regimes cited in the text, see Table 10.1.

[2] There were other important sources of Manchu legitimacy, derived from the tradition of Inner Asian conquest dynasties: see Elliott 2005.

MANDATE OF HEAVEN

Most China specialists trace the Mandate of Heaven back to the conquest of the Shang by the Zhou (*c.* 1122 BC). Power and authority during the Shang dynasty rested on birth into a small group of elite lineages that were bonded by marriage ties. Using enormously valuable vessels made of bronze, ruler-shamans offered food and drink to deified royal ancestors, who had direct access to the spirit world. To communicate with the ancestor, tortoise shells and the shoulder blades of oxen and water buffalo were chiselled and then heated until they cracked, and the cracks were interpreted; the question and the answer were then carved on the bones to serve as a written record of the exchange.[3]

Worship of royal ancestors, whose support was viewed as critical for the prosperity of the ruling house, limited eligibility for Shang rulership to direct descendants. When the Zhou conquered the Shang, they presented a different theory of political legitimacy. Heaven, a deity, determined the ruling house. The founder of the Zhou dynasty argued that the last Shang ruler had displeased Heaven, who then transferred the Mandate to the Zhou. The notion that the Mandate was conditional upon benevolent rule was further developed by the Confucian philosopher Mencius (372–289 BC). When asked by King Xuan of Qi whether a minister was ever ethically justified in killing his sovereign, Mencius replied that in the case of the last ruler of the Shang dynasty, King Zhou, his assassin killed a 'robber and a ruffian',[4] not a king: overthrowing an unworthy ruler was neither rebellion nor regicide.

Although Qin is credited with the first unification of China (221 BC), it was quickly replaced by the Former Han dynasty (206 BC – AD 8). During the reign of Han Wudi (141–87 BC), Confucianism was adopted as the doctrine of the state. Confucianism taught that the virtuous ruler exuded a charisma (*de*, virtue) that attracted subjects to him. He should rule as an exemplar, guiding others to emulate him. An ideal society was one in which each individual faithfully enacted in daily life the obligations implicit in the 'five relationships' (*wulun*) of ruler–subject, father–son, husband–wife, elder brother–younger brother and between friends. These relationships were hierarchical – even the last was usually cast as a senior–junior relationship, according to the difference in age between friends – but also involved mutuality. A subject (or a minister) was obliged to subordinate himself to his king, who must in turn nurture and protect his subordinate.

[3] Chang 1983.   [4] *Mencius*, pt 2, ch. 8 in Legge 1960: II, 167.

The failure of either party to fulfil reciprocal obligations undermined the normative social order that Confucian scholars strove to realize.[5]

The universalistic Confucian vision was embedded within a Chinese political model; its canonical texts were written in a distinctive ideographic writing system. Both the contents and the writing system were exported as a package to neighbouring groups undergoing state formation. The Chinese writing system was used by elites in Korea, Japan and Vietnam, areas that 'derived much of their higher culture and their primary system of writing from ancient China'.[6] By the middle of the fourth century AD, when Silla, Paekche and Koguryŏ emerged as 'centralized aristocratic states' on the Korean peninsula, elites in these kingdoms were familiar with Confucian texts. Political tensions with China 'did not diminish the ardor of the Korean states for the introduction of Chinese culture'.[7] A National Confucian Academy was established by Koguryŏ in 372; Chinese-style legal codes were promulgated in the three kingdoms.[8]

Relations between the Korean peninsula and the Japanese archipelago were quite intense in ancient times. During the fourth and fifth centuries, Koreans who emigrated to Japan and served the Yamato court took Chinese Confucian and other texts to Japan. Recent studies indicate that the majority of the Yamato scribes and accountants were descendants of Korean immigrants; many served on the committee that compiled the three Chinese-style penal and administrative codes (*ritsuryō*) created in Japan during the 668–701 period.[9]

Although the Korean and Japanese states quickly adopted Chinese legal and administrative codes in the state-building process, the Confucianization of other aspects of their societies occurred over a longer time span. This was because the ritual regulations intimately linked with Confucian doctrines were based on the Chinese kinship system, which was patrilineal. Koreans and Japanese seem to have organized kinship bilaterally, counting both maternal and paternal descent (as was also generally true for western Europe). What were quickly appropriated, however, were the principles by which Chinese polities regulated their relationships with other states. Inter-state relations were to be conducted according to the tributary system.

---

[5] On the role of the sage-ruler in transforming society (civilizing it), see Wang Gungwu 1991. Wang looks at Confucian ideals in the twentieth century; for an attempt to place the tributary system within a larger historiographical framework, see Wang Hui 2007.

[6] Reischauer and Fairbank 1958: 3. The same countries were identified as part of the 'East Asian cultural sphere' by the prominent Japanese scholar Nishijima Sadao in the 1960s; see Li 2004. Vietnam will not be discussed in this chapter.

[7] Lee 1984: 46.   [8] Lee 1984: 58–9.   [9] Farris 1998: 104–5; Hudson 1999: ch. 7.

Table 10.1 *Glossary of East Asian regimes*

Ashikaga	Japanese shogunate, 1356–1573
Čaqar Mongols	Mongols who inhabited present-day Inner Mongolia in the sixteenth and seventeenth centuries
Chosŏn dynasty	Korean state, 1392–1910
Former Han	Chinese dynasty, 206 BC – AD 8
'Great Yuan'	Mongol Yuan dynasty that ruled China, 1271–1368
Jin dynasty	Jurchen Jin state in north China, 1115–1234
Koguryŏ	Northeast Asian state, 37 BC – AD 668
Later Jin	Name of the Jurchen state in North-East Asia, 1616–36
Liao	Khitan Liao state in north China, 907–1125
Ming dynasty	Chinese dynasty, 1368–1644
Paekche	State on the Korean peninsula, 18 BC – AD 660
Parhae	State extending beyond the Korean peninsula into North-East Asia, 698–926
Qi	One of the Chinese regimes during the Warring States period, 770–221 BC
Qin	Regime that unified China, 221–206 BC
Qing dynasty	Conquest dynasty ruling China, 1644–1911
Shang	Regarded as the first Chinese state, 1766–1122 BC
Silla	State on the Korean peninsula, 57 BC – AD 935
Tokugawa	Japanese shogunate, 1600–1868
Xiongnu	First great 'Mongolian' nomadic empire, 209 BC – AD 91
Yamato	Japanese kingdom, *c.* 250–587 AD
Zhou	Conquest dynasty in China, 1045–256 BC

THE TRIBUTARY SYSTEM

The tributary system was described in a 1941 foundational study by John Fairbank and Ssu-yu Teng.[10] The authors used Qing administrative regulations to trace the evolution of a Sinocentric world order from the seventeenth to the nineteenth century. In a 1968 essay, Fairbank argued that the 'Chinese world order' actually originated in the Warring States (403–221 BC) period. The world was hierarchically ordered and its centre was the capital city where the 'Son of Heaven', recipient of the Mandate to rule 'all under Heaven' (the empire) received the heads of tribal groups and states. He invested vassals with hereditary titles and they in turn presented him with tribute (*gong*). Vassals were differentiated by the closeness of their ties to the imperial house. Members of the ruling lineage (*zongfan*) were first in rank; next came the heads of tribal groups within the territory directly controlled by the emperor, called *neifan* (internal vassals); and last were

---

[10] Fairbank and Teng 1941.

the *waifan* (external vassals), heads of states outside the dynasty's direct administrative control.[11]

Despite scholarly challenges, the idea of a Sinocentric world order has persisted, and appears most recently in articles by scholars in the People's Republic of China (PRC), who cite tributary missions from vassal states to argue that the current territorial boundaries of the PRC extend backwards in time.[12] While this effort is problematic, most scholars outside China accept the idea that the tributary system served as a model for the conduct of foreign relations during the 1500–1800 period, which covers the late Ming and early Qing dynasties.

According to the elaborate tributary regulations, Chinese rulers invested the rulers of vassal states with the title of 'king' (*wang*), reserving *huangdi* (emperor) for themselves. Each king received a seal of office, to be used in diplomatic correspondence, and an official calendar: Chinese reign dates were to be used in memorials (*biao*) sent from the king to the emperor on fixed occasions such as the Chinese New Year, the birthdays of the emperor and empress, etc. Embassies, sent at specified intervals, would perform the ritual 'nine knockings and three kneelings' that constituted the formal obeisance before the imperial throne. In exchange for tribute, the emperor conferred gifts on the vassal, and allowed the embassy to bring goods to trade at the frontier and in the imperial capital.

The tributary system outlined above was an idealized model which did not function when the Chinese state was weak, or when China was divided among a number of competing regional regimes. Drawing on archaeological and documentary evidence from various sites, Wang Zhenping traced inter-state relations from the second century BC to the tenth century AD, a period which spanned a full political cycle from centralization, dynastic collapse and divided rule, to recentralization. At this time, Chinese courts were preoccupied by perceived threats from pastoral peoples on the Inner Asian frontier whose military power equalled or surpassed their own. For example, the collapse of the Qin state in the third century BC allowed the Xiongnu to overcome their pastoral rivals and consolidate rule over the eastern portion of Inner Asia. Their power forced Gaozu, the founder of the Han dynasty in China, to sign a peace treaty with the Xiongnu, marry his daughter to the Xiongnu ruler, and pay annual tribute.[13] A similar situation prevailed in the tenth to fourteenth centuries and again in the sixteenth and early seventeenth centuries. When Chinese dynasties were confronted

[11] Fairbank 1968b: 5–11.
[12] For a Korean critique of this recent literature see Kwŏn 2004; also Yun 1998.
[13] Wang Zhenping 2005: ch. 2. On the Han relations with the Xiongnu, see Di Cosmo 2002a: ch. 5.

by powerful Inner Asian confederations, the Chinese had no option but
to adopt a policy of 'accommodation and collaboration'. These periods of
weakness and/or disunity represent about half of recorded Chinese history.

EMERGENCE OF A NORTH-EAST ASIAN POWER

The 1592–1644 period marks an unusual juncture of events in the history
of North-East Asia. When the unifier of Japan, Hideyoshi, invaded the
Korean peninsula in 1592 with 150,000 men, the Chosŏn king, Sŏnjo
(r. 1567–1608) was forced to flee his capital, Hansŏng, and seek refuge first
in Pyŏngyang, then in Ŭiju, right on the Ming border. In response to
Sŏnjo's pleas for aid, the Ming Wanli emperor sent troops, and a combined
Chosŏn–Ming force succeeded in pushing the Japanese forces back down
the peninsula.[14] Gratitude for this 'double grace', the military aid provided
by an overlord to its vassal state, was evoked repeatedly in later periods to
explain Chosŏn's loyalty to Ming and its reluctance to acknowledge the
Qing as overlords.

At the time of the 1592 Japanese invasion, a minor tribal chieftain named
Nurhaci was engaged in unifying the atomized Jurchen tribes in the region
of North-East Asia that lies north of the Great Wall and the northern
boundary of Chosŏn Korea, the Yalu river. Like his father and grandfather
before him, Nurhaci was part of the extensive regional military network
that the Ming had created in strategic borderlands; he offered to take his
troops to aid the Koreans but his offer was summarily rejected.[15]

The story of the expansion of Jurchen power under Nurhaci and his son
Hongtaiji is part of the narrative of the ruling house that would conquer the
Ming empire and rule as the Qing dynasty (1644–1911). Here we will focus
on the moment when the Jurchen/Qing had to explicate the ideological
grounds that justified their conquest: their exchanges with the Chosŏn
during the 1636–7 invasion.

By 1618, Nurhaci was the leader of a powerful Jurchen state. Two years
earlier (1616), he had declared himself the ruler (*Han*, the Manchu equivalent of *Khan*) of the Later Jin state, which claimed to be a successor to

---

[14] The deliberations within the Ming and Chosŏn courts are analysed in Liu 2003. For the Ming side,
see Swope 2001.

[15] Japanese troops had invaded in May 1592 and by late July they had captured the capital and pursued
the fleeing court as far north as Pyŏngyang. A token Ming force, sent in August to aid Chosŏn,
was slaughtered; reinforcements from Ming did not arrive until early December. Nurhaci offered
troops to aid Chosŏn in October 1592 and the Ming military command in the region seems to
have contemplated accepting the offer. The Chosŏn court quickly wrote to express their opposition:
Sŏnjo sillok 25/9/14 (18 October 1592), #2 and 15/9/17 (21 October 1592), #4.

the Jin dynasty which had ruled part of north China from 1115 to 1260. Nurhaci proclaimed seven grievances against the Ming, and led a 10,000-man force against the Ming garrison at Fushun (May 1618).[16] The fall of this strategic city aroused a military response from the Ming, who pressed the Chosŏn court to contribute military supplies and troops to a serious military expedition against Nurhaci. Since he would have faced armies on his western and southern flank if Chosŏn entered the fray, Nurhaci urged Chosŏn to remain neutral. Caught between the Ming and the Later Jin, the Chosŏn king, Kwanghaegun, attempted to sit on the fence. His officials were split between a pro-Ming faction and a faction that urged caution for fear that the Jurchen would punish Chosŏn if it sided with the Ming. Kwanghaegun eventually sent 13,000 men to join the Ming forces in an attack on the Later Jin, but the Ming–Chosŏn forces were routed in an epic battle at Sarhū (April 1619). Nurhaci then seized control of Liaodong, the region east of the Liao river that lay directly north of Chosŏn.[17]

After Sarhū, pressed by the Ming and by the Later Jin to choose sides, Kwanghaegun successfully resisted Nurhaci's efforts for an alliance. While remaining a tributary vassal to the Ming, he ignored their demands for more troops or more military aid. From a long-term perspective, Kwanghaegun's 'adroit foreign policy' preserved Chosŏn during extremely difficult times, but his fence-sitting provoked a successful coup d'état. He was dethroned by the pro-Ming faction in April 1623, and replaced by Injo (r. 1623–49). Injo's administration was marked by a 'blatantly pro-Ming anti-Manchu policy'. The officials of the Great Northern faction, which had dominated during Kwanghaegun's reign, were purged (many were executed) and the pro-Ming Westerners' faction took power.[18]

A change of leadership in the Later Jin regime intensified the tension with Chosŏn. After a brief period of collective rule following Nurhaci's death in 1626, Hongtaiji emerged as head of the Later Jin state. Hongtaiji first invaded Chosŏn in 1627 to remove a Ming commander, Mao Wenlong, who raided Jurchen territory from a base in Chosŏn and recruited Han Chinese fleeing Later Jin rule.[19] Korean military resistance was virtually nil; Injo was forced to enter into an alliance with the Jin, send tribute, and

---

[16] These events are described in Wakeman 1985: I, 49–66.

[17] The emergence of the Manchu power in North-East Asia is outlined in Wakeman 1985: I, 49–66.

[18] On the politics of the coup d'état, see Yi Yŏngch'un 1998: 124–42; on factional conflicts, see Yi Sŏngmu 2000: I, 155–8, 173–93.

[19] Ki-baek Lee notes that Yi Kwal, a participant in the Injo coup d'état who later turned against the coup organizers, led a failed uprising against Chosŏn. Some of his followers crossed into Liaodong and appealed to the Jurchen to 'redress the injustice of Kwanghaegun's removal from the throne'. Lee 1984: 215; Yi Sŏngmu 2000: I, 200–4.

open markets for trade on the Yalu, but he retained the Ming calendar, which meant that Chosŏn continued to acknowledge the Ming as overlord.

The Manchus did not press Chosŏn for an unconditional surrender because of the tenuous military position on their other borders. In order to send an invasion force to Chosŏn (initially of 30,000 men, with later reinforcements), the Jurchen lifted the military pressure they were exerting on Ming defences on their western border, in Liaoxi. The 1627 invasion took place during a truce between Hongtaiji and Yuan Chonghuan, the Ming governor of Liaodong.[20] The hasty withdrawal of Jurchen troops from the Korean peninsula shortly after a successful two-week campaign (1 to 19 March 1627) may have been prompted by Hongtaiji's desire to ensure that Yuan would not be able to alter substantively the military balance on the Liaoxi border. Perhaps their overall strategic situation vis-à-vis the Ming influenced the Jurchen willingness to accept a compromise.[21]

The immediate stimulus for the second Manchu invasion of 1636/7 was Chosŏn's refusal formally to recognize Hongtaiji as Son of Heaven. On the first day of the first lunar month in 1636, Hongtaiji took two major steps towards expanding the scope of his state-building activities. He adopted a dynastic name (Qing) and took the Chinese title of 'emperor' (*huangdi*). Both steps directly challenged the Ming dynasty, which was thereafter referred to in Manchu documents (rejecting the Ming as Sons of Heaven) as the 'southern dynasty'.[22] It was impossible for Chosŏn to recognize the Qing dynastic name and Hongtaiji's new imperial title. Two Chosŏn envoys that were present at Hongtaiji's court refused to perform the ritual of submission that followed the dynastic proclamation. Fearing punishment from their superiors, they abandoned a Qing state letter to Injo in a hostel, and fled home. The following month the Injo court also rebuffed an embassy of Mongol and Manchu banner princes which arrived in Hansŏng to invite the king to send a royal kinsman to the Qing capital, Shenyang, to congratulate Hongtaiji on his imperial title.[23]

---

[20] Hummel 1943: II, 954.
[21] Actually, Hongtaiji's major military operations until 1634 were directed not against the Ming but against the Čaqar Mongol leader Ligdan Khan. These campaigns had begun in 1619 and culminated in a decisive victory over Ligdan; Di Cosmo 2002b.
[22] *Injo sillok* 14/6/17 (19 July 1636), #2, records Injo's manifesto (*kyok'mun*) to Hongtaiji: in the manifesto, the Chosŏn side refers to the Ming as 'central dynasty' (*zhong chao*) while the Jurchen refer to the Ming as 'southern dynasty' (*nan chao*). *Nan chao* is also found in Hongtaiji's letter of 14 February 1637 (*Injo sillok* 15/1/20, #3), and in Injo's letter to Hongtaiji of 21 February 1637 (*Injo sillok* 15/1/27, #2).
[23] In 1635, Hongtaiji formally changed the name of his people from 'Jurchen' to 'Manchu'. Crossley 1997: 210–11.

Strategically, this second invasion aimed to deny the Ming a potential military ally and thus secure the Manchu forces from an attack on their base area during their anticipated military campaigns against the Ming. Additionally, the Manchus hoped to obtain food and military supplies from Chosŏn that had been cut off by the diplomatic fracas.[24] Finally, the subjugation of Chosŏn would be a further demonstration of Manchu charisma and military power to 'the world'.

The 1636/7 invasion, known in Korean history as the *Byongja horan*, was short and decisive. The Qing army crossed the Yalu river into Chosŏn territory on 27 December 1636 and Injo surrendered on 24 February 1637, so the campaign lasted about two months. The military confrontation was lopsided in favour of the Manchu army, which advanced rapidly down the peninsula; Chosŏn appealed for but failed to obtain military aid from the Ming; and Injo was finally forced to agree to the Manchu terms for peace. The Qing conditions were: that Chosŏn excise the Ming reign name from its official documents, discard the Ming documents and seals of investiture, and break relations with the Ming; that it accept the Qing calendar, and with it the tributary obligations, the quantity and types of tributary goods and local products being specified, to be delivered by embassies sent on New Year's Day, the emperor's birthday, the winter solstice, and the annual tribute-bearing mission.[25] Injo's eldest and second sons, and the sons of some high ministers, were taken to Shenyang as hostages. Hongtaiji also demanded that leaders of the major anti-Manchu faction should be handed over to him for punishment.[26] Hong Ik'han (1586–1637), O Dal-che (1609–37) and Yun Chib (1606–37) were executed by the Qing.[27]

UNIVERSAL EMPIRE: DIPLOMATIC EXCHANGES WITH CHOSŎN

The Chosŏn maintained a consistent stance in their diplomatic representations to Hongtaiji in 1636/7. They stressed the distinction between *sadae* (serving the great, i.e. allegiance to Ming) and *kyorin* (relations with neighbouring states).[28] Chosŏn had served as a tributary vassal to the Ming for over two centuries: their relationship was like that of father to son, in part because both states were deeply committed to Confucian ideals. Further strengthening the bond was the Wanli emperor's military aid in 1592–8, which had been crucial in expelling the Japanese invaders: this aid heaped upon Chosŏn the obligation to 'repay imperial grace'. (That was in fact

---

[24] Wakeman 1985: I, 210, n. 152.   [25] Chun 1968: 91.   [26] Sun and Li 1983: 206.
[27] Yi Hong-chik 2002: 1545, 832, 945.   [28] Watanabe 1977; Min 1998.

the message carried by Ming emissaries in 1618, when King Kwanghae was pressured to participate in a Ming military expedition against Nurhaci.) In 1636, when they rejected Hongtaiji's declaration of the Qing dynasty and the title of emperor (*huangdi*), the Chosŏn pointed out that, since Nurhaci had accepted a Ming official title, he was a vassal who had illegitimately rebelled against his overlord. Both Chosŏn and the Manchus were Ming vassals. The only proper model for Chosŏn's bilateral relations with the Manchus was therefore *kyorin*, relations with a neighbouring state.

The Manchu argument, which is laid out in Hongtaiji's missives to the Chosŏn king during the 1636–7 invasion of Korea, falls into two categories.[29] The first is based on *Realpolitik*. Responding to Chosŏn protestations that the Qing could not supplant the Ming as overlord, Hongtaiji reminded King Injo of historical precedents: the Chosŏn had after all paid tribute to the 'Great Yuan' (dynasty) and, before them, to the Liao and the Jin, conquest dynasties originating in North-East Asia who had gone on to conquer and rule portions of north China. In other words, Chosŏn had to accept *Realpolitik* as a raison d'être: 'Has there ever been a country which did not pay tribute and call itself vassal to obtain its survival?'[30]

But Hongtaiji also used the universalism of the Chinese Mandate of Heaven theory to advance his claims to supplant the Ming emperor as 'Son of Heaven'. In a letter to King Injo dated 11 February 1637, he argued that the Manchu victories were proof that the Mandate was passing from the Ming to the Qing. 'My kinsmen, the princes who have flocked to my standard, desire the dynastic name. How can you say that this ignores the proper relationship of lord and vassal [with the Ming]? . . . if Heaven favors a man, he can be the Son of Heaven; if Heaven heaps disaster on him, he is a commoner.'[31] When Hongtaiji defeated the Čaqar Mongol leader Ligdan Khan in 1634, he acquired the state seal of the former Yuan dynasty, and interpreted this as proof that Heaven favoured his cause. In 1636, Hongtaiji reported the details of his quarrel with Chosŏn to Heaven before launching the invasion, so he interpreted the Manchu victories and Chosŏn retreat as proof that Heaven also blamed Chosŏn for breaking their compact and causing war.

Hongtaiji viewed his success in battle as the ultimate demonstration that he and his followers had received the Mandate of Heaven. Earlier, in 1627, he had written to the Ming commander Yuan Chonghuan:

[29] The *Chosŏn wangjo sillok*, Injo reign, documents ten Korean–Manchu exchanges, and the Qing *Taizong shilu* records twelve written Korean–Manchu exchanges during the period of the second invasion. Five of the messages were from Hongtaiji to Injo; seven were from Injo to Hongtaiji.
[30] *Taizong shilu, juan* 33, II: 416–17.   [31] *Taizong shilu, juan* 33, II: 422–4.

The reason why our two nations have sent armies against one another was originally because the [Ming] officials quartered in Liaodong and Guangning considered their emperor to be as high as Heaven itself, while considering themselves as those who live in Heaven; and the khan of another nation merely created by Heaven was unworthy of any degree of independent standing. Not being able to bear the insults and contempt, we have taken our case to Heaven, raising troops and beginning war with you. Since Heaven is, in fact, just, and heeds not the magnitude of the nations but only the righteousness of the issue, it considers us in the right.[32]

Similarly, in his 11 February letter, he wrote to King Injo, 'The extravagant talk about Ming and your country is endless . . . as you are penned up in a mountain fortress, with disaster pressing on you, aren't you ashamed to still mouth these empty words? . . . Do you want to fight? You had better come out of the city to do battle. The two armies can face each other. Heaven can decide.'[33]

Hongtaiji's declarations reveal the paradox that lay behind the Mandate of Heaven. His letter to Injo first emphasized Confucian universalism in arguing that Heaven did not discriminate against a man because of his ethnic origins, or his past status as a vassal: 'if Heaven favors a man, he can be the Son of Heaven'. The same theme is sounded in his letter to Yuan Chonghuan, in which he notes that Heaven is just, and confers its favour on the righteous. Hongtaiji's repeated assertions that his military victories are the proof of Heaven's favour conflated the Confucian ideal of rule by 'virtue' (*de*) that Mencius (cited earlier in this chapter) emphasized with the historical reality, that dynasties are established by force.

Koreans viewed the Manchu invasions as a national catastrophe, remembered long after the Qing attitude towards Chosŏn softened. The self-image of Chosŏn officials as Confucians and the cultural equals of the Chinese literati went back to the late fourteenth-century foundations of the Chosŏn state, when Chŏng Tojŏn, a supporter of the dynastic founder, Yi Sŏnggye (r. 1392–8), stated that the dynastic name revealed that it was a 'legitimate restoration of Kija Chosŏn, which had been modeled on the glorious age of Chou'. Thus the Chosŏn 'was founded upon a standard of Confucian culture such as no later dynasty, Chinese or Korean, had ever actually attained'.[34] Since Chosŏn and the Ming shared a commitment to Confucian values, it was proper that Chosŏn should 'serve the great' (*sadae*), i.e. be a Ming vassal, in order to maintain the hierarchical Confucian world order. 'Thus Korea's tributary relationship with Ming China was to be different from its earlier relationships with the Jurchen and Mongols.

---

[32] Translation of Pamela Kyle Crossley: see Crossley 1999: 192–3.
[33] *Taizong shilu, juan* 33, II: 422–4.   [34] Chung 1985: 64.

Relationships with the Ming were to be grounded on the acceptance of common Confucian cultural values, whereas those with the non-Chinese had been based on sheer military subjugation.'[35]

In the Korean view, the Jurchen were clearly 'barbarian'. Korean accounts of the ancestors of the Jurchen, the Malgal, characterized them as an indigenous North-East Asian people who were culturally inferior and politically subordinate to those who founded the Koguryŏ kingdom and the Parhae state that succeeded it – the latter two groups being dominated by elites who were identified as Korean. Even though the Koryo king Injong (r. 1122–46) had been forced to recognize the Jin rulers as overlords in 1126, this acquiescence was based on military force, not on moral principle. With China again overrun by the barbarians, scholars in Chosŏn saw themselves as the preservers of Confucian civilization, and Korea as a 'small civilized center' (*so Hwa*) that supplanted a China ruled by the Qing.[36] Hong Ik'han, opposing recognition of Hongtaiji's claim to the imperial title, stated the case clearly in March 1636: 'our country has always viewed the world with ritual and principle, we have been called the "little China" (*so Chunghwa*), and successive rulers have transmitted the intention to *sadae* (serve the Ming) . . . to now serve the barbarian (*hono*), how could this be justified to the ancestors, to the world, and to later generations?'[37]

Chosŏn officials expressed their contempt for the Jurchen/Manchus by using homonyms like 'slave' for 'Nŭ' in the Chinese term for Jurchen, 'Nŭ-chên', or the traditional 'Yi' for the eastern barbarians. These attitudes influenced the Chosŏn court's actions after 1637 when, while outwardly fulfilling the duties of a tributary state, Confucian scholars and Chosŏn kings symbolically defied the Qing by continuing to use the Ming calendar and reign names on internal documents and erecting altars to the last two Ming emperors and even to the dynastic founder, Ming Taizu. Even though the Chosŏn court's anti-Qing sentiments cooled in the eighteenth century, the view that the Qing were not proper Sons of Heaven lingered.[38]

DIPLOMATIC EXCHANGES WITH JAPAN

Tokugawa Japan also viewed the Qing conquest with scepticism. Unlike Chosŏn, Japan had not sent an official tributary mission to Chinese courts after 1405, relying instead on a thriving illicit trade to obtain Chinese

---

[35] Chung 1985: 64. On the origins of *gyorin* in *Mencius*, see Yang 1968: 27.
[36] Kang 1997: 182–94; Haboush 2005: 115–16.
[37] *Injo sillok* 14/2/21 (27 March 1636), #1.   [38] Haboush 2005: 121–33.

goods.[39] During the breakdown of centralized authority in Japan from 1467 to the late sixteenth century, demand for Chinese goods prompted enterprising local magnates in southern Japan to present counterfeit credentials to the Ming court, claiming to represent the 'King of Japan', and sometimes their credentials were accepted by Ming officials.[40] The Hosokawa and Ōuchi, regional lords situated on the Inland Sea and northern Kyushu, presented tallies collected during the 1401–5 period of official exchanges to pass as the envoys of various Ashikaga shoguns.[41] Once in the Ming capital, Peking, they would request and receive further tallies, thereby perpetuating the system. Since these same regional lords also engaged in piracy, it is not surprising that these 'tribute missions' occasionally turned violent. The culminating episode of the false tribute missions occurred in 1523, when the Hosokawa and Ōuchi both sent embassies to the Chinese port of Ningbo, where an Office of Overseas Trade supervised the maritime tribute of Korea and Japan. The two envoys quarrelled over which was the legitimate tributary embassy. Although the Ōuchi envoy, Shusetsu Gendo, had arrived first, the Ming eunuch official gave the Hosokawa envoy, So Sokyo, priority in the customs inspection and seated him above his rival at the banquet. The enraged Shusetsu attacked his rival, who sought refuge inside the city walls of Shaoxing. Shusetsu killed some of So Sokyo's men in the affray and set fire to So's ship. His men plundered and set buildings in Ningbo on fire before setting sail in captured boats, killing some Ming naval forces who tried to arrest them.[42] The incident prompted Ming officials to investigate: they detained So Sokyo and two of Shusetsu's followers, who were captured by the Chosŏn authorities when their ship was blown off course and landed in Korea. In 1530, a Hosokawa request for a pardon for So Sokyo and for new tallies was denied; missions arriving in 1545 and 1547 were sent back because they did not comply with the tributary schedule for embassies. Ōuchi embassies in 1539–40 and 1548–9 were allowed to travel to Peking for the court audience, but their requests for new tallies were turned down. The 1549 mission marked the end of 'official' relations between the Ming dynasty and the 'King of Japan'.

[39] Japanese ambivalence towards participation in the Chinese tributary system is revealed in von Verschuer 2007. See also von Verschuer 2006.

[40] These fraudulent embassies to Ming are chronicled in Kwan-wai So's translation of the section on Japan in the Ming History (*Ming shi*), see So 1975: 172–7.

[41] So 1975: 4; the details are presented in So's translation of the section on Japan in the *Ming shi*, 161–202.

[42] So 1975: 4–5. Also Elisonas 1991: 235–9. On the structure of the Ming office to receive tributary missions in Ningbo see Shiba 1977.

Despite Ming and Qing prohibitions on trade with Japan, a non-official trade which involved Portuguese and Chinese flourished during the sixteenth century. News about Ming reached Japan through Tsushima, which managed a flourishing trade with Chosŏn Korea; through the Ryukyus, which sent embassies to Ming and to Chosŏn; and through foreign merchants sailing into Japanese ports. Japanese scholars have noted the keen interest with which Tokugawa Iyeyasu, founder of the shogunate that governed Japan from 1600 to 1868, sought intelligence about continental affairs. Indeed, the Japanese had been inquiring about the Jurchen/Manchu from the 1590s, when Iyeyasu's predecessor, Hideyoshi, sent one of his generals north of the Yalu river to obtain more precise geographic information: he and Iyeyasu wondered if there were a land bridge linking Ezochi (Hokkaido) to the mainland that the 'Orankai' (Jurchen) might use to invade Japan.[43]

News of the Manchu conquest reached Japan via Chinese traders at Nagasaki and from Korea via Tsushima. The Qing conquest of the Ming was regarded as the end of the Sinocentric world order. A three-volume Japanese compilation of intelligence reports concerning events from the 1643 capture of the Ming capital, Peking, by the Chinese rebel Li Zicheng, the 1644 Manchu takeover of Peking, and the Qing conquest up to 1678, is aptly entitled *The Metamorphosis of the Hua (Civilized) into Yi (Barbarian)* (*Ka I hentai*).[44]

Although Iyeyasu contemplated sending an embassy to Qing to request a resumption of official relations, this idea was soon dropped. Instead, the shogunate instituted policies in the 1630s and 1640s that asserted a Japan-centred world order, based on the Chinese tributary model. The shogunate invited 'the lords . . . of the various barbarian peoples of Annam, Cochin, Champa, Siam, Luzon . . . and Cambodia' to 'offer up letters and send tribute' to Edo; and used the Japanese calendar in its communications with these countries. In 1715, the shogunate issued 'New Regulations for Nagasaki' that mirrored Chinese tributary regulations. The shogunate now required Chinese merchants coming to Nagasaki to present Japanese tallies before they were permitted to trade. When the merchants reported this new requirement to the Qing emperor, he decided that the tallies were 'merely a commercial procedure of no political significance'.[45] During the

[43] Emori 1982: 159–62; Kamiya 1994.
[44] Hayashi Gahō and Hayashi Hōkō, comp. *Ka'I hentai* (Metamorphosis from civilized to barbarian), 3 vols. (Tokyo, 1958–9). Toby (1991 [1st edn 1984]: ch. 4) discusses the shogunate's intelligence-gathering concerning the Manchu conquest.
[45] Hall 1949: 456.

1689–1723 period, Qing mints used 'nothing but foreign copper' for the production of the copper cash used by citizens in daily market transactions. Japan was the major source of copper for Qing mints.[46] The Qing court's tacit acquiescence in this inversion of the Chinese tributary system was hailed by Japanese officials as proof that the new Japan-centred world order was a recognized fact.[47] Although it also drew upon the idea of Japan as a 'country of the gods' (*shinkoku*), a notion which had previously been expressed by Hideyoshi, the new Japan-centred world order was a mirror image of the Chinese one.[48]

CONCLUSION

The Mandate of Heaven doctrine enabled the Qing, outsiders of North-East Asian origins, to pacify the vast territory lying within the Great Wall. Like earlier conquest dynasties, Qing emperors became patrons of Confucian learning, revived the civil service examination system, and performed the sacrifices at state altars. They obtained the acquiescence of the educated elite by adopting Chinese Confucian norms, and they assiduously edited their written records to fit within the Chinese historical tradition. They also continued the tributary model of foreign relations, though with some strategic exceptions.[49] But it was more difficult for the Qing to persuade the Korean and Japanese of their legitimacy.

China's neighbours appropriated the Chinese model of world order for themselves in the seventeenth century. Chosŏn Korea and Tokugawa Japan each claimed that they, and not the new dynasty created by the Jurchen/Manchus, were the legitimate heirs to the civilized world order. Each constructed a new world order centred on its own ruler.[50] In their dealings with other states, each established policies that mimicked the Chinese tributary protocols, for example requiring that trade be conditional upon the establishment of overlord–vassal relations.[51] Like the Qing, Japan and Korea received embassies from the Ryukyus. Each also tried to treat the other as a subordinate. While the Tokugawa shogunate welcomed

---

[46] Hall 1949: 454.

[47] Studies based on the Chinese records suggest that the Qing were willing to overlook the diplomatic snub because they badly needed to obtain copper, a money metal which was in short supply in the early eighteenth century, before the new mines in south-west China expanded domestic production of copper: see Hall 1949.

[48] Arano 1987. For an alternative interpretation, see Thomas 2003: 309–25.

[49] The most well-known exception being early Qing relations with Russia: see Mancall 1971; Perdue 2005: ch. 4.

[50] Robinson 2000.   [51] Kang 1997: 66–8; Lewis 2002.

embassies from Chosŏn, Korea did not reciprocate by receiving embassies from Japan, instead (like the Japanese treatment of the Dutch) preferring to delegate the task to the provincial governor of Tongnae, the province surrounding Pusan.

The Sinocentric world order was a Chinese projection. The universalist aspect of Confucianism enabled conquerors who accepted its norms to win the acquiescence of the Confucian elite. Outside China, however, these universalist aspects of Confucianism were decoupled from Chinese hegemony and the Chinese hierarchy was inverted. Koreans asserted their cultural superiority over the Manchus who conquered the Ming; Japanese highlighted their cultural superiority by emphasizing the Shinto belief that Japan was a 'divine country', inferior to no continental power, especially one arising outside the civilized core region of China's Central Plain. In the polycentric universe outside China's borders, states sending tributary embassies to China also participated with impunity in bilateral relations outside the Qing tributary system. The universalist message of Confucianism enabled Korea and Japan to attack the legitimacy of the Sinocentric world order during the early Qing, on the argument that 'barbarians' could not be transformed into 'Sons of Heaven' – or, given their own status as barbarians in the eyes of Chinese, that they were more civilized than the Manchus. These seventeenth-century discourses foreshadowed the self-images that would be projected in the twentieth century. Although Japan's self-image as a 'divine country' ended in 1945, South Korea continues to proclaim its commitment to Confucian values in an implicit contrast with socialist China. Attempts to create and sustain the identities that distinguish each country from its neighbours continue to reflect the common cultural heritage that all share.

PRIMARY SOURCES

Chosŏn wangjo sillok (The annals of the Chosŏn dynasty, 1392–1911). The entire work is online, see http://sillok.history.go.kr. Documents are cited by the reign year, (lunar) month and day, followed by the Western calendrical date, then by the number of the document recorded on that date.

Hayashi, Gahō (1618–80) and Hayashi Hōkō (1644–1732), comp. *Ka'I hentai* (Metamorphosis from civilized to barbarian), 3 vols. (Tokyo, 1958–9).

Injo sillok (Veritable records of the Injo reign, 1623–49) [part of the *Chosŏn wangjo sillok*].

Legge, J. (ed. and trans.) (1960), *The Chinese Classics; with a Translation, Critical and Exegetical Notes, Prolegomena, and Copious Indexes*, 5 vols. (Hong Kong) [reprint of the 1861–72 edn].

Qing shilu (Veritable records of the Qing dynasty). Reprinted in 60 vols. by the Zhonghua shuju in 1986 (Beijing). This work is cited by the titles of individual reigns, for example *Taizong shilu*, followed by the chapter (*juan*), the volume and page number in the 1986 edn.

Sŏnjo sillok (Veritable records for the Sŏnjo reign, 1567–1608) [part of the *Chosŏn wangjo sillok*].

Taizong shilu (Veritable records of the Taizong reign, 1626–43) [vol. II of the *Qing shilu*].

PART II

Contrasting universalisms – old and new world

CHAPTER II

Aztec universalism: ideology and status symbols in the service of empire-building

Justyna Olko

The Triple Alliance, expanding in fifteenth- and early sixteenth-century Central Mexico and usually referred to as the 'Aztec empire', was no doubt one of the most powerful organizations of pre-Hispanic Mesoamerica that collapsed upon the violent encounter with the Europeans. Studies of Aztec imperialism often highlight the role of human sacrifice and ideology as a mechanism of expansion. Even if certain phenomena have been misunderstood and distorted in the historiography and contemporary studies, the importance of ritual and religion, which not only served to justify expansion but also provided a rationale for it, cannot be denied. No less significant, however, were many different strategies employed by the rulers of the Triple Alliance in order to control effectively dependent domains and assure the constant flow of tribute goods. One of their aims was to create an integrated core area and, in the outer domains, to develop procedures of acquiring new vassals with the maximal reduction of the operational cost. Of equal importance was the building of an extensive network connecting elites at both the central and the peripheral level, so as to make it possible for the conquered nobility to accommodate rapidly to the new power structure. While the common feature of most Central Mexican communities was a very localized sense of identity, considerable effort was directed to maintain and develop a universalizing elite culture (including attributes of rank or writing, artistic expressions, architecture) and pan-regional relationships among the upper group, additionally enhanced by marital alliances. This integration of the nobility throughout the empire was based on the sharing of similar concepts and dissemination of an ideology that emphasized the exceptional status of the ruling class and the cosmological supremacy of the imperial lords.

THE AZTEC EMPIRE: ORGANIZATION AND INTEGRATION MECHANISMS

The area of Central Mexico was occupied primarily by one of the most important culture groups of Mesoamerica, the Nahuas or Aztecs, who coexisted in this region with speakers of other languages. Nahuatl enjoyed considerable time-depth and importance in the pre-Hispanic world, and its speakers have survived in significant numbers to our days. Central Mexican communities shared the mythical-historical tradition of being founded by migrating ancestors, either dispersed Toltec groups settling in the Valley of Mexico after the collapse of their state or, more frequently, warlike Chichimecs identified with the barbarous north, who took possession of the land. Indeed, the archaeological record seems to support the notion that major groups of migrants arrived in Central Mexico at the onset of the Aztec period (*c.* AD 1200).[1] In the time of the Spanish conquest the Nahuas represented a highly advanced culture linked in numerous ways to other past and contemporary Mesoamerican traditions.

A terminological clarification is no doubt necessary at this point. Widely used by the public and scholars, especially anthropologists, is the term 'Aztec' or 'Aztecs' that gained popularity in the nineteenth century. Originally describing the mythical ancestors of the Mexica leaving their place of origin, Aztlan, and not serving as an ethnic name at the time of contact, it has been used in different ways, in a narrow sense referring to the Mexica-Tenochca of Tenochtitlan, but also designating other Nahuatl-speaking groups. Also today the term 'Aztecs' is commonly employed to name all inhabitants of the Valley of Mexico at the time of the Spanish conquest,[2] and sometimes even speakers of Nahuatl in neighbouring regions,[3] being more common in research focusing on the perspective of the political alliance of Tenochtitlan, Tetzcoco and Tlacopan. This term also serves as the conventional reference to archaeological 'Aztec culture' of the Middle and Late Postclassic period (*c.* 1200–1521). 'Nahuas' is a more recent name accepted by most scholars studying postconquest societies, but no less adequate in reference to preconquest times; it emphasizes the localized sense of identity of particular groups, including both wider (Acolhuaque or Tepaneca) and narrower ethnonyms (Tenochca, Tlatelolca, Quauhtin-chantlaca and many others).[4] It also emphasizes that the Nahua culture area was much wider and older than any particular imperial alliance.

The term 'Aztec empire' thus refers to the political organization of the Triple Alliance of Tenochtitlan, Tetzcoco and Tlacopan. Its core area corresponded roughly to the Valley of Mexico, and conquered imperial domains extended in almost all directions, encompassing significant portions of the present states of Hidalgo, Guerrero, Morelos, Puebla, Oaxaca and Veracruz

[1] Smith 1984: 153–80; 2008: 76–7. [2] E.g. Smith and Berdan 1996a: 3.
[3] Smith 1997. [4] Lockhart 1992.

(map 7). The Triple Alliance was probably established immediately after *c.* 1428–31, the turmoil of the 'Tepanec war' when the former regional power, the Tepanec centre of Azcapotzalco, was defeated by a broad coalition of several other groups, including its former vassals. As a result, the Mexica, Acolhuaque and Tepaneca of Tlacopan took over the domains and some of the dependencies of their former adversary, and gradually grasped control, through alliance, negotiations or direct conquests, over the remaining polities, or *altepetl*, of the Valley of Mexico (map 8).

These numerous indigenous states were central to Nahua sociopolitical organization and had a strong sense of microethnicity. Being basically groups of people holding rights to certain territories, they could be either entirely sovereign units or subordinated to other *altepetl* to which they owed tribute. In contrast to hierarchically arranged entities more typical for Spanish modes of organization, *altepetl* had a cellular structure encompassing symmetrical and self-contained parts, called *calpolli* or *tlaxilacalli*. They operated on a rotational basis, and, being themselves divided into smaller wards, replicated on a lower level the general composite structure of the whole.[5] Also, relations of personal subjugation and allegiance have been emphasized in modern reconstructions of preconquest *altepetl* structure.[6] While probably all of them had an urbanized zone with monumental architecture, the size of strictly urban populations was relatively small, with considerable numbers of people living in outlying and rural settlements. The size of the imperial metropolis, Tenochtitlan, was clearly an unequalled exception.[7]

While some scholars are reluctant to speak of the 'Aztec empire', pointing to important differences between old world terminology and indigenous concepts, the state organization created by the Mexica and their allies was no doubt a pan-regional power, unparalleled in the Mesoamerican landscape of that time, even if more attention should be given to reconstructing and understanding native perspectives and terms. The long history of research on Aztec imperialism and political organization, based on the analysis of both complex ethnohistorical sources and archaeological data, does eliminate any remaining doubts that the Triple Alliance can be described as a hegemonic empire, expanding through military conquests or sometimes by the mere threat of armed intervention.[8] Typically for organizations of a hegemonic type, the Aztec imperial infrastructure was relatively limited, rule relying instead on more subtle or indirect forms of political control.

[5] Lockhart 1992: 14–25.   [6] Smith 2008: 91.   [7] Smith 2008: 195–296.
[8] E.g. Hassig 1988; Berdan *et al.* 1996.

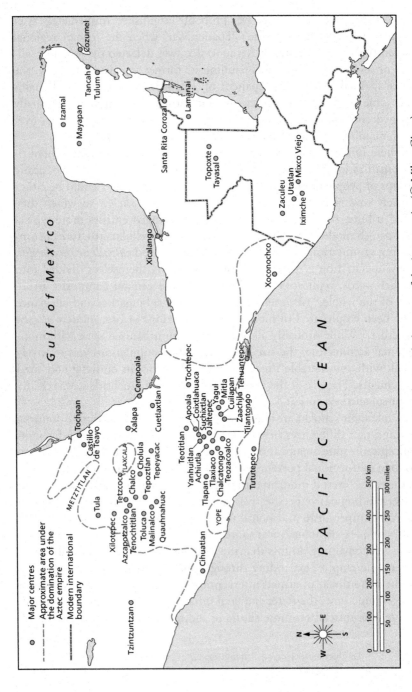

Map 7 Mesoamerica in the Late Postclassic with the extent of the Aztec empire (© Miłosz Giersz)

Map 8 Valley of Mexico (© Miłosz Giersz)

Although only later written colonial sources offer rich data on the Triple Alliance, its organization and ideology, the Aztec state, as argued by Smith and Montiel,[9] also conforms to the criteria defined by archaeologists as typical of imperialism. These include the size and complexity of the capital, proclamations of imperial ideology in different media, political control of provinces (including creation of a tribute system and sometimes also reorganization of settlement patterns in subjugated areas) or

[9] Smith and Montiel 2001: 245–65.

economic exchange between provinces and the capital. As far as the projection of economic, political and cultural influence into a pan-regional
or international context is concerned, the available evidence is ambiguous
because certain cultural traits widespread in Late Postclassic Mesoamerica
(*c.* AD 900/1000–1521) may be of 'Central Mexican' rather than specifically
imperial origin.[10]

As argued by scholars, the structure of the Aztec state and its relationship
with particular dependencies differed not only between the core (central
provinces) and periphery (outer provinces) but also within the central zone,
the Valley of Mexico. Regional political hierarchies inside this core area
varied considerably in the depth of political organization, from steep hierarchies in the Tepaneca and Mexica domains to the more shallow arrangement characteristic of the Tetzcocan sphere of influence. These differences
probably reflect distinct strategies of administrative control and varying
degrees of intervention in the appointment of subordinated rulers.[11] However, while imperial policy did not eliminate all possible sources of political
difference, tension and conflict between the main imperial allies, particularly challenging was the efficient organization of the outer provinces,
sometimes separated by natural geographical barriers and by no means
uniformly subordinated. Several unconquered enemy states remained a
permanent threat to the Triple Alliance: Tlaxcala to the east and relatively
close to the imperial core, the Tarascan state to the north-west, Metztitlan
on the north-eastern frontier of the empire, and Yopitzinco and Tututepec
along the Pacific coast. Although some modern scholars accept the propaganda of the Mexica that they would have conquered their enemies –
especially the state of Tlaxcala surrounded by areas controlled by the empire
– if they had actually wanted to,[12] there are reasons to believe these enemies
represented a serious danger which the empire was unable to overcome.[13]
There seems to be no evidence of 'neutral zones' within the empire: polities
were either subject to the empire or unconquered enemies.[14]

To control their expanding domains the rulers of the Triple Alliance
had to rely on pragmatic strategies that would facilitate the integration of
dependent areas and assure the continuous flow of tribute goods. Among
the most effective and enduring strategies were inter-dynastic marriage

[10] Mesoamerican chronology is based on the division into Preclassic (*c.* 1800 BC – AD 150/250), Classic
(*c.* 150/250–900/1000) and Postclassic (*c.* 900/1000–1521) periods with time frames differing slightly
between particular regions. Most areas also have specific chronologies based on ceramic sequences
and radiocarbon dating.
[11] Hicks 1986; Hodge 1996: 34–40.   [12] E.g. Hassig 1988: 256.
[13] Isaac 1983a and b; Smith 1996: 137.   [14] Smith 1996: 137–8.

policies and granting income-producing lands and other gains to cooper-ating elites.[15] The practice of polygamy facilitated the creation of political alliances through marriage with numerous partners. A ruler of higher rank could give one of his daughters to his vassal, while the descendant of such a union usually inherited the local throne, strengthening the bonds with the sovereign. Because the rulers of the Triple Alliance also married daughters of their allies of inferior rank, their offspring could potentially assume the throne in the places of their mothers' origin. It is also signifi-cant that the royal successors in the second capital of the Triple Alliance, Tetzcoco, were usually descendants of princesses coming from the ruling dynasty of the Mexica – but never the reverse – which implies that a higher rank was enjoyed by the latter and hence the predominance of Tenochtitlan within the alliance.[16]

Relying on more subtle mechanisms of domination reduced the degree of intervention in local political structures, where subordinated leaders were usually allowed to retain their traditional positions provided that they adhered to the conditions imposed by their imperial overlords or negoti-ated with them. While some polities did, according to surviving sources, require more direct forms of interference or the building of an imperial military infrastructure, in most cases only tribute collectors and governors were added to the local system of rule, especially in the most common form of imperial organization in the outer regions: tributary provinces. They were expected to provide a regular flow of tribute goods, and assure the safety of long-distance trading enterprises, often sponsored and con-trolled by imperial rulers, and were generally located in relatively 'safe' regions.[17] This relationship was not limited to the economic dimension: an important aim seems to have been the integration of members of the provincial elites into the imperial structure that was achieved through mar-riage alliances, gift exchange, and common participation in religious and political events.[18] Undoubtedly, this strategy made it possible for the local elites to accommodate rapidly to the new power structure after the Spanish conquest: they remained in power on the regional level, while centrally appointed officials and tribute-collectors replaced the representatives of the Triple Alliance.

Frances Berdan and Michael Smith argue that there was also another form of political organization of areas under control. Considerable evidence points to the existence of a political and military strategy for dealing with

---

[15] Hodge 1996: 43; Berdan 2006: 159.   [16] Carrasco 1984.
[17] Berdan 1996: 116; Carrasco 1996: 594–5.   [18] Berdan 1996: 122.

enemy states which was based on the creation of areas of clientship or 'strategic provinces' neighbouring hostile territories, containing important natural resources or associated with major trade routes. Strategic provinces seem to have been located frequently on imperial frontiers with tributary provinces in the interior. In the case of these 'friendly territories', military service and 'gifts' replaced the usual tribute obligations in accordance with the imperial goal to acquire secure control over such regions at relatively small expense.[19] An important factor in the creation of such client states was co-option of local elites, resulting, however, in a relatively weak integration of these areas within the empire.[20]

RELIGION AND RITUAL

An important role in the building of the Aztec empire was played by ritual and religion that provided a rationale for the expansion and justified it. According to the crucial cosmological myth shared by the Nahuas, the existence of this world (the fifth one and the most perfect in the cosmic cycle of destruction and creation) was made possible by the sacrifice of gods gathered in Teotihuacan (the monumental centre of the Classic period, revered by contemporaneous and later Mesoamerican peoples). Two of them volunteered to jump into the sacred fire so that the sun and moon could be created, while after the first dawn the rest of the gods were sacrificed to feed the newborn sun. From that time on, the offering of precious blood served as the necessary nourishment of the sun, permitting its constant movement across the horizon and the harmonious existence of the world. The blood sacrifice was referred to as *nextlahualiztli* in Nahuatl, what is commonly translated as the 'debt-payment' to the Giver of Life. However, a more careful analysis of this expression indicates it should rather be understood in terms of a moral duty as 'the paying of what behooves, what is proper'.[21] The obligations between gods and humans were reciprocal while the latter could actively participate in sustaining the cosmic order. The existence of state propaganda equating the objective of military conquests with the capture of prisoners for massive human sacrifice to feed the sun is perhaps the most widely known aspect of Aztec culture. However, this popular reading simplifies the nature of Mesoamerican religion and worldview, as well as the deeper meaning of blood offerings. A crucial concept referring to human sacrifice is *ixiptlatl* (literally, 'replacement' or 'substitute')

---

[19] Berdan 2006: 160; 2007: 3; Smith 1996: 141, 147; 2001: 143.
[20] Smith and Montiel 2001: 249.   [21] Köhler 2001.

denoting the physical form (animate or inanimate) filled with spiritual energy of divine origin. Thus, the *teteo imixiptlahuan*, literally 'substitutes of the gods', were their impersonators sacrificed during religious feasts, transformed by special rituals, way of living and insignia into the containers of the spiritual essence of the deity they embodied. Their sacrificial death released the supernatural energy that came back to the place of its origin, reintegrating with its source in the continuous process of circulation of divine substance between the earth and otherworld.[22] Apart from its esoteric dimension, the ritual of human sacrifice in imperial Tenochtitlan was also staged as a powerful political spectacle aimed to impress and terrify invited allies, vassals, potential subjects and enemies. The real scale of human sacrifice is frequently debated and difficult to estimate, because this aspect of Aztec imperialism was highlighted in early colonial sources, created in quite specific circumstances and motivated by the rhetoric of their time.

Another myth fundamental for imperial ideology relates the miraculous conception, birth and heroic fight of the Mexica patron god, Huitzilopochtli. He was born as a son of the goddess Coatlicue on the 'Serpent Mountain' (Coatepec) and immediately had to face as enemies his stepsister Coyolxauhqui and stepbrothers (or uncles, depending on the version) Centzonhuitznahua, trying to kill him as he emerged from the womb of his mother. Huitzilopochtli, equipped with a supernatural weapon, the fire serpent or *xiuhcoatl*, defeated his adversaries: the mutilated, dismembered body of his sister rolled down the slopes of Coatepec. The birth of the patron god and his mythical fight was recreated in Tenochtitlan during the annual feast of Panquetzaliztli inaugurating the time of war. According to the imperial message, all the enemies of Huitzilopochtli and his earthly representatives had to face the fate of Coyolxauhqi, whose image rested below the stairway to the main pyramid, the Huei Teocalli, representing the mountain of Coatepec (fig. 11.1). It lay on the path which war captives had to follow to the altar of sacrifice on the top of the pyramid; it was also the place where their dead bodies would fall, having been rolled down the stairway by the performing priests. In religious terms, the birth of Huitzilopochtli symbolized the emergence of the new victorious sun that defeated the moon represented by the lunar goddess Coyolxauhqui.

This myth clearly reveals the solar attributes of the Mexica patron god, who seems to have undergone a process of solarization to meet the needs of the expanding state. Thus, imperial conquests were carried out under

---

[22] See López Austin 1994; 1996.

Fig. 11.1 Archaeological remains of the Great Temple of Tenochtitlan.

the auspices of Huitzilopochtli, elevated to the rank of more ancient and important Central Mexican deities, and even usurping the position of Quetzalcoatl[23] or merging, in some contexts, with Tezcatlipoca. While it is difficult to say to what degree defeated communities were obliged to include this deity in their cults, there is no doubt that at least in some cases the Triple Alliance took control over local sanctuaries, as in the case of Tepoztecco, and appropriated earlier religious centres or sacred places in conquered areas, as in Malinalco or Calixtlahuaca (fig. 11.2).[24] It is not without reason that Mexica sculptural monuments documenting the conquests of the rulers of Tenochtitlan feature victors capturing patron deities of defeated communities: we know they were actually held captive as spiritual hostages of their people in the main temple precinct of Tenochtitlan. The dominant structure of this complex, the Huei Teocalli, was designed as the true centre of the Aztec world.[25] Its numerous rebuilding stages housed deposits from the furthest perimeters and geographical frontiers of the growing empire, such as burials of exotic animals or examples of flora. Thus, the expanding periphery was manifest in the symbolical and ideological centre of the empire, the stage for impressive ritual spectacles displaying the military

[23] Tomicki 1990.   [24] Klein and Umberger 1993; Umberger 2007.
[25] Broda, Carrasco and Matos Moctezuma 1988.

Fig. 11.2 Imperial sanctuary in Malinalco.

and economic power of the Triple Alliance. Rituals in imperial capitals, where the advantages of submission to imperial control as well as the risks associated with its rejection were consciously highlighted, also provided excellent opportunities for promoting a common elite culture.

IMPERIAL EXPANSION: THE AZTEC CONCEPT OF A 'JUST WAR'

Written sources shed interesting light on Aztec strategies associated with the mechanisms of empire-building and clearly situate them within what can be identified as a universalistic imperial ideology. While the Nahuas' own understanding or vision of their empire deserves a separate study, references to original concepts abound in the historical-rhetorical tradition recorded after the Spanish conquest, such as those alluding to the idea of uniting various peoples under a prosperous Mexica rule.[26]

Among the basic imperial strategies were ritualized negotiations on the conditions of dependence, employed in proceedings with most independent polities and described as an integral part of imperial laws and

[26] E.g. Tezozomoc 1998: 29.

Fig. 11.3 Warning and punishment of a rebellious ruler; *Codex Mendoza*,
fol. 66r, fragment.

customs.[27] Reportedly, there had to be some 'just reason' to start a war,
which, besides, could not be initiated without a formal warning. In the
written sources based specifically on the Mexica tradition, this rhetoric
goes as far as to claim that the rulers of Tenochtitlan never started wars
but were always provoked, and even in such circumstances asked for peace
several times.[28] The warning in question took the form of a highly symbolic
procedure performed by special royal messengers (fig. 11.3). The border-
line between negotiations and a ritual declaration of war sometimes seems

[27] Acuña 1988: 37–8; Casas 1971: 40; *Codex Mendoza*, fol. 66r (Bodleian Library, University of Oxford,
MS. Arch. Selden. A. 1); López de Gómara 1966: II, 410–11; Ixtlilxochitl 2000: 159–60; *Mapa
Quinatzin* (Bibliothèque Nationale de France, Ms. Mex. 396); Motolinía 1970: 157–8; Icazbalceta
1886–92: III, 312; Pomar 2000: 198–9; Torquemada 1977: IV, 110–11; Zorita 2002: 186
[28] Durán 1984: II, 82, 84.

blurred, but perhaps this was deliberate. A potential reason to initiate these proceedings could vary from the supposed or alleged attack on Aztec messengers or merchants or merely their bad reception, the refusal to send gifts to the imperial ruler, or the rejection of an invitation to the state ceremonies in Tenochtitlan.

The messengers decorated a rebellious leader with attributes associated with sacrificial victims – white chalk and down feather – thus anticipating his fate in a future military confrontation.[29] They also gave him weapons, so as to symbolically balance his chances in war. If the messengers succeeded in convincing the local elite to become 'friends' of the empire, the community 'gave tribute like friends'. However, each time they refused to accept conditions of more or less veiled dependency, the price of peace grew, and may have led to open war. According to the sources, this could happen when three diplomatic missions were ignored,[30] but sometimes apparently almost immediately. In such a case, the potential 'friends' or vassals were transformed into overt enemies and a war of conquest followed. This system of 'triple warning' emphasizes the hierarchy and internal power structure of the empire, as the successive visits were realized by messengers from Tlacopan, Tetzcoco and Tenochtitlan, the last and final 'word' being that of the dominant force in the Triple Alliance (fig. 11.4).[31] Quite telling is the range and order of negotiations directed at different social groups of the enemy polity: starting with military leaders, through the rebellious ruler and his family to the 'elders', the messengers strove for a satisfactory result for the Aztec empire: to accomplish its political and economic aims with the minimum operational costs.

Besides, the analysis of written and pictorial sources shows that the reaction to rebellion by imperial vassals (even if it involved renegotiations of the conditions of dependency) has to be differentiated from ritualized negotiations with independent territories carried out to establish relations of submission. The first case always entails an inevitable punishment,

---

[29] The symbolism of feathers and chalk as attributes (and Nahuatl metaphor) associated with human sacrifice is well grounded in Nahua culture. In the second half of the sixteenth century the expression *tiçatl ihuitl nictlalia/tiçatl ihuitl nicchihua* ['I set chalk and feathers', 'I make chalk and feathers'] appears in the dictionary of Molina, who translates it as *dar a otro buen consejo y auiso, o dar buen ejemplo* ['to give someone good advice and notice or to set a good example'] (Molina 2001: 133). There can be no doubt that Molina refers to a metaphor that was in use many years after the Spanish conquest. Its direct origin was the imperial (but perhaps not limited to the Aztec empire) procedure of warning enemies or potential opponents where the symbolism of chalk and feathers played a significant role.

[30] Ixtlilxochitl 2000: 160.

[31] As observed by Juan José Batalla Rosado, this is the actual order represented in the *Mapa Quinatzin*, misunderstood by Ixtlilxochitl (see Olko 2004: 135).

Fig. 11.4 *Mapa Quinatzin*, fol. 3, fragment.

preferably individual, which, obviously, was rarely feasible in practice unless a prior military intervention had been successful. In the second case a penalty also remained a possibility, depending on political circumstances and the internal situation of the adversary. Common for both contexts was the aspiration to reduce the costs of the operation, either punishing an individual ruler as the only one responsible, or directing warnings to different sectors of the society under pressure so as to arouse internal frictions. Even when military confrontation turned out to be unavoidable, the possibility of negotiations and the termination of war were apparently kept open at almost every moment of the ensuing hostilities, provided the opponents accepted the supremacy of Aztec rule and imperial subjugation.

The meaning and functions of this procedure are further revealed by analysis of cases of its 'practical realization' extant in available sources. In many of them, the message conveyed to an opponent is clear: recognize my supremacy or try your luck on the battlefield. It is also a manifestation of power and superiority that alludes to a specific concept of war associated with a construction of empire according to certain rules. Particularly illustrative is the employment of this act – that may have been an earlier custom, though we lack evidence on this topic – at a turning point in Mexica history during the third decade of the fifteenth century: the war of Tenochtitlan and its allies against the Tepanec centre of Azcapotzalco, the hegemon of the Valley of Mexico. As the political tension between the two cities grew and the alleged declaration of vassalage of the Mexica did not discourage the Tepanecs from planning war against Tenochtitlan, Itzcoatl – the ruler of Tenochtitlan and in reality a rebellious vassal of Azcapotzalco – ordered his close relative and collaborator Tlacaellel to carry out the procedure of ritualized warning.[32] This episode, although difficult to imagine in the then existing political circumstances, seems to have fulfilled a very important function at the key point in the historical tradition of the Mexica: their achievement of sovereign status. What is particularly striking is an inverted use of the scheme normally associated with the sovereign–vassal relationship. Although vassals themselves at the beginning of this war, the Mexica reversed the roles and hierarchy by declaring a 'just war'. This was to signal they did not act as rebellious subjects and to give them the right to victory, predetermined by the ritual proceeding of Tlacaellel.

Equally informative is the official imperial account of a Tenochca attack on the formally independent city of Tlatelolco, reportedly provoked by a Tlatelolcan plot directed against Tenochtitlan. Axayacatl, the Mexica ruler, wanted to avoid the spilling of blood, twice sending an emissary with a conventionalized symbolical message to his opponent.[33] Thus, he acted as a hegemon treating Tlatelolco as a potential vassal. The second mission met with a violent reception by the ruler of Tlatelolco, who replied that

[32] Durán 1984: II, 77–8; Tezozomoc 2001: 75–7.
[33] Durán 1984: II, 258–63; Tezozomoc 2001: 205–7.

the attributes of sacrificial victims belong rather to the sender, and had the messenger killed. This is the only case described by the available sources when the alerted ruler violently rejected his participation in the ritual behavior. However, such a situation seems more realistic than cases when enemy rulers let imperial functionaries mark them with the attributes of future sacrificial victims. The meaning of the behaviour is clear: the ruler of Tlatelolco is equated with a rebellious vassal, or, more precisely, because of his plots against the Triple Alliance the empire gives him an opportunity to become its subject without an overt war, requiring his declaration of subordination.

Undoubtedly in most cases the objective of the imperial procedure was not to give notification of an impending war, but to avoid it through intimidation and negotiation. However, the same negotiation options do not seem to have been offered to all potential vassals; some of them apparently did not get an opportunity to become 'friends'. For example, in the case of the war with the state of Tepeaca (preceded by the death of Aztec merchants in its territory), its 'fault was so great' that although it was reportedly alerted, there was neither pity shown nor space allowed for negotiations.[34] Similarly, the conquest of Ahuilizapan, which followed the assassination of Aztec merchants and messengers, was carried out without any preliminaries because the opponents 'did not deserve it'.[35] Both of these episodes clearly refer to primary conquests that occurred in the initial phase of imperial expansion, during the reign of Moteucçoma Ilhuicamina, and not to the punishment of vassals. Should we interpret these cases as examples of a different strategy or a distinct variant of the 'just war' whose objective was not the establishment of subordination but annihilation? Should we include here other examples of war where no negotiations occurred and the destruction was absolute? These cases indicate that there were different conquest strategies and that we cannot extend the 'scheme of warnings' to all conflicts, but must confine them to situations involving the acquisition of vassals. Moreover, we have to be aware that sometimes references to alerts and 'offers of peace' as integral parts of war accounts could have served a propagandistic purpose in the Mexica historical tradition, presenting these events as 'just wars'.

Another issue is the possible influence of Spanish legal terms and ideas in descriptions of pre-Hispanic history. In the sixteenth century the problem of *guerra justa* and its justified reasons – provoked by recent conquests – was frequently debated in Spanish universities and among intellectuals in

---

[34] Durán 1984: II, 156–7; Tezozomoc 2001: 133–5. [35] Durán 1984: II, 178; Tezozomoc 2001: 151.

New Spain, especially in the writings of Francisco de Vitoria, Bartolomé de las Casas and Ginés de Sepúlveda. These ideas must have had a certain impact on Spanish ecclesiastics and native intellectuals writing about pre-Hispanic customs. For example Durán, while describing Mexica war procedures, uses the contemporaneous Spanish legal term *requerimiento de la paz* ('requirement of peace'), referring to a legitimizing legal procedure employed during the conquest of America and in some respects similar to Aztec imperial customs. Nonetheless, even if descriptions of the preconquest reality were seen through European concepts, it can be argued that an independent notion of 'just war' was an integral part of the imperial strategies and the concept of the empire of the Triple Alliance. Allusions to the idea of 'just war' and its functions abound in numerous primary sources, and even if some accounts are clearly interrelated, the sample of independent versions is considerable.[36] The Spanish terms *guerra justa* and *buena guerra* appear frequently in the written accounts derived from a now lost Nahuatl *Chronicle X* transmitting the Mexica historical tradition. Although I was not able to identify an original Nahuatl term for 'just war' in the available sources, structural analysis of corresponding sections of two Spanish accounts derived directly from this original prototype[37] leaves no doubt that the terms in question are direct translations of the same native expression.

These procedures and strategies associated with imperial expansion complement the reconstructed pattern of two basic types of provinces, with different degrees of control, described earlier in this chapter: areas that became tributary provinces as a result of military subordination and those that accepted imperial superiority through negotiations and were exempted from ordinary tribute. On the pragmatic level, then, the aim was to develop procedures of acquiring new vassals with the maximal reduction of the operational cost unless political, economic or strategic factors required complete subjection or acquisition of firm control over particular areas. On the ideological level, the objective of this procedure and its associated rhetoric was to justify imperial enterprises, to present their conquests in

[36] Olko 2004: 130–6.
[37] These are the *Historia de las Indias de la Nueva España e islas de la tierra firme* by Diego Durán and *Crónica mexicana* by Fernando Alvarado Tezozomoc. The first of them was written in 1581 and, even though it is unquestionably the primary source for the Mexica, Nahuatl terms borrowed from the lost prototype are scarce. The *Crónica mexicana* by Tezozomoc (1598), like the work of Durán, relates the Mexica version of their own historical tradition. Its most recent edition (Tezozomoc 2001) is particularly valuable, for it is a modern and full transcription of a hitherto unpublished manuscript which is clearly a rough draft of Tezozomoc's final work now lost, most probably the record of the direct translation of the original Nahuatl source dictated by the author himself (Díaz Migoyo 2001). All earlier editions appear to be later copies derived from that recently published manuscript.

terms of 'just wars'. However, it has to be borne in mind that what we call
'just war' – in the Nahua version – entailed the presumption that the hegemon has the right to require the fulfilment of certain expectations, even
in respect of potential, not real vassals (compare Barjamovic, Chapter 2
above on the hierarchical conception of sovereignty by the Assyrians). In
other words, a stronger adversary has the right to carry out the procedure of ritualized negotiations on the conditions of dependence, while
his opponent can surrender or try his luck in battle. The imperial rhetoric
placing the Triple Alliance in the position of a hegemon, who seeks to avoid
direct military conflict and instead spreads affiliations with their empire
by peaceful means, can probably be considered an important part of Aztec
universalism. In practical terms, 'the imperial conquest led to the reduction
of regional warfare, and trade flourished in the *pax azteca* that followed'.[38]

STATUS SYMBOLS AND UNIVERSALIZING ELITE CULTURE

The concepts underlying the construction of the empire of the Triple
Alliance can also be seen through the spread and imposition of an elite
culture and ideology. This factor seems to have been no less important
than other mechanisms ensuring integration and expansion, even if much
more subtle. The creation of an extensive network connecting elites on both
central and peripheral levels involved such aspects of high culture as writing
or artistic expression and preceded the formation of the Aztec empire.[39]
Similar tendencies can already be observed in earlier times in large portions
of Mesoamerica. The nobility was linked by marriage alliances, exchange
of luxury goods, art styles, material culture and status items, ideology and
elite-restricted knowledge, and shared activities such as religious rituals
or elaborate ceremonies associated with the legitimization of their power.
These and other common interests crossed political boundaries and ensured
cooperation over and above local divisions and localized sense of identity.
Imperial rulers were able to benefit from these mechanisms and adjust
them to their own needs.

The integration of elites throughout the empire was based on sharing
a culture and ideology that affirmed and assured the exceptional status of
the nobility. The ruler of Tenochtitlan, bearing the title of *huei tlatoani*
('great speaker'), had jurisdiction over almost every branch of government,
including the military, civil, judicial, legislative and religious, as well as the
economic domains.[40] Subordinated or allied to him were local *tlatoque*,

[38] Smith 2001: 141.   [39] Berdan and Smith 1996: 211.   [40] Sullivan 1980: 226.

rulers of their particular *altepetl*. The position of the *huei tlatoani* was enveloped in esoteric lore expressed by elaborate ceremonies, courtly protocol, precious insignia and rich metaphoric language that referred to him. On specific occasions he was clad in the attributes of his patron gods, participating thus in their divine force. These were for example the smoking mirror of Tezcatlipoca or the flayed skin of Xipe Totec. As the substitute for and interpreter of powerful Tezcatlipoca, the king received from him not only special faculties, but also messages that he had to convey to his people.[41] But, perhaps most importantly, he was strongly associated with Xiuhteuctli ('the lord of turquoise'), the god of fire and time, manifestation of the supreme creator deity. The most prestigious royal insignia were those made of turquoise, decorated with turquoise mosaic or with designs imitating that stone. In Mesoamerican beliefs, the celestial fire, embodied by Xiuhteuctli and his fire serpent, could take the material form of turquoise, the stone explicitly linked to fire and smoke.[42]

These specifically Mexica attributes were conceived as derived from the Toltecs, glorified predecessors of the Aztecs, and actually most of them appear to have been used since at least AD 800–900, the time of formation of the Toltec state with its capital in Tula, Hidalgo. They included the turquoise diadem, *xiuhhuitzolli*, the cape with a turquoise mosaic design called *xiuhtlalpilli tilmatli*, the turquoise nose plug and other items (fig. 11.5). The origin of the most important symbol of royal power, the turquoise diadem, goes back even to the times of powerful Teotihuacan (more than a thousand years before the Nahuas), where it was used in the form of the war serpent headdress, adopted and developed by the Maya in the fourth century AD. From the beginning it symbolized the war/fire serpent, the ancestor of the Nahua fire god. Importantly, since the Classic period (*c.* 150/250–900) it was closely associated with the origin of legitimate power. Thus, the wearing of the turquoise regalia by the *huei tlatoque* of Tenochtitlan and other rulers who seem to have accepted Mexica royal insignia not only linked them to their patron, the fire deity in his manifestation of the supreme creator god, but also emphasized their role as direct inheritors of the ancient tradition of Mesoamerican rulership.

The association of kings with the divine fire was deeply rooted in the Nahua concept of nobility, but the turquoise insignia were much more than just symbolic links with the fire god. The transformations ascribed to the sovereign during coronation rites were actually equated to the increase

[41] Olivier 2002: 122–3.
[42] According to the Nahuatl text of the *Florentine Codex*, it was 'like the lovely cotinga, truly as if smoking...It smokes. It smokes like fine turquoise' (Florentine Codex XI: 224).

Fig. 11.5 The rulers of Tenochtitlan with their turquoise attributes, images from the sixteenth-century manuscript of the *Primeros Memoriales* compiled by Bernardino de Sahagún (fol. 51r, fragment © Reproducción, Real Academia de la Historia).

of that energy and personal 'heat' associated with the concentration of the *tonalli*, his spiritual entity linked to heaven and the sun. In accordance with this symbolism, coronation rites involved a direct participation of Xiuhteuctli, implying that the acquisition of celestial fire made up the nucleus of the ceremony. Thus, according to an account that accompanies the investiture scene in the *Codex Tudela* (fol. 54r),[43] 'they went to the house of him whom they had elected or who was to be the lord and put before him a costume, and this happened before the fire god . . . And they took him with a great dance before Xutecle, the fire god' (fols. 54r–54v).[44] Precious royal insignia were thus not merely signs of the high position occupied by the ruler, they were powerful means of transformation that assured the change of status associated with the accumulation of divine essence. In other words, they were conceived as physical forms capable of accumulating the celestial fire, thought to increase progressively in time as the incumbent continued to carry the burden of office and participate in various rituals.

This concept of royal power was part of an ideology that promoted a special status for elite groups. The Nahua nobility enjoyed numerous privileges, including rights to wear and exhibit elaborate clothing and

---

[43] *Codex Tudela*, Museo de América, Madrid. [44] Trans. J. Olko.

paraphernalia. The role of exuberant insignia and exotic items that served as status markers is visible in the archaeological record throughout Mesoamerica from the Preclassic period. Manifesting foreign affiliations was frequently a deliberate strategy of regional nobility. While in other Mesoamerican cultures these items were frequently acquired by means of long-distance trade, the Mexica and other dominant groups in the Triple Alliance gained a great part of these status markers by means of tribute obligations. The intense demand for luxuries as indications of rank seems to have been an important factor in conquests and tribute assessments of subjugated regions.[45] On the pragmatic level, imperial structures were complex enough to accommodate numerous members of the noble group, creating opportunities also for the subjugated aristocracy and local rulers, regardless of their ethnic affiliation.

IMPERIAL IDEOLOGY IN THE PROVINCES

Clearly, the situation of the nobility in the imperial core, often closely drawn into permanent alliance and participating in the gains of the imperial expansion, was much different from that of the subordinated peripheral aristocracy. Upon the conquest their economic profits and political status usually became limited and adjusted to the demands of the empire. However, they could also benefit from their relationship with the Aztec state in many ways.[46] For example, the archaeological data from Morelos imply that the provincial nobility in the important political centre of Yautepec became more prosperous after the Mexica conquest, whereas contemporary elites and commoners in the rural town of Cuexcomate were clearly impoverished, which corresponds with the strategies of the Triple Alliance of integrating provincial elites within the empire.[47] The pauperization of commoners and lesser elites in the conquered provinces probably resulted from the increase of tribute assessments, though not necessarily from excessive imperial demands, but because local lords could have seized the opportunity to increase their own benefits.[48] The association with the overlord could have been not only a prestigious one, but, in practical terms, helpful in local political struggles against neighbouring enemies or traditional rivals. The gains from affiliation with the Triple Alliance could therefore be quite tangible. For example, Cuauhnahuac conquered new territories after

[45] Berdan and Smith 1996: 212.   [46] Berdan 2006: 160–3.
[47] Smith and Montiel 2001: 261–2.   [48] Smith 2001: 148–50.

being subjugated by Tenochtitlan, which implies that the empire supported their new subjects in their own expansion.[49]

Particularly attractive for provincial elites cooperating in the construction of the empire was the profound symbolism and esoteric concept of rulership, as well as its powerful status grounded in the heritage of the Mesoamerican past. In a way, at the level of their polity they replicated the power of imperial overlords. This is clearly reflected in the willingness of provincial leaders to adopt and emulate the highest royal insignia associated with Tenochtitlan. While the Mexica impact is manifest throughout the empire in architectural remains, sculpture or ceramic imports, significant data on the emulation of imperial art styles and genres are found also in native pictorial manuscripts from different regions of Central Mexico,[50] even if almost all those actually known were made after the Spanish conquest based upon pre-Hispanic prototypes. The evidence of adoption of imperial status markers, at least in the iconography of power, is associated with the conquered provinces located in the present Mexican states of Guerrero, Hidalgo, Morelos, Puebla, Oaxaca and Veracruz.[51]

An illustrative example comes from the distant tributary province of Tlapan in Guerrero, adjacent to the strategic areas of Chiauhtlan, Ayotlan and Ometepec, and located in close proximity to the unconquered Yope territory.[52] In the Late and Terminal Classic periods (*c.* AD 600–900) this area received strong Mixtec influence, which continued into the Early Postclassic (*c.* 900–1150/1200) when it was combined with Toltec impact.[53] Aside from Tlapanec, the main regional language, Nahuatl, Mixtec and Yope were also spoken in the area. Ethnically mixed communities formed numerous little states, many of which were dominated by Tlachinollan before the establishment of Mexica control. The latter became formalized with the creation of the tributary province of Tlapan following the conquest carried out by the ruler Ahuitzotl in 1486. The local version of these events is given by two early colonial pictorial manuscripts, the *Codices Azoyú 1* and *2*,[54] associated with the native elite of Tlachinollan. They are examples of the native genre of historical annals and relate the story from the foundation of the kingdom through the Mexica and Spanish conquests until 1565, focusing on dynastic, military and internal community events.

While relating essentially the same story, the two documents differ slightly in style and iconographic details. In the *Codex Azoyú 1* early rulers of this mountainous region are pictured according to local conventions:

---

[49] Smith 2001: 149; 2004: 91.   [50] Boone 1996.   [51] Olko 2005; 2006.
[52] Smith and Berdan 1996b: 276.   [53] Jiménez García 2002: 391–2.
[54] Colección de Códices, Biblioteca Nacional de Antropología e Historia, Mexico.

Fig. 11.6 Imagery of the *Codex Azoyú 2*: Rain/Quiyauhtzin wearing the Mexica costume and facing Axayacatl, fol. 5, fragment.

they are seated on low stools, clad in white capes and holding fans and incense pouches. Some of them also carry tobacco gourds on their backs. An incense bag and a tobacco gourd are priestly attributes closely associated with Mesoamerican lords, and are also present in the imagery of Mexica rulers. Nonetheless, the set of attributes as a whole implies a local repertory of status items. A significant change is observed on fol. 24 marking the beginning of Mexica influence. This is signalled by the image of a local ruler 'Rain' (identified by the gloss *quiyauhtzin* in the *Codex Azoyú 2*) seated in front of the place sign of Tenochtitlan and a personage speaking to him, possibly bearing the name glyph of Axayacatl (r. 1469–81), the Mexica ruler.[55] The ruler of Tlachinollan is shown in an extended version of the formerly used costume. Unlike his predecessors, Rain/Quiyauhtzin rests on a reed throne and sports the turquoise diadem as well as a white cape bordered with eyes (*tenixyo*), in the same way as his interlocutor from Tenochtitlan. He still preserves some attributes of earlier rulers, such as an incense bag and a fan.

The same scene is recorded in the *Codex Azoyú 2,* which provides more clues for its interpretation (fig. 11.6). The sequence of earlier rulers is lacking in this manuscript, but the iconography of rank seems even

---

[55] The representative of the Aztec state is identified by an insect (fly or bee) name glyph perhaps referring to the future *huei tlatoani* Axayacatl who acceded in 1469, but probably fulfilled important military and political functions already during the rule of his predecessor Moteucçoma Ilhuicamina. The name Axayacatl means both 'water face', most commonly depicted as his name glyph, and 'marsh fly', which could be the case here. While I incline towards this interpretation, other tentative readings, such as Xicotli or Pipiyollin, have been proposed, see Gutiérrez Mendoza and Medina Lima 2008: 104.

more Mexicanized, since certain attributes, such as the turquoise diadem or the reed throne, already make their appearance before the memorable meeting with the representative of Tenochtitlan. In this very scene Rain/Quiyauhtzin is seated on the Nahua reed throne and displays a Mexica royal blue cape and the turquoise diadem, as well as a pouch tied over his arms. This last detail is strikingly similar to pouches carried by rulers in the *Códice en Cruz*[56] from Acolhuacan, which again suggests a link with the Valley of Mexico. The local leader is shown in exactly the same way as the representative of Tenochtitlan (except that the pouch is missing in the latter's image), identified by the fly or bee glyph similar to that pictured in the other manuscript. Moreover, the *xiuhhuitzolli* diadem sign is attached to his name glyph to mark the new status based on the relationship with the powerful polity. The new role of the ruler of Tlachinollan is also implied by an accompanying gloss 'quiyauhtzin tlacatecuhtli', for in accordance with the Nahua glyphic convention the turquoise diadem sign could be employed to indicate both the word *teuctli* ('lord') and the title of *tlacateuctli* ('the lord of people'), given to governors assigned to imperial provinces.

It is not clear what kind of relationship between powerful Tenochtitlan and the local kingdom alluded to by the *Codices Azoyú* was established at that point, perhaps a form of alliance or political clientship. It seems probable that the first pressures were felt around 1460, when the Tenochtitlan ruler Moteucçoma Ilhuicamina subjugated the northern province of Quiyauhteopan-Olinallan, and Tlachinollan was soon able to form an alliance with the Triple Alliance, slowing its annexation as an imperial province.[57] The 'meeting scene' seems to refer to the formation of such an alliance or veiled dependency. In the rhetoric of the *Codices Azoyú* the acceptance of an external affiliation clearly augments the prestige of local rulership. It is meaningful that the arrival of Mexica influence is expressed in the pictorial record through a change in costume and adoption of foreign insignia of rank. After this episode, followed later by an actual military conquest of Tlachinollan in 1486, the Tenochca repertory of status symbols enters the imagery of both manuscripts permanently, but is more salient in the *Codex Azoyú 2*.

It is risky to try to judge whether the Mexica insignia figure merely as part of pictorial conventions or were actually employed by the local nobility. The latter seems probable, since it is difficult to imagine the creation of numerous royal images in total detachment from the status

[56] Bibliothèque Nationale de France, Ms. Mex. 015–017.
[57] Gutiérrez Mendoza, König and Brito 2009: 51.

items actually used. Such a phenomenon fits well with the Triple Alliance policy of encouraging conquered provincial ruling groups to participate in an elevated imperial elite culture and allowing them to benefit from cooperation with the empire. This policy was no doubt helped by the universalizing spread of particular kinds of elite status items, like codices, jewelry and apparel that were frequently distributed to provincial elites as gifts during impressive ceremonies held in Tenochtitlan, and probably also on other occasions. These objects could have been crucial for the local nobility; emulation of prestigious foreign symbols of power or the actual right to use them probably played a role in strengthening their own regional status and could result in direct political and economic gains.[58] Perhaps the most salient example of this phenomenon is the emulation of Teotihuacan styles and insignia in Classic period Mesoamerica, including peripheral centres of power. The evidence from the *Codices Azoyú 1* and *2* suggests this could have actually been the case in Aztec times as well.

Also the manuscript genre itself – the year-count presentation (historical annals) – may have been adopted as an effect of Mexica imperial influence, for this was precisely the genre favoured by them to accommodate their official history.[59] However, the imperial impact in this region (part of the present state of Guerrero) is by no means limited to the annalistic genre but includes also economic and cartographic-historical documents. In other words, Aztec-inspired conventions (including imperial status symbols) are not limited to one or two particular kinds of documents that would be direct 'borrowings' or 'translations' of foreign manuscripts. They are widespread also in other documents, some of them less prestigious, which confirms their deeper and permanent inclusion in local conventions. A cartographic-historical manuscript, the *Palimpsesto Veinte Mazorcas*,[60] is another example of a creative synthesis of local tradition and imperial borrowings: local rulers sport turquoise diadems and are seated on reed thrones, but also hold bronze axes of local manufacture and display numerous captives tied by a rope (fig. 11.7). Good examples are also some tribute documents from the region, the sixteenth-century *Códices de Ohuapan* and *Tecuiciapan*[61] made in the former imperial province of Tepequaquilco, that feature early colonial native officials in a way strikingly similar to the standardized Aztec

---

[58] Interestingly enough, in 1511 Atepec was annexed to the Tlapan province, followed in 1515 by the conquest of Hueycatenango and Alcozauca, resulting in the political and spatial growth of the jurisdiction of Tlapan; Gutiérrez Mendoza, König and Brito 2009: 88–9.

[59] Boone 1996: 186–7; 2000: 198.   [60] Bibliothèque Nationale de France, Ms. Mex. 391.

[61] Latin American Library, Tulane University.

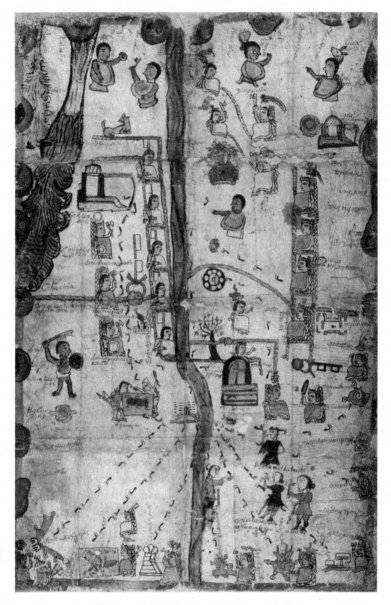

Fig. 11.7 *Palimpsesto Veinte Mazorcas* (BNF).

conventions. Governors are seated on reed thrones, wearing diadems and white capes.

The evidence of adopting the highest symbols of imperial power, and especially the turquoise diadem, in subjugated and culturally influenced areas is widespread. A telling exception to this pattern is the enemy territory of Tlaxcala, which in spite of its geographical proximity successfully resisted the expansion of the Triple Alliance. Tlaxcalans shared numerous traits of Nahua culture and historical traditions with the inhabitants of the Valley of Mexico, but seem to have deliberately rejected all the symbols associated with the imperial ideology, such as turquoise diadems, royal blue capes or reed thrones.[62] In other areas, these symbols of rank continued as prestigious status markers for numerous rulers of postconquest times, at least in the iconography of rank.

In its expansion and subsequent integration the Triple Alliance employed many complementary mechanisms based on what can be conceived as a universalistic imperial ideology. An important component of it was a concept identifying their conquests with 'just wars', a notion that, apart from obvious pragmatic advantages associated with the reduction of costs of territorial expansion, presented the imperial sovereigns as defenders of peace and of civilized norms of behaviour such as the immunity of traders and messengers. Crucial in this process was the co-optation of local aristocracies, both independent and militarily subjugated, which was effectively facilitated by the promotion of an elite ideology and material culture. Numerous provincial elites undoubtedly appreciated the advantages of such a friendly association with the empire and emulated their overlords by sharing prestigious status markers, highly valued items restricted to the noble class, royal iconography and courtly art that were frequently merged with local traditions. While upon the encounter with the Spaniards the Aztec empire did not survive long, revealing many of its weak points, the extent and nature of imperial expansion, as well as the resulting integration, are manifest in the early colonial heritage.

---

[62] Instead, they chose to portray themselves with their own insignia, white–red twisted headbands, low stools and flower bouquets.

CHAPTER 12

From empire to commonwealth(s): orders in Europe 1300–1800

Peter Haldén

I INTRODUCTION

The development of the Law of Nations and of the international political system, both of which are part of the evolution of the modern world, has been recounted many times. Nevertheless, I believe that it may be fruitfully submitted to reinterpretation by introducing other dimensions than those used in the standard accounts. This chapter argues that the development of the European order based on states during the sixteenth, seventeenth, and eighteenth centuries can be understood through changes in understanding and locating 'society' in Europe during the period. Emphasizing shifts in the concept of society clarifies how Europe came to be dominated by this kind of political system instead of, say, an imperial order. This chapter investigates how community was understood in relation to bounded systems of power.[1] Specifically it deals with the changes in the imperial heritage of universalism in the early modern period that enabled the shift to a state-centred order. To analyse this shift, the present chapter works with two ideal types of order: (1) universalist-embedding and (2) particular-atomistic. The medieval *res publica Christiana* is an order of the former kind and the classic European states-system (*c.* 1600–1900) is an order of the latter kind. In our modern age we see the inklings of a hybrid order: (3) universalist-atomistic. In all the three orders, the location of society in relation to territorially bounded units of power is a central element. Like all ideal types, these are 'pure types', and real-life historical situations are likely to contain traits of more than one type. They do so to lesser or greater degrees, which is why the images of trajectories and contrasts between them illuminate distinct traits of these historical situations.

The chapter outlines a trajectory from one kind of order, or mode of organization, to another, from the medieval *res publica Christiana* to

[1] The chapter does not deal with medieval views of society in general. For a treatment of medieval thought on the sociability of man and why society arises, see Nederman 1988.

the states-system that developed from 1500 onwards. It develops Andreas Osiander's thesis that in the *res publica Christiana* society was seen as a community existing around systems of power and hence these systems were constituted by society rather than the other way around.[2] Orders of this kind have limited capacities for expansion, which is due to the tighter coupling of the units. In the European states-system, which in our time has become global, bounded systems of power are pre-existing in relation to their common society. Society is understood as existing primarily within each unit and secondarily between the respective units. The spatial designators *around, within* and *between* will be used throughout the text as metaphors to distinguish between different conceptions of society in relation to bounded systems of power.

Modern International Relations theory[3] and historical sociology have not focused on the evolution of 'society' from a universal to an international framework between the late medieval and the early modern era as important to the organization of territorial order. There is a substantial literature on the 'international society' (social bonds and norms between territorially bounded units) and its evolution, but it is often characterized by the idea of pre-existing states.[4] By presuming the existence of an international grid that organizes political relations, this literature rules out the possibility that transformations of the way society was understood were implicated in the creation of the international. Doubtless, societal ties can and do exist in the international sphere. However, it was the redefinition of society into something that was primarily inside a bounded sphere of rule that created the precondition of the international itself. The idea of a 'world society' is central to the 'English School' of IR but it is generally seen as a modern development out of the international society of the early modern era. In contrast, this chapter analyses the idea of universal society preceding the order that sees society as contained within bounded systems of power or, secondarily, as existing between them.

Society is one of the core terms of Western political language. In this chapter I use it not in the sense of a social system but in the sense of community. Modern sociology has tended to conceptualize society primarily in terms of national societies, i.e. as existing within a bounded system of power.[5] A problem in research on the history of the formation of states

---

[2] Osiander 2001a.
[3] When referring to the academic discipline I will write 'International Relations' or 'IR'; when referring to the field of study I will use 'international relations'.
[4] See for example Bull and Watson 1984; Watson 1992; Buzan, 1993; 2004.
[5] Elias 1991: 241–2. Notable current exceptions exist, for example in the literature on cosmopolitanism. See for example Benhabib 2006; Bartelson 2009; Held 2010.

and state systems is that the modern state tends to be projected backwards into history.[6] Similarly the modern conception of society is often projected onto historical periods for which it is misleading as an analytical concept.

I understand 'universalism' as the idea that an order can, could – given the fulfilment of certain conditions – or ought to, in a normative sense, be extended to cover the entire world or, sometimes in the eyes of its adherents, the theological cosmos. I use the concept 'order' in the sense of a mode of organizing community and systems of power. In this chapter the discussion primarily pertains to political relations. Order in this sense does not imply absence of conflict or peace. It is a common framework of intersubjective rules and meanings through which actors understand their social world and through which regularized and hence relatively predictable actions take place. The understanding of order used in this chapter encompasses relations that contemporary social and historical science divides into 'domestic' and 'international'. It does so on the premise that an order will determine, in the sense of prescribing and providing, a meaning-laden framework for the understanding of the character of the component units as well as their relations to each other. Another reason for understanding 'domestic' and 'international' spheres within the same concept is that this distinction was not intelligible to thinkers previous to its codification by Emmerich de Vattel in the later eighteenth century.[7] In sum, discussing theories of the state without discussing inter-state relations, and vice versa, is misleading and hardly meaningful since they are two intrinsic parts of the same order.[8] My focus on 'inter-territorial systems'[9] means that the trajectory 'from empire to commonwealth(s)' will be drawn on a European level and not on that of individual countries, e.g. England, France or Poland. Connecting universalism with this understanding of order means that a universal order does not have to emanate from a single political centre, be backed up by a bureaucracy, or successfully claim a monopoly of legitimate violence.

Narratives of the shift from medieval to modern are stock-in-trade in the history of ideas, in social and political history and in historically oriented social sciences. A fundamental trait of most such narratives and theories is that they outline linear histories of no return. This chapter argues that such linearity is problematic with regard to universalism and inter-territorial orders in Europe. Firstly, during the early modern period the two modes of organization co-existed, as the European states-system existed side by

[6] Giddens 1985.   [7] Onuf 1989: 196.
[8] See Poggi 1978: 12; Taylor 1999: 62–79; Shaw 2000: 27–8.   [9] Schubert 1996: 102.

side with the Holy Roman Empire of the German Nation, which endured until 1806 and had inherited some of the structural traits of the medieval order. Secondly, once the connection to European civilization was dropped in the mid twentieth century, the European states-system spread across the globe to become the first truly universal way of ordering political life. In the last decades of the twentieth century we saw the beginnings of a hybrid structure: a universalist-atomistic order. This is witnessed by the recent stress on the legitimacy of intervention in the name of human rights. It is also reminiscent of a mode of organization where bounded systems of power exist within a society to which they have to answer.

2   ORDER IN EUROPE PRIOR TO THE WARS OF RELIGION

The medieval order – realms within society

It is beyond both the scope and the intent of this chapter to cover the medieval order in full but certain aspects are required as a backdrop to the processes dealt with below. Certain social sciences such as International Relations (IR) tend to simplify the Middle Ages to a binary opposition between emperor and pope. Conversely, within the historical disciplines the view that there was no 'international politics' in this era has long prevailed. Both are results of the identification of the state with the Weberian definition and of inter-state politics with institutions such as sovereignty and the 'balance of power'.[10] With this background, two options have been left to synthetic approaches, focusing on feudal relations between minor lords or concluding that Europe was governed by a unitary structure made up of the emperor and the pope until the system differentiated into fully autonomous units at the peace of Westphalia.[11] Both figures of thought give a misleading background to the formation of the European, and later, global states-system. I will avoid the choice between micro- and macro-levels. Instead I focus on the meso-level of European kingdoms, which was differently configured than in later orders in combination with a unitary conception of society that was reflected in medieval law.

The political order of Latin Christendom prior to the Reformation was not a monolith within which all centres of power were subjected to the power of the emperor. In the early fourteenth century, Dante tried to prove by means of Aristotelian logic, historical examples and biblical

---

[10] For an analysis of this predicament in earlier historical research, see Berg 1997: 1–5 and 47–9.
[11] See Buzan and Little 2000.

argument that a universal Christian empire was a theological necessity and in accordance with the will of God. The undivided and unqualified power of the emperor was a logical corollary of this necessity.[12] However, Dante's work was polemical, not factual. Of course, the office enjoyed enormous prestige and authority, by being an indispensable part of the political cosmos. Nonetheless, these attributes did not translate into power understood in the sense of the ability to issue binding commandments to the monarchs of Europe.[13] Most contemporaries distinguished between the two kinds of power, calling the former *auctoritas* and the latter *potestas*.[14] While a legitimate actor had to defer to the *auctoritas* of the emperor, it lay in the interests of the kings and other power-wielders to make sure, in words as well as deeds, that the emperor's power was not, and should not be, *potestas*.[15] Inter-territorial relations did exist on many levels, including that of kingdoms, but it should not tempt us to equate this order with an early modern or modern international system.[16] Under this order the many individual kingdoms as well as other power-wielders, such as magnates and other lords, were always considered legitimate entities within the symbolic universe endowed with meaning by the *auctoritas* of the empire and of Christendom.[17] The writings of Nicholas of Cusa from the mid fifteenth century express this view more clearly. Like Dante he yearned for and supported the universal Christian empire but was careful to note that the authority of the emperor over the kings of Christendom (and hence the empire itself) was spiritual, not temporal and political. Each *natio* or country was a distinct entity which had the right to its particular customs and mode of rule.[18] Interestingly, in Cusa's view the Christian character of the empire placed definite limits upon its reach. Since it was spiritual in kind, rulers outside of Christendom were legitimate and the emperor could not claim global authority.

The unity of the Latin medieval order consisted not in a unified system of hierarchical action emanating from a single centre but rather in the idea that Latin Christendom was a single society and in the lack of a separation between power and society. Both aspects were expressed in the uniformity of Roman Law. It made no distinction between public and private law; the *Code of Justinian* applied to all legal relations.[19] This meant

---

[12] Dante 1996.

[13] My term 'command power' corresponds to the power successfully and on a routine basis to create binding rules by making directive speech acts. See Onuf 1989: 87–90.

[14] Berg 1997: 51; Osiander 2001a: 123.   [15] Osiander 2001a: 135.   [16] Berg 1997.

[17] Grewe 2000: 54; Osiander 2001: 143.   [18] Nederman 2005: 10–11.

[19] There were other kinds of law during the Middle Ages, such as customary, local, feudal and city laws. Two important collections of feudal and city law were, respectively, the German *Sachsenspiegel*

that legal as well as political acts and relations were, in modern conceptual terms, simultaneously private and public.[20] According to Osiander,
the significance of this feature was that there was no distinction between
spheres of power and society in the Middle Ages. Rather, Latin Christendom was a single society in which different bounded systems of power
existed and interacted. Rulers were members of this society and considered
themselves as having a joint responsibility for its maintenance, stability and
survival.[21]

The distinction between natural law and legal positivism is fundamental
to understanding the development of law in the European tradition and
in particular as regards the interplay between different concepts of society
and power.[22] Since this important distinction has been a topic of research
for many centuries, only a cursory summary can be given here. Both
positions originate in twelfth- and thirteenth-century theology. St Thomas
Aquinas argued that the natural order of being, in which relations we
today would call 'social' were included, was identical with the will of
God and divine reason.[23] This order could not be changed, not even
by God since He could not be in conflict with Himself. Translated to
the world of men, upholding the eternal law became a moral obligation.
Against Aquinas, Duns Scotus propagated a more dynamic theology by
arguing that the will of God and the natural law, the *lex naturalis*, were
identical. Hence that law could not bind God's will. William of Occam
drew the consequence that the natural law was the positive law of the
divine legislator.[24] The implications of the two positions were profound.
While the scholastic natural law position claimed that human law existed
in a hierarchy with natural and divine law, positive law would later be

---

(see Eckhardt 1955) and the *Magdeburger Stadtrecht*. Concerning the influence of Roman law on
peace treaties in the Middle Ages, see Ziegler 2004.

[20] Stolleis (1988: 86) thus summarizes the unity of law in the Middle Ages: 'das Gewicht des *ius
civile* fiel in Streitigkeiten zwischen Bürgern ebenso in der Waagschale wie im Konflikt zwischen
dem Kaiser und einer freien Reichsstadt. Private und Öffentliche Sphäre waren nicht und wurden
dabei nicht getrennt. "Privatfeuden" gab es nicht; denn jede Fehde war zwar die Sache einzelner
Personen, zugleich aber öffentliche Erklärung und Aktion in und mit der Gesamtheit. Ebenso war
ein gekauftes Lehen zwar ein geldwerter Titel für Einzelnen, zugleich ordnete sich der Käufer in die
Lehenspyramide, also in die verfassungsähliche Makrostruktur der feudalen Welt ein.'

[21] Osiander 2001a: 144–5. Lesaffer (2004b: 32) also states the importance of this idea in the sixteenth
century.

[22] 'The antithetical intellectual structure of the natural and positivist schools of legal thought, which
has been presented here, reappeared time and again in the basic conceptions of the classics of the
modern Law of Nations. Sometimes the idea of natural law prevailed; at other times legal positivism
prevailed or, alternatively, a compromise was reached in the form of a 'synthesist' school of thought'
(Grewe 2000: 87).

[23] Grewe 2000: 86.   [24] Grewe 2000: 87.

understood as identical with the will of the person or institution possessing command power.[25] The connection of law and power, in the sense of making the former dependent on the latter, enabled a differentiation of legal orders, as each power-wielder could be seen as a divine legislator within the territory that he commanded. Thereby an order based on separate legal systems that required laws between them was made possible, replacing the idea of order as an all-encompassing hierarchy of human, natural and divine law. The strong notion of a common society in the medieval order had effects that restrained the scope of conflict as well as creating conditions for collective action, the most important of which were the crusades.[26] Naturally the shared religion was the major uniting component, but also the idea of a common Latin occidental culture of chivalry was important.[27] In effect, all Latins, as they called themselves, formed one community in which distinct territories of power existed.[28] Having Latin Christianity as its most fundamental feature and membership criterion, the medieval order had only conquest and conversion as its means of expansion.[29]

The Reformation – separating the spheres of power and society

The sixteenth century was an age of unprecedented territorial expansion as well as augmentation of the material power base of Spain, one of the many European *regna*. By the end of the 1530s Spain had conquered the Aztec and Inca empires in America and was tapping their enormous resources and mineral wealth. Overseas expansion in combination with a number of fortunate marriages dramatically increased the holdings, power and prestige of the House of Habsburg. This severely disrupted relations of strength and raised hopes as well as fears that Europe would become united under the political power of Spain.[30] In the terms of the framework used in this chapter, such a united Europe would only know one system of command power and its society would become co-extensive with it in the manner of classical and eastern empires. In medieval conceptual usage, *potestas* and *auctoritas* would be fused. The project of creating a *monarchia universalis* was never realized, for reasons too complex to deal with in full here. However, the main reasons were the resistance of the Dutch Republic,

---

[25] Grewe 2000: 349–50. [26] Grewe 2000: 52. [27] Grewe 2000: 51–7. [28] Grewe 2000: 56–9.
[29] According to Grewe (2000: 71–82), papal approbation was highly important for the legitimacy of a ruler, but mutual acts of recognition between the 'independent polities' were also crucial to legitimate membership in the European 'family of nations'.
[30] Pagden 1995: 44.

England and France, as well as the abdication of Charles V in 1555 which separated the Spanish and Austrian branches of the House of Habsburg.[31] The attempts of Charles V to achieve supremacy over other Christian princes came close to succeeding in the 1520s but failed as spectacularly later in the century.[32] After the crushing military defeats and growing insolvency of Spain towards the end of the sixteenth century, it was clear that 'empire' as we know it from the Roman and Mughal cases, a vast more or less unified system of rule, would not be possible to pursue in Europe. Rather, this became a form of rule[33] that individual European *regna* would pursue overseas, in the Americas, in Asia and, with time, in Africa.[34]

The Spanish expansion, which upset the balance in Europe, coincided with a tremendous ideational upheaval: the Reformation. On a structural level although not immediately at a conceptual one, the Reformation created several distinctions that paved the way for a new order. I argue that these distinctions can be understood as changes in the nature of society that were to have a profound impact on the relations between the *regna*. The Reformation led to a prolonged period of destructive and bitter religious warfare between as well as within European realms. The wars of religion introduced an element of hostility in intra-European warfare that had hitherto been confined to external wars against the Saracens and pagans or to marginal conflicts against heretics. Not only was the idea of unrestrained warfare, advocated by some legal scholars, potentially disrupting, but so also were the actual intra- and extra-territorial conflicts that took place. The wars of religion that wracked the main powers of Europe for almost a century seemed to threaten England, France and the Holy Roman Empire as systems of governance.[35] The threat of anarchy prompted a solution that would contain the conflicts. The differentiation and demarcation of the interior politics of each territory from those of others that after 1555 emerged as a solution to the religious wars have been interpreted as a means of preventing and mitigating conflicts.[36] The peace of Augsburg established the formula 'Cuius regio, eius religio' as a guiding principle for ordering the relations between the princes of the Holy Roman Empire, which later came

---

[31] However, fears that the two branches of the House of Habsburg would become united persisted up until 1658. Article xiv of the electoral capitulation signed by Leopold I upon becoming Holy Roman Emperor in 1658 compelled him to neutrality in foreign policy issues. This article was primarily intended to prevent Leopold I from allying with the other Habsburg power, Spain, in order for the dynasty to dominate the European continent. Aretin 1997a: 184ff.

[32] Taylor 1999: 65; Lesaffer 2004b: 32.   [33] See Giddens 1985: 57.

[34] As Jönsson, Tägil and Törnqvist (2000) suggest, it is also possible to understand Napoleon's and Hitler's 'projects' as attempts to impose imperial orders in Europe.

[35] Lesaffer 2004b: 13.   [36] Bartelson 1995: 139, 164, 243.

to be accepted in the wider European context. It inhibited religious warfare by insulating each principality from outside intervention owing to or on the pretext of religion. The need for stability is a prevalent interpretation of the projects of order launched by Jean Bodin and Thomas Hobbes, which I discuss in the next section.[37] With respect to the legal situation at mid sixteenth century, Lesaffer notes that:

> By 1550 the old European order had collapsed and no new international system was in place yet ... the old legal system that governed the international relations between ... princes and rulers had crumbled away.[38]

This development was based on, and hence reflected, a fundamental shift in the conception of society that made the changes during this period so profound. No longer was it possible to see Europe as completely unitary with respect to its most important cultural element, Christendom, although we know that the idea of a common Christianity played an important role until the end of the eighteenth century. The division of Europe into Catholic and Protestant (Lutheran and Reformed/Calvinist) camps meant that the differences between European societies were increased, which probably strengthened the conception that western Europe consisted of several societies, each co-terminous with an institutionalized coercive apparatus, rather than of one society within which several realms were embedded. However, our analysis cannot stop at this point, but must go further.

In fact, the question raised by the Reformation created a deeper division, one that contemporary thinking and conceptual apparatus takes as a natural starting-point, namely the one between the spheres of coercive power and society, since the 1820s formulated as the distinction between 'state' and 'society'.[39] The Reformation introduced a new dimension of conflict that was played out between princes, between the subjects of each prince, and between the prince and his subjects. The appearance of different versions of the Christian religion, and hence two kinds of society, meant that princes had to choose between them as well as to devise new kinds of policies vis-à-vis their subjects. The actualization of the question of how each realm should be governed created a new dimension of governance as well as society itself as an object of governance.

Instead of personal rule (*Herrschaft*) being exercised in a common sphere, we can discern a growing alienation and differentiation between rulers and the ruled.[40] The kind of society that was emerging was co-extensive with the extent of the power apparatus of each prince. In fact, the rule emanating

---

[37] Cf. Stolleis 1988: 174.   [38] Lesaffer 2004b: 13.
[39] See Riedel 1979a: 763.   [40] Stolleis 1988: 71.

from this apparatus rose above the subjects as public law (*potestas publica*) and was effectively bounding a given society.[41] Thus a feedback loop can be discerned in whose first phase society 'arises', and in its second phase is bounded by the territorial limits of effective rule; finally, in its third phase, this society, co-extensive with effective rule, reinforces the distinction and boundaries between systems of power. Over the years, this completely new kind of choice that faced rulers would generate a conceptual apparatus and an institutional framework that would evolve into the modern state. This development was not completed in the sixteenth century but took place throughout the early modern period. Nevertheless, the basis of the division between systems of coercive power and society, which in turn reinforced the distinction between different systems of coercive power, lies in the Reformation.

The creation of two separate spheres, coercive power and society, is reflected in the distinction between public and private legal spheres during this time.[42] No longer was there one legal sphere within which all relations were handled. The significance of the emergence of public law as a response to the new questions and object of power can hardly be overstated since it played a major part in creating socio-political realities.[43] The Reformation was not the sole cause of this distinction; rather, the increasing emphasis on the individual in Renaissance thinking also played a part. This interpretation of the formation of a European states-system as driven by ideational factors, in particular the changing conception of society, could be called into question by arguing that it was the violence and threatening disruptiveness of the religious wars that prompted the division of Europe as a functional solution. Thereby, only the first of the changes outlined above, the 'containment' argument, would become relevant. If this objection would hold true, then an order characterized by violent conflict would not be able to hold together but would split up into smaller units and thus come to resemble the European states system.[44] It needs to be emphasized that the existence of a society that ties individuals or formally institutionalized groups of individuals, such as realms, together does not preclude war or violent conflict.[45]

---

[41] Stolleis 1988: 71.   [42] Stolleis 1988: 70.

[43] Stolleis 1988: 67 ('Die rechtswissenschaftliche Argumentation verengte, wie auch noch heute, die Handlungsspielräume dadurch, daß sie faktisch vorhandene Alternativen ausschloß, verdeckte oder durch einfache Nichterwähnung, unsichtbar machte') and 394–5.

[44] This would be the reply of the structural realist school of IR, which sees systems of states as a perennial feature of non-pacified social systems. See Waltz 1979 and Mearsheimer 2001.

[45] Hence Carl Schmitt's definition of war and civil war as 'Krieg ist bewaffneter Kampf zwischen organisierten politischen Einheten, Bürgerkrieg bewaffneter Kampf innerhalb einer (*dadurch aber problematisch werdenden*) organisierten Einheit' (my italics) is a statement of an age in which

The coexistence of the notion of a single society and extensive warfare in medieval Europe as well as its post-Reformation successors can be more easily understood through the terms of modern systems theory than through theories that consider societies in terms of system–subsystem. A key figure of thought in the former is that systems can be nested in one another, i.e. joined as well as isolated from each other although along different dimensions. This conception allows us to see that imbalance in one dimension may not lead to disruption in another, as a set–subset model would lead us to assume. Conversely, violent conflict within a society does not have to lead to its break-up. In other words, the rather high frequency of warfare in medieval Europe could take place without breaking up the unitary social order.[46] For example, feuding, an important part of many medieval social systems, is a kind of organized combat which sustains rather than dismantles the social system. The isolation of levels, this 'double-think', can be stable as long as certain factors, which are usually only visible in retrospect, are not introduced. I believe that the Reformation introduced just such a dimension into the *res publica Christiana* that upset the terms of the nestedness of the *regna* in the *imperio*.

After the Reformation, Europe was no longer one society that existed on different levels of scale – continental, regional and local – in which power-apparatuses were embedded. Two alternative models of society, Catholic and Protestant, had emerged and the princes had to choose one of them. This moment created a differentiation between the spheres of coercive power and society that opened up for a connection and interaction between them. Society in the form it developed from the Reformation onwards became the object of governance. The problem of how these two spheres should relate to each other was to become a dominant theme in European history over the coming centuries, especially during the ones this chapter deals with. I argue that the different conceptions of how the spheres of coercive power and society should be combined were to entail consequences for how the different systems of coercive power, that we in retrospect tend to call 'states', should relate to each other.

3   RESTORING AND RECREATING ORDER

The post-Reformation projects of order were not only counter-projects to the older medieval order and to the Spanish imperial project of the

---

an armed struggle within an organised unity renders that unity problematic. That age is the contemporary one and his verdict cannot be applied to the unity represented by medieval Europe. Schmitt 1938: 15.
[46] See Brunner 1981; Poulsen and Netterstrøm 2007.

sixteenth century. Rather, I understand them as ways not only to make sense of the new political and ontological landscape, but also to replace the old order with something that may fill the void of meaning left by it.[47] These projects differed from the older universalism with respect to language and in terms of the specific configuration of elements, but not in terms of purpose.

The Reformation had brought considerable upheavals to the major countries of Europe, and as religious strife went into a second round in France in the 1570s, establishing stability seemed paramount. Arguably, the most important writer in this period was Jean Bodin, the inventor of the modern concept of sovereignty. His views were favourably received in his native country and would supply absolutist reformers and government with an invaluable arsenal of arguments in later centuries.[48] In a manner revolutionary to his time, Bodin understood sovereignty as 'absolute and perpetual power over citizens and subjects in a commonwealth'.[49] This definition meant that the power apparatus of the prince was recognized as distinct from other institutions and wielders of power that existed within a realm. At the time, European realms were characterized by an extreme 'pluralism' of institutions and actors that could, and did, exercise rule. These were noblemen who exercised seigniorial rights in their lands as well as in local and central estates and courts of law, and also in cities, city-leagues and corporate bodies such as guilds.[50] Not only was sovereignty absolute and unlimited power, it was also indivisible. This meant that commanding power could only have one locus in a realm. It did not matter whether this locus took the form of a parliamentary assembly or a king, but the power to command and coerce could not be shared among many holders.[51] A hallmark of sovereignty was that he who possessed it was bound by no law but was rather the source of law himself.[52]

Since Aristotle, Western political theory had worked with the idea that human societies were ascending orders of associations, starting with individual households and continuing upwards. The theory of corporations usually granted different degrees of self-rule to each corporation. In Bodin's case, however, his conception of sovereignty made all bodies beneath the

---

[47] For a description of the general sense of dislocation and metaphysical crisis that prevailed during the later sixteenth and early seventeenth centuries, see Toulmin 1992.

[48] Franklin 2003: x.   [49] Dyson 1980: 34; Stolleis 1988: 173.

[50] For the first category see Major 1980.

[51] Franklin 2003: xii, xxii. Bodin vigorously attacked the idea that France was composed of three kinds of government (aristocracy, democracy and monarchy) each of which exercised power and thus had a share in the rule of the realm. France was not a 'mixed state' and it was tantamount to *lèse-majesté* to advocate it since that would 'make subjects the colleagues of a sovereign prince'. Bodin 2003: 100 (Book II, ch. 1).

[52] Bodin 2003: 11 (Book I, ch. 8).

level of the sovereign irrelevant.[53] Concerning the issue of society, Bodin
argued that a society (*civitas, societas civilis*) gained a political organization
only once it achieved the highest power (*puissance souveraine*). Riedel sees
this as a fundamental change in the relationship between political rule and
society as it allows the former to begin to emerge as an independent sphere.
This independence replaced the older idea of an equal relationship between
rulers and ruled.[54]

The singularity of the monarch in Bodin's work was based on his unique
position in the divinely created and maintained order.[55] This idea could
not be rejected without breaking with the Christian cosmology which,
obviously, no one was prepared to do. Bodin claimed that the empire was
a pure 'aristocracy', i.e. sovereignty rested exclusively with the estates. Such
a position might hazard disrupting the unity of the empire and therefore few authors were willing to concede this point. Instead of reducing the
empire to either aristocracy, monarchy or democracy, scholars of the empire
sought to fortify the idea that the empire was a *status mixta*, a combination
of all three kinds.[56] To argue so without rejecting the idea of sovereignty –
and thus severing the links with natural law – demanded considerable virtu-
osity of conceptual analysis.[57] A distinction was drawn between *majestas*,[58]
which was the indispensable quality of a social entity (*Gemeinwesen*), and
imperium, commanding power as the factual manifestation of *majestas*.
By distinguishing between entitlement to and practice of what we with
a blunter conceptual toolkit call 'power' the empire retained sovereignty
at the same time as the actual distribution of power and lordship rights
in the empire was fitted into a philosophical-legal system.[59] This distinction between different kinds of power was very much in the spirit of the
medieval order dealt with above and very much at odds with the emerging
paradigm of order. A coherent solution was thereby found that retained
the link to natural law without conceding to Bodin's claim that sovereignty
was unitary and that all loci and kinds of power must converge, at least in
principle. It also laid the foundations for later debates on the location of
majestas in the empire.

Bodin's argument made the systems of power bounded and closed to
the outside and clearly hierarchical with respect to the newly created inside
through his doctrine of sovereignty. The latter, of course, was a kind of

[53] Onuf 1998: 71–2.   [54] Riedel 1979a: 733–4.   [55] Stolleis 1988: 181.
[56] Stolleis 1988: 182.   [57] Stolleis 1988: 179–80.
[58] For a closer definition see 'Majestät – Majestas', in Speer 1992–6, Heft 1/2: *Mahlgericht – Martin*,
37–41.
[59] Stolleis 1988: 178.

closure of the top level, that of the monarch and his court, from other levels of power, such as the estates and the judicial courts. However, he still operated in the framework of association theory, where society extended outwards and upwards from the domain controlled by the power system. Later, Hobbes reacted upon, codified and strengthened the distinction between 'power' and the newly created idea of civil society.

The systems of power as well as distinct societies had become bounded. Nevertheless, much of Europe still very much shared a common culture of religion, language, customs, noble and dynastic family ties, etc. Therefore, in this new context, relations between the newly constructed configurations of society/community and power systems had to be forged, both in the sense of ordering a legal system for the relations between peoples, a *ius inter gentes*, and in the sense of creating an intersubjective framework enabling the understanding of such relations. Efforts to do so had been made by Spanish legal scholars of the sixteenth century such as Francisco de Vitoria (1486–1546) and Francisco Suárez (1548–1617). Their work laid the foundations for later legal scholars, the most renowned, in his age as well as to posterity, being Hugo Grotius.[60]

The differences between Vitoria and Suárez replicated the disagreement between St Thomas Aquinas and William of Occam on the nature of law and the divine order. More specifically relevant to the present problem, the two Spanish jurists disagreed concerning the character of the Law of Nations. Vitoria argued that it was a natural and divinely pre-ordained community independent of the will of the states, that is, the princes of each *regnum*.[61] The laws of this community were binding, but rather by force of their moral standing than by the capacity of enforcement. Suárez, writing a generation later, took a voluntarist position which saw the Law of Nations as derived from the consensus of the wills of the sovereigns. Its foundations were treaties and custom, not natural law.[62] The two conceptions of order presupposed as well as prescribed radically different ontologies. In the first case, community is pre-existent to the individual units, and overrides them. In the second, community is formed voluntarily by pre-existing *regna*, and depends on their interest in maintaining it.

These ideational developments laid the foundations of a new order but they did not have immediate effects on state practice. Rather, between 1618 and 1648 much of continental Europe was drawn into the conflagration of the Thirty Years War: a complex of conflicts that involved inter-territorial struggles between great powers, the political form of the Holy Roman

[60] See Kingsbury and Roberts 1990. [61] Grewe 2000: 189–90. [62] Grewe 2000: 190.

Empire and religion. With the peace of Westphalia in 1648, the war came to an end. Recent research on the peace has disputed the standard account that the treaties marked the starting-point of a modern international system based on sovereign national states. The latter position held that the system created in 1648 was in its basic forms identical with the current system of international law.[63] In contrast, the 'revisionist' turn stresses that the treaties were primarily constitutional documents pertaining to the Holy Roman Empire and it is only in this context that any references to sovereignty are found.[64] In the second instance, however, the treaties of Westphalia were between powers external to the empire and the emperor and the estates of the realm. The net result of the treaties was a relative pacification of large areas of Europe, which enabled the gradual construction of a stable order for the continent through law. What this order should look like in terms of relations between its constituent members and how far it would stretch was, however, far from clear in 1648.

4   ORDERS IN EUROPE 1648–1800

Establishing societies within realms

The thought of Thomas Hobbes is identified as a distinct break between early modern and modern political thought.[65] Hobbes is a pivotal figure in the political theory of international relations, but most commentators have focused on his views of the state of nature as a precondition of commonwealths and on the analogy between the state of nature and relations between states.[66] Discussions of the relations between commonwealths have mostly focused on the passages in his writings that deal with relations that make no mention of religion. I believe that a useful entry into his view of the social element as such can be found in his views on Christianity and Christendom.

Hobbes identified *civitas*, which he translated into English as 'commonwealth', not with the community of Christendom, but with the territorially bounded power-structure of the prince, to whom Bodin's conception of

[63] This view has featured in numerous works; for the classical statement see Gross 1948. For examples of more recent statements in International Relations see Holsti 1991; Watson 1992; Krasner 1993. For a synthesis between the interpretation of the peace of Westphalia as a break with the past and the interpretation of it as being in continuity with earlier practices, see Duchhardt 2004: 46.

[64] Osiander 1994, Teschke 2002; 2003; Lesaffer 2004b: 10; Haldén 2006. See also Aretin 1997a: 22–3. The peace treaties regulated the political relations within the Empire, between the emperor and the estates, and from another point of view between the Habsburgs and the other principalities.

[65] See Skinner 2002.   [66] See for example Williams 1996; Boucher 1998: 145–70.

sovereignty had given absolute pre-eminence.[67] In contrast to the idea that Christendom formed one community beyond the realms that existed within this communal sphere, Hobbes argued that 'there are Christians, *in* the dominions of several princes and states'.[68] This spatial shift pointed in an entirely different direction as it made the shared community of Christians, i.e. of the vast majority of Europeans and the audience for which Hobbes was writing, subordinate to their belonging to separate commonwealths. Thus, in contrast to the earlier conception, community was now postulated as existing within each commonwealth, not between or above them. This move proved to be a decisive shift: community could exist within the territory commanded, at least in theory, by a military-political system, whereas outside of it, in Hobbes' words, no right or wrong could exist.[69] This conception of society was very different from the medieval order and, as we shall see, from the order of the Holy Roman Empire that contained numerous territorial power systems within the same community. As such, Hobbes' notion of society as something existing within the state had powerful ramifications for his conception of the Law of Nations and of inter-territorial politics.

Concerning his conceptualization of society and the power apparatus of the sovereign ('state'), Hobbes' treatment of heresy is instructive. In his philosophical system heresy did not have an objective existence, but was relative to each sovereign. Basing his argument on the acceptance by early Christians of their subservient position vis-à-vis their Roman rulers, Hobbes maintained that any belief held by the sovereign was the public doctrine and, as such, it could not be heresy.[70] Thereby, a question as important as religion was made relative by postulating that every realm had its own measure of religious correctness and by placing the sovereign as a yard-stick. Furthermore, heresy could only be understood as opposition to the religious commands of the sovereign and as such it was an opinion held by 'private men'.[71] Firstly, this move clearly identifies what was still, arguably, the most important cultural element, with the opinion of the sovereign. In other words, the sovereign bounds society by bounding its most important element, religion (a move which is strengthened by Hobbes' argument that every Christian prince is the pastor of his subjects, which means that religion becomes identified with the bounded realm).[72]

[67] Hobbes 1996: 114; Grewe 2000: 349–50.
[68] Hobbes 1996: 311 (ch. xxxix:5) (my italics).   [69] Grewe 2000: 350.
[70] Hobbes 1996: 388: 'for I cannot call anyone whose doctrine is the public doctrine, an heretic'.
[71] Hobbes also rejects the idea that kings could be deposed for being heretics or failing to root out heretics: 1996: 383–4.
[72] See Hobbes 1996: 387–8.

This claim further diminishes societal elements outside the bounded sphere of the realm since communication with the Divine proceeds 'vertically' from each realm and through its hierarchies rather than bypassing them. In other words, each realm by virtue of its sovereign became the conduit for religion rather than existing within the Christian cosmos.[73] Secondly, it reinforces the supreme position of the sovereign by absolving him, *prima facie*, from heresy. Thirdly, it reinforces the distinction between power and society by moving heresy from the sphere of the former to that of the latter. Hence, the postulation of the power-structure of a realm and society as two separate spheres, which had begun by the emergence of the idea of 'public law', was substantially reinforced by implicating religion in it.

Hobbes' conceptions of law and of power were intimately connected since he saw law only as existing where there was a command mechanism to enforce it.[74] The association of law with the command of the sovereign has been understood as a perception of law as distinctly voluntaristic and positive in a way that Grewe traced to William of Occam's philosophy.[75] By making enforcement a precondition of law, Hobbes denied the existence of a natural legal order between powers in Europe and saw only a web of positive law joining them.[76] Either the relations between commonwealths were inimical or this condition had been solved by a contract between two commonwealths.[77]

Regarding inter-territorial relations I believe that Hobbes' view of Christendom is once again central. As discussed above, he rejected the idea that Christianity is one commonwealth and rather argued that individual realms constituted separate commonwealths. This claim rested on a sophisticated fusion of argument pertaining to law, Protestant theology and power. If Christendom was one commonwealth, then its head, the pope, would be the temporal and spiritual sovereign and thus possess the power to 'command, judge and punish'.[78] This argument, effective as it may have been in feeding on fears of 'popery' and Catholicism, required the identification between commanding and lawgiving power. Hobbes fused command power with lawgiving power.[79] As we saw above, the distinction between

---

[73] Another interpretation is the school that Seaman calls 'Hobbes-as-eliminator-of-Christianity' (Leo Strauss, among others), which argues that by the subjection of Christianity to the political sovereign it was virtually eliminated, at least as a motivational force for politics. See Seaman 1999, esp. 228 and 231. For a contrary point, see Milner 1988.

[74] Hobbes 1996: 179 and 181. For a critique of the Hobbesian argument see Kratochwil 1989: 184.

[75] Grewe 2000: 189 and 349. For a contrary opinion that Hobbes was not antithetical to the natural law tradition, see Murphy 1995.

[76] Grewe 2000: 350.   [77] Hobbes 1996: 210.   [78] Hobbes 1996: 385.   [79] Hobbes 1996: 141.

two kinds of power was a central part of the medieval order and, as will be argued below, an important trait of the Holy Roman Empire.

The classical European states-system and its society

The changes in the location of society corresponded to changes in the European order, or as we may call it the European system of states. The European system in the eighteenth century has been seen as an order tempered by the new international law, the *ius gentium*, which underlay the limited 'cabinet wars' of the time.[80] Although it is indisputable that international law and natural law had made great headway intellectually and that the conflagrations of the seventeenth century were not repeated in the next, international relations correspond to this orderly image only in western Europe between 1763 and the outbreak of the Revolutionary Wars in 1792. Previous eighteenth-century conflicts were bitter, prolonged and intense, and included numerous infringements of the *ius gentium*.[81]

A new legal framework had been put in place that regulated the affairs of the European powers and it had made the enormously destructive religious warfare into a thing of the past. This had come as a result of the closure of each component part, through the doctrine of sovereignty, a closure that was accepted by all actors of the system. This closure, however, had effects on how the external relations between these actors, once members of one Christian community, came to be perceived. Closing off each realm from each other had freed Europe of the risk of systemic religiously motivated disruptions, but it contained other risks. By making each monarch answerable only to himself and to his God, the sense of a common community had been seriously weakened. The conception of the European system, or 'republic of Europe' as it began to be called, as offering each unit a high degree of autonomy meant that system-sustaining policies were becoming not only less profitable, but also less thinkable. We can see this very clearly in a feature of eighteenth-century Europe that is often highly lauded, the balance of power.

The idea of a *iustum potentiae aequilibrium* – a just balance of power – was pronounced as a key rule in the peace of Utrecht in 1713, which reordered relations among the European great powers after the Spanish

---

[80] Stolleis 1988: 196.
[81] E.g. the War of the Spanish Succession (1700–13), the Great Northern War (1700–21), the War of the Austrian Succession (1740–8) and the Seven Years War (1756–63).

War of Succession, and became incorporated into the public law of the 'republic of Europe' of the eighteenth century.[82] The order of the eighteenth century was dominated by the idea of the balance of power and references to it are found in most major peace treaties of the time. It rested on two fundamental principles, that a certain amount of restraint must be observed in warfare between European powers[83] and that no power should be allowed to achieve a position from which it could dominate the European continent.

The principle of the balance of power required that if the force of any of the units increased, then that of the other units had to increase as well in order to maintain the equilibrium. In Europe at the time, the two factors that accounted for the force and gravity of a power were land and money. So if the territorial possessions of one power increased, then others could, and did, raise rightful claims to be compensated. A power could be compensated either by a share in the spoils of war gained by the first state or by itself expanding at the expense of a third party, subsequently subject to approval by the other powers of Europe. Closely linked to the idea of compensations was the practice of demanding and receiving indemnities not only from defeated enemies but also from allies, either through territory or by monetary means.[84]

Although celebrated by later generations of historians and political scientists, this system contained numerous disadvantages. It could hardly have been perceived as a just, stable or equitable order by the powers whose territories were used as a reserve for compensations and indemnities. The most famous example was the three partitions of Poland, which contemporaries saw as highly destructive to the system as a whole. The system of compensations also contained an inherent weakness since sooner or later the continent would run out of its stabilizing buffer of distributable territory. A final reason why it was difficult to sustain was that restraining functions were externalized, in the sense of being entrusted to the willingness and – above all – the capacity of other states to check the expansion of hungry neighbours. The willingness to assert oneself and expand was also the factor that, according to the logic of the balance of power, maintained the system since it constituted the countervailing force that held others in check. Therefore, restraint was externalized and the value that was

---

[82] Grewe 2000: 282. For a contrary opinion, see Duchhardt 2004: 56–7.

[83] Kunisch 2004: 110–11. One representative seventeenth-century proponent of this view was Pufendorf and one of the eighteenth was Vattel, see Little 1989: 94. Cf. Grotius' view that European states had obligations to each other that were not extended to powers outside the system such as the Ottomans: Reus-Smit 1999: 103.

[84] Schroeder 1994: 6–7.

internalized by each power was expansion, which made the system inherently unstable.[85]

Some preconditions of this system can be found in the conception of society that had become dominant in Europe at the turn of the eighteenth century. In terms of the kind of society that the balance of power system represented we can discern an analogy to the foundations of the Hobbesian commonwealth as well as to the individuals that make up Locke's civil society. Since Hobbes and Spinoza, a new conception of society had become established. Instead of nature, i.e. the divine plan,[86] as the base of human community and organization, Hobbes saw human society as the product of circumstance and accident.[87] The organization of human individuals was not part of a pre-existing plan or order but was now seen as fulfilling a distinct function, that of security. In Locke's political philosophy we see the definite transition from a traditional natural law to modern rational conceptual language. For the classical Aristotelian foundation of society as a purposeful fulfilling of a pre-existing form ($\tau\acute{\epsilon}\lambda o\varsigma$), he substituted a society whose purpose is the fulfilment of its members' functional needs, in this case of security of life and property.[88]

Of primary interest for this chapter is not this break in the history of ideas itself, nor the exact purpose of the social contract. What is important is that the units began to be seen as existing prior to society and entering into it in order to fulfil previously existing interests. The older kind of society was seen as pre-existing to the members and not reducible to the members' individual relations. Society was seen as a precondition of the members and their attributes, not the other way around. This conception of society also restrained the autonomy of the members, that is, the European realms. In the newer kind of order the realms were more autonomous and their actions less restrained. The greater degree of autonomy stemmed from the view that realms were in command of society and thus were their own moral arbiters. Although the new kind of order was becoming established and settled on the level of state practice, it was not quite settled on the level of ideas.

Between 1648 and 1800, the basis of recognition of new states – and thereby the membership criteria of the European order – changed into a question of whether control over a given territory was exercised by an organized political body or not.[89] Previously, membership, seen as a function of criteria for recognition, had depended on whether a new power morally

---

[85] See also Haldén 2011.   [86] Riedel 1979a: 733.   [87] Riedel 1979b: 810.
[88] Riedel 1979b: 810.   [89] Grewe 2000: 343ff.

and legally corresponded to the values of the system and whether the circumstances through which it came into being were legally and morally acceptable. After 1650, the internal character of a state was of decreasing importance as to whether it would be recognized or not. Emmerich de Vattel, widely regarded as one of most important figures in early modern international law, stressed sovereignty as the most important criterion for membership in the 'society' of Europe.[90] In 1776 the debates on whether the United States should be recognized became a litmus test of the criteria for membership. It was the French opinion that came to prevail: that effective control was the defining criterion, not legitimate procedure of establishment.[91] Nevertheless, the idea of a Christian community remained important in the eighteenth century, although the paramount position it enjoyed in previous centuries had declined somewhat.[92] It was only in the nineteenth century that it would be replaced by the much more inclusive idea a 'community of civilized nations'.[93]

Continuities and returns

Throughout this chapter I have argued that the development from the order where bounded units of power were embedded in society to the kind of order where society is embedded in bounded units of power was not linear. There was no complete break between the tradition of ordering bounded systems of power within society and ordering society within bounded units of power. The medieval empire of the Ottonians and the Staufen dynasties lived on in the late medieval and early modern Holy Roman Empire of the German Nation, although in a very changed form until 1806.[94] A constant feature throughout the changes that it went through was that it was a society, a community, in which many different centres of power were embedded. In this sense it was analogous to the medieval *res publica Christiana*. It was an order that contained many territorially bounded systems of military-political power, but they were embedded in a common system of law and a conception of a shared society. Despite its imperial trappings, symbols and sometimes discourse, the early modern Holy Roman Empire differed sharply from other universal orders in the sense that it could not expand.

[90] Grewe 2000: 345–6 and 348. Vattel also used the criterion of effective rule in the question of the rights of non-European populations, arguing that 'natives' in the Americas and Africa did not exercise effective rule and therefore had no claims to their lands. See Grewe 2000: 401.
[91] Grewe 2000: 348.   [92] Grewe 2000: 287–8.   [93] Grewe 2000: 289.
[94] I deal with this issue at length in my book *Stability without Statehood: Lessons from Europe's History before the Sovereign State* (Haldén 2011). See also Aretin 1997a and b.

Its individual members, like Austria or Prussia, could expand on their own but they could not extend the empire. Hence, the Holy Roman Empire lacked many of the central traits of empire and most crucially universalism.

Even with the end of the Holy Roman Empire, the universalistic heritage in Europe has lived on but it has materialized itself in unexpected ways. The universal heritage of imperial thought in European history has travelled along a trajectory that is everything but straightforward. The European states-system is often portrayed as a radical break with all imperial traditions of the Middle Ages. In most narratives of the Valois–Habsburg wars, the wars of religion, the Thirty Years War and the subsequent struggles against Louis XIV, Napoleon and Hitler, the European states-system is portrayed as an anti-imperial system. The workings of the balance of power, by many seen as a core feature of the European system, mitigated against the emergence of a single European ruler. Indeed, why Europe unlike India or China has not seen an institutionalized empire since the Romans has been a major topic of research for several centuries. However, in one crucial respect the European states-system is the successor of universal empire – its universality.

Membership criteria in the two orders were very different. In the case of the European states-system at the end of the eighteenth century membership hinged on having effective control over a territory and conforming to certain practices. These criteria ultimately enabled the expansion of the European system of states and the *ius publicum europeum*. First it admitted Russia in the eighteenth century, then Turkey, Oman, Japan and Siam in the nineteenth, and eventually it came to encompass the entire world once the global system of European overseas empires dissolved in the twentieth. Although significantly anti-imperial in its aversion to a single centralized power system dominating the continent, the European system of states was much more universal than the medieval order or the Holy Roman Empire. In the absence of a priori limits to its extension, it resembled the Roman idea of the *civitas* whose boundaries were concomitant with what we today would call civilization and could be extended almost indefinitely.[95] The greater degree of inclusiveness of the European system of states, and thus the possibility of spreading a web of rules and laws, regulating and to some extent restraining state actions, across the globe, can be understood as made possible by a more loose coupling of the units. Without a looser system in Europe after the mid seventeenth century we would perhaps not have had the current global system of law and diplomacy. Drawing up a

---

[95] See Pagden 2001: 175–6.

balance sheet of a period as long as the one surveyed in this chapter is difficult but it seems that the trade-off between strong community and inclusiveness may be hard to surmount.

The European states-system is the only form of order that has truly become global. Of all the major templates of order in European and indeed world history, the European states-system is the only one that has had the potential to organize the entire globe. The modern states-system is not an empire in the sense of a territorial order with a centre that exercises rule in the sense of command. Its configuration differs strongly from the universal model of the *res publica Christiana* since society is understood primarily within and secondarily between bounded systems of power. However, in its universality it is an heir of the imperial traditions of Europe.

Concurrent with but not necessarily causally connected to the universal extension of the states-system are developments that point towards an emergent hybrid of the two historical forms of order surveyed in this chapter: a 'universalist-atomistic' order. Two late twentieth-century developments can be invoked to show the return of conceptions of a global society existing above bounded systems. Firstly there is the case of increased restraints of rulers through international law and the doctrine of human rights.[96] During the 1990s there was a shift in emphasis from the inviolability of borders to the right of military intervention if a ruler or a government abused his sovereignty and violated the population's human rights. This has not been translated into a general doctrine and one could argue that the cases where interventions have taken place are few and far between. Still, the shift towards intervention represents a historical return of the idea that bounded systems of power exist within a single society. Secondly, the inviolability of frontiers as agreed by the Helsinki Conference in 1975[97] was a major step in the self-binding of states. The conference was directly aimed at easing tensions during the Cold War and to exclude the possibility that states like Germany and Poland would try to revise their borders which were changed after the Second World War.

CONCLUSIONS

I have tried to show how different ideas of society and its location (*within*, *between* or *around* bounded political systems) have influenced political

---

[96] There is a substantial literature on intervention. See, for example, Finnemore 2003; Feste 2003; Haass 1999.

[97] Conference on Security and Co-operation in Europe. Final Act (Helsinki, 1975) (available on www.osce.org/mc/39501).

orders. Changes in this idea have in a number of crucial breaks transformed the conditions of politics on the European continent. What, then, is the difference between this argument and the idea that norms and values concerning the behaviour of states have changed over the years, and that, through the course of that process, so have the actions of states? Firstly, it introduces precision by pointing to the locus of change: that it has been the conception of society that has changed rather than ideas and values between and supposedly within pre-existing separate systems. Rather than putting states, and before that *regna*, at the analytical forefront, I believe that the commonly held idea of society has influenced the configuration of the different political orders. Concomitant with this change were changes in the nature of the units (*regna*, states). Changes in the idea of society at the level of order have shaped the framework within which preferences and actions are formed at a lower level, namely that of units. Secondly, when comparing the different kinds of order on the basis of what forms the communal element, we see that they are structurally very different. The communal element, or conception of society, forms the raison d'être of that order and is central to how the relations of the members are regulated.

The contemporary order, which I have tentatively called the 'universalist-atomistic', combines ideas of society within and between as well as above bounded systems of power. This compound is not a decisive break with other universal conceptions of order but an heir of the medieval universalism as well as of early modern attempts to break with it. Whether it will be robust and flexible enough to accommodate the rising powers like China and India in a densely knit world will be a central concern of the twenty-first century. That, however, is beyond the scope of this chapter.

CHAPTER 13

Imperial universalism – further thoughts

John A. Hall

I came to these papers somewhat in the spirit of Kierkegaard, touched by anxiety, even dread. My professional formation has tended to privilege structural explanations, in terms of power and wealth rather than in terms of belief – whose varied contours, made universal as part of the cosmic or religious order, form the core of this volume. One notes that the spirit of Foucault appears on several occasions, and feels more generally the presence of the cultural turn characteristic of so much of contemporary approaches to social understanding. Would this set of authors naively presume that meaning makes the world go round? Let me say immediately that my doubts were soon dissipated. For one thing, the volume does not seek to suggest that meaning alone matters, but rather to offer sustained analysis of the origin, character and maintenance of the symbolic aspects of power. The proof of the pudding here is in Peter Bang's chapter which reminds us that the symbolic displays of the monarchs of the Hellenistic world were yet another dimension of an intensely competitive geopolitical order at the heart of which was military confrontation.[1] For another, these excellent papers are extremely challenging, especially to the mainstream tradition of comparative historical analysis. Several points in this regard need highlighting.

We can arrive at a first point by turning Foucault on his head, right side up. Reality is of course complex, and there is something to be said for his insistence that 'modernity' seeks to control and reformulate every part of social and personal life, making us the subjects of some sort of total surveillance, externally imposed but felt just as much internally. Equally, it is clearly the case that high levels of 'governmentality' were ruled out in pre-modern circumstances, as will be stressed in a moment, given the lack of infrastructural powers available to political elites. But a general

---

[1] It is worth noting in this connection that this book is complemented by another volume from the same research project, *Tributary Empires in Global History* (Bang and Bayly 2011), which concentrates on structural aspects of power.

claim can nonetheless be made, to Foucault's disadvantage. Many of the readers of this volume will be European, accordingly members of a world bereft of great ideological ambition. The continent's last great ideology, Marxism, is dead, replaced by the duller command for consumers of the world to unite. The contrast with the universal claims made by the empires considered here is very great. Rule mattered, power had purpose. Increasing growth rates seem almost pathetic in comparison to the need to feed the gods, or to preserve the Mandate of nothing less than Heaven. It might seem as if there is an exception in the modern world to this generalization, apparent above all in the language employed by Donald Rumsfeld when Secretary of Defense under Bush the Younger. But the United States as a whole is no real exception. Here is a country with capacities of all sorts controlled by categories that stress societal virtue, a social formation which denies the brute power it possesses. Insofar as self-belief has an autonomous impact on social life there is a good deal to be said for the concentration here on the ideologies of the empires under scrutiny. In this context, it is important to offer perhaps the most striking finding of the whole volume. Every empire under consideration here took the ritualistic and symbolic aspects of power utterly seriously. We are clearly dealing here with more than superstructural excrescences. The self-images we are shown were quite simply what these empires were, in a certain sense, about, their very raison d'être.

If the tributary empires discussed and analysed in this collection had a visceral sense of power and purpose, this is not for a moment to say that they found it easy to exercise control. All rule depends upon co-operation with subordinates, upon different power sources pointing in the same direction. But one such source generally available in the modern world, professionalized bureaucracy, was largely missing in pre-modern conditions. It may be this very fact that explains the very subject matter of this volume, namely the ways in which rituals and symbols shaped power relations. The very lack of the resources and capacities which the modern world takes for granted made the performative aspects of power vitally important. Peter Bang is surely right in this connection to make use of Clifford Geertz's description of the seemingly endless competitive rituals and displays that appeared to make up the nineteenth-century Balinese state.[2]

The contributors help us to understand why these aspects of power mattered so very much. The most important power connection in

[2] Geertz 1980.

pre-modern conditions was that between the elite and the state. The chapters in this volume cast much light here, making one realize how crucial it was to unify the elite, to make it feel that it was part of the imperial construct. Sentiments doubtless came often from the possibilities of advantage and advance, as Justyna Olko so clearly demonstrates for the Aztecs. Royal pageantry served to publicize the wealth and capacity of the ruler, thereby establishing models of comportment to be emulated by elites wishing to stake a claim for attention and power. If this is the world of Clifford Geertz, it is also that of the unduly neglected American social theorist Thorstein Veblen – whose analyses of seemingly useless displays demonstrated that conspicuous consumption could be used to claim status and power.[3] But the Assyrian case suggests that fear mattered quite as much. The elite of that social formation had to move around a palace whose wall reliefs privileged scenes of destruction and torture, Gojko Barjamovic tells us – a lurid world for once not so far from Hollywood representations.

One social theorist who recognized the importance of elite unity in preindustrial circumstances was Ernest Gellner, and it is useful to recall his comments here, both for their inherent interest and as a means to pointing out the contributions made by the authors of this volume.[4] Gellner made us realize that elites sat on top of laterally insulated groups of primary producers, all caged *vertically* within particular local cultures. The elites themselves were linked *horizontally* over large territorial spaces, and they were prone to share a great deal in cultural terms. Of course, sharing does not mean continual agreement. Relations between military, ideological and political actors might be consensual but might as easily be riddled with tension. In this matter, Gellner himself offered a neat set of four contrasts: centralized/uncentralized, stallions/gelded, open/closed and fused/non-fused. Each contrast had an illustration: the papacy compared to the ulamas of Islam; feudal warriors contrasted to the eunuchs so prominent in the Roman and Chinese cases; the meritocratic, examined Mandarinate of China compared to the hereditary Brahmins of the classical Hindu world; and the military orders of Europe pushing expansion to the East seen as so very different from the division of function characteristic of the caste system. These are striking contrasts, deeply thought-provoking – in part, of course, because they were not mere constructs but rather the distillation of a good deal of comparative historical knowledge. The chapters in this volume add a great deal of detail to this ideal typical model. Most of all, however, they support the first general point, the horizontal nature of elite

---

[3] Veblen 1899.   [4] Gellner 1983: ch. 2.

power, and the constant interactions between different sections of the elite and the pretensions of the state. Several points deserve highlighting.

Gellner's viewpoint, essentially static in character, is here replaced by a processual, dynamic view. Peter Bang shows Alexander attempting to bring the Persian elite into the fold of his new empire, a move which clearly put the backs up of the members of his own conquering elite, fearful both of the loss of privilege and the possibility of being outnumbered and submerged in an entity other than their own. A very similar story can be told of the Qing empire, where the Manchus for long maintained an identity separate from the Chinese so as to preserve their ruling position. All of this is to say that the popular image of agrarian empires as all-powerful is woefully far from the truth. These were puny leviathans, constantly engaged in negotiation and compromise. One striking way in which this can be seen is in the varied mechanisms the empires used when trying to integrate elites into their core. Ebba Koch offers a stimulating account of the use of visual means to attract elites, and this is neatly paralleled by the account of the role of poetry in state building in Vijayanagara in south India offered by N. Rao and Sanjay Subrahmanyam. Garth Fowden's account of the incorporation of Aristotle within early Islam makes exactly the same point about philosophy. Still what mattered most is probably the attempt to incorporate through religious means, a topic that deserves special treatment.

Pre-modern empires had to deal with very great diversity, having emerged in areas of rich cultural contact. The limited power resources available to emperors meant that it was almost never possible to imagine universalism in the strongest sense, as the imposition of a single set of beliefs held in the metropole. If the endlessly varied beliefs and customs of the vertically insu-lated sets of peasant producers could be ignored, as long as they kept quiet, the practices of those elites who came within the empire as conquest pro-ceeded were an entirely different matter. Hence we learn a great deal about the complexity of belief 'systems', the composite nature of the ideologies involved. The incorporation of the Trojan legend in Rome, together with Orientalist attitudes par excellence, is a clear example, brilliantly described by Schneider. Similar linking of very varied worldviews is equally appar-ent in Dariusz Kołodziejczyk's treatment of the Ottomans. Most striking of all is the contribution of Garth Fowden, describing nothing less than exchange, the adoption within Islam of ideas of rule originating in the Late Classical period in Greece. And there is a further point. We can see on occasion a positive appreciation of diversity, even a measure of revelling in different traditions whilst standing above all of them – as exemplified most famously in the palatial architecture of the Achaemenids described in Barjamovic's chapter. So the univeralism internal to these empires is best seen in terms of pluralism and polyethnicity rather than in terms of standardization and uniformity.

A final point must be made about the relations between religion and empire. A basic analytic point is clear, namely that religion can both help and hinder imperial consolidation. Dimiter Angelov and Judith Herrin describe with the greatest lucidity the contrast in Christianity between the Caesaropapism of Byzantium and the attempt, short-lived though it was, to establish a spiritual empire in the West. It is as well to remember in this context that this polar opposition does not exhaust the possibilities within Christianity. The rule of Philip II saw an astonishingly close symbiosis between rule and religion, it being impossible to separate one force from the other.[5] Even a casual visit to the Escorial – at one and the same time palace and monastery, with Philip's own bedroom allowing him to see the altar below – makes the point with brutal clarity.

A further comment about universalism is necessary. Agrarian empires have very often been seen as universal in the sense of being worlds unto themselves, lacking links with others for infrastructural reasons, prone to celebrate themselves and to ignore outsiders. Ebba Koch and Evelyn Rawski undermine this view for the Mughal and Qing empires, both of which faced genuine rivals, making their social worlds very far from complete. What is noticeable in both cases is that the central tenets of belief in both cases were played down. Ideology here seems, as so often, less a conceptual cage than a tool box which can be used according to circumstance. But the point is in fact a more general one. Many emperors wrote to nothing less than their peers, often referring to them as 'brothers' when diplomatic expediency dictated a more cordial and respectful tone. Modern historiography has made much of cultural contact, and these chapters suggest that peer polity emulation, in which kings competed with each other for supremacy so as to increase their own standing, was present here, thereby diminishing claims about the uniqueness of the better-known competitive multipolar system of European history. It is often claimed that not all world religions and ethics are so flexible, with Islam sometimes being singled out as particularly rigid on the grounds that its doctrine, established in a very short period and late in the record of monotheisms, insists that rule be godly. There may be something to this, but both the Ottomans and the Mughals presented here reveal themselves to be quite flexible. This seems strikingly true of

[5] Elliott 2007.

Dariusz Kołodziejczyk's portrait of nothing less than the multiple identities of the Ottoman sultan. Equally, Ebba Koch shows us the Mughals drawing on illuminationist thinking, with Akbar, of course, famously preaching tolerance to the more bigoted Safavids. Equally relevant in this regard is the demonstration provided by Rao and Sanjay Subrahmanyam of the emulation in the early modern period of historic models of kingship.

Universal empire is sometimes seen as an anomaly, as an oddity of history naturally replaced by the nation-state. Nothing could be further from the truth. Empire is probably the default option of the historical record, with the nation-state being the oddity – created by and suited for only modern circumstances. It is worth noting in this regard recent literatures about the character of the current growth of Chinese power. An optimistic American view holds that this power presents no threat to a fully globalized world, stressing that the interdependence between the two economies is so great that little will change. A more realistic view has emerged, stressing Chinese desire for a measure of hegemony in its own near-abroad. When one looks into the details of this latter view, one discovers that it resembles nothing so much as the classical tributary system of the Chinese imperial past.[6] And Peter Haldén's concluding chapter suggests that we now live in a world in which the pre-eminence of the nation-state may be coming to an end. He is surely right to say that European nation-states *aimed* to be complete power containers in the first half of the twentieth century, in large part because they were the bearers of moral projects.[7] This is not the world of the European Union, happily humbler and wiser. But this does not mean that universal ideals have died out. Very much to the contrary, such ideals abound, above all in the related emphasis on human rights and on cosmopolitan citizenship. This is a combination that makes one feel a little uneasy. The desirability of the former fits ill with the social base of the latter – so limited in fact that it reminds us of the horizontal quality of pre-industrial elites, theorized by Gellner and described at length in the contributions to this volume.

---

[6] Friedberg 2011.

[7] The idea of the state as the bearer of a moral project was proposed by Víctor Pérez-Díaz in his *The Return of Civil Society: The Emergence of Democratic Spain* (Pérez-Díaz 1993) and then used by Michael Mann as an intellectual cornerstone of his *The Dark Side of Democracy* (Mann 2005).

General bibliography

'Abbās, I. (1988), *'Abd al-Ḥamīd b. Yaḥyā al-Kātib wa-mā tabaqqā min rasā'ilihi wa-rasā'il Sālim Abī 'l-Alā'* (Amman).

Abbott, N. (1957–72), *Studies in Arabic Literary Papyri*, 3 vols. (Chicago).

Abulafia, D. (1992), *Frederick II: A Medieval Emperor*, new revised edn (London).

Abu'l Fazl 'Allāmī (1998), *Mukātabāt-i 'Allāmī (Inshā'ī Abu'l Fazl), Daftar I*, English trans. and ed. M. Haidar (New Delhi).

   (1979), *The Akbar Nāma of Abu-l-Fazl*, trans. H. Beveridge, 3 vols. (New Delhi) [reprint; originally published in Calcutta, 1902–39].

   (1873), *The Ā'in-i Akbari*, vol. I, trans. H. Blochmann (Calcutta) [also available on: http://persian.packhum.org/persian/main?url=pf%3Ffile%3D00701020%26ct%3D0].

Acuña, R. (1988), *Relaciones geográficas del siglo XVI: Nueva Galicia* (Mexico City).

Adamson, P. (2002), *The Arabic Plotinus: A Philosophical Study of the Theology of Aristotle* (London).

Adrados, F. (1984), 'Aśoka's Inscriptions and Persian, Greek and Latin Epigraphy', in S. D. Joshi (ed.), *Amrtadhara: Prof. R. N. Dandekar Felicitation Volume* (Delhi), pp. 1–15.

Ágoston, G. (2007), 'Information, Ideology, and Limits of Imperial Policy: Ottoman Grand Strategy in the Context of Ottoman–Habsburg Rivalry', in Aksan and Goffman, pp. 75–103.

Ahmad, A. (1965), 'Dīn-i ilāhī', in *The Encyclopaedia of Islam*, 2nd edn (Leiden and London), vol. II, pp. 296–7.

Ahrweiler, H. (1975), *Idéologie politique de l'Empire byzantin* (Paris).

Aksan, V. H. and Goffman, D. (eds.) (2007), *The Early Modern Ottomans: Remapping the Empire* (Cambridge).

Alam, M. (2004), *The Languages of Political Islam in India, c. 1200–1800* (Delhi).

Alam, M. and Subrahmanyam, S. (2007), *Indo-Persian Travels in the Age of Discoveries 1400–1800* (Cambridge).

   (2006), 'Envisioning Power: The Political Thought of a Late Eighteenth-Century Mughal Prince', *Indian Economic and Social History Review*, 43, no. 2, pp. 131–61.

Alcock, S., D'Altroy, T., Morrison, K. and Sinopoli, C. (eds.) (2001), *Empires: Perspectives from Archaeology and History* (New York and Cambridge).

310

Alef, G. (1966), 'The Adoption of the Muscovite Two-Headed Eagle: A Discordant View', *Speculum*, 41, pp. 1–22.

Alexander, P. (1985), *The Byzantine Apocalyptic Tradition*, ed. D. Abrahamse (Berkeley).

Alföldi, A. (1970), *Die monarchische Repräsentation im römischen Kaiserreiche* (Darmstadt).

Algar, H. (ed.) (1985), *Islam and Revolution: Writings and Declarations, Imam Khomeini* (London).

Allsen, T. T. (2006), *The Royal Hunt in Eurasian History* (Philadelphia).

Althoff, G. (2003), *Otto III*, trans. P. Jestice (Philadelphia).

Anderson, B. (1983), *Imagined Communities: Reflections on the Origin and Spread of Nationalism* (New York).

Anderson, M. S. (1970), 'Eighteenth Century Theories of the Balance of Power', in R. Hatton and M. S. Anderson (eds.), *Studies in Diplomatic History* (Harlow), pp. 183–99.

Andreae, B. (2001), *Skulptur des Hellenismus: Aufnahmen Albert Hirmer und Irmgard Ernstmeier-Hirmer* (Munich).

(1999), *Odysseus: Mythos und Erinnerung* (Mainz).

(1995), *Praetorium Speluncae: l'antro di Tiberio a Sperlonga ed Ovidio* (Soveria Mannelli).

Angelov, D. (2007), *Imperial Ideology and Political Thought in Byzantium, 1204–1330* (Cambridge).

Anghie, A. (2005), *Imperialism, Sovereignty and the Making of International Law* (Cambridge).

Ansari, A. S. B. (1965), 'Djahāngīr', in *The Encyclopaedia of Islam*, 2nd edn (Leiden and London), vol. II, pp. 379–81.

Arano, Y. (1987), 'Nihongata Ka-I chitsujo no keisei' [The formation of a Japanese-style civilized/barbarian order], in A. Naohiro *et al.* (eds.), *Nihon no shakaishi*, vol. I: *Rettō naigai no kōtsū to kokka* [A social history of Japan, I: The state and transportation within and beyond the archipelago] (Tokyo), pp. 183–226.

Aretin, K. O. von (1997a), *Das Alte Reich 1648–1806*, vol. I: *Föderalistische oder hierarchische Ordnung (1648–1684)* (Stuttgart).

(1997b), *Das Alte Reich 1648–1806*, vol. II: *Kaisertradition und österreichische Großmachtpolitik (1684–1745)* (Stuttgart).

(1975), 'Die Kreisassoziationen in der Politik der Mainzer Kurfürsten Johann Philipp und Lothar Franz von Schönborn 1648–1711', in Aretin (ed.), *Der Kurfürst von Mainz und die Kreisassoziationen 1648–1746: Zur verfassungsmässigen Stellung der Reichskirche nach dem Westfälischen Frieden* (Wiesbaden), pp. 31–68.

Arnason, J. P. (2005), 'The Axial Age and its Interpreters: Reopening a Debate', in Arnason, Eisenstadt and Wittrock, pp. 19–49.

Arnason, J. P., Eisenstadt, S. N. and Wittrock, B. (eds.) (2005), *Axial Civilizations and World History* (Leiden).

Arnold, B. (2003), 'Eschatological Imagination and the Program of Roman Imperial and Ecclesiastical Renewal at the End of the Tenth Century', in

R. Landes, A. Gow and D. C. Van Meter (eds.), *The Apocalyptic Year 1000: Religious Expectation and Social Change, 950–1050* (Oxford), pp. 271–88.

(1997), *Medieval Germany 500–1300: A Political Interpretation* (London).

Asher, C. (2004), 'A Ray from the Sun: Mughal Ideology and the Visual Construction of the Divine', in M. T. Kapstein (ed.), *The Presence of Light: Divine Radiance and Religious Experience* (Chicago and London), pp. 161–94.

Austin, M. M. (1981), *The Hellenistic World from Alexander to the Roman Conquest* (Cambridge).

Azevedo, M. C. de (1951), *Le antichità di Villa Medici* (Rome).

Babayan, K. (2002), *Mystics, Monarchs, and Messiahs: Cultural Landscapes of Early Modern Iran* (Cambridge, Mass.).

Babinger, F. (1978), *Mehmed the Conqueror and his Time* (trans. R. Manheim) (Princeton).

Badāuni, ʿAbd al-Qādir (1973), *Muntakhabu-t-tawārīkh by ʿAbdu-l-Qādir-ibn-i Mulūk Shāh known as Al-Badāoni*, trans. G. S. A. Ranking, W. Haig and W. H. Lowe, 3 vols. (New Delhi) [reprint; originally published in Calcutta, 1884–1925].

Badian, E. (1958), 'Alexander the Great and the Unity of Mankind', *Historia: Zeitschrift für Alte Geschichte*, 7, pp. 425–44.

Bagnall, R. (1997), 'Decolonising Ptolemaic Egypt', in P. Cartledge, P. Garnsey and E. Gruen (eds.), *Hellenistic Constructs: Essays in Culture, History, and Historiography* (Berkeley), pp. 225–41.

Bahrani, Z. (2008), *Rituals of War: The Body and Violence in Mesopotamia* (New York).

Bailey, G. and Mabbett, I. W. (2003), *The Sociology of Early Buddhism* (Cambridge).

Baldry, H. C. (1965), *The Unity of Mankind in Greek Thought* (Cambridge).

Balensiefen, L. (2009), 'Apollo Palatinus: Ein Kultgründungsvorhaben des jungen Caesar Divi Filius', in C. Schmitz and A. Bettenworth (eds.), *Mensch – Heros – Gott: Weltentwürfe und Lebensmodelle im Mythos der Vormoderne* (Stuttgart), pp. 67–89.

Ball, W. (2000), *Rome in the East: The Transformation of an Empire* (London).

Balsdon, J. P. V. D. (1979), *Romans and Aliens* (London and Chapel Hill).

Bang, P. F. (2011a), 'Lord of All the World – The State, Heterogeneous Power and Hegemony in the Roman and Mughal Empires,' in Bang and Bayly, pp. 171–92.

(2011b), 'The King of Kings: Universal Hegemony, Imperial Power, and a New Comparative History of Rome', in J. P. Arnason and K. A. Raaflaub (eds.), *The Roman Empire in Context: Historical and Comparative Perspectives* (Chichester), pp. 322–50.

(2010), 'Imperial Ecumene and Polyethnicity', in W. Scheidel and A. Barchiesi (eds.), *The Oxford Handbook of Roman Studies* (Oxford), pp. 671–84.

(2008), *The Roman Bazaar: A Comparative Study of Trade and Markets in a Tributary Empire* (Cambridge).

Bang, P. F. and Bayly, C. A. (eds.) (2011), *Tributary Empires in Global History* (Basingstoke).

(eds.) (2003), *Tributary Empires in History: Comparative Perspectives from Antiquity to the Late Medieval = Medieval History Journal*, 6, no. 2 (special issue), 2003 [the editors' introduction 'Comparing Pre-Modern Empires', pp. 169–87].

Barbantani, S. (2003), 'Review of Susan A. Stephens: Seeing Double', *Bryn Mawr Classical Review* 2003.06.43: http://bmcr.brynmawr.edu/2003/2003-06-43.html.

Barchiesi, A. (2009), 'Phaeton and the Monsters', in P. Hardie (ed.), *Paradox and the Marvellous in Augustan Literature and Culture* (Oxford), pp. 163–88.

(2005), 'Learned Eyes: Poets, Viewers, Image Makers', in K. Galinsky (ed.), *The Cambridge Companion to the Age of Augustus* (Cambridge), pp. 281–305.

Barjamovic, G. (2011), 'Pride, Pomp and Circumstance: Palace, Court and Household in Assyria 879–612 BCE', in Duindam, Artan and Kunt, pp. 27–61.

(2004), 'Civic Institutions and Self-government in Southern Mesopotamia in the Mid-first Millennium BC', in Dercksen, pp. 47–98.

Barkey, K. (2008), *Empire of Difference: The Ottomans in Comparative Perspective* (Cambridge).

Barnes, T. D. (1981), *Constantine and Eusebius* (Cambridge, Mass.).

Barraclough, G. (1950), *The Medieval Empire: Idea and Reality* (London).

Bartelson, J. (2009), *Visions of World Community* (Cambridge).

(1995), *A Genealogy of Sovereignty* (Cambridge).

Barzegar, K. N. (2000), *Mughal–Iranian Relations during Sixteenth Century* (Delhi).

Bauer, H. (1993), 'Basilica Paul(l)i', in M. Steinby (ed.), *Lexicon Topographicum Urbis Romae*, vol. I: *A–C* (Rome), pp. 183–7.

Bayly, C. A. (2004), *The Birth of the Modern World 1780–1914: Global Connections and Comparisons*, The Blackwell History of the World (Oxford).

(2002), '"Archaic" and "Modern" Globalization in the Eurasian and African Arena, c. 1750–1850', in Hopkins, pp. 47–73.

(1996), *Empire and Information: Intelligence Gathering and Social Communication in India, 1780–1870* (Cambridge).

Baynes, N. (1955), 'Eusebius and the Christian Empire', in Baynes, *Byzantine Studies and Other Essays* (London), pp. 168–72.

(1925), *The Byzantine Empire* (London).

Beach, M. C., Koch, E. and Thackston, W. M. (1997), *King of the World: The Padshahnama. An Imperial Mughal Manuscript from the Royal Library, Windsor Castle* (London).

Beard, M. (2007), *The Roman Triumph* (Cambridge, Mass.).

(1994), 'The Roman and the Foreign: The Cult of the "Great Mother" in Imperial Rome', in N. Thomas and C. Humphrey (eds.), *Shamanism, History and the State* (Ann Arbor), pp. 164–90.

Beard, M., North, J., and Price, S. (1998a), *Religions of Rome*, vol. I: *A History* (Cambridge).

(1998b), *Religions of Rome*, vol. II: *A Sourcebook* (Cambridge).

Beck, H., Bol, P. C. and Bückling, M. (eds.) (2005), *Ägypten – Griechenland – Rom: Abwehr und Berührung, Ausstellung Städelsches Kunstinistut und Städtische Galerie, Frankfurt am Main, 26. November 2005–26. Februar 2006* (Frankfurt and Tübingen).

Bederman, D. J. (2001), *International Law in Antiquity* (Cambridge).

Bellinger, A. R. (1961), *Troy: The Coins*, Supplementary Monograph 2 (Princeton).

Benhabib, S. (2006), *Another Cosmopolitanism*, with commentaries by J. Waldron, B. Honig and W. Kymlicka, ed. R. Post (Oxford).

Bennison, A. K. (2002), 'Muslim Universalism and Western Globalization', in Hopkins, pp. 74–97.

Benson, R. L. (1982), 'Political Renovatio: Two Models from Roman Antiquity', in Benson and Constable, pp. 339–86.

Benson, R. L. and Constable, G., with Lanham, C. D. (eds.) (1982), *Renaissance and Renewal in the Twelfth Century* (Cambridge, Mass.).

Benveniste, É (1964), 'Édits d'Asoka en traduction grecque', *Journal Asiatique*, 252, pp. 137–57.

Berdan, F. F. (2007), 'Continuity and Change in Aztec Culture. From Imperial Lords to Royal Subjects', in G. Spindler and J. Stockard (eds.), *Globalization and Change in Fifteen Cultures: Born in One World, Living in Another* (Belmont, Calif.), pp. 1–23.

(2006), 'The Role of Provincial Elites in the Aztec Empire', in C. Elson and R. A. Covey (eds.), *Intermediate Elites in Pre-Columbian States and Empires* (Tucson), pp. 154–65.

(1996), 'The Tributary Provinces', in Berdan *et al.*, pp. 115–35.

Berdan, F. F. *et al.* (eds.) (1996), *Aztec Imperial Strategies* (Washington, DC).

Berdan, F. F. and Smith, M. E. (1996), 'Imperial Strategies and Core–Periphery Relations', in Berdan *et al.*, pp. 209–17.

Berg, D. (1997), *Deutschland und seine Nachbarn 1200–1500* (Munich).

Bergmann, B. (2008), 'Pictorial Narratives of the Roman Circus', in J. Nelis-Clément and J.-M. Roddaz (eds.), *Le cirque romain et son image: Actes du colloque tenu à l'Institut Ausonius, Bordeaux, 2006* (Bordeaux), pp. 361–91.

Bernard, P. (1973–87), *Fouilles D'Ai Khanoum. Mémoires de la Délégation archéologique française en Afghanistan*, vols. XXI, XXVI–XXXI (Paris).

Bernoulli, J. J. (1886), *Römische Ikonographie*, pt II: *Die Bildnisse der römischen Kaiser*, vol. I: *Das julisch-claudische Kaiserhaus* (Berlin and Stuttgart).

Bersani, L. and Dutoit, U. (1985), *The Forms of Violence: Narrative in Assyrian Art and Modern Culture* (New York).

Bertolacci, A. (2005), 'On the Arabic Translations of Aristotle's *Metaphysics*', *Arabic Sciences and Philosophy*, 15, pp. 241–75.

Besnier, B. (2003), '*De Mundo*. Tradition grecque', in Goulet, pp. 475–80.

Bilde, P. *et al.* (eds.) (1996), *Aspects of Hellenistic Kingship* (Aarhus).

Billows, R. A. (1990), *Antigonos the One-Eyed and the Creation of the Hellenistic State* (Berkeley and Los Angeles).

Bing, P. (1988), *The Well-Read Muse: Present and Past in Callimachus and the Hellenistic Poets* (Göttingen).

Bisson, T. N. (1966), 'The Military Origins of Mediaeval Representation', *American Historical Review*, 71, no. 4, pp. 1199–1218.

Bitterer, T. (2007), 'Neue Forschungen zur Basilica Aemilia auf dem Forum Romanum. Ein Vorbericht. Die Orientalenstatuen', *Mitteilungen des Deutschen Archäologischen Instituts, Römische Abteilung*, 113, pp. 535–51.

Black, A. (2001), *The History of Islamic Political Thought: From the Prophet to the Present* (New York).

(1992), *Political Thought in Europe, 1250–1450* (Cambridge).

Bladel, K. van (2007), 'The Syriac Sources of the Early Arabic Narratives of Alexander', in Ray and Potts, pp. 54–75.

(2004), 'The Iranian Characteristics and Forged Greek Attributions in the Arabic *Sirr al-asrār* (*Secret of secrets*)', *Mélanges de l'Université Saint-Joseph*, 57, pp. 151–72.

Blake, S. P. (1991), *Shahjahanabad: The Sovereign City in Mughal India 1639–1739* (Cambridge).

Blankinship, K. Y. (1994), *The End of the Jihād State: The Reign of Hishām Ibn 'Abd al-Malik and the Collapse of the Umayyads* (Albany, NY).

Bloch, M. (1973), *The Royal Touch: Sacred Monarchy and Scrofula in England and France*, trans. J. E. Anderson (London) [originally published as *Les rois thaumaturges* (Strasbourg, 1924)].

Blois, F. de (1998), '*Eskandar-Nāma* of Neżāmī', in *Encyclopaedia Iranica*, 8, pp. 612–14.

Blythe, J. M. (trans.) (1997), Ptolemy of Lucca, *On the Government of Rulers* (Philadelphia).

Böckenförde, E.-W. (1969), 'Der Westfälische Frieden und das Bündnisrecht der Reichsstände', *Der Staat*, 8, pp. 449–78.

Bodde, D. (1986), 'The State and Empire of Ch'in', in D. Twitchett, M. Loewe and J. K. Fairbank (eds.), *The Cambridge History of China*, vol. I: *The Ch'in and Han Empires (221 B.C.–A.D. 220)* (Cambridge), pp. 20–102.

Bodin, J. (2003), *On Sovereignty: Four Chapters from the Six Books of the Commonwealth*, ed. and trans. J. H. Franklin, Cambridge Texts in the History of Political Thought (Cambridge).

Bohrer, F. N. (2003), *Orientalism and Visual Culture: Imagining Mesopotamia in Nineteenth-Century Europe* (Cambridge).

Bojović, B. (1987), 'Dubrovnik et les Ottomans (1430–1472). 20 actes de Murad II et de Mehmed II en médio-serbe', *Turcica. Revue d'Études Turques*, 19, pp. 119–73.

Bonaud, Y. C. (1997), *L'Imam Khomeyni, un gnostique méconnu du XXe siècle: métaphysique et théologie dans les œuvres philosophiques et spirituelles de l'Imam Khomeyni* (Beirut).

Boone, E. H. (2000), *Stories in Red and Black: Pictorial Histories of the Aztecs and Mixtecs* (Austin).

(1996), 'Manuscript Painting in Service of Imperial Ideology', in Berdan *et al.*, pp. 181–206.

Boretius, A. and Krause, V. (eds.) (1883–97) *Capitularia Regum Francorum*, 2 vols., Monumenta Germaniae Historica: Leges (Hanover).

Borger, R. (1996), *Beiträge zum Inschriftenwerk Assurbanipals: Die Prismenklassen A, B, C = K, D, E, F, G, H, J und T sowie andere Inschriften* (Wiesbaden).

Boschung, D. (1993), *Die Bildnisse des Augustus*, Das römische Herrscherbild, 1. Abteilung (Berlin).

Bosworth, A. B. (1999), 'Augustus, the Res Gestae and Hellenistic Theories of Apotheosis', *Journal of Roman Studies*, 89, pp. 1–18.

(1996), *Alexander and the East: The Tragedy of Triumph* (Oxford).

Boucher, D. (1998), *Political Theories of International Relations: From Thucydides to the Present* (Oxford).

Bourdieu, P. (1974), *Zur Soziologie der symbolischen Formen* (Frankfurt) [1st edn 1970].

Boyce, M. (1968), *The Letter of Tansar* (Rome).

Braccesi, L. (2006), *L'Alessandro occidentale: Il Macedone e Roma* (Rome).

Bradley, M. (2009a), 'The Importance of Colour on Ancient Marble Sculpture', *Art History*, 32, no. 3, pp. 427–57.

(2009b), *Colour and Meaning in Ancient Rome* (Cambridge).

Brand, C. (1962), 'The Byzantines and Saladin, 1185–1192: Opponents of the Third Crusade', *Speculum*, 37, pp. 167–81.

Braude, B. and Lewis, B. (eds.) (1982), *Christians and Jews in the Ottoman Empire: The Functioning of a Plural Society*, vol. 1: *The Central Lands* (New York and London).

Braund, S. (2009), *Seneca, De Clementia: Edited with Text, Translation, and Commentary* (Oxford).

Bremmer, J. N. (2004), 'Attis: A Greek God in Anatolian Pessinous and Catullan Rome', *Mnemosyne*, 57, pp. 534–73.

Briant, P. (2009), 'Alexander the Great and the Persian Empire, between "Decline" and "Renovation"', in W. Heckel and L. A. Tritle (eds.), *Alexander the Great: A New History* (Chichester), pp. 171–88.

(2003), *Darius dans l'ombre d'Alexandre* (Paris).

(2002), *From Cyrus to Alexander: A History of the Persian Empire* (Winona Lake) [updated English trans. of Briant 1996].

(1996), *Histoire de l'Empire perse: de Cyrus à Alexandre* (Paris) [also English trans. 2002].

(1982), *Rois, tributs et paysans: études sur les formations tributaires du Moyen-Orient ancient* (Paris).

Briant, P., Henkelman, W. F. M. and Stolper, M. W. (eds.) (2008), *Les archives des fortifications de Persépolis dans le contexte de l'Empire achéménide et de ses prédécesseurs*, Persika 12 (Paris).

Bridges, M. and Bürgel, J. C. (eds.) (1996), *The Problematics of Power: Eastern and Western Representations of Alexander the Great* (Berne).

Brisch, N. (ed.) (2008), *Religion and Power: Divine Kingship in the Ancient World and Beyond*, Oriental Institute Seminars 4 (Chicago).

Brock, S. (1984), *Syrian Perspectives on Late Antiquity* (London).

Broda, J., Carrasco, D. and Matos Moctezuma, E. (1988), *The Great Temple of Tenochtitlan: Center and Periphery in the Aztec World* (Berkeley).

Brosius, M. (2007), 'New out of Old? Court and Court Ceremonies in Achaemenid Persia', in A. J. S. Spawforth (ed.), *The Court and Court Society in Ancient Monarchies* (Cambridge), pp. 17–57.

(2006), *The Persians: An Introduction* (London and New York).

(2003), 'Alexander and the Persians', in J. Roisman (ed.), *Brill's Companion to Alexander the Great* (Leiden), pp. 169–93.

Browning, R. (1975), 'Enlightenment and Repression in Byzantium in the Eleventh and Twelfth Centuries', *Past and Present*, 69, pp. 3–23.

Brumfiel, E. M. (2001), 'Aztec Hearts and Minds: Religion and the State in the Aztec Empire', in Alcock *et al.*, pp. 283–310.

Brummett, P. (2007), 'Imagining the Early Modern Ottoman Space, from World History to Piri Reis', in Aksan and Goffman, pp. 15–58.

Brunner, O. (1981), *Land und Herrschaft: Grundfragen der territorialen Verfassungsgeschichte Österreichs im Mittelalter* (Darmstadt) [originally published in 1939].

Brunner, O., Conze, W. and Koselleck, R. (eds.) (1979), *Geschichtliche Grundbegriffe: Historisches Lexicon zur politisch-sozialen Sprache in Deutschland*, vol. II: *E–G* (Stuttgart).

Buchner, R. (1963), 'Der Titel *rex Romanorum* in deutschen Königsurkunden des 11. Jahrhunderts', *Deutsches Archiv*, 19, pp. 327–38.

Buckler, F. W. (1924), 'A New Interpretation of Akbar's "Infallibility Decree" of 1579', *Journal of the Royal Asiatic Society*, New Series, 56, pp. 591–608 [reprinted in Pearson 1985].

Bull, H. and Watson, A. (eds.) (1984), *The Expansion of International Society* (Oxford).

Bulst, N. (1989), 'Finanzwesen–verwaltung. B. Westliches Europa, II. Deutschland', in *Lexikon des Mittelalters*, vol. IV (Munich), pp. 458–61.

Burghart, R. (1987), 'Gifts to the Gods: Power, Property and Ceremonial in Nepal', in Cannadine and Price, pp. 237–70.

Burke, P. (1999), 'Presenting and Representing Charles V and the Mythification of the Emperor', in H. Soly (ed.), *Charles V 1500–1558 and his Time* (Antwerp).

Burkert, W. (2003), *Die Griechen und der Orient: Von Homer bis zu den Magiern* (Munich).

(1992), *The Orientalizing Revolution: Near Eastern Influence on Greek Culture in the Early Archaic Age* (Cambridge).

Burkhardt, J. (1992), *Der Dreißigjährige Krieg* (Frankfurt).

Burns, T. S. (2003), *Rome and the Barbarians, 100 B.C. – A.D. 400* (Baltimore and London).

Burton, P. J. (1996), 'The Summoning of the Magna Mater to Rome, 205 BC', *Historia: Zeitschrift für Alte Geschichte*, 45, pp. 36–63.

Burzacchini, G. (ed.) (2005), *Troia tra realtà e leggenda*, con la collaborazione di G. Alvoni and M. Magnani (Parma).

Buzan, B. (2004), *From International to World Society? English School Theory and the Social Structure of Globalisation* (Cambridge).

(1993), 'From International System to International Society: Structural Realism and Regime Theory Meet the English School', *International Organization*, 47, no. 3, pp. 327–52.

Buzan, B. and Little, R. (2000), *International Systems in World History. Remaking the Study of International Relations* (Oxford).

Cain, P. (1993), *Männerbildnisse neronisch-flavischer Zeit* (Munich).

Cameron, G. G. (1948), *Persepolis Treasury Tablets*, Oriental Institute Publications 65 (Chicago).

Campbell, B. (1993), 'War and Diplomacy: Rome and Parthia, 31 BC–AD 235', in J. Rich and G. Shipley (eds.), *War and Society in the Roman World* (London), pp. 213–40.

Canepa, M. P. (2009), *The Two Eyes of the Earth: Art and Ritual of Kingship between Rome and Sasanian Iran* (Berkeley and Los Angeles).

Cannadine, D. (2001), *Ornamentalism: How the British Saw their Empire* (London).

(1983), 'The Context, Performance and Meaning of Ritual: The British Monarchy and the "Invention of Tradition", c. 1820–1977', in Hobsbawm and Ranger, pp. 101–64.

Cannadine, D. and Price, S. (eds.) (1987), *Rituals of Royalty: Power and Ceremonial in Traditional Societies* (Cambridge).

Capdetrey, L. (2008), 'Le royaume séleucide: une empire impossible?', in Hurlet, pp. 57–80.

(2007), *Le pouvoir séleucide: territoire, administration, finances, d'un royaume hellénistique (312–129 avant J.-C.)* (Rennes).

Capezzone, L. (2004), 'Note su alcuni romanzi di ambientazione bizantino-sasanide nel *Fihrist* di Ibn al-Nadīm', in *Convegno internazionale La Persia e Bisanzio, Roma, 14–18 ottobre 2002* (Rome), pp. 137–60.

Carlier, P. (1980), 'Étude sur la prétendue lettre d'Aristote à Alexandre transmise par plusieurs manuscrits arabes (1)', *Ktema*, 5, pp. 277–88.

Carr, E. H. (1946), *The Twenty Years' Crisis, 1919–1939: An Introduction to the Study of International Relations*, 2nd edn (London).

Carrasco, P. (1996), *Estructura político-territorial del Imperio tenochca: La Triple Allianza de Tenochtitlan, Tetzcoco y Tlacopan* (Mexico City).

(1984), 'Royal Marriages in Ancient Mexico', in H. R. Harvey and H. J. Prem (eds.), *Explorations in Ethnohistory: Indians of Central Mexico in the Sixteenth Century* (Albuquerque), pp. 41–81.

Carsten, F. L. (1959), *Princes and Parliaments in Germany: From the Fifteenth to the Eighteenth Century* (Oxford).

Casas, B. de las (1971), *Los Indios de México y Nueva España: antología* (Mexico City).

Cassieri, N. (2000), *La Grotta di Tiberio e il Museo Archeologico Nazionale Sperlonga*, Itinerari dei musei, gallerie, scavi e monumenti d'Italia, nuova seria no. 52 (Rome).

Castella, D. and Flutsch, L. (1990), 'Sanctuaires et monuments funéraires à Avenches – en Chaplix VD', *Archäologie der Schweiz*, 13, pp. 2–30.

Castriota, D. (1995), *The Ara Pacis Augustae and the Imagery of Abundance in Later Greek and Early Roman Imperial Art* (Princeton).

Chaisemartin, N. de (2001), 'Le retour des Troyens: l'exemple d'Aphrodisias', in V. Fromentin and S. Gotteland (eds.), *Origines gentium: Séminaire Bordeaux, 1996–1997* (Paris), pp. 187–206.

Chang, K. C. (1983), *Art, Myth, and Ritual: The Path to Political Authority in Ancient China* (Cambridge, Mass.).

Charanis, P. (1941), 'Coronation and its Constitutional Significance in the Later Roman Empire', *Byzantion*, 15, pp. 49–66.

(1939), *Church and State in the Later Roman Empire: The Religious Policy of Anastasius the First, 491–518* (Madison).

Charles, R. H. (1920), *A Critical and Exegetical Commentary on the Revelation of St. John*, vol. II (New York).

Charlesworth, J. H. (ed.) (1985), *The Old Testament Pseudepigrapha*, vol. II: *Expansions of the 'Old Testament' and Legends, Wisdom and Philosophical Literature, Prayers, Psalms, and Odes, Fragments of Lost Judeo-Hellenistic Works* (London).

Chotzakoglou, C. (1996), 'Die Palaiologen und das früheste Auftreten des byzantinischen Doppeladlers', *Byzantinoslavica*, 57, pp. 60–8.

Christian, D. (1998), *A History of Russia, Central Asia and Mongolia*, vol. I: *Inner Eurasia from Prehistory to the Mongol Empire* (Oxford).

Christophilopoulou, E. (1956), *Ekloge, anagoreusis kai stepsis tou byzantinou autokratoros* (Athens).

Chun, Hae-jong (1968), 'Sino-Korean Tributary Relations in the Ch'ing Period', in Fairbank, pp. 90–111.

Chung, Chai-sik (1985), 'Chŏng Tojŏn: "Architect" of Yi Dynasty Government and Ideology', in W. T. de Bary and J. Kim Haboush (eds.), *The Rise of Neo-Confucianism in Korea* (New York), pp. 59–88.

Cifola, B. (1995), *Analysis of Variants in the Assyrian Royal Titulary: From the Origins to Tiglath-Pileser III*, Istituto Universitario Orientale. Series Minor 47 (Naples).

Classen, P. (1985), *Karl der Grosse, das Papsttum und Byzanz: Die Begründung des Karolingischen Kaisertums* (Sigmaringen).

(1982), 'Res Gestae, Universal History, Apocalypse', in Benson and Constable, pp. 387–417.

Clauss, M. (2001), *The Roman Cult of Mithras: The God and his Mysteries* (London and New York) [first published as *Mithras: Kult und Mysterien* (Munich, 1990)].

(1999), *Kaiser und Gott: Herrscherkult im römischen Reich* (Stuttgart and Leipzig).

Cohen, G. (2006), *The Hellenistic Settlements in Syria, the Red Sea Basin, and North Africa* (Berkeley).

(1995), *The Hellenistic Settlements in Europe, the Islands, and Asia Minor* (Berkeley).

Cohn, B. S. (1983), 'Representing Authority in Victorian India', in Hobsbawm and Ranger, pp. 165–210.

Collins, N. L. (2000), *The Library in Alexandria and the Bible in Greek* (Leiden).

Colvin, S. (2011), 'The Koine: A New Language for a New World', in Erskine and Llewellyn-Jones, pp. 31–45.

Constantinides, C. (1982), *Higher Education in Byzantium in the Thirteenth and Early Fourteenth Centuries (1204–ca. 1310)* (Nicosia).

Conticello, B., Andreae, B. and Bol, P. C. (1974), *Antike Plastik 14: Die Skulpturen von Sperlonga* (Berlin).

Corbin, H. (1971–2), *En Islam iranien: aspects spirituels et philosophiques*, 4 vols. (Paris).

Corcoran, S. (2006), 'Before Constantine', in N. Lenski (ed.), *The Cambridge Companion to the Age of Constantine* (Cambridge), pp. 35–58.

Coutre, J. de (1991), *Andanzas asiáticas*, ed. Eddy Stols, B. Teensma and J. Verberckmoes (Madrid).

Crawford, M. (1974), *Roman Republican Coinage*, 2 vols. (Cambridge).

Creveld, M. van (1999), *The Rise and Decline of the State* (Cambridge).

Crib, J. and Herrmann, G. (eds.) (2007), *After Alexander: Central Asia before Islam*, Proceedings of the British Academy 133 (Oxford).

Crone, P. (forthcoming), *The Nativist Prophets of Early Islamic Iran: Rural Revolt and Regional Zoroastrianism* (Cambridge).

(2004), *Medieval Islamic Political Thought* (Edinburgh).

Crone, P. and Hinds, M. (1986), *God's Caliph: Religious Authority in the First Centuries of Islam* (Cambridge).

Crossley, P. (1999), *A Translucent Mirror: History and Identity in Qing Imperial Ideology* (Berkeley and Los Angeles).

(1997), *The Manchus* (Oxford).

(1992), 'The Rulerships of China: A Review Article', *American Historical Review*, 97, no. 5, pp. 1468–83.

Çulpan, C. (1970), 'İstanbul Süleymaniye camii kitabesi', in *Kanunî Armağanı* (Ankara), pp. 291–9.

Cunningham, A. (1877), *Inscriptions of Asoka*, Corpus Inscriptionum Indicarum, vol. 1 (Calcutta).

Dadvar, A. (1999), *Iranians in Mughal Politics and Society (1606–1658)* (New Delhi).

Dagron, G. (2007), 'From the *Mappa* to the *Akakia*: Symbolic Drift', in H. Amirav and B. ter Haar Romeny (eds.), *From Rome to Constantinople: Studies in Honour of Averil Cameron* (Louvain and Paris), pp. 203–20.

(2003), *Emperor and Priest: The Imperial Office in Byzantium*, trans. J. Birrell (Cambridge).

Dahlmann, H. (1954), *Der Bienenstaat in Vergils Georgica* (Mainz).

Dakhlia, J. (2002), 'Les miroirs des princes islamiques: une modernité sourde?', *Annales. Histoire, Sciences Sociales*, 57, pp. 1191–1206.

Dallapiccola, A. L. and Zingel-Avé Lallemant, S. (eds.) (1985), *Vijayanagara – City and Empire: New Currents of Research*, 2 vols. (Stuttgart).

D'Altroy, T. (1992), *Provincial Power in the Inca Empire* (Washington).

D'Ancona, C. (2005a), 'La filosofia della tarda antichità e la formazione della "falsafa"', in D'Ancona, pp. 5–47.

(ed.) (2005b), *Storia della filosofia nell'Islam medievale* (Turin).

(2005c), 'Le traduzioni di opere greche e la formazione del corpus filosofico arabo', in D'Ancona, pp. 180–258.

(ed.) (2003a), *Plotino: la discesa dell'anima nei corpi (Enn. IV 8 [6]). Plotiniana Arabica (Pseudo-Teologia di Aristotele, capitoli 1 e 7; 'Detti del sapiente greco')* (Padua).

(2003b), 'The *Timaeus'* model for creation and providence: an example of continuity and adaptation in Arabic philosophical literature', in G. J. Reydams-Schils (ed.), *Plato's Timaeus as Cultural Icon* (Notre Dame, Ind.), pp. 206–37.

D'Ancona, C. and Taylor, R. C. (2003), '*Liber de causis*', in Goulet, pp. 599–647.

Dante (1996), *Monarchy*, ed. and trans. P. Shaw, Cambridge Texts in the History of Political Thought (Cambridge).

Darbandi, S. M. R. and Zournatzi, A. (eds.) (2008), *Ancient Greece and Ancient Iran: Cross-Cultural Encounters. 1st International Conference (Athens, 11–13 November 2006)* (Athens).

Dardenay, A. (2010), *Les mythes fondateurs de Rome: images et politique dans l'Occident romain* (Paris).

Das, A. K. (1978), *Mughal Painting during Jahangir's Time* (Calcutta).

Davids, A. (ed.) (1995), *The Empress Theophano: Byzantium and the West at the Turn of the First Millennium* (Cambridge).

Dawson, C. (ed.) (1955), *The Mongol Mission: Narratives and Letters of the Franciscan Missionaries in Mongolia and China in the Thirteenth and Fourteenth Centuries* (New York).

Deér, J. (1961), 'Der Globus des spätrömischen und des byzantinischen Kaisers. Symbol oder Insigne?', *Byzantinische Zeitschrift*, 54, pp. 53–85 [reprinted in Deér, *Byzanz und das abendländische Herrschertum*, ed. P. Classen (Sigmaringen, 1977), pp. 70–124].

(1950) 'Der Ursprung der Kaiserkrone', *Schweizer Beiträge zur allgemeinen Geschichte*, 8, pp. 51–87 [reprinted in Deér, *Byzanz und das abendländische Herrschertum*, ed. P. Classen (Sigmaringen, 1977), pp. 11–41].

Degrassi, A. (1963), *Inscriptiones Italiae*, vol. XIII: *Fasti et elogia, fasc. II: Fasti anni Numani et Iuliani* (Rome).

Dench, E. (2005), *Romulus' Asylum: Roman Identities from the Age of Alexander to the Age of Hadrian* (Oxford).

Dennis, G. T. (ed.) (1981), *Das Strategikon des Maurikios* (Vienna).

Dercksen, J. G. (ed.) (2004), *Assyria and Beyond: Studies Presented to Mogens Trolle Larsen*, Publications de l'Institut historique-archéologique néerlandais de Stanboul 100 (Leiden).

Deringil, S. (1998), *The Well-Protected Domains: Ideology and the Legitimation of Power in the Ottoman Empire, 1876–1909* (London and New York).

Desai, Z. A. (1999), 'A Foreign Dignitary's Visit to Akbar's Tomb: A First-Hand Account', in I. A. Khan (ed.), *Akbar and his Age*, Indian Council of Historical Research Monograph Series 5 (New Delhi), pp. 188–97.

Dewing, H. B. (trans.) (1940), Procopius, *Buildings* (London).

Díaz Migoyo, G. (2001), 'El manuscrito #117 de la colección Hans P. Kraus', in Tezozomoc, pp. 7–27.

Di Cosmo, N. (2002a), *Ancient China and its Enemies: The Rise of Nomadic Power in East Asian History* (Cambridge).

  (2002b), 'Military Aspects of the Manchu Wars against the Čaqars', in Di Cosmo (ed.), *Warfare in Inner Asian History, 500–1800* (Leiden), pp. 337–65.

  (1999), 'State Formation and Periodization in Inner Asian History', *Journal of World History*, 10, no. 1, pp. 1–40.

Di Cosmo, N., Frank, A. J. and Golden, P. B. (eds.) (2009), *The Cambridge History of Inner Asia: The Chinggisid Age* (Cambridge).

Dihle, A. (1994), *Die Griechen und die Fremden* (Munich).

Dölger, F. (1953a), 'Die "Familie der Könige" im Mittelalter', in Dölger, *Byzanz und die europäische Staatenwelt: ausgewählte Vorträge und Aufsätze* (Ettal), pp. 34–70.

  (1953b), 'Die mittelalterliche "Familie der Fürsten und Völker" und der Bulgarenherrscher', in Dölger, *Byzanz und die europäische Staatenwelt: ausgewählte Vorträge und Aufsätze* (Ettal), pp. 159–82.

Doufikar-Aerts, F. (2003), 'Alexander Magnus Arabicus. Zeven eeuwen arabische Alexandertraditie: Van Pseudo-Callisthenes tot Ṣūrī' (Leiden) [doctoral dissertation].

Drake, H. A. (2007), 'Church, Society and Political Power', in A. Casiday and F. W. Norris (eds.), *The Cambridge History of Christianity*, vol. II (Cambridge), pp. 403–30.

  (2000), *Constantine and the Bishops: The Politics of Intolerance* (Baltimore).

Dreyer, E. L. (2007), *Zheng He: China and the Oceans in the Early Ming Dynasty, 1405–1433* (New York).

Droysen, J. G. (2008), *Geschichte des Hellenismus*, 3 vols., edn E. Bayer, introduced by H.-J. Gehrke (Darmstadt) [based on the 2nd edn from 1877].

Duchhardt, H. (2004), 'Peace Treaties from Westphalia to the Revolutionary Era', in Lesaffer, pp. 45–58.

Dueck, D., Lindsay, H. and Pothecary, S. (eds.) (2005), *Strabo's Cultural Geography: The Making of a Kolossourgia* (Cambridge).

Duindam, J., Artan, T. and Kunt, M. (eds.) (2011), *Royal Courts in Dynastic States and Empires: A Global Perspective*, Rulers and Elites: Comparative Studies in Governance I (Leiden).

Dumont, L. (1970), 'The Conception of Kingship in Ancient India', in Dumont, *Religion, Politics and History in India* (Paris), pp. 62–88.

Dunne, T. (1998), *Inventing International Society: A History of the English School* (London).

Durán, D. (1984), *Historia de las Indias de la Nueva España e islas de la tierra firme*, 2 vols. (Mexico City).

Durrans, P. J. (1982), 'A Two-Edged Sword: The Liberal Attack on Disraelian Imperialism', *Journal of Imperial and Commonwealth History*, 10, pp. 262–84.

Dvornik, F. (1970), *Byzantine Missions among the Slavs* (New Brunswick).

(1966), *Early Christian and Byzantine Political Philosophy*, 2 vols. (Washington, DC).

(1958), *The Idea of Apostolicity in Byzantium and the Legend of the Apostle Andrew* (Washington, DC).

(1948), *The Photian Schism: History and Legend* (Cambridge).

Dwyer, E. J. (1982), *Pompeian Domestic Sculpture: A Study of Five Pompeian Houses and their Contents* (Rome).

Dyson, K. H. F. (1980), *The State Tradition in Western Europe: A Study of an Idea and Institution* (Oxford).

Eckhardt, K. A. (ed.) (1955), *Das Landrecht des Sachsenspiegels* (Göttingen, Berlin and Frankfurt).

Edwards, M. (trans.) (2003), *Constantine and Christendom* (Liverpool).

Eicher, J. B. (ed.) (1995), *Dress and Ethnicity: Change across Space and Time*, Berg Ethnicity and Identity Series (Oxford).

Eichmann, E. (1942), *Die Kaiserkrönung im Abendland, ein Beitrag zur Geistesgeschichte des Mittelalters, mit besonderer Berücksichtigung des kirchlichen Rechts, der Liturgie und der Kirchenpolitik*, 2 vols. (Würzburg).

Elezović, G. (1932), *Tursko-srpski spomenici dubrovačkog arhiva* (Belgrade).

Elias, N. (1991), *The Society of Individuals* (Oxford).

Elisonas, J. (1991), 'The Inseparable Trinity: Japan's Relations with China and Korea', in J. W. Hall and J. L. McClain (eds.), *The Cambridge History of Japan*, vol. IV: *Early Modern Japan* (Cambridge), pp. 235–300.

Elliott, J. H. (2007), *Empires of the Atlantic World: Britain and Spain in America 1492–1830* (New Haven).

Elliott, M. C. (2005), 'Whose Empire Shall It Be? Manchu Figurations of Historical Process in the Early Seventeenth Century', in Struve, pp. 31–72.

Elze, R. (ed.) (1960), *Die Ordines für die Weihe und Krönung des Kaisers und der Kaiserin* (Hanover).

Emori, S. (1982), *Hokkaidō kinseishi no kenkyū – Bakuhan taisei to Ezochi* [The early modern history of Hokkaido – the shogunal system and Ezochi] (Sapporo).

Endress, G. (2001), 'Philosophische Ein-Band-Bibliotheken aus Isfahan', *Oriens*, 36, pp. 10–58.

Ensslin, W. (1942), 'Zur Torqueskrönung und Schilderhebung bei der Kaiserwahl', *Klio*, 35, pp. 268–98.

Erskine, A. (ed.) (2003), *A Companion to the Hellenistic World* (Oxford).

(2001), *Troy between Greece and Rome: Local Tradition and Imperial Power* (Oxford).

(1995), 'Culture and Power in Ptolemaic Egypt: The Museum and Library of Alexandria', *Greece and Rome*, 42, pp. 38–48.

Erskine, A. and Llewellyn-Jones, L. (eds.) (2011), *Creating a Hellenistic World* (Swansea).

Ess, J. van (1991–7), *Theologie und Gesellschaft im 2. und 3. Jahrhundert Hidschra: Eine Geschichte des religiösen Denkens im frühen Islam*, 6 vols. (Berlin).

Ettinghausen, R. (1961a), *Paintings of the Sultans and Emperors of India in American Collections* (New Delhi).

(1961b), 'The Emperor's Choice', in M. Meiss (ed.), *De Artibus Opuscula XL: Essays in Honor of Erwin Panofsky* (New York), pp. 98–120.

Eusebius (1976), *In Praise of Constantine: A Historical Study and New Translation of Eusebius' Tricennial Orations*, trans. H. A. Drake (Berkeley).

Fairbank, J. K. (ed.) (1968a), *The Chinese World Order: Traditional China's Foreign Relations* (Cambridge, Mass.).

(1968b), 'A Preliminary Framework', in Fairbank, pp. 1–19.

Fairbank, J. K. and Teng, S. Y. (1941), 'On the Ch'ing Tributary System', *Harvard Journal of Asiatic Studies*, 6, no. 2, pp. 135–246.

Fales, F. M. (2009), '"To Speak Kindly to Him/Them" as Item of Assyrian Political Discourse', in M. Luukko, S. Svärd and R. Mattila (eds.), *Of God(s), Trees, Kings and Scholars: Neo-Assyrian and Related Studies in Honour of Simo Parpola* (Helsinki).

Fales, F. M. and Postgate, J. N. (1992), *Imperial Administrative Records*, Part 1: *Palace and Temple Administration*, State Archives of Assyria 7 (Helsinki).

Falkenhausen, V. von (1997), 'Bishops', in G. Cavallo (ed.), *The Byzantines* (Chicago), pp. 172–96.

Fantuzzi, M. and Hunter, R. (2004), *Tradition and Innovation in Hellenistic Poetry* (Cambridge).

Farooqi, N. R. (1989), *Mughal–Ottoman Relations (A Study of Political and Diplomatic Relations between Mughal India and the Ottoman Empire, 1556–1748)* (Delhi).

Farris, W. (1998), *Sacred Texts and Buried Treasures: Issues in the Historical Archaeology of Ancient Japan* (Honolulu).

Fejfer, J. (2008), *Roman Portraits in Context*, ICON 2 (Berlin and New York).

(2005), 'Bust of an Oriental', in M. Moltesen (ed.), *Catalogue Imperial Rome III. Ny Carlsberg Glyptotek* (Copenhagen), pp. 192–6.

Ferrari, C. (2005), 'La scuola aristotelica di Baghdad', in D'Ancona, pp. 352–79.

Ferris, M. I. (2000), *Enemies of Rome: Barbarians through Roman Eyes* (Stroud).

Feste, K. A. (2003), *Intervention: Shaping the Global Order* (Westport, Conn.).

Filliozat, V. (1973), *L'épigraphie de Vijayanagara du début à 1377* (Paris).

Finnemore, M. (2003), *The Purpose of Intervention: Changing Beliefs about the Use of Force* (Ithaca, NY).

Fisch, J. (1984), 'Der märchenhafte Orient: Die Umwertung einer Tradition von Marco Polo bis Macaulay', *Saeculum: Jahrbuch für Universalgeschichte*, 35, pp. 246–66.

Flaig, E. (1999), 'Über die Grenzen der Akkulturation. Wider die Verdinglichung des Kulturbegriffs', in Vogt-Spira and Rommel, pp. 81–112.

Fleischer, C. H. (1992), 'The Lawgiver as Messiah: The Making of the Imperial Image in the Reign of Süleymân', in G. Veinstein (ed.), *Soliman le Magnifique et son temps* (Paris), pp. 159–78.

Fletcher, J. (1995), *Studies on Chinese and Islamic Inner Asia* (Aldershot).

Florentine Codex (1950–82), *Florentine Codex: General History of the Things of New Spain*, ed. and trans. A. J. O. Anderson and C. Dibble, 12 vols. (Santa Fe).

Flügel, J. C. (1930), *The Psychology of Clothes* (London).

Forrest, A. and Wilson, P. H. (eds.) (2008), *The Bee and the Eagle: Napoleonic France and the End of the Holy Roman Empire, 1806* (Basingstoke).

Forster, R. (2006), *Das Geheimnis der Geheimnisse: Die arabischen und deutschen Fassungen des pseudo-aristotelischen Sirr al-asrār/Secretum secretorum* (Wiesbaden).

Fortuin, R. W. (1996), *Der Sport im augusteischen Rom: philologische und sporthistorische Untersuchungen (mit einer Sammlung, Übersetzung und Kommentierung der antiken Zeugnisse zum Sport in Rom)*, Palingenesia LVII (Stuttgart).

Fowden, G. (2004), *Quṣayr 'Amra: Art and the Umayyad Elite in Late Antique Syria* (Berkeley).

(1993), *Empire to Commonwealth: Consequences of Monotheism in Late Antiquity* (Princeton).

Fowler, R. (2005), 'Most Fortunate Roots: Tradition and Legitimacy in Parthian Royal Ideology', in Hekster and Fowler, pp. 125–55.

Fragner, B. (1999), *Die 'Persephonie': Regionalität, Identität und Sprachkontakt in der Geschichte Asiens* (Berlin).

Frahm, E. (1997), *Einleitung in die Sanherib-Inschriften*, Archiv für Orientforschung, Beiheft 26 (Vienna).

Franklin, J. (2003), 'Introduction', in Bodin, pp. ix–xxvi.

Fraser, P. M. (1996), *Cities of Alexander the Great* (Oxford).

(1972), *Ptolemaic Alexandria*, 3 vols. (Oxford).

Frazer, J. G. (1890), *The Golden Bough: A Study in Comparative Religion*, 1st edn, 2 vols. (London).

Freeman, P., Bennett, J., Fiema, T. and Hoffmann, B. (eds.) (2002), *Limes: 18. Proceedings of the XVIIIth International Congress of Roman Frontier Studies held in Amman, Jordan, September 2000*, British Archaeological Reports, International Series 1084 (II) (Oxford).

Freyberger, K. S. and Ertel, C. (2007), 'Neue Forschungen zur Basilica Aemilia auf dem Forum Romanum. Ein Vorbericht', *Mitteilungen des Deutschen Archäologischen Instituts, Römische Abteilung*, 113, pp. 493–524.

Fried, J. (2007), *Donation of Constantine and Constitutum Constantini: The Misinterpretation of a Fiction and its Original Meaning*, with a contribution by W. Brandes (Berlin).

Friedberg, Aaron (2011), 'The New Era of U.S.–China Rivalry', *Wall Street Journal*, 17 January.

Frieder, B. K. (2008), *Chivalry and the Perfect Prince: Tournaments, Art and Armor at the Spanish Habsburg Court* (Kirksville).

Friedrich, J. (1940), *Die Inschriften vom Tell Halaf: Keilschrifttexte und aramäische Urkunden aus einer assyrischen Provinzhauptstadt*, Archiv für Orientforschung, Beiheft 6 (Berlin).

Fritz, J., Michell, G. and Nagaraja Rao, M. S. (1984), *Where Kings and Gods Meet: The Royal Centre at Vijayanagara, India* (Tucson).

Fritz, W. D. (ed.) (1972), *Die Goldene Bulle Kaiser Karls IV. vom Jahre 1356* (Weimar).

Fuchs, A. (1994), *Inschriften Sargons II. aus Khorsabad* (Göttingen).

Fuchs, H. (1990), *Lusus Troiae* (Cologne).

Fuhrmann, H. (1986), *Germany in the High Middle Ages, c. 1050–1200*, trans. T. Reuter (Cambridge).

(1966), 'Konstantinische Schenkung und abendländisches Kaisertum', *Deutsches Archiv für Erforschung des Mittelalters*, 22, pp. 63–178.

Gallivan, P. A. (1973), 'The False Neros: A Re-Examination', *Historia*, 22, pp. 364–5.

Galtung, J. (1971), 'A Structural Theory of Imperialism', *Journal of Peace Research*, 2, pp. 81–117.

Ganzert, J. (2000), *Im Allerheiligsten des Augustusforums: Fokus 'oikoumenischer Akkulturation'* (Mainz).

(1996), *Der Mars-Ultor-Tempel auf dem Augustusforum in Rom*, mit einem Beitrag von Peter Herz (Mainz).

Geertz, C. (1980), *Negara: The Theatre State in Nineteenth-Century Bali* (Princeton).

Gehrke, H.-J. (1982), 'Der siegreiche König. Überlegungen zur hellenistischen Monarchie', *Archiv für Kulturgeschichte*, 64, pp. 247–77.

Geiger, J. (2008), *The First Hall of Fame: A Study of the Statues in the Forum Augustum*, Mnemosyne, Supplement 295 (Leiden).

Gellner, E. (1983), *Nations and Nationalism* (Ithaca, NY).

Georganteli, E. and Cook, B. (2006), *Encounters: Travel and Money in the Byzantine World* (London).

Ghini, G. (1994), 'Il Mitreo di Marino: considerazioni sul culto e sull'iconografia', in L. Devoti (ed.), *Il Mitreo di Marino* (Marino), pp. 51–84.

Giard, J. B. (1998), *Le Grand Camée de France* (Paris).

Giddens, A. (1985), *A Contemporary Critique of Historical Materialism*, vol. II: *The Nation State and Violence* (Cambridge).

Giuliani, L. (2009), *Ein Geschenk für den Kaiser: Das Geheimnis des grossen Kameo* (Munich).

(2006), 'Macht und Ohnmacht der Bilder: Eine frisch gewaschene Schürze und die gemordeten Mamelucken', in C. Maar and H. Burda (eds.), *Iconic World: Neue Bilderwelten und Wissensräume* (Cologne), pp. 185–204.

(2003), *Bild und Mythos: Geschichte der Bilderzählung in der griechischen Kunst* (Munich).

Goar, J. (ed.) (1730), *Euchologion sive Rituale Graecorum* (Venice).

Goffman, D. (2002), *The Ottoman Empire and Early Modern Europe* (Cambridge).

Gommans, J. (2007), 'Warhorse and Post-nomadic Empire in Asia, c. 1000–1800', *Journal of Global History*, 2, pp. 1–21.

(2002), *Mughal Warfare: Indian Frontiers and High Roads to Empire 1500–1700* (London).

Gordon, R. (2001), 'Ritual and Hierarchy in the Mysteries of Mithras', *ARYS. Antigüedad: Religiones y Sociedades*, 4, pp. 245–74.

(1996), *Image and Value in the Graeco-Roman world: Studies in Mithraism and Religious Art* (Aldershot).

Görich, K. (1998), 'Otto III. öffnet das Karlsgrab in Aachen. Überlegungen zu Heiligenverehrung, Heiligsprechung und Traditionsbildung', in G. Althoff and E. Schubert (eds.), *Herrschaftsrepräsentation im ottonischen Sachsen* (Sigmaringen), pp. 381–430.

Goulet, R. (ed.) (2003), *Dictionnaire des philosophes antiques*, Supplément (Paris).

(ed.) (1989), *Dictionnaire des philosophes antiques*, vol. I (Paris).

Grabar, A. (1936), *L'empereur dans l'art byzantin* (Paris) [repr. London 1971].

Gradel, I. (2002), *Emperor Worship and Roman Religion* (Oxford).

Graillot, H. (1912), *Le culte de Cybèle mère des dieux à Rome et dans l'empire romaine*, Bibliothèque des Écoles françaises d'Athènes et de Rome 107 (Paris).

Grala, H. (1996), 'Uniwersalizm wschodni (idea Cesarstwa Powszechnego w kręgu cywilizacji bizantyńskiej)', in J. Staszewski (ed.), *Pamiętnik XV Powszechnego Zjazdu Historyków Polskich*, vol. I, pt I (Toruń), pp. 139–65.

Grassinger, D. (1999), *Die mythologischen Sarkophage*, pt I: *Achill – Adonis – Aeneas – Aktaion – Alkestis – Amazonen*, Die antiken Sarkophagreliefs, vol. XII, pt I (Berlin).

Grayson, A. K. (1991), *Assyrian Rulers of the Early First Millennium BC*, vol. I: *1114–859 BC*, Royal Inscriptions of Mesopotamia, Assyria 2 (Toronto).

Grewe, W. G. (2000), *Epochs of International Law* (Berlin and New York).

Grierson, P. (1999), *Catalogue of the Byzantine Coins in the Dumbarton Oaks Collection and in the Whittemore Collection (= DOC)*, vol. V: *Michael VIII to Constantine XI, 1258–1453*, pt I (Washington, DC).

(1973), *Catalogue of the Byzantine Coins in the Dumbarton Oaks Collection and in the Whittemore Collection (= DOC)*, vol. III: *Leo III to Nicephorus III, 717–1081*, pt. I (Washington, DC).

(1968), *Catalogue of the Byzantine Coins in the Dumbarton Oaks Collection and in the Whittemore Collection (= DOC)*, vol. II: *Phocas to Theodosius III, 602–717*, pt. I (Washington, DC).

Grierson, P. and Mays, M. (1992), *Catalogue of Late Roman Coins in the Dumbarton Oaks Collection and in the Whittemore Collection: from Arcadius and Honorius to the Accession of Anastasius* (Washington, DC).

Grignaschi, M. (1996), 'Un roman épistolaire gréco-arabe: la correspondance entre Aristote et Alexandre', in Bridges and Bürgel, pp. 109–23.

(1993), 'La figure d'Alexandre chez les arabes et sa genèse', *Arabic Sciences and Philosophy*, 3, pp. 205–34.

(1975), 'La "Siyâsatu-l-'âmmiyya" et l'influence iranienne sur la pensée politique islamique', in *Monumentum H. S. Nyberg*, vol. III [= Acta Iranica 6] (Leiden), pp. 33–287.

(1967), 'Le roman épistolaire classique conservé dans la version arabe de Sâlim Abû 'l-'Alâ', *Le Muséon*, 80, pp. 211–64.

(1965–6), 'Les *Rasā'il Aristātālīsa 'ilā-l-Iskandar* de Sālim Abū-l-'Alā' et l'activité culturelle à l'époque omayyade', *Bulletin d'Études Orientales de Damas*, 19, pp. 7–83.

Gross, L. (1948), 'The Peace of Westphalia, 1648–1948', *American Journal of International Law*, 42, no. 1, pp. 20–41.

Gruen, E. S. (1992), *Culture and National Identity in Republican Rome*, Cornell Studies in Classical Philology 52 (Ithaca, NY).

(1990), *Studies in Greek Culture and Roman Policy*, Cincinnati Classical Studies, New Series, 7 (Leiden).

Guboglu, M. (1958), *Paleografia și diplomatica turco-osmană: studiu și album* (Bucharest).

Guilland, R. (1967), *Recherches sur les institutions byzantines*, vol. 1 (Berlin and Amsterdam).

Günay, R. (1998), *Sinan the Architect and his Works* (Istanbul).

Gutas, D. (2009), 'On Graeco-Arabic Epistolary "novels"', *Middle Eastern Literatures*, 12, pp. 59–70.

(1998), *Greek Thought, Arabic Culture: The Graeco-Arabic Translation Movement in Baghdad and Early 'Abbāsid Society (2nd–4th/8th–10th centuries)* (London).

Gutiérrez Mendoza, G., König, V. and Brito, B. (2009), *Códice Humboldt Fragmento 1, Ms. amer. 2 y Códice Azoyú 2, Reverso. Nómina de tributos de Tlapa y su provincia al Imperio Mexicano* (Mexico City and Berlin).

Gutiérrez Mendoza, G. and Medina Lima, C. (2008), *Toponimia nahuatl en los codices Azoyú 1 y 2: un estudio crítico de los nombres de lugar de los antiguos señoríos del oriente de Guerrero* (Mexico City).

Haarer, F. K. (2006), *Anastasius I: Politics and Empire in the Late Roman World* (Leeds).

Haass, R. N. (1999), *Intervention: The Use of American Military Force in the Post-Cold War World*, revised edn (Washington).

Haberkorn, H. (1940), *Beiträge zur Beurteilung der Perser in der griechischen Literatur* (Greifswald).

Haboush, J. Kim (2005), 'Contesting Chinese Time, Nationalizing Temporal Space: Temporal Inscription in Late Chosŏn Korea', in Struve, pp. 115–41.

Hadot, I. (2002), 'Der fortlaufende philosophische Kommentar', in W. Geerlings and C. Schulze (eds.), *Der Kommentar in Antike und Mittelalter: Beiträge zu seiner Erforschung* (Leiden), pp. 183–99.

Hadot, P. (1972), 'Fürstenspiegel' (trans. J. Engemann), in *Reallexicon für Antike und Christentum*, vol. VIII, pp. 555–632.

Haldén, P. (2011), *Stability without Statehood: Lessons from Europe's History before the Sovereign State* (Basingstoke).

(2006), 'Compound Republics as Viable Political Systems: A Comparison of the Holy Roman Empire of the German Nation and the European Union'. Ph.D. thesis, European University Institute.

Hall, E. (1989), *Inventing the Barbarian: Greek Self-Definition through Tragedy* (Oxford).

(1988), 'When Did the Trojans Turn into Phrygians? Alcaeus 42.15', *Zeitschrift für Papyrologie und Epigraphik*, 73, pp. 15–18.

Hall, J. M. (2002), *Hellenicity. Between Ethnicity and Culture* (Chicago).

Hall, J. W. (1949), 'Notes on the Early Ch'ing Copper Trade with Japan', *Harvard Journal of Asiatic Studies*, 12, no. 3/4, pp. 444–61.

Hallett, C. H. (2005), *The Roman Nude: Heroic Portrait Statuary 200 B.C. – A.D. 300* (Oxford).

Hallock, R. T. (1969), *Persepolis Fortification Tablets*, Oriental Institute Publications 92 (Chicago).

Hamilton, K. R. and Langhorne, R. (1995), *The Practice of Diplomacy: Its Evolution, Theory and Administration* (New York).

Hanaway, W. L. (1998), 'Eskandar-Nāma', in *Encyclopaedia Iranica*, vol. VIII, pp. 609–12.

Haneda, M. (1997), 'Emigration of Iranian Elites to India during the 16th–18th Centuries', in M. Szuppe (ed.), *L'heritage timouride: Iran – Asie centrale – Inde, XVe–XVIIe siècles = Cahiers d'Asie Centrale* vol. 3/4, pp. 129–43.

Harbsmeier, M. (1994), *Wilde Völkerkunde: Andere Welten in deutschen Reiseberichten der Frühen Neuzeit* (Frankfurt and New York).

Hardie, P. (ed.) (2009), *Paradox and the Marvellous in Augustan Literature and Culture* (Oxford).

(2006), 'Virgil's Ptolemaic Relations', *Journal of Roman Studies*, 96, pp. 25–41.

Hartog, F. (1980), *Le miroir d'Hérodote: essai sur la représentation de l'autre* (Paris).

Haselberger, L. and Humphrey, J. (eds.) (2006), *Imaging Ancient Rome: Documentation – Vizualization – Imagination, Proceedings of the Third Williams Symposium on Classical Architecture held at the American Academy in Rome, the British School at Rome, and the Deutsches Archäologisches Institut, Rom, on May 20–23, 2004, Journal of Roman Archaeology*, Supplementary Series 61 (Portsmouth, RI).

Hassig, R. (1988), *Aztec Warfare: Imperial Expansion and Political Control* (Norman).

(1985), *Trade, Tribute, and Transportation: The Sixteenth-Century Political Economy of the Valley of Mexico* (Norman).

Hauser, S. R. (2001), 'Orientalismus', in *Der Neue Pauly*, vol. XV, pt 1 (Stuttgart and Weimar), pp. 1233–43.

Headley, J. M. (1997), *Tommaso Campanella and the Transformation of the World* (Princeton).

Heitz, C. (2009), *Die Guten, die Bösen und die Hässlichen: Nördliche 'Barbaren' in der römischen Bildkunst* (Hamburg).

Hekster, O. and Fowler, R. (eds.) (2005), *Imaginary Kings: Royal Images in the Ancient Near East, Greece and Rome*, Oriens et Occidens 11 (Stuttgart).

Held, D. (2010), *Cosmopolitanism: Ideals and Realities* (Cambridge).

Hendy, M. F. (1985), *Studies in the Byzantine Monetary Economy c. 300–1450* (Cambridge).

Henkelman, W. F. M. (2008), *The Other Gods Who Are: Studies in Elamite–Iranian Acculturation based on the Persepolis Fortification Texts*, Achaemenid History 14 (Leiden).

Henten, J. W. van (2000), 'Nero Redivivus Demolished: The Coherence of the Nero Traditions in the Sibylline Oracles', *Journal for the Study of Pseudoepigrapha*, 11, no. 3, pp. 3–17.

Hentsch, T. (1988), *L'Orient imaginaire: la vision politique occidentale de l'Est méditerranéen* (Paris).

Heras, H. (1927), *The Aravidu Dynasty of Vijayanagara* (Madras).

Herman, G. (1997), 'The Court Society of the Hellenistic Age', in P. Cartledge, P. Garnsey and E. S. Gruen (eds.), *Hellenistic Constructs: Essays in Culture, History and Historiography* (Berkeley and Los Angeles), pp. 199–224.

Herrin, J. (1987), *The Formation of Christendom* (Oxford).

(1975), 'Realities of Byzantine Provincial Government: Hellas and Peloponnesos, 1180–1205', *Dumbarton Oaks Papers*, 29, pp. 253–84.

Hertel, D. (2003), *Die Mauern von Troia: Mythos und Geschichte im antiken Ilion* (Munich).

Hevia, J. L. (1995), *Cherishing Men from Afar: Qing Guest Ritual and the Macartney Embassy of 1793* (Durham, NC).

Hicks, F. (1986), 'Prehispanic Background of Colonial Political and Economic Organization in Central Mexico', in R. Spores (ed.), *Supplement to the Handbook of Middle American Indians*, vol. IV: *Ethnohistory* (Austin), pp. 35–54.

Hingley, R. (2005), *Globalizing Roman Culture: Unity, Diversity and Empire* (London).

Hinüber, O. von (2010), 'Did Hellenistic Kings Send Letters to Aśoka?', *Journal of the American Oriental Society*, 130, no. 2, pp. 261–6.

Hinz, W. (1974), 'Tiara', in *Paulys Realencyclopädie der classischen Altertumswissenschaft*, Supplementband XIV (Munich), pp. 786–96.

Hobbes, T. (1996), *Leviathan*, ed. with an introduction and notes J. C. A. Gaskin (Oxford).

Hobsbawm, E. and Ranger, T. (eds.) (1983), *The Invention of Tradition* (Cambridge).

Hocart, A. M. (1970), *Kings and Councillors: An Essay in the Comparative Anatomy of Human Society*, ed. R. Needham (Chicago).

Hodge, M. G. (1996), 'Political Organization of the Central Provinces', in Berdan *et al.*, pp. 17–45.

Hodgson, M. G. S. (1974), *The Venture of Islam: Conscience and History in a World Civilization*, 3 vols. (Chicago).

Hölbl, G. (2001), *A History of the Ptolemaic Empire*, trans. T. Saavedra (London and New York).

Hölkeskamp, K.-J. (2010), review of Beard 2007, *Gnomon*, 82, pp. 130–6.

(2008), 'Hierarchie und Konsens. *Pompae* in der politischen Kultur der römischen Republik', in A. H. Arweiler and B. M. Gauly (eds.), *Machtfragen: Zur kulturellen Repräsentation und Konstruktion von Macht in Antike, Mittelalter und Neuzeit* (Stuttgart), pp. 79–126.

(2004), 'Römische *gentes* und griechische Genealogien', in Hölkeskamp, *SENATVS POPVLVSQVE ROMANVS: Die politische Kultur der Republik – Dimensionen und Deutungen* (Stuttgart), pp. 199–217 [first published in Vogt-Spira and Rommel, pp. 3–21].

Holloway, S. W. (2002), *Aššur Is King! Aššur Is King! – Religion in the Exercise of Power in the Neo-Assyrian Empire*, Culture and History of the Ancient Near East 10 (Leiden).

Hölscher, T. (2009), *Herrschaft und Lebensalter: Alexander der Grosse: Politisches Image und anthropologisches Modell* (Basel).

(2006), 'Das Forum Romanum – die monumentale Geschichte Roms', in E. Stein-Hölkeskamp and K.-J. Hölkeskamp (eds.), *Erinnerungsorte der Antike: Die römische Welt* (Munich), pp. 100–22.

(1988), 'Historische Reliefs', in *Kaiser Augustus und die verlorene Republik: Eine Ausstellung im Martin-Gropius-Bau, Berlin 7. Juni – 14. August 1988* (Mainz), pp. 351–400.

Holsti, K. J. (1991), *Peace and War: Armed Conflicts and International Order, 1648–1989* (Cambridge).

Holt, F. L. (1999), *Thundering Zeus: The Making of Hellenistic Bactria* (Berkeley).

Hommel, P. (1954), *Studien zu den römischen Figurengiebeln* (Berlin).

Honigman, S. (2003), *The Septuagint and Homeric Scholarship in Alexandria: A Study in the* Letter of Aristeas (London and New York).

Hopkins, A. G. (ed.) (2002), *Globalization in World History* (London).

Horsfall, N. M. (1987), 'The Aeneas-Legend from Homer to Vergil', in J. N. Bremmer and N. M. Horsfall (eds.), *Roman Myth and Mythography*, Bulletin of the Institute of Classical Studies of the University of London, Supplement 52 (London), pp. 12–24.

Howard, D. A. (2007), 'Genre and Myth in the Ottoman Advice for Kings Literature', in Aksan and Goffman, pp. 137–66.

Howard-Johnston, J. (1995), 'The Two Great Powers in Late Antiquity: A Comparison', in A. Cameron (ed.), *The Byzantine and Early Islamic Near East*, vol. III: *States, Resources and Armies* (Princeton), pp. 157–226.

Hudson, M. J. (1999), *Ruins of Identity: Ethnogenesis in the Japanese Islands* (Honolulu).

Huet, V. (1999), 'Napoleon I: A New Augustus?', in C. Edwards (ed.), *Roman Presences: Receptions of Rome in European Culture, 1789–1945* (Cambridge), pp. 53–69.

Hugonnard-Roche, H. (2004), 'Éthique et politique au premier âge de la tradition syriaque', *Mélanges de l'Université Saint-Joseph*, 57, pp. 99–119.

Hultzsch, E. (1925), *Inscriptions of Asoka*, new edn, Corpus Inscriptionum Indicarum 1 (Oxford).

Humfress, C. (2007), *Orthodoxy and the Courts in Late Antiquity* (Oxford).

Hummel, A. W. (ed.) (1943), *Eminent Chinese of the Ch'ing Period (1644–1912)*, 2 vols. (Washington).

Hunger, H. (1964), *Prooimion: Elemente der byzantinischen Kaiseridee in den Arengen der Urkunden* (Vienna).

Hunter, R. (2011), 'The Letter of Aristeas', in Erskine and Llewellyn-Jones, pp. 47–60.

Hurlet, F. (ed.) (2008), *Les Empires: Antiquité et Moyen Âge. Analyse comparée* (Rennes).

Huyghebaert, N. (1979), 'Une légende de fondation: le Constitutum Constantini', *Le Moyen Âge*, 85, pp. 177–209.

Huyse, P. (2006), 'Die sasanidische Königstitulatur: Eine Gegenüberstellung der Quellen', in Wiesehöfer and Huyse, pp. 181–202.

Hye, F.-H. (1973), 'Der Doppeladler als Symbol für Kaiser und Reich', *Mitteilungen des Instituts für Österreichische Geschichtsforschung*, 81, pp. 63–100.

Iacopi, G. (1963), *L'antro di Tiberio a Sperlonga* (Rome).

Ibn Battūta (1993), *The Travels of Ibn Battūta A.D. 1325–1354*, trans. H. A. R. Gibb, 3 vols. (New Delhi) [reprint].

Icazbalceta, J. García (ed.) (1886–92), *Nueva colección de documentos para la historia de México*, 5 vols. (Mexico City) [also reprinted in 1971].

Imber, C. (1997), *Ebu's-su'ud: The Islamic Legal Tradition* (Edinburgh).

İnalcık, H. (1993), 'State and Ideology under Sultan Süleyman I', in İnalcık, *The Middle East and the Balkans under the Ottoman Empire: Essays on Economy and Society* (Bloomington), pp. 70–94.

(1993/1986), 'Power Relationships between Russia, the Crimea, and the Ottoman Empire as Reflected in Titulature', in İnalcık, *The Middle East and the Balkans under the Ottoman Empire: Essays in Economy and Society* (Bloomington), pp. 369–411 [originally published in C. Lemercier-Quelquejay, G. Veinstein and S. E. Wimbusch (eds.), *Passé Turco-Tatar présent soviétique: études offertes à Alexandre Bennigsen* (Louvain and Paris), pp. 175–211].

(1992), 'Islamization of Ottoman Laws on Land and Land Tax', in C. Fragner and K. Schwarz (eds.), *Festgabe an Josef Matuz: Osmanistik–Turkologie–Diplomatik* (Berlin), pp. 101–18.

(1991), 'Mehemmed II', in *The Encyclopaedia of Islam*, 2nd edn, vol. VI (Leiden and London), pp. 978–81.

(1973), *The Ottoman Empire: The Classical Age 1300–1600* (New York and London).

(1965), 'Girāy', in *The Encyclopaedia of Islam*, 2nd edn, vol. II (Leiden and London), pp. 1112–14.

Invernizzi, A. (2001), 'Die Kunst der Partherzeit', in W. Seipel (ed.), *7000 Jahre persische Kunst: Meisterwerke aus dem Iranischen Nationalmuseum in Teheran*, eine Ausstellung des Kunsthistorischen Museums Wien und des Iranischen Nationalmuseums in Teheran, Kunsthistorisches Museum, 22. November 2000 bis 25. März 2001 (Milan).

Isaac, B. (2004), *The Invention of Racism in Classical Antiquity* (Princeton).

Isaac, B. L. (1983a), 'Aztec Warfare: Goals and Battlefield Comportments', *Ethnology*, 22, pp. 121–31.

(1983b), 'The Aztec "Flowery War": A Geopolitical Explanation', *Journal of Anthropological Research*, 39, pp. 415–32.

Islam, R. (1979–82), *A Calendar of Documents on Indo-Persian Relations (1500–1750)*, 2 vols. (Teheran and Karachi).

(1970), *Indo-Persian Relations: A Study of the Political and Diplomatic Relations between the Mughal Empire and Iran* (Teheran).

Itgenshorst, T. (2005), *Tota illa pompa: Der Triumph in der römischen Republik*, Hypomnemata 161 (Göttingen).

Ivantchik, A. I. (2005), 'Who Were the "Scythian" Archers on Archaic Attic Vases?', in D. Braund (ed.), *Scythians and Greeks: Cultural Interactions in Scythia*,

Athens and the Early Roman Empire (Sixth Century BC to First Century AD) (Exeter), pp. 100–13.

Ixtlilxochitl, F. de Alva (2000), *Historia de la nación chichimeca* (Madrid).

Jackson, P. (1999), *The Delhi Sultanate: A Political and Military History* (Cambridge).

Jahangir (1999), *The Jahangirnama: Memoirs of Jahangir, Emperor of India*, trans. and ed. W. Thackston (New York and Oxford).

Jardine, L. and Brotton, J. (2000), *Global Interests: Renaissance Art between East and West* (London).

Jaspers, K. (1955), *Vom Ursprung und Ziel der Geschichte: Bücher des Wissens, Fischer Edition* (Frankfurt) [1st edn 1949].

Jiménez García, E. (2002), 'Apuntes sobre la arqueología de Tlapa, Guerrero', in C. Niederberger and R. M. Reyna Robles (eds.), *El pasado arqueológico de Guerrero* (Mexico City), pp. 387–403.

Johnson, S. R. (2004), *Historical Fictions and Hellenistic Jewish Identity: Third Maccabees in its Cultural Context* (Berkeley).

Jones, A. H. M. (1964), *The Later Roman Empire, 284–602*, 3 vols. (Oxford).

Jones, W. (1807), *The Works of Sir William Jones*, vol. III (London).

Jönsson, C., Tägil, S. and Törnqvist, G. (2000), *Organizing European Space* (London).

Jordanov, I. (1976), 'Ednostranni zlatni moneti-medalioni s imeto na khan Omurtag', *Numizmatika*, 1976, no. 4, pp. 18–34.

Jouanno, C. (2002), *Naissance et métamorphoses du Roman d'Alexandre: domaine grec* (Paris).

Kacunov, V. (1996), 'On the Ethnic Self-Consciousness of the Bulgarians during the 15th–17th Century', *Bulgarian Historical Review*, 1996, no. 2, pp. 3–24.

Kafadar, C. (1995), *Between Two Worlds: The Construction of the Ottoman State* (Berkeley, Los Angeles and London).

Kähler, H. (1959), *Die Augustusstatue von Primaporta*, Monumenta Artis Romanae I (Cologne).

Kaiser, W. B. (1968), 'Die Göttin mit der Mauerkrone', *Schweizer Münzblätter*, 18, pp. 25–36.

Kaldellis, A. (2005a), 'Republican Theory and Political Dissidence in Ioannes Lydos', *Byzantine and Modern Greek Studies*, 29, pp. 1–16.

(2005b), 'The Works and Days of Hesychios the Illoustrios of Miletos', *Greek, Roman and Byzantine Studies*, 45, pp. 381–403.

(2004a), 'Identifying Dissident Circles in Sixth-Century Byzantium: The Friendship of Prokopios and Ioannes Lydos', *Florilegium*, 21, pp. 1–17.

(2004b), *Procopius of Caesarea: Tyranny, History, and Philosophy at the End of Antiquity* (Philadelphia).

(1999), 'The Historical and Religious Views of Agathias: A Reinterpretation', *Byzantion*, 69, pp. 206–52.

Kalhaṇa (1991), *Kalhaṇa's Rājataraṅgiṇī: A Chronicle of the Kings of Kaśmīr*, trans. M. A. Stein, 2 vols. (Lahore) [reprint; originally published 1900].

Kamiya, N. (1994), 'Japanese Control of Ezochi and the Role of Northern Koryŏ', *Acta Asiatica*, 67, pp. 49–68.

Kang, E. Hae-jin (1997), *Diplomacy and Ideology in Japanese–Korean Relations from the Fifteenth to the Eighteenth Century* (New York).

Kantor, M. (trans.) (1983), *Medieval Lives of Slavic Saints and Princes* (Ann Arbor).

Kantorowicz, E. (1957), *The King's Two Bodies: A Study in Mediaeval Political Theology* (Princeton).

Käppel, L. (2001), "Rhea Silvia", in *Der Neue Pauly*, vol. x (Stuttgart and Weimar), pp. 950–1.

Karashima, N. (1999), 'Vijayanagar Nāyakas in Tamil Nadu and the King', in Karashima (ed.), *Kingship in Indian History* (New Delhi), pp. 143–62.

  (1992), *Towards a New Formation: South Indian Society under Vijayanagar Rule* (Delhi).

Karateke, H. (2005), 'Legitimizing the Ottoman Sultanate: A Framework for Historical Analysis', in H. Karateke and M. Reinkowski (eds.), *Legitimizing the Order: The Ottoman Rhetoric of State Power* (Leiden), pp. 13–52.

Kazhdan, A. P. (ed.) (1991), *The Oxford Dictionary of Byzantium*, 3 vols. (Oxford and New York).

Keenan, E. (1967), 'Muscovy and Kazan: Some Introductory Remarks on the Patterns of Steppe Diplomacy', *Slavic Review*, 26, pp. 548–58.

Kejariwal, O. P. (1988), *The Asiatic Society of Bengal and the Discovery of India's Past, 1784–1838* (New Delhi).

Kennedy, H. (2004), *The Prophet and the Age of the Caliphates: The Islamic Near East from the Sixth to the Eleventh Century*, 2nd edn (Harlow).

Kennedy, P. (1987), *The Rise and Fall of the Great Powers: Economic Change and Military Conflict from 1500 to 2000* (New York).

Kent, R. G. (1953), *Old Persian: Grammar, Texts, Lexicon*, American Oriental Series 53 (New Haven).

Kern, F. (1939), *Kingship and Law in the Middle Ages*, trans. S. B. Chrimes (Oxford).

Khan, I. A. (1997), 'Akbar's Personality Traits and World Outlook – A Critical Reappraisal', in I. Habib (ed.), *Akbar and his India* (Delhi), pp. 79–96.

Khwāndamīr, Ghiyās al-Dīn (1940), *Qānūn-i Humāyūnī (also known as Humāyūn Nāma) of Khwāndamīr*, 2 vols. (Persian text ed. M. Hidāyat Hosain; English trans. B. Prashad) (Calcutta).

Kingsbury, B. and Roberts, A. (1990), 'Introduction: Grotian Thought in International Relations', in H. Bull, B. Kingsbury and A. Roberts (eds.), *Hugo Grotius and International Relations* (Oxford), pp. 1–65.

Kinnier Wilson, J. V. (1972), *The Nimrud Wine Lists: A Study of Men and Administration at the Assyrian Capital in the Eighth Century BC*, Cuneiform Texts from Nimrud 1 (London).

Klein, C. and Umberger, E. (1993), 'Aztec Art and Imperial Expansion', in D. S. Rice (ed.), *Latin American Horizons* (Washington, DC), pp. 295–336.

Koch, E. (in press), 'The Symbolic Possession of the World: European Cartography in Mughal Allegory', in C. Lefèvre and I. G. Županov (eds.), *Cultural*

Dialogue in South Asia and Beyond: Narratives, Images and Community (16th–19th centuries), special issue of *Journal of the Economic and Social History of the Orient*.

(2011), 'The Mughal Audience Hall: A Solomonic Revival of Persepolis in the Form of a Mosque', in Duindam *et al.*, pp. 313–38.

(2010), 'The Mughal Emperor as Solomon, Majnun and Orpheus or the Album as a Think-Tank for Allegory', *Muqarnas*, 27, pp. 278–311.

(2009), 'Jahangir as Francis Bacon's Ideal of the King as an Observer and Investigator of Nature', *Journal of the Royal Asiatic Society*, Series 3, 19, pt 3, pp. 293–338.

(2006), 'The Influence of the Jesuit Mission on Symbolic Representations of the Mughal Emperors', in A. Hagedorn (ed.), *The Phenomenon of 'Foreign' in Oriental Art* (Wiesbaden), pp. 117–34 [earlier version published in C. W. Troll (ed.), *Islam in India: Studies and Commentaries*, vol. 1 (New Delhi, 1982), pp. 14–29; also reprinted in Koch 2001, pp. 1–11].

(2002), 'The Intellectual and Artistic Climate at Akbar's Court', in J. Seyller (ed.), *The Adventures of Hamza: Painting and Storytelling in Mughal India*, exhibition catalogue (London and Washington), pp. 18–31.

(2001), *Mughal Art and Imperial Ideology: Collected Essays* (New Delhi).

(1998), *Dara Shikoh Shooting Nilgai: Hunt and Landscape in Mughal Painting*, Freer Gallery of Art Occasional Papers, New Series 1 (Washington).

Kockel, V. (1995), 'Forum Augustum', in E. M. Steinby (ed.), *Lexicon Topographicum Urbis Romae*, vol. II: *D–G* (Rome), pp. 289–95.

Koeppel, G. M. (1983), 'Die historischen Reliefs der römischen Kaiserzeit I', *Bonner Jahrbücher*, 183, pp. 61–144.

Köhbach, M. (1992), '*Çasar* oder *imperator*? – Zur Titulatur der römischen Kaiser durch die Osmanen nach dem Vertrag von Zsitvatorok (1606)', *Wiener Zeitschrift für die Kunde des Morgenlandes*, 82, pp. 223–34.

Köhler, U. (2001), '"Debt Payment" to the Gods among the Aztec. The Misrendering of the Spanish Expression and its Effects', *Estudios de Cultura Náhuatl*, 32, pp. 125–33.

Kołodziejczyk, D. (2012), 'Between Universalistic Claims and Reality: Ottoman Frontiers in the Early Modern Period', in C. Woodhead (ed.), *The Ottoman World* (London and New York), pp. 205–19.

(2011), *The Crimean Khanate and Poland-Lithuania: International Diplomacy on the European Periphery (15th–18th Century). A Study of Peace Treaties Followed by Annotated Documents* (Leiden).

(2009), 'Obraz sułtana tureckiego w publicystyce staropolskiej', in F. Wolański and R. Kołodziej (eds.), *Staropolski ogląd świata: Rzeczpospolita między okcydentalizacją a orientalizacją*, vol. i: *Przestrzeń kontaktów* (Toruń), pp. 11–19.

(2006), 'The "Turkish Yoke" Revisited: The Ottoman Non-Muslim Subjects between Loyalty, Alienation, and Riot', *Acta Poloniae Historica*, 93, pp. 177–95.

(2004), *The Ottoman Survey Register of Podolia (ca. 1681)*. Defter-i Mufassal-i Eyalet-i Kamaniçe, 2 pts (Cambridge, Mass.).

(2000), *Ottoman–Polish Diplomatic Relations (15th–18th Century): An Annotated Edition of* 'Ahdnames *and Other Documents* (Leiden).

König, H.-J. (1969), *Monarchia Mundi und Res Publica Christiana: Die Bedeutung des mittelalterlichen Imperium Romanum für die politische Ideenwelt Kaiser Karls V und seiner Zeit dargestellt an ausgewählten Beispielen* (Hamburg).

Koselleck, R. (2000), 'Begriffsgeschichte und Sozialgeschichte', in Koselleck, *Vergangene Zukunft: Zur Semantik geschichtlicher Zeiten* (Frankfurt), pp. 107–29.

——— (1975), 'Zur historisch-politischen Semantik asymmetrischer Gegenbegriffe', in H. Weinreich (ed.), *Positionen der Negativität*, Poetik und Hermenutik 6 (Munich), pp. 65–104 [reprinted in R. Koselleck, *Vergangene Zukunft: Zur Semantik geschichtlicher Zeiten* (numerous editions)].

Kossatz-Deissmann, A. (1994), 'Paridis Iudicium', in *Lexicon Iconographicum Mythologiae Classicae*, vol. vii (Zurich and Munich), pp. 176–88.

Kränzle, P. (1994), 'Der Fries der Basilica Aemilia', in A. H. Borbein (ed.), *Antike Plastik*, vol. 23 (Munich), pp. 93–130.

Krasner, S. D. (1993), 'Westphalia and All That', in J. Goldstein and R. O. Keohane (eds.), *Ideas and Foreign Policy: Beliefs, Institutions, and Political Change* (Ithaca, NY), pp. 235–64.

Kratochwil, F. (2002), 'Souveränität und Moderne: Eine begriffliche Analyse des semantischen Feldes', in M. Jachtenfuchs and M. Knodt (eds.), *Regieren in internationalen Institutionen* (Opladen), pp. 29–51.

——— (1989), *Rules, Norms, and Decisions: On the Conditions of Practical and Legal Reasoning in International Relations and Domestic Affairs* (Cambridge).

Krierer, K. R. (2004), *Antike Germanenbilder*, Österreichische Akademie der Wissenschaften, Philosophisch-Historische Klasse 318 (Vienna).

Kroll, W. (1917), 'Iulius (Germanicus)', in *Paulys Realencyclopädie der classischen Altertumswissenschaft*, vol. x, pt 1 (Stuttgart), pp. 435–64 (no. 138).

Krumeich, R. (2001), 'Dokumente orientalischen Selbstbewusstseins in Rom: Die Weihreliefs des Iuppiter Dolichenus-Priesters parthischer Herkunft M. Ulpius Chresimus', *Bonner Jahrbücher*, 201, pp. 69–92.

Kuhrt, A. (2007), *The Persian Empire: A Corpus of Sources from the Achaemenid Period*, 2 vols. (London).

——— (1996), 'The Seleucid Kings and Babylonia: New Perspectives on the Seleucid Realm in the East', in Bilde *et al.*, pp. 41–54.

Kuhrt, A. and Sherwin-White, S. (eds.) (1987), *Hellenism in the East: The Interaction of Greek and Non-Greek Civilizations from Syria to Central Asia after Alexander* (London).

Kulke, H. (1997), 'Introduction: The Study of the State in Pre-modern India', in Kulke (ed.), *The State in India, 1000–1700* (Delhi).

——— (1993a), 'Mahārājas, Mahants and Historians: Reflections on the Historiography of early Vijayanagara and Sringeri', in Kulke, *Kings and Cults: State Formation and Legitimation in India and Southeast Asia* (New Delhi), pp. 208–39.

——— (1993b), 'The Devarāja Cult: Legitimation and Apotheosis of the Ruler in the Kingdom of Angkor', in Kulke, *Kings and Cults: State Formation and Legitimation in India and Southeast Asia* (New Delhi), pp. 327–81.

Kumar, S. (2007), *The Emergence of the Delhi Sultanate 1190–1290* (New Delhi).

Kunisch, J. (2004), *Friedrich der Grosse: Der König und seine Zeit* (Munich).

Kunze, C. (1996), 'Zur Datierung des Laokoon und der Skyllagruppe aus Sperlonga', *Jahrbuch des Deutschen Archäologischen Instituts*, 111, pp. 139–223.

Kwŏn, Chung-dal (2004), 'Chungguk ŭi hwakdae wa Hanjok gwan' [The expansion of China and views of the Han people], *Han'guk sahaksa hakbo*, 10, pp. 147–62.

Lamprichs, R. (1995), *Die Westexpansion des neuassyrischen Reiches – Eine Strukturanalyse*, Alter Orient und Altes Testament 239 (Neukirchen-Vluyn).

Lampros, S. (1909), 'Dikephalos aetos sto Byzantio', *Neos Hellenomnemon*, 6, pp. 433–73.

Lancellotti, M. G. (2002), *Attis: Between Myth and History. King, Priest and God* (Leiden).

Landes, R. (1988), 'Lest the Millennium Be Fulfilled: Apocalyptic Expectations and the Pattern of Western Chronography, 100–800 C.E.', in W. Verbeke, D. Verhelst and A. Welkenhuysen (eds.), *The Use and Abuse of Eschatology in the Middle Ages* (Louvain), pp. 137–211.

Landskron, A. (2006), 'Repräsentantinnen des *orbis* Romanus auf dem sog. Partherdenkmal von Ephesos. Personifikationen und Bildpropaganda', in W. Seipel (ed.), *Das Partherdenkmal von Ephesos*, Schriften des Kunsthistorisches Museums 10 (Vienna and Milan), pp. 103–28.

(2005), *Parther und Sasaniden: Das Bild der Orientalen in der römischen Kaiserzeit*, Wiener Forschungen zur Archäologie 7 (Vienna).

Landwehr, C. (2000), *Die römischen Skulpturen von Caesarea Mauretaniae*, vol. 11: *Idealplastik: Männliche Figuren* (Mainz).

Lane Fox, R. (2011), 'The First Hellenistic Man', in Erskine and Llewellyn-Jones, pp. 1–29.

(2007), 'Alexander the Great: Last of the Achaemenids?', in C. J. Tuplin (ed.), *Persian Responses: Political and Cultural Interaction with(in) the Achaemenid Empire* (Swansea), pp. 267–311.

Lanfranchi, G. B. and Parpola, S. (1990), *The Correspondence of Sargon II, Part II*, State Archives of Assyria 5 (Helsinki).

Larner, J. (1980), *Italy in the Age of Dante and Petrarch, 1216–1380* (London and New York).

La Rocca, E. (2002), 'Silenzio e compianto dei morti nell'Ara Pacis', Αρχαία ελληνική γλυπτική. Αφιέρωμα στη μνήμη του γλύπτη Στέλιου Τριάντη, Μουσείο Μπενάκι, 10 Παράρτημα (Athens), pp. 269–313.

(2001), 'La nuova immagine dei fori imperiali. Appunti in margine agli scavi', *Mitteilungen des Deutschen Archäologischen Instituts, Römische Abteilung*, 108, pp. 171–213.

Larsen, M. T. (2000), 'The City-States of the Early Neo-Babylonian Period', in M. H. Hansen (ed.), *A Comparative Study of Thirty City-state Cultures: An Investigation Conducted by the Copenhagen Polis Centre*, Historisk-filosofiske skrifter 21 (Copenhagen), pp. 117–27.

Latham, J. D. (1983), 'The Beginnings of Arabic Prose Literature: The Epistolary Genre', in A. F. L. Beeston, T. M. Johnstone, R. B. Serjeant and G. R. Smith (eds.), *Arabic Literature to the End of the Umayyad Period* (Cambridge), pp. 154–79.

Latour, B. (2007), *We Have Never Been Modern*, trans. C. Porter (Cambridge, Mass.).

Laube, I. (2006), *Thorakophoroi: Gestalt und Semantik des Brustpanzers in der Darstellung des 4. bis 1. Jhs. v. Chr.*, Tübinger archäologische Forschungen 1 (Rahden).

Laurent, V. (ed. and trans.) (1971), *Les 'Mémoires' du Grand Ecclésiarque de l'Église de Constantinople Sylvestre Syropoulos sur le concile de Florence (1438–1439)* (Paris and Rome).

(1955), 'Les droits de l'empereur en matière ecclésiastique. L'accord de 1380/82', *Revue des Études Byzantines*, 13, pp. 5–20.

Laurenti, R. (2003), 'Les "Dialogues"', in Goulet, pp. 379–471.

Leach, L. Y. (1995), *Mughal and Other Indian Paintings from the Chester Beatty Library*, 2 vols. (London).

Lecoq, P. (1997), *Les inscriptions de la Perse achéménide* (Paris).

Leder, S. (1999), 'Aspekte arabischer und persischer Fürstenspiegel. Legitimation, Fürstenethik, politische Vernunft', in A. De Benedictis (ed.), *Specula principum* (Frankfurt), pp. 21–50.

Lee, K. (1984), *A New History of Korea*, trans. E. W. Wagner with E. J. Shultz (Cambridge, Mass.).

Lefèvre, C. (2010), 'Jahangir et son frère Šah 'Abbas: compétition et circulation entre deux puissances de l'Asie musulmane de la première modernité', in D. Hermann and F. Speziale (eds.), *Muslim Cultures in the Indo-Iranian World during the Early-Modern and Modern Periods*, Islamkundliche Untersuchungen, Band 290 = Bibliothèque Iranienne 69 (Berlin), pp. 23–56.

Lefort, J. (1981), *Documents grecs dans les Archives de Topkapı Sarayı. Contribution à l'histoire de Cem Sultan/Topkapı Sarayı Arşivlerinin Yunanca belgeleri. Cem Sultan'ın tarihine katkı* (Ankara).

Leichty, E. (2011), *The Royal Inscriptions of Esarhaddon, King of Assyria (680–669 BC)*, The Royal Inscriptions of the Neo-Assyrian Period 4 (Winona Lake).

Lemerle, P. (1986), *Byzantine Humanism*, trans. H. Lindsay and A. Moffatt (Canberra).

Lesaffer, R. (ed.) (2004a), *Peace Treaties and International Law in European History: From the Late Middle Ages to World War One* (Cambridge).

(2004b), 'Peace Treaties from Lodi to Westphalia', in Lesaffer, pp. 9–45.

Levin, H. (1969), *The Myth of the Golden Age in the Renaissance* (New York).

Lewis, J. B. (2002), 'Late Chosŏn-Era Korean Interaction with Japanese in Pusan: Defining Boundaries', in *Embracing the Other: The Interaction of Korean and Foreign Culture*, Proceedings of the 1st World Congress of Korean Studies, vol. III (Songnam), pp. 1275–88.

Li, Sŏngsi (2004), *Higashi Ajia bunkaken no keisei* [The formation of the East Asian cultural sphere] (Tokyo).

Lieberman, V. (2010), *Strange Parallels: Southeast Asia in Global Context, c.800–1830*, vol. ɪɪ: *Mainland Mirrors: Europe, Japan, China, South Asia, and the Islands* (Cambridge).

(2008), 'Protected Rimlands and Exposed Zones: Reconfiguring Premodern Eurasia', *Comparative Studies in Society and History*, 50, no. 3, pp. 692–723.

Lipps, J. (2011), *Basilica Aemilia: Der kaiserzeitliche Bau und seine Ornamentik*, Palilia 24 (Wiesbaden).

Little, R. (1989), 'Deconstructing the Balance of Power: Two Traditions of Thought', *Review of International Studies*, 15, pp. 87–100.

Liu, Baoquan (2003), 'Imjin waeran si pabyŏng ui silsang e daehan ilgo – ge donggi wa sigi rul chungsimŭro' [An investigation of the Ming dynasty's dispatch of troops during the Japanese invasion – focused on the motives and timing], *Han'guksa hakbo*, 14, pp. 151–84.

Liverani, M. (2001), *International Relations in the Ancient Near East, 1600–1100 BC*, Studies in Diplomacy (Basingstoke and New York).

Lockhart, J. (1992), *The Nahuas after the Conquest: A Social and Cultural History of the Indians of Central Mexico, Sixteenth through Eighteenth Centuries* (Stanford).

Lopez, R. S. (1951), 'The Dollar of the Middle Ages', *Journal of Economic History*, 11, pp. 209–34.

López Austin, A. (1996), *Cuerpo humano e ideología: las concepciones de los antiguos nahuas*, Serie Antropológica 39 [reedition], Universidad Nacional Autónoma de México (Mexico City).

(1994), *Tamoanchan y Tlalocan* (Mexico City).

López de Gómara, F. (1966), *Historia general de las Indias*, 2 vols. (Barcelona).

L'Orange, H. P. (1953), *Studies on the Iconography of Cosmic Kingship* (Oslo).

Losensky, P. E. (1998), *Welcoming Fighānī: Imitation and Poetic Individuality in the Safavid-Mughal Ghazal* (Costa Mesa, Calif.).

Losty, J. P. (1991), 'Abu'l Hasan', in P. Pal (ed.), *Master Artists of the Imperial Mughal Court* (Bombay), pp. 69–86.

Lowry, H. (2008), *The Shaping of the Ottoman Balkans, 1350–1550: The Conquest, Settlement and Infrastructural Development of Northern Greece* (Istanbul).

(2003), *The Nature of the Early Ottoman State* (Albany).

Luckenbill, D. D. (1924), *The Annals of Sennacherib*, Oriental Institute Publications 2 (Chicago).

Lumsden, S. P. (2004), 'Narrative Art and Empire: The Throneroom of Aššurnaṣirpal II', in Dercksen, pp. 359–85.

(2001), 'Power and Identity in the Neo-Assyrian World', in I. Nielsen (ed.), *The Royal Palace Institution in the First Millennium BC: Regional Development and Cultural Interchange between East and West*, Monographs of the Danish Institute at Athens 4 (Athens).

Lund, H. S. (1992), *Lysimachus: A Study in Early Hellenistic Kingship* (London).

Luukko, M. and van Buylaere, G. (2002), *The Political Correspondence of Esarhaddon*, State Archives of Assyria 16 (Helsinki).

Ma, J. (in press), 'Macedon and the Hellenistic Empires', in P. Bang and W. Scheidel (eds.), *The Oxford Handbook of the Ancient State: Near East and Mediterranean* (New York).

(2003), 'Kings', in Erskine, pp. 177–95.

(2000), *Antiochos III and the Cities of Western Asia Minor* (Oxford).

Machinist, P. (1993), 'Assyrians on Assyria in the First Millennium B.C.', in K. Raaflaub and E. Müller-Luckner (eds.), *Anfänge politischen Denkens in der Antike: Die nahöstlichen Kulturen und die Griechen* (Oldenburg), pp. 77–104.

Mackenzie, C. (1844), 'View of the Principal Political Events that Occurred in the Carnatic, from the Dissolution of the Ancient Hindoo Government in 1564 till the Mogul Government was Established, in 1687, . . . Compiled from Various Authentic Memoirs and Original Mss., Collected Chiefly within the Last Ten Years . . . ', *Journal of the Asiatic Society of Bengal*, 13, pp. 421–63 and 578–609.

Mackenzie, J. (1995), *Orientalism: History, Theory and the Arts* (Manchester and New York).

Maclagan, E. (1990), *The Jesuits and the Great Mogul* (New Delhi) [reprint; originally published in 1932].

Macrides, R. (1992), 'Bad Historian or Good Lawyer? Demetrios Chomatenos and Novel 131', *Dumbarton Oaks Papers*, 46, pp. 187–96.

Mair, V. H. (1985), 'Language and Ideology in the Written Popularizations of the Sacred Edict', in D. Johnson, A. Nathan and E. Rawski (eds.), *Popular Culture in Late Imperial China* (Berkeley), pp. 325–59.

Major, J. Russell (1980), *Representative Government in Early Modern France* (New Haven).

Malanczuk, P. (1997), *Akehurst's Modern Introduction to International Law*, 7th revised edn (London and New York).

Malinowski, B. (1922), *Argonauts of the Western Pacific* (London).

Mancall, M. (1971), *Russia and China: Their Diplomatic Relations to 1728* (Cambridge, Mass.).

Mango, C. (ed.) (2002), *The Oxford History of Byzantium* (Oxford).

Mann, M. (2005), *The Dark Side of Democracy: Explaining Ethnic Cleansing* (Cambridge).

(1986), *The Sources of Social Power*, vol. I: *A History of Power from the Beginning to A.D. 1760* (Cambridge).

(1984), 'The Autonomous Power of the State: Its Origins, Mechanisms and Results', *Archives Européennes de Sociologie*, 25, pp. 185–213.

Manning, C. A. W. (1962), *The Nature of International Society* (New York).

Manning, J. G. (2010), *The Last Pharaohs: Egypt under the Ptolemies, 305–30 BC* (Princeton).

Manrique, S. (1927), *Travels of Fray Sebastien Manrique, 1629–1643*, 2 vols., trans. C. E. Luard and H. Hosten (Oxford).

Manucci, N. (1990), *Mogul India (1653–1708) or Storia do Mogor*, trans. W. Irvine, 4 vols. (Delhi).

Manz, B. F. (2002), 'Tamerlane's Career and its Uses', *Journal of World History*, 13, no. 1, pp. 1–25.

Manzalaoui, M. (1974), 'The Pseudo-Aristotelian *Kitāb sirr al-asrār:* Facts and Problems', *Oriens*, 23–24, pp. 147–257.

Markus, R. A. (1997), *Gregory the Great and his World* (Cambridge).

Maróth, M. (ed.) (2006), *The Correspondence between Aristotle and Alexander the Great: An Anonymous Greek Novel in Letters in Arabic Translation* (Pilisc-saba) [Introduction printed separately under the same title in *Acta Antiqua Academiae Scientiarum Hungaricae*, 45 (2005), pp. 231–315].

(2004), 'Literature in the Rising Ottoman Empire', in M. Maróth (ed.), *Problems in Arabic Literature* (Piliscsaba), pp. 103–21.

(2002), 'The Library of Sultan Bayazit II', in É. M. Jeremiás (ed.), *Irano-Turkic Cultural Contacts in the 11th–17th Centuries* (Piliscsaba), pp. 111–32.

Martin, A. (1989), 'La *Métaphysique.* Tradition syriaque et arabe', in Goulet, pp. 528–34.

Martin, V. (2000), *Creating an Islamic State: Khomeini and the Making of a New Iran* (London).

Martini Bonadeo, C. (2003), 'La *Métaphysique.* Tradition syriaque et arabe', in Goulet, pp. 259–64.

Martini Bonadeo, C. and Ferrari, C. (2005), 'Al-Fārābī', in D'Ancona, pp. 380–448.

Mathiesen, H. E. (1992), *Sculpture in the Parthian Empire: A Study in Chronology* (Aarhus).

Mattern, S. (1999), *Rome and the Enemy: Imperial Strategy in the Principate* (Berkeley and Los Angeles).

Matz, F. and von Duhn, F. (1881), *Antike Bildwerke in Rom mit Ausschluss der grösseren Sammlungen*, vol. III (Leipzig).

Mavrogiannis, T. (2003), *Aeneas und Euander: Mythische Vergangenheit und Politik im Rom vom 6. Jh. v. Chr. bis zur Zeit des Augustus* (Naples).

Maxim, M. (2001), 'The Ottoman Legacy in Romania', in Maxim, *Romano-Ottomanica: Essays and Documents from the Turkish Archives* (Istanbul), pp. 207–13.

McCormick, M. (1987), 'Byzantium's Role in the Formation of Early Medieval Civilization: Approaches and Problems', *Illinois Classical Studies*, 12, pp. 207–20.

(1986), *Eternal Victory: Triumphal Rulership in Late Antiquity, Byzantium, and the Early Medieval West* (Cambridge).

McEwan, I. K. (2003), *Vitruvius: Writing the Body of Architecture* (Cambridge, Mass.).

McKitterick, R. (2008), *Charlemagne: The Formation of a European Identity* (Cambridge).

(1989), *The Carolingians and the Written Word* (Cambridge).

McNeill, W. H. (1986), *Polyethnicity and National Unity in World History* (Toronto).

Mearsheimer, J. (2001), *The Tragedy of Great Power Politics* (New York).

Megow, W. R. (1987), *Kameen von Augustus bis Alexander Severus*, Antike Münzen und geschnittene Steine II (Berlin).

Meier, C. (1990), *The Greek Discovery of Politics* (Cambridge, Mass.).

Meier, H. (1994), *Die Lehre Carl Schmitts: Vier Kapitel zur Unterscheidung politischer Theologie und politischer Philosophie* (Stuttgart and Weimar).

Melikian-Chirvani, A. S. (1971), 'Le royaume de Salomon: les inscriptions persanes de sites achémenides', in *Le monde iranien et l'Islam*, vol. I (Paris), pp. 1–41.

Ménage, V. (1985), 'On the Constituent Elements of Certain Sixteenth-century Ottoman Documents', *Bulletin of the School of Oriental and African Studies*, 48, pp. 283–304.

Meneghini, R. (2009), *I Fori Imperiali e i Mercati di Traiano: storia e descrizione dei monumenti alla luce degli studi e degli scavi recenti* (Rome).

Meyendorff, J. (1981), *Byzantium and the Rise of Russia: A Study of Byzantino-Russian Relations in the Fourteenth Century* (Cambridge).

Meyer, H. (2000), *Prunkkameen und Staatsdenkmäler römischer Kaiser: Neue Perspektiven zur Kunst der frühen Prinzipatszeit* (Munich).

Mielsch, H. (2001), *Römische Wandmalerei* (Darmstadt).

Miklosich, F. and Müller, J. (eds.) (1865), *Acta et diplomata graeca medii aevi sacra et profana*, vol. III: *Acta et diplomata graeca res graecas italasque illustrantia* (Vienna).

Millar, F. (2006), *A Greek Roman Empire: Power and Belief under Theodosius II (408–450)* (Berkeley and Los Angeles).

Miller, F. D. (1995), *Nature, Justice, and Rights in Aristotle's Politics* (Oxford).

Miller, M. C. (1997), *Athens and Persia in the Fifth Century BC: A Study in Cultural Receptivity* (Cambridge).

Milner, B. (1988), 'Hobbes: On Religion', *Political Theory*, 16, no. 3, pp. 400–25.

Min, Dŏkgi (1998), 'Chosŏn sidae kyorin ŭi rinyŏn gwa gukje sahŭi ŭi gyorin' [The concept of 'kyorin' in the Chosŏn period and international social relations with neighbours], *Minjok munhwa*, 21, pp. 28–55.

Minorsky, V. (1940), 'A Civil and Military Review in Fārs in 881/1476', *Bulletin of the School of Oriental and African Studies*, 10, pp. 141–78.

Mitchell, C. P. (2009), *The Practice of Politics in Safavid Iran: Power, Religion and Rhetoric* (London).

Mitchell, W. J. T. (1986), *Iconology: Image, Text, Ideology* (Chicago).

Moin, B. (1999), *Khomeini: Life of the Ayatollah* (London).

Molina, A. de (2001), *Vocabulario en lengua Castellana y Mexicana y Mexicana y Castellana* (Mexico City).

Momigliano, A. (1971), *Alien Wisdom: The Limits of Hellenization* (Cambridge).

Monfasani, J. (1976), *George of Trebizond: A Biography and a Study of his Rhetoric and Logic* (Leiden).

Monserrate, A. (1993), *The Commentary of Father Monserrate, S.J., on his Journey to the Court of Akbar*, trans. J. S. Hoyland, annotated by S. N. Banerjee (Jalandhar) [reprint, originally published in 1922; Latin text published in *Mongolicae Legationis Commentarius or The First Jesuit Mission to Akbar*, ed.

H. Hosten, Memoirs of the Asiatic Society of Bengal III, no. 9 (Calcutta, 1914), pp. 513–704].

Mookerjee, G. K. (1973), *Diplomacy: Theory and History* (New Delhi).

Moravcsik, G. (ed.) (1967), Constantine Porphyrogenitus, *De Administrando Imperio* (Washington).

Mørkholm, O. (1991), *Early Hellenistic Coinage: From the Accession of Alexander to the Peace of Apamea (336–186 B.C.)* (Cambridge).

Morris, I. and Scheidel, W. (2009), *The Dynamics of Ancient Empires: State Power from Assyria to Byzantium*, Oxford Studies in Early Empires (New York).

Morrison, K. D. (2001), 'Coercion, Resistance and Hierarchy: Local Processes and Imperial Strategies in the Vijayanagara Empire', in Alcock *et al.*, pp. 252–78.

Moseley, C. W. R. D. (trans.) (1983), *The Travels of Sir John Mandeville* (Harmondsworth).

Motolinía, T. [de Benavente] (1970), *Memoriales e historia de los Indios de la Nueva España*, Biblioteca de autores españoles 240 (Madrid).

Mueller, K. (2006), *Settlements of the Ptolemies: City Foundations and New Settlement in the Hellenistic World*, Studia Hellenistica 43 (Leuven).

Muldoon, J. (1999), *Empire and Order: The Concept of Empire, 800–1800* (Basingstoke).

Murphey, R. (2009), 'Ottoman Imperial Identity in the Post-foundation Era: Coming to Terms with the Multiculturalism Associated with the Empire's Growth and Expansion, 1450–1650', *Archivum Ottomanicum*, 26, pp. 83–108.

Murphy, M. C. (1995), 'Was Hobbes a Legal Positivist?', *Ethics*, 105, no. 4, pp. 846–73.

Murray, A. (1978), *Reason and Society in the Middle Ages* (Oxford).

Murray, O. (1996), 'Hellenistic Royal Symposia', in Bilde *et al.*, pp. 15–27.

Mutschler, F.-H. and Mittag, A. (2008), *Conceiving the Empire: China and Rome Compared* (Oxford).

Načev, V. and Fermandžiev, N. (eds.) (1984), *Pisaxme da se znae: pripiski i letopisi* (Sofia).

Nagel, T. (1978), *Alexander der Grosse in der frühislamischen Volksliteratur* (Walldorf-Hessen).

Narayana Rao, V. and Shulman, D. (2002), *Classical Telugu Poetry: An Anthology* (Delhi).

Narayana Rao, V., Shulman, D. and Subrahmanyam, S. (2004), 'A New Imperial Idiom in the Sixteenth Century: Krishnadeva Raya and his Political Theory of Vijayanagara', in J.-L. Chevillard and E. Wilden (eds.), *South Indian Horizons: Felicitation Volume for François Gros on the Occasion of his 70th Birthday* (Pondicherry), pp. 597–625.

(2001), *Textures of Time: Writing History in South India, 1600–1800* (New Delhi).

(1992), *Symbols of Substance: Court and State in Nayaka-period Tamilnadu* (Delhi).

Nava'i, 'A. (ed.) (1974), *Shāh 'Abbās: Majmu'a-yi asnād va mukātabāt-i tārīkhī*, 3 vols. (Teheran).

Necipoğlu, G. (1993), 'Framing the Gaze in Ottoman, Safavid, and Mughal Palaces', in Necipoğlu (ed.), *Pre-modern Islamic Palaces = Ars Orientalis*, 23 (special issue), pp. 303–42.

(1989), 'Süleyman the Magnificent and the Representation of Power in the Context of Ottoman–Hapsburg–Papal Rivalry', *Art Bulletin*, 71, pp. 401–27.

Nedergaard, E. (1988), 'The Four Sons of Phraates IV in Rome', in T. Fischer-Hansen (ed.), *East and West: Cultural Relations in the Ancient World*, Danish Studies in Classical Archaeology: Acta Hyperborea 1 (Copenhagen), pp. 102–15.

Nederman C. J. (2005), 'Empire and the Historiography of European Political Thought: Marsiglio of Padua, Nicholas of Cusa, and the Medieval/Modern Divide', *Journal of the History of Ideas*, 66, no. 1, pp. 1–15.

(1988), 'Nature, Sin and the Origins of Society: The Ciceronian Tradition in Medieval Political Thought', *Journal of the History of Ideas*, 49, no. 1, pp. 3–26.

Nelson, J. L. (2001), 'Aachen', in M. de Jong and F. Theuws, with C. van Rhijn (eds.), *Topographies of Power in the Early Middle Ages*, Transformation of the Roman World 6 (Leiden), pp. 217–41.

(1988), 'Kingship and Empire', in J. H. Burns (ed.), *The Cambridge History of Medieval Political Thought, c. 350–c. 1450* (Cambridge), pp. 211–51.

(1986a), 'National Synods, Kingship as Office, and Royal Anointing: An Early Medieval Syndrome', in Nelson, *Politics and Ritual in Early Medieval Europe* (London), pp. 239–57.

(1986b), 'Symbols in Context: Rulers' Inauguration in Byzantium and the West in the Early Middle Ages', in Nelson, *Politics and Ritual in Early Medieval Europe* (London), pp. 259–82.

Netton, I. R. (1997), 'Siyāsa', in *The Encyclopaedia of Islam*, 2nd edn, vol. IX (Leiden and London), pp. 693–4.

Neudecker, R. (1988), *Die Skulpturenausstattung römischer Villen in Italien*, Beiträge zur Erschließung hellenistischer und kaiserzeitlicher Skulptur und Architektur 9 (Mainz).

Nicol, D. M. (1976), '*Kaisersalbung*: The Unction of Emperors in Late Byzantine Coronation Ritual', *Byzantine and Modern Greek Studies*, 2, pp. 37–52.

Nicolet, J. (1991), *Space, Geography, and Politics in the Early Roman Empire* (Ann Arbor).

Nicolet, J. and Tardieu, M. (1980), 'Pletho arabicus: identification et contenu du manuscrit arabe d'Istanbul, *Topkapi Serāi, Ahmet III 1896*', *Journal Asiatique*, 268, pp. 35–57.

Nicolson, H. (1969), *Diplomacy*, 3rd edn (London).

Niehoff-Panagiotidis, J. (2003), *Übersetzung und Rezeption: Die byzantinisch-neugriechischen und spanischen Adaptionen von Kalīla wa-Dimna* (Wiesbaden).

Nizām al-Mulk (1891–3), *Siyāsatnāma*, ed. and French trans. C. Schefer [under the title *Siasset namèh: Traité de gouvernement*] (Paris).

Noble, T. (1995), 'The Papacy in the Eighth and Ninth Centuries', in R. McKitterick (ed.), *The New Cambridge Medieval History*, vol. II: *c.700–c.900* (Cambridge), pp. 563–86.

Norden, E. (1924), *Die Geburt des Kindes: Geschichte einer religiösen Idee*, Studien der Bibliothek Warburg 3 (Leipzig and Berlin).

(1916), *P. Vergilius Maro Aeneis Buch VI, erklärt von*, 2nd edn (Leipzig).

Noreña, C. (2001), 'The Public Communication of the Emperor's Virtues', *Journal of Roman Studies*, 91, pp. 146–68.

Nouvel-Kammerer, O. (2007), *Symbols of Power: Napoleon and the Art of the Empire Style, 1800–1815* (New York).

Novák, M. (2002), 'The Artificial Paradise: Programme and Ideology of Royal Gardens', in S. Parpola and R. M. Whiting (eds.), *Sex and Gender in the Ancient Near East* (Helsinki), pp. 443–60.

Noy, D. (2000), *Foreigners at Rome: Citizens and Strangers* (London).

Oates, J. and Oates, D. (2001), *Nimrud: An Assyrian Imperial City Revealed* (London).

Oberländer-Târnoveanu, E. (2005), 'Notes on the Beginnings of the Bulgarian Medieval Coinage', in *The Bulgarian Lands in the Middle Ages, 7th–18th Centuries. International Conference: A Tribute to the 70th Anniversary of Prof. Alexander Kuzev. Varna, 12–14 September*, Acta Musei Varnaensis III.1 (Varna), pp. 183–214.

Obolensky, D. (1971), *The Byzantine Commonwealth: Eastern Europe, 500–1453* (London).

Offler, H. S. (1965), 'Aspects of Government in the Late Medieval Empire', in J. R. Hale, J. R. L. Highfield and B. Smalley (eds.), *Europe in the Late Middle Ages* (London), pp. 217–47.

Okada, A. (1992), *Indian Miniatures of the Mughal Court*, trans. D. Dusinberre (New York).

Olivelle, P. (2012), 'Aśoka's Inscriptions as Text and Ideology', in Olivelle (ed.), *Reimagining Aśoka: Memory and History* (Oxford).

Olivier, G. (2002), 'Hidden King and the Broken Flutes: Mythical and Royal Dimensions of the Feast of Tezcatlipoca in Toxcatl', in E. Quiñones Keber (ed.), *Representing Aztec Ritual: Performance, Text, and Image in the Work of Sahagún* (Boulder), pp. 107–42.

Olko, J. (2006), '¿Imitación, patrimonio pan-regional o distorsión colonial? Influencia mexica en manuscritos pictográficos del centro de México', *Revista Española de Antropología Americana*, 36, pp. 139–74.

(2005), *Turquoise Diadems and Staffs of Office: Elite Costume and Insignia of Power in the Aztec and Early Colonial Mexico* (Warsaw).

(2004), 'Los mensajeros reales y negociaciones de la paz. En concepto de la guerra justa entre los aztecas', *Revista Española de Antropología Americana*, 34, pp. 125–48.

Olmstead, A. T. (1918), 'The Calculated Frightfulness of Ashur Nasir Apal', *Journal of the American Oriental Society*, 38, pp. 209–63.

O'Meara, D. (2003), *Platonopolis: Platonic Political Philosophy in Late Antiquity* (Oxford).

Onuf, N. (1998), *The Republican Heritage in International Thought* (Cambridge). (1989), *World of Our Making* (Princeton).

Oppenheim, A. L. (1960), 'The City of Assur in 714 B.C.', *Journal of Near Eastern Studies*, 19, pp. 133–47.

Osiander, A. (2001a), 'Before Sovereignty: Society and Politics in Ancien Régime Europe', *Review of International Studies*, 27, pp. 119–45.

(2001b), 'Sovereignty, International Relations, and the Westphalian Myth', *International Organization*, 55, no. 2, pp. 251–87.

(1994), *The States System of Europe, 1640–1990: Peacemaking and the Conditions of International Stability* (Oxford).

Östenberg, I. (2003), *Staging the World: Rome and the Other in the Triumphal Procession* (Lund).

Ostrogorsky, G. (1956–7), 'The Byzantine Emperor and the Hierarchical World Order', *Slavonic and East European Review*, 35, pp. 1–14.

(1955), 'Zur Kaisersalbung und Schilderhebung im spätbyzantinischen Krönungszeremoniell', *Historia: Zeitschrift für Alte Geschichte*, 4, pp. 246–56.

Pagden, A. (2001), *Peoples and Empires: A Short History of European Migration, Exploration, and Conquest, from Greece to the Present* (New York).

(1995), *Lords of All the World: Ideologies of Empire in Spain, Britain and France c.1500–c.1800* (New Haven).

(1990), *Spanish Imperialism and the Political Imagination* (New Haven).

Pal, P., Leoshko, J. Dye III, J. M. and Markel, S. (1989), *Romance of the Taj Mahal*, exhibition catalogue (Los Angeles and London).

Palaver, W. (1998), *Die mythischen Quellen des Politischen: Carl Schmitts Freind-Feind-Theorie*, Beiträge zur Friedensethik 27 (Stuttgart, Berlin and Cologne).

Pamuk, Ş. (2004), *Monetary History of the Ottoman Empire* (Cambridge).

Pani, M. (1975), 'Troia resurgens: mito troiano e ideologia del principato', *Annali della Facoltà di Lettere e Filosofia, Università degli Studi, Bari*, 18, pp. 63–85.

Papamastorakis, T. (2005), 'Orb of the Earth. Images of Imperial Universality', in E. Chrysos (ed.), *Byzantium as Oecumene* (Athens), pp. 79–105.

Parker, B. J. (2001), *The Mechanics of Empire: The Northern Frontier of Assyria as a Case Study in Imperial Dynamics* (Helsinki).

Parker, G. (2008), *The Making of Roman India* (Cambridge).

Parpola, S. (2003), 'International Law in the First Millennium', in Westbrook, pp. 1047–66.

Parpola, S. and Watanabe, K. (1988), *Neo-Assyrian Treaties and Loyalty Oaths*, State Archives of Assyria 2 (Helsinki).

Parpola, S. and Whiting, R. M. (eds.) (1997), *ASSYRIA 1995: Proceedings of the 10th Anniversary Symposium of the Neo-Assyrian Text Corpus Project, Helsinki, September 7–11, 1995* (Helsinki).

Parsons, T. (1968), *The Structure of Social Action* (Glencoe) [originally published in 1937].

Patroni, G. (1898), 'Sperlonga. Costruzioni appartenenti ad una villa romana e sculture marmoree scoperte presso la grotta di Tiberio', *Notizie degli Scavi di Antichità*, p. 493.

Pearson, M. N. (ed.) (1985), *Legitimacy and Symbols: The South Asian Writings of F. W. Buckler* (Ann Arbor).

(1976), 'Shivaji and the Decline of the Mughal Empire', *Journal of Asian Studies*, 35, no. 2, pp. 221–35.

Pedani Fabris, M. (1998), 'Ottoman *Fetihname*s: The Imperial Letters Announcing a Victory', *Tarih İncelemeleri Dergisi*, 13, pp. 183–92.

(1994), *I 'Documenti turchi' dell'Archivio di Stato di Venezia. Inventario... con l'edizione dei regesti di Alessio Bombaci* (Venice).

Peddanna, A. (1966), *Manucaritramu* (Hyderabad).

Pellegrin, P. (2003), 'Les politiques', in Goulet, pp. 199–202.

Pensabene, P. (2004), 'Das Heiligtum der Kybele und die Untergeschoßbauten im Südwesten des Palatin', in A. Hoffmann and U. Wulf (eds.), *Die Kaiserpaläste auf dem Palatin in Rom: Das Zentrum der römischen Welt und seine Bauten* (Mainz), pp. 18–31.

(1996), 'Magna Mater, Aedes', in M. Steinby (ed.), *Lexicon Topographicum Urbis Romae*, vol. iii: *H–O* (Rome), pp. 206–8.

Perdue, P. C. (2005), *China Marches West: The Qing Conquest of Central Eurasia* (Cambridge, Mass.).

Pérez-Díaz, V. M. (1993), *The Return of Civil Society: The Emergence of Democratic Spain* (Cambridge, Mass.).

Pfeiffer, R. (1968), *History of Classical Scholarship: From the Beginnings to the End of the Hellenistic Age* (Oxford).

Plezia, M. (ed.) (1977), *Aristotelis privatorum scriptorum fragmenta* (Leipzig).

Podskalsky, G. (1972), *Byzantinische Reichseschatologie: Die Periodisierung der Weltgeschichte in den vier Grossreichen (Daniel 2 und 7) und dem tausendjährigen Friedensreiche (Apok. 20). Eine motivgeschichtliche Untersuchung* (Munich).

Poggi, G. (1978), *The Development of the Modern State: A Sociological Introduction* (Stanford).

Pollini, J. (2004), 'The Caelian Hill Ministrant: A Marble Head of an Imperial Slave-boy from the Antiquarium Comunale on the Caelian Hill in Rome. With an Appendix on the Pseudo-Otho', *Mitteilungen des Deutschen Archäologischen Instituts, Römische Abteilung*, 111, pp. 513–36.

(2002), 'Frieden-durch-Sieg-Ideologie und die Ara Pacis Augustae: Bildrhetorik und die Schöpfung einer dynastischen Erzählweise', in *Krieg und Sieg: Narrative Wanddarstellungen von Altägypten bis ins Mittelalter*, Internationales Kolloquium im Schloss Haindorf bei Langenlois 29–30. Juli 1997 (Vienna), pp. 137–59.

Pollock, S. (2006), *The Language of the Gods in the World of Men: Sanskrit, Culture, and Power in Premodern India* (Berkeley and Los Angeles).

(2005), 'Axialism and Empire', in J. P. Árnason, S. N. Eisenstadt and B. Wittrock (eds.), *Axial Civilizations and World History* (Leiden), pp. 397–450.

(ed.) (2003), *Literary Cultures in History: Reconstructions from South Asia* (Berkeley and Los Angeles).

(1996), 'The Sanskrit Cosmopolis, 300–1300: Transculturation, Vernacularization, and the Question of Ideology', in J. E. M. Houben (ed.), *Ideology and Status of Sanskrit: Contributions to the History of the Sanskrit Language* (Leiden), pp. 197–247.

Pomar, J. B. de (2000), 'Relación de Juan Bautista de Pomar (Tetzcoco, 1582)', in Á. M. Garibay Kintana (ed.), *Poesía Náhuatl*, vol. 1: *Romances de los Señores de la Nueva España* (Mexico City), pp. 149–219.

Popescu Vornicul, R. (1963), *Istoriile domnilor Țării Romînești*, ed. C. Grecescu (Bucharest).

Poulsen, B. and Netterstrøm, J. B. (eds.) (2007), *Feud in Medieval and Early Modern Europe* (Aarhus).

Price, S. (2003), 'Homogénéité et diversité dans les religions à Rome', *Archiv für Religionsgeschichte*, 5, pp. 180–97.

(1987), 'From Noble Funerals to Divine Cult: The Consecration of Roman Emperors', in Cannadine and Price, pp. 56–105.

Prinsep, J. (1838), 'Discovery of the Name of Antiochus the Great, in Two of the Edicts of Asoka, King of India', *Journal of the Asiatic Society of Bengal*, 7, pp. 156–67.

(1837a), 'II. – Note on the Facsimiles of Inscriptions from Sanchi near Bhilsa, Taken for the Society by Captain Ed. Smith, Engineers; and on the Drawings of the Buddhist Monument Presented by Captain W. Murray, at the Meeting of the 7th June', *Journal of the Asiatic Society of Bengal*, 6, pp. 451–77.

(1837b), 'VI. – Interpretation of the Most Ancient of the Inscriptions on the Pillar Called the Lát of Feroz Sháh, near Delhi, and of the Allahabad Radhia and Matthiah Pillar, or Lát, Inscriptions which Agree Therewith.', *Journal of the Asiatic Society of Bengal*, 6, pp. 566–609.

Pritsak, O. (1967), 'Moscow, the Golden Horde, and the Kazan Khanate from a Polycultural Point of View', *Slavic Review*, 26, pp. 577–83.

Pugliesi Carratelli, G. (1997), *Pompei: pitture e mosaici 7 Regio VII, 2. Enciclopedia dell'arte antica classica e orientale* (Rome).

Pugliese Carratelli, G. and Garbini, G. (1964), *A Bilingual Graeco-Aramaic Edict by Aśoka: The First Greek Inscription Discovered in Afghanistan*, Serie Orientale Roma 29 (Rome).

Purcell, N. (1995), 'Forum Romanum', in M. Steinby (ed.), *Lexicon Topographicum Urbis Romae*, vol. II: *D–G* (Rome), pp. 325–36.

Raby, J. (1983), 'Mehmed the Conqueror's Greek Scriptorium', *Dumbarton Oaks Papers*, 37, pp. 15–34.

Raby, J. and Tanindi, Z. (ed. Stanley, T.) (1993), *Turkish Bookbinding in the 15th Century: The Foundation of an Ottoman Court Style* (London).

Radner, K. (2003), 'Neo-Assyrian Period', in Westbrook, pp. 883–910.

Raeck, W. (1981), *Zum Barbarenbild in der Kunst Athens im 6. und 5. Jahrhundert v. Chr.*, Habelts Dissertationsdrucke, Reihe klassische Archäologie, 14 (Bonn).

Ramaswamy, S. (2007), 'Conceit of the Globe in Mughal Visual Practice', *Comparative Studies in Society and History*, 49, pp. 751–82.

Randelzhofer, A. (1967), *Völkerrechtliche Aspekte des Heiligen Römischen Reiches nach 1648* (Berlin).

Rapp, C. (2005), *Holy Bishops in Late Antiquity* (Berkeley).

Raven, W. (2003), '*De mundo*. Tradition syriaque et arabe', in Goulet, pp. 481–3.

Rawski, E. S. (1998), *The Last Emperors: A Social History of Qing Imperial Institutions* (Berkeley).

Ray, H. P. (2007), 'Alexander's Campaign (327–326 BC): A Chronological Marker in the Archaeology of India', in Ray and Potts, pp. 105–21.

Ray, H. P. and Potts, D. T. (eds.) (2007), *Memory as History: The Legacy of Alexander in Asia* (Delhi).

Redford, S. (2004), 'Byzantium and the Islamic World', in H. Evans (ed.), *Byzantium: Faith and Power (1261–1557)* (New York), pp. 385–413.

Reeves, M. (1961), 'Joachimist Influences on the Idea of a Last World Emperor', *Traditio*, 17, pp. 323–70.

Rehatsek, E. (1887), 'A Letter of the Emperor Akbar Asking for the Christian Scriptures', *The Indian Antiquary*, 16, pp. 135–9.

Reinhold, M. (1970), *History of Purple as a Status Symbol in Antiquity* (Brussels).

Reinink, G. J. (2002), 'Heraclius, the New Alexander: Apocalyptic Prophecies during the Reign of Heraclius', in G. J. Reinink and B. H. Stolte (eds.), *The Reign of Heraclius (610–641): Crisis and Confrontation* (Leuven), pp. 81–94.

Reischauer, E. and Fairbank, J. K. (1958), *East Asia: The Great Tradition* (Boston).

Reiske, J. J. (ed.) (1829), Constantine Porphyrogenitus, *De cerimoniis aulae byzantinae, libri duo* (Bonn).

Reus-Smit, C. (1999), *The Moral Purpose of the State: Culture, Social Identity and Institutional Rationality in International Relations* (Princeton).

Reuter, T. (1991), *Germany in the Early Middle Ages, c. 800–1056* (London and New York).

Rice, E. E. (1983), *The Grand Procession of Ptolemy Philadelphus* (Oxford).

Rich, J. W. (1998), 'Augustus's Parthian Honours, the Temple of Mars Ultor, and the Arch in the Forum Romanum', *Papers of the British School at Rome*, 66, pp. 71–128.

Richards, J. F. (1978), 'The Formulation of Imperial Authority under Akbar and Jahangir', in Richards (ed.), *Kingship and Authority in South Asia* (Madison), pp. 252–85.

Riedel, Manfred (1979a), 'Gesellschaft, bürgerliche', in Brunner, Conze and Koselleck, pp. 719–800.

(1979b), 'Gesellschaft, Gemeinschaft', in Brunner, Conze and Koselleck, pp. 801–62.

Rivière, Y. (2006), 'Pouvoir impérial et vengeance: de Mars Ultor à la diuina uindicta (1er–1ve siècle ap. J.-C.)', in *La vengeance: 400–1200*, Actes du Colloque La vengeance: 400–1200 réuni á Rome les 18, 19 et 20 septembre 2003, Collection de l'École française de Rome 357 (Rome), pp. 7–42.

Rizvi, S. A. A. (1975), *Religious and Intellectual History of the Muslims in Akbar's Reign, with Special Reference to Abu'l Fazl (1556–1605)* (New Delhi).

  (1964), *Muslim Revivalist Movements in Northern India in the Sixteenth and Seventeenth Centuries* (Agra).

Robert, L. (1968), 'De Delphes à l'Oxus, inscriptions grecques nouvelles de la Bactriane', *Comptes-rendus des Séances de l'Académie des Inscriptions et Belles-Lettres*, 112e année, no. 3, pp. 416–57.

Roberts, F. S. (1897), *Forty-One Years in India: From Subaltern to Commander-in-Chief* (London).

Robinson, K. R. (2000), 'Centering the King of Chosŏn: Aspects of Korean Maritime Diplomacy, 1392–1592', *Journal of Asian Studies*, 59, no. 1, pp. 109–25.

Rogers, M. (2009), 'Mehmet II. und die Naturwissenschaften', in N. Asutay-Effenberger and U. Rehm (eds), *Sultan Mehmed II. Eroberer Konstantinopels – Patron der Künste* (Cologne), pp. 77–92.

Roller, L. E. (1999), *In Search of God the Mother: The Cult of Anatolian Cybele* (Berkeley).

  (1998), 'The Ideology of the Eunuch Priest', in M. Wyke (ed.), *Gender and the Body in the Ancient Mediterranean* (Oxford), pp. 118–35.

Roller, M. B. (2001), *Constructing Autocracy: Aristocrats and Emperors in Julio-Claudian Rome* (Princeton).

Root, M. C. (1979), *The King and Kingship in Achaemenid Art: Essays on the Creation of an Iconography of Empire*, Acta Iranica, textes et mémoires 9 (Leiden).

Rose, C. B. (2008), 'Forging Identity in the Roman Republic: Trojan Ancestry and Veristic Portraiture', in I. Lyse Hansen and S. Bell (eds.), *Role Models in the Roman World: Identity and Assimilation*, Memoirs of the American Academy in Rome, Supplementary Volume 7 (Ann Arbor), pp. 97–131.

  (2005), 'The Parthians in Augustan Rome', *American Journal of Archaeology*, 109, pp. 21–75.

  (2002a), 'Bilingual Trojan Iconography', in *Mauerschau: Festschrift für Manfred Korfmann*, vol. 1 (Remshalden-Grunbach), pp. 329–50.

  (2002b), 'Ilion in the Early Empire', in C. Berns *et al.* (eds.), *Patris und Imperium: Kulturelle und politische Identität in den Städten der römischen Provinzen Kleinasiens in der frühen Kaiserzeit, Kolloquium Köln, November 1998*, Bulletin antieke beschaving, Supplement 8 (Leuven), pp. 33–47.

  (1990), '"Princes" and Barbarians on the Ara Pacis', *American Journal of Archaeology*, 94, pp. 453–67.

Rosenthal, E. (1971), 'Plus Ultra, Non Plus Ultra, and the Columnar Device of Emperor Charles V', *Journal of the Warburg and Courtauld Institutes*, 34, pp. 204–28.

Rossini, O. (2006), *Ara Pacis* (Milan).
Roth, R. (2007), *Styling Romanisation: Pottery and Society in Central Italy* (Cambridge).
Rozen, M. (2002), *A History of the Jewish Community in Istanbul: The Formative Years, 1453–1566* (Leiden).
Ryholt, K. (forthcoming) 'Libraries in Ancient Egypt', in J. König, K. Oikonomopolou and G. Woolf (eds.), *Ancient Libraries* (Cambridge).
Sahlins, M. (1988), 'Cosmologies of Capitalism: The Trans-Pacific Sector of "The World System"', *Proceedings of the British Academy*, 74, pp. 1–51.
Said, E. (1978), *Orientalism* (London).
Saletore, B. A. (1934), *Social and Political Life in the Vijayanagara Empire (A.D. 1346–A.D. 1646)*, 2 vols. (Madras).
Sancisi-Weerdenburg, H. (1993), 'Persian Food: Stereotypes and Political Identity', in J. Wilkins, D. Harvey and M. Dobson (eds.), *Food in Antiquity* (Exeter), pp. 286–302.
Sande, S. (1985), 'Römische Frauenporträts mit Mauerkrone', *Acta ad Archaeologiam et Artium Historiam Pertinentina, Series Altera*, 5, pp. 151–245.
Sardar, Z. (1999), *Orientalism* (Buckingham).
Sawyer, C. (1996), 'Sword of Conquest, Dove of the Soul: Political and Spiritual Values in Aḥmadī's *Iskandarnāma*', in Bridges and Bürgel, pp. 135–47.
Schaendlinger, A. (1983), *Die Schreiben Süleymans des Prächtigen an Karl V., Ferdinand I. und Maximilian II. aus dem Haus-, Hof- und Staatsarchiv zu Wien*, 2 pts (Vienna).
Scheer, T. (1997), 'Darnaidai', in *Der Neue Pauly*, vol. iii (Stuttgart and Weimar), pp. 318–19.
Scheidel, W. (2009), *Rome and China: Comparative Perspectives on Ancient World Empires* (New York).
Schimmel, A. (1993), 'Mughals 6. Religious Life', in *The Encyclopaedia of Islam*, 2nd edn, vol. vii (Leiden and London), pp. 327–8.
Schlumberger, D. (1964), 'Une nouvelle inscription grecque d'Açoka', *Comptesrendus des Séances de l'Académie des Inscriptions et Belles-Lettres*, 108e année, no. 1, pp. 126–40.
Schlumberger, D. *et al.* (1958), 'Une bilingue gréco-araméenne d'Asoka', *Journal Asiatique*, 246, pp. 1–48.
Schmitt, C. (1938), *Der Begriff des Politischen* (Hamburg).
Schmitz, T. (1997), *Bildung und Macht: Zur sozialen und politischen Funktion der zweiten Sophistik in der griechischen Welt der Kaiserzeit* (Munich).
Schneider, R. M. (2007), 'Friend and Foe. The Orient in Rome', in V. Sarkhosh and S. Stewart (eds.), *The Age of the Parthians*, The Idea of Iran Series 2 (London), pp. 50–86.
(2006), 'Orientalism in Late Antiquity: The Oriental in Imperial and Christian Imagery', in Wiesehöfer and Huyse, pp. 241–78.
(2004), 'Nicht mehr Ägypten, sondern Rom. Der neue Lebensraum der Obelisken', *Städel Jahrbuch*, 19 (new series), pp. 155–79.

(2002), 'Nuove immagini del potere romano: sculture in marmo colorato nell'impero romano', in M. De Nuccio and L. Ungaro (eds.), *I marmi colorati della Roma imperiale: Roma, Mercati di Traiano, 28 settembre 2002 – 19 gennaio 2003* (Venice), pp. 82–105.

(2001), 'Coloured Marble: The Splendour and Power of Imperial Rome', *Apollo: The International Magazine of the Arts*, July, pp. 3–10.

(1999), 'Marmor', in *Der Neue Pauly*, vol. VII (Stuttgart and Weimar), pp. 928–38.

(1998), 'Die Faszination des Feindes: Bilder der Parther und des Orients in Rom', in J. Wiesehöfer (ed.), *Das Partherreich und seine Zeugnisse: Beiträge des internationalen Colloquiums, Eutin 27.–30. Juni 1996*, Historia – Einzelschriften 122 (Stuttgart), pp. 95–146.

(1997), 'Roma Aeterna – Aurea Roma: Der Himmelsglobus als Zeitzeichen und Machtsymbol', in J. Assmann and E. W. B. Hess-Lüttich (eds.), *Kult, Kalender und Geschichte: Semiotisierung von Zeit als kulturelle Konstruktion = Kodikas/Code. Ars Semeiotica. An International Journal of Semiotics*, 20, nos. 1–2 (special issue), pp. 103–33.

(1992a), 'Barbar II (ikonographisch)', in *Reallexikon für Antike und Christentum*, Supplement 1 (Stuttgart), pp. 895–962.

(1992b), 'Orientalische Tischdiener als römische Tischfüsse', *Archäologischer Anzeiger*, pp. 295–305.

(1986), *Bunte Barbaren: Orientalenstatuen aus farbigem Marmor in der römischen Repräsentationskunst* (Worms).

Schofield, M. (1991), *The Stoic Idea of the City* (Chicago).

Scholz, U. W. (1970), *Studien zum altitalischen und altrömischen Marskult und Marsmythos*, Bibliothek der klassischen Altertumswissenschaften, Neue Folge 2, Reihe 35 (Heidelberg).

Schopen, L. (ed.) (1829–55), *Nicephori Gregorae Byzantina historia*, 3 vols. (Bonn).

Schramm, P. E. (1968–71), *Kaiser, Könige und Päpste: gesammelte Aufsätze*, 4 vols. (Stuttgart).

(1958), *Sphaira, Globus, Reichsapfel: Wanderung und Wandlung eines Herrschaftszeichens von Caesar bis zu Elisabeth II. Ein Beitrag zum 'Nachleben' der Antike* (Stuttgart).

Schroeder, P. (1994), *The Transformation of European Politics 1763–1848* (Oxford).

Schubert, E. (1996), *Fürstliche Herrschaft und Territorium im späten Mittelalter* (Munich).

(1977), 'Königswahl und Königtum im spätmittelalterlichen Reich', *Zeitschrift für Historische Forschung*, 4, pp. 257–338.

Schwarzenberg, E. (2001/2), 'Ganymède', *Hephaistos: Kritische Zeitschrift zu Theorie und Praxis der Archäologie und Angrenzender Gebiete*, 19–20, pp. 159–201.

Scullard, H. H. (1974), *The Elephant in the Greek and Roman World* (Ithaca, NY).

Seaman, J. W. (1999), 'Hobbes and the Liberalization of Christianity', *Canadian Journal of Political Science/Revue Canadienne de Science Politique*, 32, no. 2, pp. 227–46.

Searle, J. R. (1969), *Speech Acts: An Essay in the Philosophy of Language* (Cambridge).

Seiterle, G. (1985), 'Die Urform der phrygischen Mütze', *Antike Welt: Zeitschrift für Archäologie und Kulturgeschichte*, 16, no. 3, pp. 2–13.

Seneviratne, S. (1978), 'The Mauryan State', in H. J. M. Claessen and P. Skalnik (eds.), *The Early State* (The Hague), pp. 381–402.

Sewell, Robert (1972), *A Forgotten Empire (Vijayanagar): A Contribution to the History of India* (New York) [reprint].

Shaked, S. (1995), *From Zoroastrian Iran to Islam: Studies in Religious History and Intercultural Contacts* (Aldershot).

    (1984), 'From Iran to Islam: Notes on Some Themes in Transmission', *Jerusalem Studies in Arabic and Islam*, 4, pp. 31–67 [reprinted in Shaked 1995: VI].

Shaw, M. (2000), *Theory of the Global State: Globality as an Unfinished Revolution* (Cambridge).

Sherwin-White, A. N. (1973), *The Roman Citizenship*, rev. edn (Oxford) [1st edn 1939].

Sherwin-White, S. (1987), 'Seleucid Babylonia: A Case Study for the Installation and Development of Greek Rule', in Kuhrt and Sherwin-White, pp. 1–31.

Sherwin-White, S. and Kuhrt, A. (eds.) (1993), *From Samarkand to Sardis: A New Approach to the Seleucid Empire* (Berkeley).

Shiba, Y. (1977), 'Ningpo and its Hinterland', in G. W. Skinner (ed.), *The City in Late Imperial China* (Palo Alto), pp. 391–439.

Shichiji, Y. (ed.) (1991), 'Orientalismus, Exotismus, koloniale Diskurse', in E. Iwasaki (ed.), *Begegnung mit dem 'Fremden': Grenzen – Traditionen – Vergleiche, Akten des VIII. internationalen Germanisten-Kongresses, Tokyo 1990* (Munich), pp. 253–502.

Shipley, G. (2000), *The Greek World after Alexander, 323–30 BC* (London and New York).

Shmuelevitz, A. (1984), *The Jews of the Ottoman Empire in the Late Fifteenth and the Sixteenth Centuries: Administrative, Economic, Legal, and Social Relations as Reflected in the Responsa* (Leiden).

Shulman, D. (2001), *The Wisdom of Poets: Studies in Tamil, Telugu, and Sanskrit* (Delhi).

Sichtermann, H. (1988), 'Ganymedes', in *Lexicon Iconographicum Mythologiae Classicae*, vol. IV (Zurich and Munich), pp. 154–69.

Sick, D. H. (2007), 'When Socrates Met the Buddha: Greek and Indian Dialectic in Hellenistic Bactria and India', *Journal of the Royal Asiatic Society*, Series 3, 17, no. 3, pp. 253–78.

Sickel, W. (1905), 'Diadema', in *Paulys Realencyclopädie der classischen Altertumswissenschaft*, vol. V (Stuttgart), pp. 458–91.

[Sidi Ali Reis] (1975), *The Travels and Adventures of the Turkish Admiral Sidi Ali Reïs in India, Afghanistan, Central Asia, and Persia, during the Years 1553–1556*, trans. A. Vámbéry (Lahore).

Siebler, M. (1988), *Studien zum augusteischen Mars Ultor*, Münchener Arbeiten zur Kunstgeschichte und Archäologie 1 (Munich).

Silver, L. (2008), *Marketing Maximilian: The Visual Ideology of a Holy Roman Emperor* (Princeton).

Simon, E. (2001), 'Rom und Troia: Der Mythos von den Anfängen bis in die römische Kaiserzeit', in M. Korfmann (ed.), *Troia – Traum und Wirklichkeit: Begleitband zur Ausstellung, 17. März bis 17. Juni 2001, Archäologisches Landesmuseum Baden-Württemberg, Stuttgart* (Stuttgart), pp. 154–73.

(1990), *Die Götter der Römer* (Munich).

(1967), *Ara Pacis Augustae* (Tübingen).

Singana, M. (1970), *Sakala-nīti-sammatamu*, ed. N. Venkataravu and P. S. R. Apparao (Hyderabad).

Skelton, R. (1988), 'Imperial Symbolism in Mughal Painting', in P. Soucek (ed.), *Content and Context of Visual Arts in the Islamic World: Papers from a Colloquium in Memory of Richard Ettinghausen, Institute of Fine Arts, New York University, 2–4 April 1980* (University Park, Penn. and London), pp. 177–87.

Skilliter, S. (1971), 'The Hispano-Ottoman Armistice of 1581', in C. E. Bosworth (ed.), *Iran and Islam (in Memory of the late Vladimir Minorsky)* (Edinburgh), pp. 491–516.

Skinner, Q. (2002), *Visions of Politics*, vol. III: *Hobbes and Civil Science* (Cambridge).

Smith, M. E. (2008), *Aztec City-State Capitals* (Gainesville).

(2004), 'Los hogares de Morelos en el sistema mundial mesoamericano postclásico', *Relaciones. Estudios de Historia y Sociedad*, 25 (= no. 99), pp. 79–113.

(2001), 'The Aztec Empire and the Mesoamerican World System', in Alcock *et al.*, pp. 128–54.

(1997), *The Aztecs* (Malden, Mass.).

(1996), 'The Strategic Provinces', in Berdan *et al.*, pp. 137–50.

(1984), 'The Aztlan Migrations of Nahuatl Chronicles: Myth or History?', *Ethnohistory* 31, no. 3, pp. 153–86.

Smith, M. E. and Berdan, F. F. (1996a), 'Introduction', in Berdan *et al.*, pp. 1–9.

(1996b), 'Province Descriptions', in Berdan *et al.*, pp. 265–323.

Smith, M. E. and Montiel, L. M. (2001), 'The Archaeological Study of Empires and Imperialism in Prehispanic Central Mexico', *Journal of Anthropological Archaeology*, 20, pp. 245–84.

Smith, R. R. R. (2002), 'The Use of Images: Visual History and Ancient History', in T. P. Wiseman (ed.), *Classics in Progress: Essays on Ancient Greece and Rome*, British Academy Centenary Monographs (Oxford), pp. 59–102.

(1987), 'The Imperial Reliefs from the Sebasteion at Aphrodisias', *Journal of Roman Studies*, 77, pp. 88–138.

So, Kwan-wai (1975), *Japanese Piracy in Ming China during the 16th Century* (Dearborn, Mich.).

Sommer, M. (2005), *Roms Orientalische Steppengrenze* (Stuttgart).

Sonnabend, H. (1986), *Fremdenbild und Politik: Vorstellungen der Römer von Ägypten und dem Partherreich in der späten Republik und frühen Kaiserzeit* (Frankfurt, Berne and New York).

Soudavar, A. (2003), *The Aura of Kings: Legitimacy and Divine Sanction in Iranian Kingship* (Costa Mesa, Calif.).

Southern, R. W. (1970), *Western Society and the Church in the Middle Ages* (Harmondsworth).

Spagnolis, M. de' (1983), 'Sculture da Sperlonga e Formia nella Ny Carlsberg Glyptothek di Copenhagen', *Bollettino d'Arte*, 21, pp. 75–84.

Spannagel, M. (1999), *Exemplaria Principis: Untersuchungen zu Entstehung und Ausstattung des Augustusforums*, Archäologie und Geschichte 9 (Heidelberg).

Spawforth, A. (1994), 'Symbol of Unity? The Persian-Wars Tradition in the Roman Empire', in S. Hornblower (ed.), *Greek Historiography* (Oxford), pp. 233–69.

Speer, H. (1992–6), *Deutsches Rechtswörterbuch: Wörterbuch der älteren deutschen Rechtssprache*, vol. ix: *Mahlgericht bis Notrust* (Weimar).

Spengler, W. F. and Sayles, W. G. (1996), *Turkoman Figural Bronze Coins and their Iconography*, vol. ii: *The Zengids* (Lodi, Wis.).

Spivey, N. and Squire, M. (2004), *Panorama of the Classical World* (London).

Spufford, P. (1988), *Money and its Use in Medieval Europe* (Cambridge).

Squire, M. (2011), *The Iliad in a Nutshell: Visualizing Epic on the Tabulae Iliacae* (Oxford).

(2009), *Image and Text in Graeco-Roman Antiquity* (Cambridge).

Stambaugh, J. E. (1988), *The Ancient Roman City* (Baltimore).

Stanwick, P. E. (2002), *Portraits of the Ptolemies: Greek Kings as Egyptian Pharaohs* (Austin).

Stein, B. (1996), *A History of India* (Oxford).

(1989), *The New Cambridge History of India*, vol. 1.2: *Vijayanagara* (Cambridge).

(1980), *Peasant State and Society in Medieval South India* (Delhi).

Stephens, S. A. (2002), *Seeing Double: Intercultural Poetics in Ptolemaic Alexandria*, Hellenistic Culture and Society 37 (Berkeley).

Stevens, A. (1994), *Jung: A Very Short Introduction* (Oxford).

Stewart, A. (1993), *Faces of Power: Alexander's Image and Hellenistic Politics* (Berkeley and Los Angeles).

Stocking, G. W. Jr (1995), *After Tylor: British Social Anthropology, 1888–1951* (Madison).

Stojanović, L. (1934), *Stare srpske povelje i pisma*, BOOK I: *Dubrovnik i susedi njegovi*, pt 2 (Belgrade and Sremski Karlovci).

Stolleis, M. (1988), *Geschichte des öffentlichen Rechts in Deutschland*, vol. i: *Reichspublizistik und Policeywissenschaft 1600–1800* (Munich).

Stolper, M. W. (1984), *Texts from Tall-i Malyan*, vol. i: *Elamite Administrative Texts (1972–1974)*, Occasional Publications of the Babylonian Fund 6 (Philadelphia).

Strocka, V. M. (2007), 'Vergils *tibicenes*', *Gymnasium: Zeitschrift für Kultur der Antike und Humanistische Bildung*, 114, pp. 523–33.

Strong, J. S. (1983), *The Legend of King Aśoka: A Study and Translation of the Aśokāvadāa* (Princeton).

Strootman, R. (2011), 'Hellenistic Court Society: The Seleukid Imperial Court under Antiochos the Great, 223–187 BCE', in T. Artan, J. Duindam and M.

Kunt (eds.), *Royal Courts in Dynastic States and Empires: A Global Perspective* (Leiden), pp. 63–89.

(2010), 'Queen of Kings: Kleopatra VII and the Donations of Alexandria', in M. Facella and T. Kaizer (eds.), *Kingdoms and Principalities in the Roman Near East* (Stuttgart), pp. 139–57.

Struve, L. A. (ed.), *Time, Temporality, and Imperial Transition: East Asia from Ming to Qing* (Honolulu).

Subrahmanyam, S. (2009), 'The Fate of Empires: Rethinking Mughals, Ottomans and Habsburgs', in H. Islamoğlu and P. C. Perdue (eds.), *Shared Histories of Modernity: China, India and the Ottoman Empire* (New Delhi), pp. 74–108.

(2000), 'Sobre uma carta de Vira Narasimha Raya, rei de Vijayanagar (1505–1509), a Dom Manuel I de Portugal (1495–1521)', in I. de Riquer, E. Losada and H. González (eds.), *Professor Basilio Losada: ensinar a pensar con liberdade e risco* (Barcelona), pp. 677–83.

(1997a), 'Connected Histories: Notes towards a Reconfiguration of Early Modern Eurasia', *Modern Asian Studies*, 31, no. 3, pp. 735–62.

(1997b), 'Agreeing to Disagree: Burton Stein on Vijayanagara', *South Asia Research*, 17, no. 2, pp. 127–39.

(1995), 'The Politics of Fiscal Decline: A Reconsideration of Maratha Tanjavur, 1676–1799', *Indian Economic and Social History Review*, 37, no. 2, pp. 177–217.

(1986), 'Aspects of State Formation in South India and Southeast Asia, 1500–1650', *Indian Economic and Social History Review*, 23, no. 4, pp. 357–77.

Sullivan, R. (ed.) (1995), *'The Gentle Voices of Teachers': Aspects of Learning in the Carolingian Age* (Columbus).

(1994), *Christian Missionary Activity in the Early Middle Ages* (Aldershot).

Sullivan, T. D. (1980), 'Tlatoani and Tlatocayotl in the Sahagun Manuscript', *Estudios de Cultura Náhuatl*, 14, pp. 225–38.

Sun, Wenliang and Li, Zhiting (1983), *Qing Taizong quanzhuan* [Biography of Qing Taizong] (Changchun).

Swain, S. (1996), *Hellenism and Empire: Language, Classicism and Power in the Greek World, AD 50–250* (Oxford).

Swope, K. M. (2001), 'The Three Great Campaigns of the Wanli Emperor, 1592–1600: Court, Military, and Society in Late Sixteenth-Century China'. Ph.D. thesis, University of Michigan.

[Synadinos] (1996), *Conseils et mémoires de Synadinos, prêtre de Serrès en Macédoine (XVIIe siècle)*, ed. P. Odorico *et al.* (Paris).

Szajnocha, K. (1877), 'Dwa lata dziejów naszych', in Szajnocha, *Dzieła*, vol. IX (Warsaw).

Taagepera, R. (1978), 'Size and Duration of Empires: Systematics of Size', *Social Science Research*, 7, pp. 108–27.

Tadmor, H. (1997), 'Propaganda, Literature, Historiography: Cracking the Code of the Assyrian Royal Inscriptions', in Parpola and Whiting, pp. 328–38.

(1994), *The Inscriptions of Tiglath-Pileser III, King of Assyria* (Jerusalem).

Takács, S. A. (1999), 'Kybele', in *Der Neue Pauly*, vol. VI (Stuttgart and Weimar), pp. 950–6.

(1996), 'Magna Deum Mater Idaea, Cybele, and Catullus' Attis', in E. M. Lane (ed.), *Cybele, Attis and Related Cults: Essays in Memory of M. J. Vermaseren* (Leiden), pp. 367–86.

Talbot, C. (2001), 'The Nayakas of Vijayanagara Andhra: A Preliminary Prosopography', in K. R. Hall (ed.), *Structure and Society in Early South India: Essays in Honour of Noboru Karashima* (Delhi), pp. 251–75.

Tanner, M. (1993), *The Last Descendant of Aeneas: The Hapsburgs and the Mythic Image of the Emperor* (New Haven).

Tarn, W. W. (1951), *The Greeks in Bactria and India*, 2nd edn (Cambridge).

(1933), 'Alexander the Great and the Unity of Mankind', *Proceedings of the British Academy*, 19, pp. 123–66.

Taylor, M. (2004), 'Queen Victoria and India 1837–61', *Victorian Studies*, 47, no. 1, pp. 264–74.

Taylor, P. J. (1999), *Modernities: A Geohistorical Approach* (Cambridge).

Teschke, B. (2003), *The Myth of 1648: Class, Geopolitics and the Making of Modern International Relations* (London and New York).

(2002), 'Theorizing the Westphalian System of States: International Relations from Absolutism to Capitalism', *European Journal of International Relations*, 8, no. 1, pp. 5–48.

Tezcan, B. (2011), 'The Frank in the Ottoman Eye of 1583', in J. G. Harper (ed.), *The Turk and Islam in the Western Eye, 1450–1750: Visual Imagery before Orientalism* (Farnham and Burlington, Vt.), pp. 267–96.

(2000), 'The Development of the Use of "Kurdistan" as a Geographical Description and the Incorporation of this Region into the Ottoman Empire in the 16th Century', in K. Çiçek (ed.), *The Great Ottoman-Turkish Civilisation*, vol. III (Ankara), pp. 540–53.

Tezozomoc, F. Alvarado (2001), *Crónica Mexicana* (Madrid).

(1998), *Crónica Mexicayotl* (Mexico City).

Thackeray, H. St. J. (1917), *The Letter of Aristeas, Translated with an Appendix of Ancient Evidence on the Origin of the Septuagint* (London).

Thackston, W. M. (1989), *A Century of Princes: Sources on Timurid History and Art* (Cambridge, Mass.).

Thapar, R. (2002), *Early India: From the Origins to AD 1300* (London).

(1997), *Aśoka and the Decline of the Mauryas: With a New Afterword*, 2nd edn (Oxford and New Delhi).

(1981), 'The State as Empire', in H. J. M. Claessen and P. Skalnik (eds.), *The Study of the State* (The Hague), pp. 409–26.

Theophanes (1883), *Chronographia*, vol. 1, ed. C. de Boor (Leipzig).

Thomann, M. (1987), 'Christian Wolff', in M. Stolleis (ed.), *Staatsdenker im 17. und 18. Jahrhundert: Reichpublizistik, Politik, Naturrecht* (Frankfurt), pp. 257–83.

Thomas, J. A. (2003), 'High Anxiety: World History as Japanese Self-Discovery', in B. Stuchtey and E. Fuchs (eds.), *Writing World History, 1800–2000* (Oxford), pp. 309–25.

Tierney, B. (1964), *The Crisis of Church and State 1050–1300* (Englewood Cliffs).

Timmanna, N. (1978), *Pārijātāpaharanamu*, ed. N. Kuppusvamayya (Hyderabad).

Toby, R. (1991), *State and Diplomacy in Early Modern Japan: Asia in the Development of the Tokugawa Bakufu* (Stanford) [1st edn Princeton, 1984].

Tomei, M. A. (2004), 'Die Residenz des ersten Kaisers – Der Palatin in auguste-ischer Zeit', in A. Hoffmann and U. Wulf (eds.), *Die Kaiserpaläste auf dem Palatin in Rom: Das Zentrum der römischen Welt und seine Bauten* (Mainz), pp. 6–17.

Tomicki, R. (1990), *Ludzie i bogowie: Indianie meksykańscy wobec Hiszpanów we wczesnej fazie konkwisty* (Wrocław).

Torelli, M. (1999), 'Pax Augusta, Ara', in M. Steinby (ed.), *Lexicon Topographicum Urbis Romae*, vol. IV: *P–S* (Rome), pp. 70–4.

Torquemada, J. de (1977), *Monarquía indiana*, 4 vols. (Mexico City).

Toulmin, S. (1992), *Cosmopolis: The Hidden Agenda of Modernity* (Chicago).

Toynbee, A. (1969), 'If Alexander the Great Had Lived On', in Toynbee, *Some Problems of Greek History* (London), pp. 441–86.

Tracy, T. (1989), 'Who Stands behind Aeneas on the Ara Pacis?', in R. F. Sutton (ed.), *Daidalikon: Studies in Memory of Raymond V. Schoder* (Wauconda, Ill.), pp. 375–96.

Turnheim, Y. (2004), 'Visual Art as Text: The Rape of Ganymede', in M. Fano Santi (ed.), *Studi di archeologia in onore di Gustavo Traversari*, vol. II (Rome), pp. 895–905.

Turnour, G. (1837), 'An Examination of the Pálí Buddhistical Annals', *Journal of the Asiatic Society of Bengal*, 6, pp. 501–27.

Tybjerg, K. (2003), 'Wonder-making and Philosophical Wonder in Hero of Alexandria', *Studies in History and Philosophy of Science*, 34, pp. 443–66.

Ullmann, W. (1975), 'A Greek Démarche on the Eve of the Council of Florence', *Journal of Ecclesiastical History*, 26, pp. 337–52.

(1955), *The Growth of Papal Government in the Middle Ages: A Study in the Ideological Relation of Clerical to Lay Power* (London).

Umberger, E. (2007), 'Historia del arte e Imperio Azteca: la evidencia de las esculturas', *Revista Española de Antropología Americana*, 37, pp. 165–202.

Umur, S. (1980), *Osmanlı padişah tuğraları* (Istanbul).

Ungaro, L. (2007), 'The Forum of Augustus', in Ungaro (ed.), *The Museum of the Imperial Forums in Trajan's Market* (Rome and Milan).

Valenzuela Montenegro, N. (2004), *Die Tabulae Iliacae: Mythos und Geschichte im Spiegel einer Gruppe frühkaiserzeitlicher Miniaturreliefs* (Berlin).

Varisco, D. M. (2007), *Reading Orientalism: Said and the Unsaid* (Washington, DC).

Vasiliev, A. A. (1932), 'Was Old Russia a Vassal State of Byzantium', *Speculum*, 7, pp. 350–60.

Veblen, T. (1899), *The Theory of the Leisure Class: A Study of Economic Institutions* (New York).

Venetis, E. (2008), 'Greco-Persian Literary Interactions in Classical Persian Literature', in S. M. R. Darbandi and A. Zournatzi (eds.), *Ancient Greece and Ancient Iran: Cross-Cultural Encounters* (Athens), pp. 59–63.

Venkataramanayya, N. (1935), *Studies in the Third Dynasty of Vijayanagara* (Madras).

(1933), *Vijayanagara: The Origin of the City and the Empire* (Madras).

Vermaseren, M. J. (1982), *Mithraica III: The Mithraeum at Marino*, Études préliminaires aux religions orientales dans l'empire romain 16 (Leiden).

Verpeaux, J. (ed.) (1966), *Pseudo-Kodinos: traité des offices* (Paris).

Verschuer, C. von (2007), 'Ashikaga Yoshimitsu's Foreign Policy 1398 to 1408 AD: A Translation from *Zenrin Kokuhōki*, the Cambridge Manuscript', *Monumenta Nipponica*, 62, no. 3, pp. 261–97.

(2006), *Across the Perilous Sea: Japanese Trade with China and Korea from the Seventh to the Sixteenth Centuries*, trans. K. L. Hunter (Ithaca, NY).

Vogt-Spira, G. and Rommel, B. (eds.) (1999), *Rezeption und Identität: Die kulturelle Auseinandersetzung Roms mit Griechenland als europäisches Paradigma* (Stuttgart).

Vos, M. F. (1963), *Scythian Archers in Archaic Attic Vase Painting* (Groningen).

Wagoner, P. B. (2000), 'Harihara, Bukka and the Sultan: The Delhi Sultanate in the Political Imaginary of Vijayanagara', in D. Gilmartin and B. B. Lawrence (eds.), *Beyond Turk and Hindu: Rethinking Religious Identities in Islamicate South Asia* (Gainesville), pp. 300–26.

(1996), '"Sultan among Hindu Kings": Dress, Titles and the Islamicization of Hindu Culture at Vijayanagara', *Journal of Asian Studies*, 55, no. 4, pp. 851–80.

Wakeman, F. (1985), *The Great Enterprise: The Manchu Reconstruction of Imperial Order in Seventeenth-Century China*, 2 vols. (Berkeley).

Walbank, F. W. (2002), *Polybius, Rome and the Hellenistic World* (Cambridge).

(1992), *The Hellenistic World*, rev. edn (Cambridge, Mass.).

(1957), *A Historical Commentary on Polybius*, vol. 1 (Oxford).

Walbridge, J. (2005), 'Suhrawardī and Illuminationism', in P. Adamson and R. C. Taylor (eds.), *The Cambridge Companion to Arabic Philosophy* (Cambridge), pp. 201–23.

Wallace-Hadrill, A. (2008), *Rome's Cultural Revolution* (Cambridge).

(2004), 'The Golden Age and Sin in Augustan Ideology', in R. Osborne (ed.), *Studies in Ancient Greek and Roman Society* (Cambridge), pp. 159–76.

(1997), 'Mutatio morum: The Idea of a Cultural Revolution', in T. Habinek and A. Schiesaro (eds.), *The Roman Cultural Revolution* (Cambridge), pp. 3–22.

Walter, C. (1975), 'Raising on a Shield in Byzantine Iconography', *Revue des Études Byzantines*, 33, pp. 133–75.

Walter, U. (2006), 'Die Rache der Priamos-Enkel? Troia und Rom', in M. Zimmermann (ed.), *Der Traum von Troia: Geschichte und Mythos einer ewigen Stadt* (Munich), pp. 89–103 and 233–4.

Waltz, K. (1979), *Theory of International Politics* (New York).

Wang Gungwu (1991), 'The Chinese Urge to Civilize: Reflections on Change', in Wang Gungwu, *The Chineseness of China: Selected Essays* (Oxford), pp. 145–64.

Wang Hui (2007), 'The Politics of Imagining Asia: A Genealogical Analysis', *Inter-Asia Cultural Studies*, 8, no. 1, pp. 1–33.

Wang Zhenping (2005), *Ambassadors from the Islands of Immortals: China–Japan Relations in the Han-Tang Period* (Honolulu).

Warraq, I. (2007), *Defending the West: A Critique of Edward Said's Orientalism* (Amherst).

Watanabe, M. (1977), 'The Concept of *Sadae Kyorin* in Korea', *Japan Quarterly*, 24, no. 4, pp. 411–21.

Watson, A. (1992), *The Evolution of International Society: A Comparative Historical Analysis* (London).

Weber, G. (1995), 'Herrscher, Hof und Dichter. Aspekte der Legitimierung und Repräsentation hellenistischer Könige am Beispiel der ersten drei Antigoniden', *Historia: Zeitschrift für Alte Geschichte*, 44, pp. 283–316.

  (1993), *Dichtung und höfische Gesellschaft: Die Rezeption von Zeitgeschichte am Hof der ersten drei Ptolemäer* (Stuttgart).

Weil, R. (1985), 'Sur la "Lettre d'Aristote à Alexandre"', in J. Wiesner (ed.), *Aristoteles Werk und Wirkung Paul Moraux gewidmet*, vol. 1 (Berlin), pp. 485–98.

Weiland, L. (ed.) (1896), *Constitutiones et acta publica imperatorum et regum inde ab a. MCXCVIII usque a. MCCLXXII*, Monumenta Germaniae Historica: Leges IV (Hanover).

Weinstock, S. (1960), 'Pax and the Ara Pacis', *Journal of Roman Studies*, 50, pp. 44–58.

Weis, H. A. (2000), 'Odysseus at Sperlonga: Hellenistic Hero or Roman Heroic Foil?', in N. T. de Grummond and B. S. Ridgway (eds.), *From Pergamon to Sperlonga: Sculpture and Context* (Berkeley and Los Angeles), pp. 111–65.

Weissert, E. (1997), 'Royal Hunt and Royal Triumph in a Prism Fragment of Ashurbanipal (82-5-22,2)', in Parpola and Whiting, pp. 339–58.

Welles, C. B. (1934), *Royal Correspondence in the Hellenistic Period: A Study in Greek Epigraphy* (London).

Westbrook, R. (ed.) (2003), *A History of Ancient Near Eastern Law*, Handbook of Oriental Studies, Section 1: The Near and Middle East, vol. 72/II (Leiden).

Wheeler, E. L. (2002), 'Roman Treaties with Parthia: Völkerrecht or Power Politics?', in Freeman *et al.*, pp. 287–92.

Whitmarsh, T. (2001), *Greek Literature and the Roman Empire: The Politics of Imitation* (Oxford).

Whittaker, C. R. (1994), *Frontiers of the Roman Empire: A Social and Economic Study* (Baltimore and London).

Wiemer, H.-U. (2007), 'Alexander – der letzte Achaimenide? Eroberungspolitik, lokale Eliten und altorientalische Traditionen im Jahr 323', *Historische Zeitschrift*, 284, pp. 283–309.

Wiesehöfer, J. (2009), 'The Achaemenid Empire', in I. Morris and W. Scheidel (eds.), *The Dynamics of Ancient Empires: State Power from Assyria to Byzantium*, Oxford Series in Ecology and Evolution (Oxford), pp. 66–98.

  (2006), 'Statt einer Einleitung: "Randkultur" oder "Nabel der Welt"? Das Sasanidenreich und der Westen. Anmerkungen eines Althistorikers', in Wiesehöfer and Huyse, pp. 9–28.

(2003), 'Iraner und Hellenen: Bemerkungen zu einem umstrittenen kulturellen Verhältnis', in S. Conermann and J. Kusber (eds.), *Studia Eurasiatica: Kieler Festschrift für Hermann Kulke zum 65. Geburtstag*, Asien und Afrika, Beiträge des Zentrums für Asiatische und Afrikanische Studien (ZAAS) der Christian-Albrechts-Universität zu Kiel 10 (Hamburg), pp. 497–524.

(2002), 'Die Sklaven des Kaisers und der Kopf des Crassus: Römische Bilder des Ostens und parthische Bilder des Westens in augusteischer Zeit', in Freeman *et al.*, pp. 293–300.

(2001), *Ancient Persia from 550 BC to 650 AD*, new edn (London and New York) [English trans. of Wiesehöfer 1994].

(1994), *Das antike Persien: Von 550 v. Chr. bis 650 n. Chr.* (Munich and Zurich) [also English trans. 2001].

Wiesehöfer, J. and Huyse, P. (eds.) (2006), *Ērān ud Anērān: Studien zu den Beziehungen zwischen dem Sasanidenreich und der Mittelmeerwelt. Beiträge des Internationalen Colloquiums, Eutin 7.–9. Juni 2000*, Oriens et Occidens 13 (Stuttgart).

Wight, M. (1977), *Systems of States* (Leicester).

Wilhelm, R. M. (1988), 'Cybele: The Great Mother of Augustan order', *Vergilius: The Journal of the Vergilian Society of America*, 34, pp. 77–101.

Will, E. (1985), 'Pour une "anthropologie coloniale" du monde hellénistique', in J. W. Eadie and J. Ober (eds.), *The Craft of the Ancient Historian: Essays in Honor of Chester G. Starr* (Lanham, Md.), pp. 273–301.

(1979–1982), *Histoire politique du monde hellénistique*, 2 vols. (Nancy).

Williams, M. C. (1996), 'Hobbes and International Relations: A Reconsideration', *International Organization*, 50, no. 2, pp. 213–36.

Williams, S. (2003), *The Secret of Secrets: The Scholarly Career of a Pseudo-Aristotelian Text in the Latin Middle Ages* (Ann Arbor).

Wink, A. (2011), 'Postnomadic Empires: From the Mongols to the Mughals', in Bang and Bayly, pp. 120–31.

(1986), *Land and Sovereignty in India: Agrarian Society and Politics under the Eighteenth-century Maratha Svarājya* (Cambridge).

Winter, I. J. (1997), 'Art in Empire: The Royal Image and the Visual Dimensions of Assyrian Ideology', in Parpola and Whiting, pp. 359–81.

Wiseman, T. P. (1984), 'Cybele, Vergil and Augustus', in T. Woodman and D. West (eds.), *Poetry and Politics in the Age of Augustus* (Cambridge), pp. 117–28.

Wissemann, M. (1981), *Die Parther in der augusteischen Dichtung* (Frankfurt, Berne and New York).

Wittek, P. (1938), *The Rise of the Ottoman Empire* (London).

Wittke, A.-M., Olshausen, E. and Szydlak, R. (2007), *Historischer Atlas der antiken Welt*, Der Neue Pauly, Supplementum, 3 (Stuttgart and Weimar).

Wohl, A. S. (1995), '"Dizzi-Ben-Dizzi": Disraeli as Alien', *Journal of British Studies*, 34, no. 3, pp. 375–411.

Wolff, H. (2007), 'Die römische Bürgerrechtspolitik nach den Militärdiplomen', in M. A. Speidel, H. Lieb and A. M. Hirt (eds.), *Militärdiplome: Die*

Forschungsbeiträge der Berner Gespräche von 2004, Roman Army Researches 15 (Stuttgart), pp. 345–72.

Woolf, G. (2011), *Tales of the Barbarians: Ethnography and Empire in the Roman West* (Chichester).

   (2009), 'World Religion and World Empire in the Ancient Mediterranean', in H. Cancik and J. Rüpke (with F. Fabricius) (eds.), *Die Religion des Imperium Romanum: Koine und Konfrontationen* (Tübingen), pp. 19–34.

   (2008), 'Divinity and Power in Ancient Rome', in Brisch, pp. 243–60.

   (2003), 'The City of Letters', in C. Edwards and G. Woolf (eds.), *Rome the Cosmopolis* (Cambridge), pp. 203–21.

   (1994), 'Becoming Roman, Staying Greek: Culture, Identity and the Civilizing Process in the Roman East', *Proceedings of the Cambridge Philological Society*, 40, pp. 116–43.

Wrigley, R. (1997), 'Transformations of a Revolutionary Emblem: The Liberty Cap in the French Revolution', *French History*, 11, pp. 131–69.

Wu Hung (1995), 'Emperor's Masquerade – "Costume Portraits" of Yongzheng and Qianlong', *Orientations*, 26, no. 7, pp. 25–41.

Wünsche, R. (2011), *Kampf um Troja: 200 Jahre Ägineten in München* (Munich).

Yailenko, V.-P. (1990), 'Les maximes delphiques d'Aï Khanoum et la formation de la doctrine du *dhamma* d'Asoka', *Dialogues d'Histoire Ancienne*, 16, no. 1, pp. 239–56.

Yang, Lien-sheng (1968), 'Historical Notes on the Chinese World Order', in Fairbank, pp. 20–33.

Yates, F. A. (1975), *Astraea: The Imperial Theme in the Sixteenth Century* (London and Boston).

Yi Hong-chik (2002), *Saeguksa sajŏn* [New Korean history dictionary] (Seoul).

Yi Sŏngmu (2000), *Chosŏn sidae tangjaengsa* [History of factional disputes in the Chosŏn period], 2 vols. (Seoul).

Yi Yŏngch'un (1998), *Chosŏn hugi wangwi gyesŭng yŏn'gu* [Research on royal succession in the Later Chosŏn period] (Seoul).

Yun, P. I. (1998), 'Rethinking the Tribute System: Korean States and Northeast Asian Interstate Relations, 600–1600'. Ph.D. thesis, University of California, Los Angeles.

Zakeri, M. (2004), '*Ādāb al-falāsifa*: The Persian Context of an Arabic Collection of Aphorisms', *Mélanges de l'Université Saint-Joseph*, 57, pp. 173–90.

Zanker, P. (2000), 'Die Gegenwelt der Barbaren und die Überhöhung der häuslichen Lebenswelt, Überlegungen zum System der kaiserzeitlichen Bilderwelt', in T. Hölscher (ed.), *Gegenwelten zu den Kulturen Griechenlands und Roms in der Antike* (Munich and Leipzig), pp. 409–33.

   (1988), *The Power of Images in the Age of Augustus* (Ann Arbor) [first published as *Augustus und die Macht der Bilder* (Munich, 1987)].

   (1987), *Augustus und die Macht der Bilder* (Munich).

   (1969), *Forum Augustum: Das Bildprogramm*, Monumenta Artis Antiquae II (Tübingen).

Ziegler, K.-H. (2004), 'The Influence of Medieval Roman Law on Peace Treaties', in Lesaffer, pp. 147–61.

Zilio-Grandi, I. (2005), 'Temi e figure dell'apologia musulmana ("'ilm al-kalām") in relazione al sorgere e allo sviluppo della "falsafa"', in D'Ancona, pp. 137–79.

Zink, S. and Piening, H. (2009), 'Haec aurea templa: The Palatine Temple of Apollo and its Polychromy', *Journal of Roman Archaeology*, 22, pp. 109–22.

Ziolkowski, J. M. and Putnam, M. C. J. (2008), *The Virgilian Tradition: The First Fifteen Hundred Years* (New Haven).

Zonta, M. (2003), 'Pseudo-Aristote, *Secretum secretorum*', in Goulet, pp. 648–51.

Zorita, A. de (2002), *Edición crítica de la Relación de la Nueva España y de la Breve y Sumaria Relación escritas por Alonso de Zorita*, ed. W. Ahrndt (Mexico City and Bonn).

Index

Index